THE COMPLETE WRITINGS
OF AN ITALIAN HERETIC

THE OTHER VOICE IN EARLY MODERN EUROPE

A Series Edited by Margaret L. King and Albert Rabil Jr.

RECENT BOOKS IN THE SERIES

TULLIA D'ARAGONA
Dialogue on the Infinity of Love
Edited and translated by Rinaldina Russell and Bruce Merry

CASSANDRA FEDELE
Letters and Orations
Edited and translated by Diana Robin

VERONICA FRANCO
Poems and Selected Letters
Edited and translated by Ann Rosalind Jones and Margaret F. Rosenthal

MARIE LE JARS DE GOURNAY
"Apology for the Woman Writing" and Other Works
Edited and translated by Richard Hillman and Colette Quesnel

LUCREZIA MARINELLA
The Nobility and Excellence of Women, and the Defects and Vices of Men
Edited and translated by Anne Dunhill with Letizia Panizza

ANNE-MARIE-LOUISE D'ORLÉANS, DUCHESSE DE MONTPENSIER
Against Marriage: The Correspondence of La Grande Mademoiselle
Edited and translated by Joan DeJean

FRANÇOIS POULLAIN DE LA BARRE
Three Cartesian Feminist Treatises
Introductions and Annotations by Marcelle Maistre Welch
Translation by Vivien Bosley

SISTER BARTOLOMEA RICCOBONI
Life and Death in a Venetian Convent: The Chronicle and Necrology of Corpus Domini, 1395–1436
Edited and translated by Daniel Bornstein

MARÍA DE SAN JOSÉ SALAZAR
Book for the Hour of Recreation
Introduction and Notes by Alison Weber
Translation by Amanda Powell

ANNA MARIA VAN SCHURMAN
"Whether a Christian Woman Should Be Educated" and Other Writings from Her Intellectual Circle
Edited and translated by Joyce L. Irwin

LUCREZIA TORNABUONI DE' MEDICI
Sacred Narratives
Edited and translated by Jane Tylus

JUAN LUIS VIVES
"The Education of a Christian Woman": A Sixteenth-Century Manual
Edited and translated by Charles Fantazzi

Olympia Morata

THE COMPLETE WRITINGS
OF AN ITALIAN HERETIC

*Edited and Translated
by Holt N. Parker*

THE UNIVERSITY OF CHICAGO PRESS
Chicago & London

Olympia Fulvia Morata, 1526/27–55

Holt N. Parker is Fellow of the American Academy in Rome and associate professor of classics at the University of Cincinnati. He has published widely in the areas of ancient gender and sexuality and the Greek and Latin authors.

The University of Chicago Press, Chicago 60637
The University of Chicago Press, Ltd., London
© 2003 by The University of Chicago
All rights reserved. Published 2003
Printed in the United States of America
12 11 10 09 08 07 06 05 04 03   1 2 3 4 5

ISBN: 0-226-53668-8 (cloth)
ISBN: 0-226-53669-6 (paper)

Library of Congress Cataloging-in-Publication data

Morata, Olympia Fulvia, 1526–1555.
 [Works. English]
 The complete writings of an Italian heretic / edited and translated by Holt N. Parker.
   p.   cm.—(The other voice in early modern Europe)
Includes bibliographical references and index.
Works translated from the Latin.
 ISBN 0-226-53668-8 (hard : alk. paper)—ISBN 0-226-53669-6 (pbk. : alk. paper)
 1. Morata, Olympia Fulvia, 1526–1555. 2. Humanists—Italy—Biography. 3. Women intellectuals—Italy—Biography. 4. Reformation—Biography. I. Title: Complete writings of an Italian heretic. II. Parker, Holt N. III. Title. IV. series.
DG540.8.M7 M67 2003
305.42'0945'09031—dc21   2002151322

⊗The paper used in this publication meets the minimum requirements of the American National Standard for Information Sciences—Permanence of Paper for Printed Library Materials, ANSI Z39.48–1992.

PARENTIBUS
PIISSIMIS
AMANTISSIMIS
—Isa. 51:1–2

CONTENTS

Acknowledgments ix
Editors' Introduction to the Series xi
Key to Abbreviations xxxiii
Introduction: Olympia Fulvia Morata (1526/27–55) 1

I Olympia Morata: Works and Letters
Documents 61
Dedications 65
Juvenilia: Ferrara, c. 1539–41, Age 12–14 75
Letters: Italy 84
Letters: Germany 104
Poetry 178
Psalms 184

II Writings about Olympia Morata or in Honor of Her
Letters after the Death of Olympia Morata 195
Poems in Honor of Olympia Morata Written during Her Lifetime 208
Epitaphs by Learned Men 214
The Tombstones 224

Volume Editor's Bibliography 227
Series Editors' Bibliography 245
Biblical References Index 257
Classical References Index 261
General Index 263

ACKNOWLEDGMENTS

Research for this book began during a Fellowship at the American Academy in Rome. I wish to thank the American Academy and the National Endowment for the Humanities. Further support was provided by generous grants from the Semple Fund of the University of Cincinnati.

My greatest thanks are due to the superb librarians of the John Miller Burnam Classical Library, Jean Wellington and Michael Braunlin. Their patience and helpfulness in getting obscure volumes and microfilms was inexhaustible and invaluable.

I am grateful to Albert Rabil, editor of "The Other Voice in Early Modern Europe," and Sandra Hazel, of the University of Chicago Press, who have done Herculean labors in bringing this book to print. Thanks also to Brian Sowers for help with proofreading and indexing.

The edition of Morata's works by Doctor Professor Rainer Kössling and Gertrude Weiss-Stählin (1990) has been a model of presentation. I am also indebted to Doctor Professor Kössling for having sent me a copy of the extremely rare text of letter 61.

Finally, my thanks to Barbara Burrell: "Is [illae] eruditionem singularem, moresque castissimos admiratus, eam (quae vicissim nihil in homine praeter ingenii dotes admiretur) uxorem delegit, sibique pulchro connubio copulavit."

THE OTHER VOICE
IN EARLY MODERN EUROPE:
INTRODUCTION TO THE SERIES
Margaret L. King and Albert Rabil Jr.

THE OLD VOICE AND THE OTHER VOICE

In western Europe and the United States, women are nearing equality in the professions, in business, and in politics. Most enjoy access to education, reproductive rights, and autonomy in financial affairs. Issues vital to women are on the public agenda: equal pay, child care, domestic abuse, breast cancer research, and curricular revision with an eye to the inclusion of women.

These recent achievements have their origins in things women (and some male supporters) said for the first time about six hundred years ago. Theirs is the "other voice," in contradistinction to the "first voice," the voice of the educated men who created Western culture. Coincident with a general reshaping of European culture in the period 1300–1700 (called the Renaissance or early modern period), questions of female equality and opportunity were raised that still resound and are still unresolved.

The other voice emerged against the backdrop of a three-thousand-year history of the derogation of women rooted in the civilizations related to Western culture: Hebrew, Greek, Roman, and Christian. Negative attitudes toward women inherited from these traditions pervaded the intellectual, medical, legal, religious, and social systems that developed during the European Middle Ages.

The following pages describe the traditional, overwhelmingly male views of women's nature inherited by early modern Europeans and the new tradition that the "other voice" called into being to begin to challenge reigning assumptions. This review should serve as a framework for understanding the texts published in the series "The Other Voice in Early Modern Europe." Introductions specific to each text and author follow this essay in all the volumes of the series.

TRADITIONAL VIEWS OF WOMEN, 500 B.C.E.–1500 C.E.

Embedded in the philosophical and medical theories of the ancient Greeks were perceptions of the female as inferior to the male in both mind and body. Similarly, the structure of civil legislation inherited from the ancient Romans was biased against women, and the views on women developed by Christian thinkers out of the Hebrew Bible and the Christian New Testament were negative and disabling. Literary works composed in the vernacular of ordinary people, and widely recited or read, conveyed these negative assumptions. The social networks within which most women lived—those of the family and the institutions of the Roman Catholic Church—were shaped by this negative tradition and sharply limited the areas in which women might act in and upon the world.

GREEK PHILOSOPHY AND FEMALE NATURE. Greek biology assumed that women were inferior to men and defined them as merely childbearers and housekeepers. This view was authoritatively expressed in the works of the philosopher Aristotle.

Aristotle thought in dualities. He considered action superior to inaction, form (the inner design or structure of any object) superior to matter, completion to incompletion, possession to deprivation. In each of these dualities, he associated the male principle with the superior quality and the female with the inferior. "The male principle in nature," he argued, "is associated with active, formative and perfected characteristics, while the female is passive, material and deprived, desiring the male in order to become complete."[1] Men are always identified with virile qualities, such as judgment, courage, and stamina, and women with their opposites—irrationality, cowardice, and weakness.

The masculine principle was considered superior even in the womb. The man's semen, Aristotle believed, created the form of a new human creature, while the female body contributed only matter. (The existence of the ovum, and with it the other facts of human embryology, was not established until the seventeenth century.) Although the later Greek physician Galen believed there was a female component in generation, contributed by "female semen," the followers of both Aristotle and Galen saw the male role in human generation as more active and more important.

---

1. Aristotle, *Physics* 1.9.192a20–24, in *The Complete Works of Aristotle*, ed. Jonathan Barnes, rev. Oxford trans., 2 vols. (Princeton, 1984), 1:328.

In the Aristotelian view, the male principle sought always to reproduce itself. The creation of a female was always a mistake, therefore, resulting from an imperfect act of generation. Every female born was considered a "defective" or "mutilated" male (as Aristotle's terminology has variously been translated), a "monstrosity" of nature.[2] For Greek theorists, the biology of males and females was the key to their psychology. The female was softer and more docile, more apt to be despondent, querulous, and deceitful. Being incomplete, moreover, she craved sexual fulfillment in intercourse with a male. The male was intellectual, active, and in control of his passions.

These psychological polarities derived from the theory that the universe consisted of four elements (earth, fire, air, and water), expressed in human bodies as four "humors" (black bile, yellow bile, blood, and phlegm) considered respectively dry, hot, damp, and cold and corresponding to mental states ("melancholic," "choleric," "sanguine," "phlegmatic"). In this scheme, the male, sharing the principles of earth and fire, was dry and hot; the female, sharing the principles of air and water, was cold and damp.

Female psychology was further affected by her dominant organ, the uterus (womb), *hystera* in Greek. The passions generated by the womb made women lustful, deceitful, talkative, irrational, indeed—when these affects were in excess—"hysterical."

Aristotle's biology also had social and political consequences. If the male principle was superior and the female inferior, then in the household, as in the state, men should rule and women must be subordinate. That hierarchy did not rule out the companionship of husband and wife, whose cooperation was necessary for the welfare of children and the preservation of property. Such mutuality supported male preeminence.

Aristotle's teacher Plato suggested a different possibility: that men and women might possess the same virtues. The setting for this proposal is the imaginary and ideal Republic that Plato sketches in a dialogue of that name. Here, for a privileged elite capable of leading wisely, all distinctions of class and wealth dissolve, as, consequently, do those of gender. Without households or property, as Plato constructs his ideal society, there is no need for the subordination of women. Women may therefore be educated to the same level as men to assume leadership. Plato's Republic remained imaginary, however. In real societies, the subordination of women remained the norm and the prescription.

The views of women inherited from the Greek philosophical tradition became the basis for medieval thought. In the thirteenth century,

---

2. Aristotle, *Generation of Animals* 2.3.737a27–28, in *The Complete Works*, 1:1144.

the supreme Scholastic philosopher Thomas Aquinas, among others, still echoed Aristotle's views of human reproduction, of male and female personalities, and of the preeminent male role in the social hierarchy.

ROMAN LAW AND THE FEMALE CONDITION. Roman law, like Greek philosophy, underlay medieval thought and shaped medieval society. The ancient belief that adult property-owning men should administer households and make decisions affecting the community at large is the very fulcrum of Roman law.

About 450 B.C.E., during Rome's republican era, the community's customary law was recorded (legendarily) on twelve tablets erected in the city's central forum. It was later elaborated by professional jurists, whose activity increased in the imperial era, when much new legislation was passed, especially on issues affecting family and inheritance. This growing, changing body of laws was eventually codified in the *Corpus of Civil Law* under the direction of the emperor Justinian, generations after the empire ceased to be ruled from Rome. That *Corpus*, read and commented on by medieval scholars from the eleventh century on, inspired the legal systems of most of the cities and kingdoms of Europe.

Laws regarding dowries, divorce, and inheritance pertain primarily to women. Since those laws aimed to maintain and preserve property, the women concerned were those from the property-owning minority. Their subordination to male family members points to the even greater subordination of lower-class and slave women, about whom the laws speak little.

In the early republic, the *paterfamilias*, or "father of the family," possessed *patria potestas*, "paternal power." The term *pater*, "father," in both these cases does not necessarily mean biological father but denotes the head of a household. The father was the person who owned the household's property and, indeed, its human members. The *paterfamilias* had absolute power—including the power, rarely exercised, of life or death—over his wife, his children, and his slaves, as much as his cattle.

Male children could be "emancipated," an act that granted legal autonomy and the right to own property. Those over fourteen could be emancipated by a special grant from the father or automatically by their father's death. But females could never be emancipated; instead, they passed from the authority of their father to that of a husband or, if widowed or orphaned while still unmarried, to a guardian or tutor.

Marriage in its traditional form placed the woman under her husband's authority, or *manus*. He could divorce her on grounds of adultery, drinking wine, or stealing from the household, but she could not divorce him. She could neither possess property in her own right nor bequeath any to her children upon her death. When her husband died, the household property passed not to her but to his male heirs. And when her father died, she had no claim to any family inheritance, which was directed to her brothers or more remote male relatives. The effect of these laws was to exclude women from civil society, itself based on property ownership.

In the later republican and imperial periods, these rules were significantly modified. Women rarely married according to the traditional form. The practice of "free" marriage allowed a woman to remain under her father's authority, to possess property given her by her father (most frequently the "dowry," recoverable from the husband's household on his death), and to inherit from her father. She could also bequeath property to her own children and divorce her husband, just as he could divorce her.

Despite this greater freedom, women still suffered enormous disability under Roman law. Heirs could belong only to the father's side, never the mother's. Moreover, although she could bequeath her property to her children, she could not establish a line of succession in doing so. A woman was "the beginning and end of her own family," said the jurist Ulpian. Moreover, women could play no public role. They could not hold public office, represent anyone in a legal case, or even witness a will. Women had only a private existence and no public personality.

The dowry system, the guardian, women's limited ability to transmit wealth, and total political disability are all features of Roman law adopted by the medieval communities of western Europe, although modified according to local customary laws.

CHRISTIAN DOCTRINE AND WOMEN'S PLACE. The Hebrew Bible and the Christian New Testament authorized later writers to limit women to the realm of the family and to burden them with the guilt of original sin. The passages most fruitful for this purpose were the creation narratives in Genesis and sentences from the Epistles defining women's role within the Christian family and community.

Each of the first two chapters of Genesis contains a creation narrative. In the first "God created man in his own image, in the image of God he created him; male and female he created them" (Gen. 1:27). In the second, God created Eve from Adam's rib (2:21–23). Christian theologians relied principally on Genesis 2 for their understanding of the relation between man and woman, interpreting the creation of Eve from Adam as proof of her subordination to him.

The creation story in Genesis 2 leads to that of the temptations in Genesis 3: of Eve by the wily serpent and of Adam by Eve. As read by Christian theologians from Tertullian to Thomas Aquinas, the narrative made Eve responsible for the Fall and its consequences. She instigated the act; she deceived her husband; she suffered the greater punishment. Her disobedience made it necessary for Jesus to be incarnated and to die on the cross. From the pulpit, moralists and preachers for centuries conveyed to women the guilt that they bore for original sin.

The Epistles offered advice to early Christians on building communities of the faithful. Among the matters to be regulated was the place of women. Paul offered views favorable to women in Gal. 3:28: "There is neither Jew nor Greek, there is neither slave nor free, there is neither male nor female; for you are all one in Christ Jesus." Paul also referred to women as his coworkers and placed them on a par with himself and his male coworkers (Phil. 4:2–3; Rom. 16:1–3; 1 Cor. 16:19). Elsewhere Paul limited women's possibilities: "But I want you to understand that the head of every man is Christ, the head of a woman is her husband, and the head of Christ is God" (1 Cor. 11:3).

Biblical passages by later writers (though attributed to Paul) enjoined women to forgo jewels, expensive clothes, and elaborate coiffures; and they forbade women to "teach or have authority over men," telling them to "learn in silence with all submissiveness" as is proper for one responsible for sin, consoling them, however, with the thought that they will be saved through childbearing (1 Tim. 2:9–15). Other texts among the later Epistles defined women as the weaker sex and emphasized their subordination to their husbands (1 Pet. 3:7; Col. 3:18; Eph. 5:22–23).

These passages from the New Testament became the arsenal employed by theologians of the early church to transmit negative attitudes toward women to medieval Christian culture—above all, Tertullian ("On the Apparel of Women"), Jerome (*Against Jovinian*), and Augustine (*The Literal Meaning of Genesis*).

THE IMAGE OF WOMEN IN MEDIEVAL LITERATURE. The philosophical, legal, and religious traditions born in antiquity formed the basis of the medieval intellectual synthesis wrought by trained thinkers, mostly clerics, writing in Latin and based largely in universities. The vernacular literary tradition that developed alongside the learned tradition also spoke about female nature and women's roles. Medieval stories, poems, and epics also portrayed women negatively—as lustful and deceitful—while praising good housekeepers and loyal wives as replicas of the Virgin Mary or the female saints and martyrs.

There is an exception in the movement of "courtly love" that evolved in southern France from the twelfth century. Courtly love was the erotic love between a nobleman and noblewoman, the latter usually superior in social rank. It was always adulterous. From the conventions of courtly love derive modern Western notions of romantic love. The tradition has had an impact disproportionate to its size, for it affected only a tiny elite, and very few women. The exaltation of the female lover probably does not reflect a higher evaluation of women or a step toward their sexual liberation. More likely it gives expression to the social and sexual tensions besetting the knightly class at a specific historical juncture.

The literary fashion of courtly love was on the wane by the thirteenth century, when the widely read *Romance of the Rose* was composed in French by two authors of significantly different dispositions. Guillaume de Lorris composed the initial four thousand verses about 1235, and Jean de Meun added about seventeen thousand verses—more than four times the original—about 1265.

The fragment composed by Guillaume de Lorris stands squarely in the tradition of courtly love. Here the poet, in a dream, is admitted into a walled garden where he finds a magic fountain in which a rosebush is reflected. He longs to pick one rose, but the thorns prevent his doing so, even as he is wounded by arrows from the god of love, whose commands he agrees to obey. The rest of this part of the poem recounts the poet's unsuccessful efforts to pluck the rose.

The longer part of the *Romance* by Jean de Meun also describes a dream. But here allegorical characters give long didactic speeches, providing a social satire on a variety of themes, some pertaining to women. Love is an anxious and tormented state, the poem explains: women are greedy and manipulative, marriage is miserable, beautiful women are lustful, ugly ones cease to please, and a chaste woman is as rare as a black swan.

Shortly after Jean de Meun completed *The Romance of the Rose*, Mathéolus penned his *Lamentations*, a long Latin diatribe against marriage translated into French about a century later. The *Lamentations* sum up medieval attitudes toward women and provoked the important response by Christine de Pizan in her *Book of the City of Ladies*.

In 1355 Giovanni Boccaccio wrote *Il Corbaccio*, another antifeminist manifesto, though ironically by an author whose other works pioneered new directions in Renaissance thought. The former husband of his lover appears to Boccaccio, condemning his unmoderated lust and detailing the defects of women. Boccaccio concedes at the end "how much men naturally surpass women in nobility" and is cured of his desires.[3]

WOMEN'S ROLES: THE FAMILY. The negative perceptions of women expressed in the intellectual tradition are also implicit in the actual roles that women played in European society. Assigned to subordinate positions in the household and the church, they were barred from significant participation in public life.

Medieval European households, like those in antiquity and in non-Western civilizations, were headed by males. It was the male serf (or peasant), feudal lord, town merchant, or citizen who was polled or taxed or succeeded to an inheritance or had any acknowledged public role, although his wife or widow could stand as a temporary surrogate. From about 1100, the position of property-holding males was further enhanced: inheritance was confined to the male, or agnate, line—with depressing consequences for women.

A wife never fully belonged to her husband's family, nor was she a daughter to her father's family. She left her father's house young to marry whomever her parents chose. Her dowry was managed by her husband, and at her death it normally passed to her children by him.

A married woman's life was occupied nearly constantly with cycles of pregnancy, childbearing, and lactation. Women bore children through all the years of their fertility, and many died in childbirth. They were also responsible for raising young children up to six or seven. In the propertied classes that responsibility was shared, since it was common for a wet nurse to take over breast-feeding, and servants performed other chores.

Women trained their daughters in the household duties appropriate to their status, nearly always tasks associated with textiles: spinning, weaving, sewing, embroidering. Their sons were sent out of the house as apprentices or students, or their training was assumed by fathers in later childhood and adolescence. On the death of her husband, a woman's children became the responsibility of his family. She generally did not take "his" children with her to a new marriage or back to her father's house, except sometimes in the artisan classes.

Women also worked. Rural peasants performed farm chores, merchant wives often practiced their husbands' trades, the unmarried daughters of the

---

3. Giovanni Boccaccio, *The Corbaccio, or The Labyrinth of Love*, trans. and ed. Anthony K. Cassell, rev. ed. (Binghamton, N.Y., 1993), 71.

urban poor worked as servants or prostitutes. All wives produced or embellished textiles and did the housekeeping, while wealthy ones managed servants. These labors were unpaid or poorly paid but often contributed substantially to family wealth.

WOMEN'S ROLES: THE CHURCH. Membership in a household, whether a father's or a husband's, meant for women a lifelong subordination to others. In western Europe, the Roman Catholic Church offered an alternative to the career of wife and mother. A woman could enter a convent, parallel in function to the monasteries for men that evolved in the early Christian centuries.

In the convent, a woman pledged herself to a celibate life, lived according to strict community rules, and worshiped daily. Often the convent offered training in Latin, allowing some women to become considerable scholars and authors as well as scribes, artists, and musicians. For women who chose the conventual life, the benefits could be enormous, but for numerous others placed in convents by paternal choice, the life could be restrictive and burdensome.

The conventual life declined as an alternative for women as the modern age approached. Reformed monastic institutions resisted responsibility for related female orders. The church increasingly restricted female institutional life by insisting on closer male supervision.

Women often sought other options. Some joined the communities of laywomen that sprang up spontaneously in the thirteenth century in the urban zones of western Europe, especially in Flanders and Italy. Some joined the heretical movements that flourished in late medieval Christendom, whose anticlerical and often antifamily positions particularly appealed to women. In these communities, some women were acclaimed as "holy women" or "saints," whereas others often were condemned as frauds or heretics.

In all, though the options offered to women by the church were sometimes less than satisfactory, they were sometimes richly rewarding. After 1520 the convent remained an option only in Roman Catholic territories. Protestantism engendered an ideal of marriage as a heroic endeavor and appeared to place husband and wife on a more equal footing. Sermons and treatises, however, still called for female subordination and obedience.

THE OTHER VOICE, 1300–1700

When the modern era opened, European culture was so firmly structured by a framework of negative attitudes toward women that to dismantle it was a monumental labor. The process began as part of a larger cultural movement that entailed the critical reexamination of ideas inherited from the ancient and medieval past. The humanists launched that critical reexamination.

THE HUMANIST FOUNDATION. Originating in Italy in the fourteenth century, humanism quickly became the dominant intellectual movement in Europe. Spreading in the sixteenth century from Italy to the rest of Europe, it fueled the literary, scientific, and philosophical movements of the era and laid the basis for the eighteenth-century Enlightenment.

Humanists regarded the Scholastic philosophy of medieval universities as out of touch with the realities of urban life. They found in the rhetorical discourse of classical Rome a language adapted to civic life and public speech. They learned to read, speak, and write classical Latin and, eventually, classical Greek. They founded schools to teach others to do so, establishing the pattern for elementary and secondary education for the next three hundred years.

In the service of complex government bureaucracies, humanists employed their skills to write eloquent letters, deliver public orations, and formulate public policy. They developed new scripts for copying manuscripts and used the new printing press to disseminate texts, for which they created methods of critical editing.

Humanism was a movement led by males who accepted the evaluation of women in ancient texts and generally shared the misogynist perceptions of their culture. (Female humanists, as we will see, did not.) Yet humanism also opened the door to a reevaluation of the nature and capacity of women. By calling authors, texts, and ideas into question, it made possible the fundamental rereading of the whole intellectual tradition that was required in order to free women from cultural prejudice and social subordination.

A DIFFERENT CITY. The other voice first appeared when, after so many centuries, the accumulation of misogynist concepts evoked a response from a capable female defender: Christine de Pizan (1365–1431). Introducing her *Book of the City of Ladies* (1405), she described how she was affected by reading Mathéolus's *Lamentations*: "Just the sight of this book . . . made me wonder how it happened that so many different men . . . are so inclined to express both in speaking and in their treatises and writings so many wicked insults about women and their behavior."[4] These statements impelled her to detest herself "and the entire feminine sex, as though we were monstrosities in nature."[5]

The rest of *The Book of the City of Ladies* presents a justification of the female sex and a vision of an ideal community of women. A pioneer, she has received the message of female inferiority and rejected it. From the fourteenth to the seventeenth century, a huge body of literature accumulated that responded to the dominant tradition.

The result was a literary explosion consisting of works by both men and women, in Latin and in the vernaculars: works enumerating the achievements of notable women; works rebutting the main accusations made against women; works arguing for the equal education of men and women; works defining and redefining women's proper role in the family, at court, in public; works describing women's lives and experiences. Recent monographs and articles have begun to hint at the great range of this movement, involving probably several thousand titles. The protofeminism of these "other voices" constitutes a significant fraction of the literary product of the early modern era.

THE CATALOGS. About 1365 the same Boccaccio whose *Corbaccio* rehearses the usual charges against female nature wrote another work, *Concerning Famous Women*. A humanist treatise drawing on classical texts, it praised 106 notable women, ninety-eight of them from pagan Greek and Roman antiquity, one (Eve) from the Bible, and seven from the medieval religious and cultural tradition; his book helped make all readers aware of a sex normally condemned or forgotten. Boccaccio's outlook nevertheless was unfriendly to women, for it singled out for praise those women who possessed the traditional virtues of chastity, silence, and obedience. Women who were active in the public realm—for example, rulers and warriors—were depicted as usually being lascivious and as suffering terrible punishments for entering the masculine sphere. Women were his subject, but Boccaccio's standard remained male.

Christine de Pizan's *Book of the City of Ladies* contains a second catalog, one responding specifically to Boccaccio's. Whereas Boccaccio portrays female virtue as exceptional, she depicts it as universal. Many women in history

---

4. Christine de Pizan, *The Book of the City of Ladies*, trans. Earl Jeffrey Richards, foreword by Marina Warner (New York, 1982), 1.1.1, pp. 3–4.

5. Ibid., 1.1.1–2, p. 5.

were leaders, or remained chaste despite the lascivious approaches of men, or were visionaries and brave martyrs.

The work of Boccaccio inspired a series of catalogs of illustrious women of the biblical, classical, Christian, and local pasts, among them Filippo da Bergamo's *Of Illustrious Women*, Pierre de Brantôme's *Lives of Illustrious Women*, Pierre Le Moyne's *Gallerie of Heroic Women*, and Pietro Paolo de Ribera's *Immortal Triumphs and Heroic Enterprises of 845 Women*. Whatever their embedded prejudices, these works drove home to the public the possibility of female excellence.

THE DEBATE. At the same time, many questions remained: Could a woman be virtuous? Could she perform noteworthy deeds? Was she even, strictly speaking, of the same human species as men? These questions were debated over four centuries, in French, German, Italian, Spanish, and English, by authors male and female, among Catholics, Protestants, and Jews, in ponderous volumes and breezy pamphlets. The whole literary genre has been called the *querelle des femmes*, the "woman question."

The opening volley of this battle occurred in the first years of the fifteenth century, in a literary debate sparked by Christine de Pizan. She exchanged letters critical of Jean de Meun's contribution to *The Romance of the Rose* with two French royal secretaries, Jean de Montreuil and Gontier Col. When the matter became public, Jean Gerson, one of Europe's leading theologians, supported de Pizan's arguments against de Meun, for the moment silencing the opposition.

The debate resurfaced repeatedly over the next two hundred years. *The Triumph of Women* (1438) by Juan Rodríguez de la Camara (or Juan Rodríguez del Padron) struck a new note by presenting arguments for the superiority of women to men. *The Champion of Women* (1440–42) by Martin Le Franc addresses once again the negative views of women presented in *The Romance of the Rose* and offers counterevidence of female virtue and achievement.

A cameo of the debate on women is included in *The Courtier*, one of the most widely read books of the era, published by the Italian Baldassare Castiglione in 1528 and immediately translated into other European vernaculars. *The Courtier* depicts a series of evenings at the court of the duke of Urbino in which many men and some women of the highest social stratum amuse themselves by discussing a range of literary and social issues. The "woman question" is a pervasive theme throughout, and the third of its four books is devoted entirely to that issue.

In a verbal duel, Gasparo Pallavicino and Giuliano de' Medici present the main claims of the two traditions. Gasparo argues the innate inferiority of women and their inclination to vice. Only in bearing children do they profit the world. Giuliano counters that women share the same spiritual and mental capacities as men and may excel in wisdom and action. Men and women are of the same essence: just as no stone can be more perfectly a stone than another, so no human being can be more perfectly human than others, whether male or female. It was an astonishing assertion, boldly made to an audience as large as all Europe.

THE TREATISES. Humanism provided the materials for a positive counterconcept to the misogyny embedded in Scholastic philosophy and law and inherited from the Greek, Roman, and Christian pasts. A series of humanist treatises on marriage and family, on education and deportment, and on the nature of women helped construct these new perspectives.

The works by Francesco Barbaro and Leon Battista Alberti—*On Marriage* (1415) and *On the Family* (1434–37)—far from defending female equality, reasserted women's responsibility for rearing children and managing the housekeeping while being obedient, chaste, and silent. Nevertheless, they served the cause of reexamining the issue of women's nature by placing domestic issues at the center of scholarly concern and reopening the pertinent classical texts. In addition, Barbaro emphasized the companionate nature of marriage and the importance of a wife's spiritual and mental qualities for the well-being of the family.

These themes reappear in later humanist works on marriage and the education of women by Juan Luis Vives and Erasmus. Both were moderately sympathetic to the condition of women without reaching beyond the usual masculine prescriptions for female behavior.

An outlook more favorable to women characterizes the nearly unknown work *In Praise of Women* (ca. 1487) by the Italian humanist Bartolommeo Goggio. In addition to providing a catalog of illustrious women, Goggio argued that male and female are the same in essence, but that women (reworking the Adam and Eve narrative from quite a new angle) are actually superior. In the same vein, the Italian humanist Maria Equicola asserted the spiritual equality of men and women in *On Women* (1501). In 1525 Galeazzo Flavio Capra (or Capella) published his work *On the Excellence and Dignity of Women*. This humanist tradition of treatises defending the worthiness of women culminates in the work of Henricus Cornelius Agrippa *On the Nobility and Preeminence of the Female Sex*. No work by a male humanist more succinctly or explicitly presents the case for female dignity.

THE WITCH BOOKS. While humanists grappled with the issues pertaining to women and family, other learned men turned their attention to what they perceived as a very great problem: witches. Witch-hunting manuals, explorations of the witch phenomenon, and even defenses of witches are not at first glance pertinent to the tradition of the other voice. But they do relate in this way: most accused witches were women. The hostility aroused by supposed witch activity is comparable to the hostility aroused by women. The evil deeds the victims of the hunt were charged with were exaggerations of the vices to which, many believed, all women were prone.

The connection between the witch accusation and the hatred of women is explicit in the notorious witch-hunting manual *The Hammer of Witches* (1486) by two Dominican inquisitors, Heinrich Krämer and Jacob Sprenger. Here the inconstancy, deceitfulness, and lustfulness traditionally associated with women are depicted in exaggerated form as the core features of witch behavior. These traits inclined women to make a bargain with the devil—sealed by sexual intercourse—by which they acquired unholy powers. Such bizarre claims, far from being rejected by rational men, were broadcast by intellectuals. The German Ulrich Molitur, the Frenchman Nicolas Rémy, and the Italian Stefano Guazzo all coolly informed the public of sinister orgies and midnight pacts with the devil. The celebrated French jurist, historian, and political philosopher Jean Bodin argued that because women were especially prone to diabolism, regular legal procedures could properly be suspended in order to try those accused of this "exceptional crime."

A few experts such as the physician Johann Weyer, a student of Agrippa's, raised their voices in protest. In 1563 he explained the witch phenomenon thus, without discarding belief in diabolism: the devil deluded foolish old women afflicted by melancholia, causing them to believe they had magical powers. Weyer's rational skepticism, which had good credibility in the community of the learned, worked to revise the conventional views of women and witchcraft.

WOMEN'S WORKS. To the many categories of works produced on the question of women's worth must be added nearly all works written by women. A woman writing was in herself a statement of women's claim to dignity.

Only a few women wrote anything before the dawn of the modern era, for three reasons. First, they rarely received the education that would enable them to write. Second, they were not admitted to the public roles—as administrator, bureaucrat, lawyer or notary, or university professor—in which they might gain knowledge of the kinds of things the literate public thought worth writing about. Third, the culture imposed silence on women, considering speaking out a form of unchastity. Given these conditions, it is remarkable that any women wrote. Those who did before the fourteenth century were almost always nuns or religious women whose isolation made their pronouncements more acceptable.

From the fourteenth century on, the volume of women's writings rose. Women continued to write devotional literature, although not always as cloistered nuns. They also wrote diaries, often intended as keepsakes for their children; books of advice to their sons and daughters; letters to family members and friends; and family memoirs, in a few cases elaborate enough to be considered histories.

A few women wrote works directly concerning the "woman question," and some of these, such as the humanists Isotta Nogarola, Cassandra Fedele, Laura Cereta, and Olympia Morata, were highly trained. A few were professional writers, living by the income of their pens; the very first among them was Christine de Pizan, noteworthy in this context as in so many others. In addition to *The Book of the City of Ladies* and her critiques of *The Romance of the Rose*, she wrote *The Treasure of the City of Ladies* (a guide to social decorum for women), an advice book for her son, much courtly verse, and a full-scale history of the reign of King Charles V of France.

WOMEN PATRONS. Women who did not themselves write but encouraged others to do so boosted the development of an alternative tradition. Highly placed women patrons supported authors, artists, musicians, poets, and learned men. Such patrons, drawn mostly from the Italian elites and the courts of northern Europe, figure disproportionately as the dedicatees of the important works of early feminism.

For a start, it might be noted that the catalogs of Boccaccio and Alvaro de Luna were dedicated to the Florentine noblewoman Andrea Acciaiuoli and to Doña María, first wife of King Juan II of Castile, while the French translation of Boccaccio's work was commissioned by Anne of Brittany, wife of King Charles VIII of France. The humanist treatises of Goggio, Equicola, Vives, and Agrippa were dedicated, respectively, to Eleanora of Aragon, wife of Ercole I d'Este, duke of Ferrara; to Margherita Cantelma of Mantua; to Catherine of Aragon, wife of King Henry VIII of England; and to Margaret, duchess of Austria and regent of the Netherlands. As late as 1696, Mary Astell's *Serious Proposal to the Ladies, for the Advancement of Their True and Greatest Interest* was dedicated to Princess Anne of Denmark.

These authors presumed that their efforts would be welcome to female patrons, or they may have written at the bidding of those patrons. Silent themselves, perhaps even unresponsive, these loftily placed women helped shape the tradition of the other voice.

THE ISSUES. The literary forms and patterns in which the tradition of the other voice presented itself have now been sketched. It remains to highlight the major issues around which this tradition crystallizes. In brief, there are four problems to which our authors return again and again, in plays and catalogs, in verse and letters, in treatises and dialogues, in every language: the problem of chastity, the problem of power, the problem of speech, and the problem of knowledge. Of these the greatest, preconditioning the others, is the problem of chastity.

THE PROBLEM OF CHASTITY. In traditional European culture, as in those of antiquity and others around the globe, chastity was perceived as woman's quintessential virtue—in contrast to courage, or generosity, or leadership, or rationality, seen as virtues characteristic of men. Opponents of women charged them with insatiable lust. Women themselves and their defenders—without disputing the validity of the standard—responded that women were capable of chastity.

The requirement of chastity kept women at home, silenced them, isolated them, left them in ignorance. It was the source of all other impediments. Why was it so important to the society of men, of whom chastity was not required, and who more often than not considered it their right to violate the chastity of any woman they encountered?

Female chastity ensured the continuity of the male-headed household. If a man's wife was not chaste, he could not be sure of the legitimacy of his offspring. If they were not his and they acquired his property, it was not his household, but some other man's, that had endured. If his daughter was not chaste, she could not be transferred to another man's household as his wife, and he was dishonored.

The whole system of the integrity of the household and the transmission of property was bound up in female chastity. Such a requirement pertained only to property-owning classes, of course. Poor women could not expect to maintain their chastity, least of all if they were in contact with high-status men to whom all women but those of their own household were prey.

In Catholic Europe, the requirement of chastity was further buttressed by moral and religious imperatives. Original sin was inextricably linked with the sexual act. Virginity was seen as heroic virtue, far more impressive than, say, the avoidance of idleness or greed. Monasticism, the cultural institution that dominated medieval Europe for centuries, was grounded in the renunciation of the flesh. The Catholic reform of the eleventh century imposed a similar standard on all the clergy and a heightened awareness of sexual requirements on all the laity. Although men were asked to be chaste, female unchastity was much worse: it led to the devil, as Eve had led mankind to sin.

To such requirements, women and their defenders protested their innocence. Furthermore, following the example of holy women who had escaped the requirements of family and sought the religious life, some women began to conceive of female communities as alternatives both to family and to the cloister. Christine de Pizan's city of ladies was such a community. Moderata Fonte and Mary Astell envisioned others. The luxurious salons of the French *précieuses* of the seventeenth century, or the comfortable English drawing rooms of the next, may have been born of the same impulse. Here women not only might escape, if briefly, the subordinate position that life in the family entailed but might also make claims to power, exercise their capacity for speech, and display their knowledge.

THE PROBLEM OF POWER. Women were excluded from power: the whole cultural tradition insisted on it. Only men were citizens, only men bore arms, only men could be chiefs or lords or kings. There were exceptions that did not disprove the rule, when wives or widows or mothers took the place of men, awaiting their return or the maturation of a male heir. A woman who attempted to rule in her own right was perceived as an anomaly, a monster, at once a deformed woman and an insufficient male, sexually confused and consequently unsafe.

The association of such images with women who held or sought power explains some otherwise odd features of early modern culture. Queen Elizabeth I of England, one of the few women to hold full regal authority in European history, played with such male/female images—positive ones, of course—in representing herself to her subjects. She was a prince, and manly, even though she was female. She was also (she claimed) virginal, a condition absolutely essential if she was to avoid the attacks of her opponents. Catherine de' Medici, who ruled France as widow and regent for her sons, also adopted such imagery in defining her position. She chose as one symbol the figure of Artemisia, an androgynous ancient warrior-heroine who combined a female persona with masculine powers.

Power in a woman, without such sexual imagery, seems to have been indigestible by the culture. A rare note was struck by the Englishman Sir Thomas Elyot in his *Defence of Good Women* (1540), justifying both women's participation in civic life and their prowess in arms. The old tune was sung by the Scots reformer John Knox in his *First Blast of the Trumpet against the Monstrous Regiment of Women* (1558); for him rule by women, defects in nature, was a hideous contradiction in terms.

The confused sexuality of the imagery of female potency was not reserved for rulers. Any woman who excelled was likely to be called an Amazon, recalling the self-mutilated warrior women of antiquity who repudiated all men, gave up their sons, and raised only their daughters. She was often said to have "exceeded her sex" or to have possessed "masculine virtue"—as the very fact of conspicuous excellence conferred masculinity even on the female subject. The catalogs of notable women often showed those female heroes dressed in armor, armed to the teeth, like men. Amazonian heroines romp through the epics of the age—Ariosto's *Orlando Furioso* (1532) and Spenser's *Faerie Queene* (1590–1609). Excellence in a woman was perceived as a claim for power, and power was reserved for the masculine realm. A woman who possessed either one was masculinized and lost title to her own female identity.

THE PROBLEM OF SPEECH. Just as power had a sexual dimension when it was claimed by women, so did speech. A good woman spoke little. Excessive speech was an indication of unchastity. By speech, women seduced men. Eve had lured Adam into sin by her speech. Accused witches were commonly accused of having spoken abusively, or irrationally, or simply too much. As enlightened a figure as Francesco Barbaro insisted on silence in a woman, which he linked to her perfect unanimity with her husband's will and her unblemished virtue (her chastity). Another Italian humanist, Leonardo Bruni, in advising a noblewoman on her studies, barred her not from speech but from public speaking. That was reserved for men.

Related to the problem of speech was that of costume—another, if silent, form of self-expression. Assigned the task of pleasing men as their primary occupation, elite women often tended toward elaborate costume, hairdressing, and the use of cosmetics. Clergy and secular moralists alike condemned these practices. The appropriate function of costume and adornment was to announce the status of a woman's husband or father. Any further indulgence in adornment was akin to unchastity.

THE PROBLEM OF KNOWLEDGE. When the Italian noblewoman Isotta Nogarola had begun to attain a reputation as a humanist, she was accused of incest—a telling instance of the association of learning in women with unchastity. That chilling association inclined any woman who was educated to deny that she was or to make exaggerated claims of heroic chastity.

If educated women were pursued with suspicions of sexual misconduct, women seeking an education faced an even more daunting obstacle: the assumption that women were by nature incapable of learning, that reasoning was a particularly masculine ability. Just as they proclaimed their chastity, women and their defenders insisted on their capacity for learning. The major work by a male writer on female education—that by Juan Luis Vives, *On the*

Education of a Christian Woman (1523)—granted female capacity for intellection but still argued that a woman's whole education was to be shaped around the requirement of chastity and a future within the household. Female writers of the following generations—Marie de Gournay in France, Anna Maria van Schurman in Holland, Mary Astell in England—began to envision other possibilities.

The pioneers of female education were the Italian women humanists who managed to attain a literacy in Latin and a knowledge of classical and Christian literature equivalent to that of prominent men. Their works implicitly and explicitly raise questions about women's social roles, defining problems that beset women attempting to break out of the cultural limits that had bound them. Like Christine de Pizan, who achieved an advanced education through her father's tutoring and her own devices, their bold questioning makes clear the importance of training. Only when women were educated to the same standard as male leaders would they be able to raise that other voice and insist on their dignity as human beings morally, intellectually, and legally equal to men.

THE OTHER VOICE. The other voice, a voice of protest, was mostly female, but it was also male. It spoke in the vernaculars and in Latin, in treatises and dialogues, in plays and poetry, in letters and diaries, and in pamphlets. It battered at the wall of prejudice that encircled women and raised a banner announcing its claims. The female was equal (or even superior) to the male in essential nature—moral, spiritual, intellectual. Women were capable of higher education, of holding positions of power and influence in the public realm, and of speaking and writing persuasively. The last bastion of masculine supremacy, centered on the notions of a woman's primary domestic responsibility and the requirement of female chastity, was not as yet assaulted—although visions of productive female communities as alternatives to the family indicated an awareness of the problem.

During the period 1300–1700, the other voice remained only a voice, and one only dimly heard. It did not result—yet—in an alteration of social patterns. Indeed, to this day they have not entirely been altered. Yet the call for justice issued as long as six centuries ago by those writing in the tradition of the other voice must be recognized as the source and origin of the mature feminist tradition and of the realignment of social institutions accomplished in the modern age.

We thank the volume editors in this series, who responded with many suggestions to an earlier draft of this introduction, making it a collaborative enterprise. Many of their suggestions and criticisms have resulted in revisions of this introduction, though we remain responsible for the final product.

PROJECTED TITLES IN THE SERIES

Isabella Andreini, *Mirtilla*, edited and translated by Laura Stortoni

Tullia d'Aragona, *Complete Poems and Letters*, edited and translated by Julia Hairston

Tullia d'Aragona, *The Wretch, Otherwise Known as Guerrino*, edited and translated by Julia Hairston and John McLucas

Giuseppa Eleonora Barbapiccola and Diamante Medaglia Faini, *The Education of Women*, edited and translated by Rebecca Messbarger

Francesco Barbaro et al., *On Marriage and the Family*, edited and translated by Margaret L. King

Laura Battiferra, *Selected Poetry, Prose, and Letters*, edited and translated by Victoria Kirkham

Giulia Bigolina, *Urania*, edited and translated by Valeria Finucci

Francesco Buoninsegni and Arcangela Tarabotti, *Menippean Satire: "Against Feminine Extravagance" and "Antisatire,"* edited and translated by Elissa Weaver

Elisabetta Caminer Turra, *Writings on and about Women*, edited and translated by Catherine Sama

Maddalena Campiglia, *Flori*, edited and translated by Virginia Cox with Lisa Sampson

Rosalba Carriera, *Letters, Diaries, and Art*, edited and translated by Shearer West

Madame du Chatelet, *Selected Works*, edited by Judith Zinsser

Gabrielle de Coignard, *Spiritual Sonnets*, edited and translated by Melanie E. Gregg

Vittoria Colonna, *Sonnets for Michelangelo*, edited and translated by Abigail Brundin

Vittoria Colonna, Chiara Matraini, and Lucrezia Marinella, *Marian Writings*, edited and translated by Susan Haskins

Marie Dentière, *Epistles*, edited and translated by Mary B. McKinley

Marie-Catherine Desjardins (Madame de Villedieu), *Memoirs of the Life of Henriette-Sylvie de Molière*, edited and translated by Donna Kuizenga

Princess Elizabeth of Bohemia, *Correspondence with Descartes*, edited and translated by Lisa Shapiro

Isabella d'Este, *Selected Letters*, edited and translated by Deanna Shemek

Fairy-Tales by Seventeenth-Century French Women Writers, edited and translated by Lewis Seifert and Domna C. Stanton

Moderata Fonte, *Floridoro*, edited and translated by Valeria Finucci

Moderata Fonte and Lucrezia Marinella, *Religious Narratives*, edited and translated by Virginia Cox

Francisca de los Apostoles, *Visions on Trial: The Inquisitional Trial of Francisca de los Apostoles*, edited and translated by Gillian T. W. Ahlgren

Catharina Regina von Greiffenberg, *Meditations on the Life of Christ*, edited and translated by Lynne Tatlock

Annibal Guasco, *Discourse to Lady Lavinia His Daughter concerning the Manner in Which She Should Conduct Herself at Court*, edited and translated by Peggy Osborn

In Praise of Women: Italian Fifteenth-Century Defenses of Women, edited and translated by Daniel Bornstein

Louise Labé, *Complete Works*, edited and translated by Annie Finch and Deborah Baker
Madame de Maintenon, *Lectures and Dramatic Dialogues*, edited and translated by John Conley, S.J.
Lucrezia Marinella, *L'Enrico, or Byzantium Conquered*, edited and translated by Virginia Cox
Lucrezia Marinella, *Happy Arcadia*, edited and translated by Susan Haskins and Letizia Panizza
Chiara Matraini, *Selected Poetry and Prose*, edited and translated by Elaine MacLachlan
Isotta Nogarola, *Selected Letters*, edited and translated by Margaret L. King and Diana Robin
Jacqueline Pascal, *"A Rule for Children" and Other Writings*, edited and translated by John Conley, S.J.
Eleonora Petersen von Merlau, *Autobiography* (1718), edited and translated by Barbara Becker-Cantarino
Alessandro Piccolomini, *Rethinking Marriage in Sixteenth-Century Italy*, edited and translated by Letizia Panizza
Christine de Pizan et al., *Debate over the "Romance of the Rose,"* edited and translated by Tom Conley with Elisabeth Hodges
Christine de Pizan, *Life of Charles V*, edited and translated by Charity Cannon Willard
Christine de Pizan, *The Long Road of Learning*, edited and translated by Andrea Tarnowski
Madeleine and Catherine des Roches, *Selected Letters, Dialogues, and Poems*, edited and translated by Anne Larsen
Oliva Sabuco, *The New Philosophy: True Medicine*, edited and translated by Gianna Pomata
Margherita Sarrocchi, *La Scanderbeide*, edited and translated by Rinaldina Russell
Madeleine de Scudéry, *Orations and Rhetorical Dialogues*, edited and translated by Jane Donawerth with Julie Strongson
Madeleine de Scudéry, *The "Histoire de Sapho,"* edited and translated by Karen Newman
Justine Siegemund, *The Court Midwife of the Electorate of Brandenburg* (1690), edited and translated by Lynne Tatlock
Gabrielle Suchon, *"On Philosophy" and "On Morality,"* edited and translated by Domna Stanton with Rebecca Wilkin
Sara Copio Sullam, *Sara Copio Sullam: Jewish Poet and Intellectual in Early Seventeenth-Century Venice*, edited and translated by Don Harrán
Arcangela Tarabotti, *Convent Life as Inferno: A Report*, introduction and notes by Francesca Medioli, translated by Letizia Panizza
Arcangela Tarabotti, *Paternal Tyranny*, edited and translated by Letizia Panizza
Laura Terracina, *Works*, edited and translated by Michael Sherberg
Katharina Schütz Zell, *Selected Writings*, edited and translated by Elsie McKee

KEY TO ABBREVIATIONS

ADB   *Allgemeine deutsche Biographie.* Hrsg. durch die Historische Commission bei der Koniglichen Akademie der Wissenschaften. 1875–1912. Reprint, Berlin: Duncker & Humblot, 1967–1971.

BBK   *Biographisch-Bibliographisches Kirchenlexikon.* Edited by Friedrich Wilhelm Bautz. Hamm: Bautz, 1970—.

CMH   *Cambridge Modern History.* Cambridge: Cambridge University Press, 1957—.

CR   *Corpus Reformatorum.* Halle and Braunschweig: Schwetschke, 1834—.

DBI   *Dizionario biografico degli Italiani.* Roma: Istituto della Enciclopedia italiana, 1960—.

DBF   *Dictionnaire de biographie francaise.* Paris: Letouzey et Ane, 1933—.

DNB   *The Dictionary of National Biography.* London: Oxford University Press, 1882—.

NDB   *Neue deutsche Biographie.* Berlin: Duncker & Humblot, 1953—.

NCMH *The New Cambridge Modern History.* Edited by G. R. Elton. 2d ed. Cambridge: Cambridge University Press, 1990—.

OLYMPIA FULVIA MORATA
(1526/27–55)

Disse allor madonna Margherita Gonzaga: «Parmi che voi narriate troppo brevemente queste opere virtuose fatte da donne; ché se ben questi nostri nemici l'hanno udite e lette, mostrano non saperle e vorriano che se ne perdesse la memoria: ma se fate che noi altre le intendiamo, almen ce ne faremo onore».

[Then the lady Margherita Gonzaga said, "In my opinion, you tell these virtuous deeds done by women much too quickly; for our enemies, although they've heard of them and read them, pretend that they don't know about them and would like the memory of them to be lost. But if you let us women hear them, then at least we can do them honor."]

—Castiglione, *The Book of the Courtier*, 3.23

THE VOICE OF ONE CRYING IN THE WILDERNESS

She was raised in a court of unmatched splendor. She was the childhood companion of nobility. A brilliant scholar, she gave public lectures on Cicero, wrote commentaries on Homer, and composed poems, dialogues, and orations in both Latin and Greek. She was one of the most sophisticated and flexible Latin stylists of her age.

She was also a Protestant in papal lands, a profound student of the Bible, who underwent a crisis of faith to emerge stronger. Thrown into disfavor at court, she married for love and love of learning. In search of religious freedom, she and her husband went over the Alps to Germany. There she communicated with leading Reformation theologians, continued her studies, wrestled with the mysteries of predestination and the Eucharist, and wrote Greek poems that won praise across Europe. She was a vivid eyewitness to the horrors of the wars of religion. She suffered siege and bombardment at Schweinfurt, making a perilous escape to Heidelberg, where she continued to write and teach. She spoke with singular authority within the church.

2 Introduction

But the disease contracted during her terrible adventures killed her before her thirtieth birthday. By that time most of her works had been destroyed. Those that remained were gathered by an old family friend as a memorial to the genius he had loved as a daughter. After her death she was attacked as a "Calvinist Amazon," but other women scholars viewed her as a light shining in the darkness.

LIFE AND TIMES

> cuius hic vitam describerem, nisi ex sequentibus epistolis, facile colligi et cognosci posset.
>
> [I would write her biography at this point, but it can be easily gathered and understood from the letters that follow.]
> ———Caelius Secundus Curio, "Dedication to Isabella of Bresengna," 1558

Olympia Morata first stepped onto the stage of history at the age of fourteen. It was a literal stage, set in what her friend and biographer, Caelius Secundus Curio, called "the private Academy of the Queen of Ferrara." At Renée de France's secluded villa, which she called Il Consolando, some time between April and October of 1541, before a select audience of French, German, and Italian heretics, Morata lectured in Latin on Cicero's *Stoic Paradoxes*.[1]

We know little of Morata's life before her own letters begin to tell the story, but we can see something of the background to her life and thought by examining the two most important influences during her formative years: her father, Fulvio Pellegrino Morato, and the besieged and heterodox court in which she was raised.

FULVIO PELLEGRINO MORATO (C. 1483–1548). I cannot here give a summary of the Protestant Reformation or even a sketch of the birth-strangled progress of "evangelism" in Italy.[2] Yet the life of Pellegrino Moretto

---

1. "Dedication to Isbella Bresegna" (1558): "in privata Reginae Ferrariensis Academia." This is doubtless Renée's country retreat near Argenta, twenty-five miles south of Ferrara, which the duke had given her in July 1540. It was the center for most of Renée's clandestine activities in aid of the Protestants, according to the testimony of an Inquisition spy: Rodocanachi 1896 [1970], 153–54; Blaisdell 1969, 200–201; Caponetto 1999, 25.

2. The best introductions to the period are by Miccoli 1974, 975–1075 (esp. 1013–71); Cantimori in *NCMH* 2:288–312; and Cameron 1992. The best general work in English on the Italian Reformation is Caponetto 1999; Brown 1933 and (to a lesser extent) Church 1932 remain useful. The complex idea of "evangelism" is discussed more fully below.

is almost exemplary in showing how the ideas of the Reform spread in Italy.[3] He was originally from Mantua, and in keeping with humanist practice he Latinized his name to Fulvius Peregrinus Moratus.[4] A talented teacher with considerable fame as a poet,[5] he was exiled from Mantua for unknown reasons, and as early as 1517 he had made his way to the Este court in Ferrara to seek aid from Duke Alfonso I for his return.[6] He seems instead to have remained, and in 1522 was employed by the duke's cousin Sigismondo. In the same year he was appointed by the duke himself to oversee the education of his two youngest sons, Ippolito d'Este, later to become cardinal (1509–72), and Francesco, prince of Massa (1516–78).[7] While in service at Ferrara he contributed not only to classical studies but also to the philological study of Italian. His *Rimario di tutte le cadentie di Dante e Petrarca* (1528) was the first study and dictionary of rhyme in Italian.

At Ferrara Morato married a certain Lucrezia, and late in 1526 or early 1527, the first of their children, Olympia, was born.[8] In that same year, he dedicated an explication of the Our Father and the Hail Mary to the nun Teofila Gozi of S. Gabriello in Ferrara, possibly Lucrezia's sister.[9] In this he attacked

---

3. For Morato, see principally Capori 1875; Puttin 1974; Olivieri 1992, 300–46; briefly, Caretti 1940, 50 n. 1.

4. He made the change as early as 1526 (Olivieri 1992, 317 n. 128). Calcagnini (1544, 189) in an undated letter teases him about it and makes it appear that the "metamorphosis" happened while Morato was at Venice.

5. For the social status of such schoolteachers, see Seidel Menchi 1987, 122–42. For his poetry see, for example, Calcagnini 1544, 124, and the letter of Pietro Bembo praising Morato's poetry as "facetum et elegans" (the letter thanks Morato for a gift of letters and *versiculi*, which Morato sent as a way of asking admission to Bembo's friendship: Bembo 1729, 4:230: Liber VI, prid. id. Sex., 1534). I have been unable to locate a copy of Morato's *Carmina Quaedam Latina* (Venice, 1533).

6. Puttin 1974, 113, with documentation.

7. Ibid., 114. See documents 1 and 2 in the present text (Giraldus, *On the Poets of Our Time* and Caelius Secundus Curio to Sixtus Betulius); Bonnet 1856, 24; Kössling and Weiss-Stählin 1990, 10; Flood and Shaw 1997, 101.

8. The marriage may have occurred in 1525, the year in which he acquired some property: Puttin, 1974, 114. Olympia was born after 26 October 1526; see letters 72, 73, and Note on Chronology.

9. Barotti [1792–93] 1970, 2:165; Caretti 1940, 51 n. 1; Puttin 1974, 122 and 125 n. 40. Moretto refers to her as "Cognata anzi Sirochia soa amatissima" (1st ed., Ferrara: Francesco Rosso da Valenza, 1526. I have not been able to locate a copy). Two other works were published in a 1540 edition of short works by Luther and Amsdorf circulating under the less alarming name of Erasmus: *La dichiaratione di i dieci commandamenti dil credo e dil pater noster con una breve Annotatione dil vivere Christiano per Erasmo Rotedamo, utile e necessaria a caiscuno fedele Christiano*. The frontispiece lists an *Opera nuova dilla dichiaratione dil nome di Giesù mirabile* (A new work on the explanation of the wonderful name of Jesus) and *Da mihi bibere dilla Samaritana* (The Samaritan woman's "give me to

a piece of mud covered in a monk's hood. I'm talking about Brother Martin Luther with his muck[10] and mud. In our time he has so encrusted our faith that almost the whole thing is transformed. And out of the multitude of ecclesiastics there has not appeared up till now even one who has completely taken up the challenge of controverting him.[11]

This seems an orthodox enough work, but Morato was already following in the footsteps of such forerunners of the Reformation as Savonarola, Pico della Mirandola, Erasmus, and even Luther himself, all of whom had written expositions on the Lord's Prayer for a vernacular audience.[12]

However, when Morata was five, her father took her and her family away from Ferrara for six years (1532–39).[13] The reason is unclear, but it seems to have been the result of professional jealousy rather than religious persecution.[14] His friend, the scholar and astronomer Celio Calcagnini (1479–1541), spoke of various secret enemies and proclaimed Morato's departure a great loss; the youth of the city were dissatisfied with all the other private teachers.[15]

To the great delight of the local humanists, Morato opened a school in Vicenza in April 1532, where he gave public lectures on Cicero's *Stoic Paradoxes* and Horace's *Art of Poetry*. He also spent time in Venice and Cesena.[16] While in exile he wrote further works: *On the Significance of the Colors* (1535), an allegorical handbook, as well as his book of Latin poems (1533).[17] But by

---

drink" [John 4:10]) by Peregrino Moretto Mantoano e Ferrarese. This exists as a unique copy in Florence: the part containing Morato's works was damaged in the 1966 flood. Seidel Menchi 1987, 83, 377–78 n. 44; 1993, 86 n. 44; Olivieri 1992, 304–5.

10. *luto*, punning on Luther.

11. Text trans. from Prosperi 1990, 267 (also at Puttin 1974, 123).

12. Olivieri 1992, 304–5.

13. Calcagnini 1544, 199, for the date of return; Olivieri 1967, 55 n. 5.

14. Contra the impression given by Kutter 1955, 35 (very speculative) and Blaisdell 1969, 178 (citing also Church 1932, 65, who offers no evidence). Baruffaldi (cited from Tiraboschi 1822, 12 [= VII, pt. 3]:1746 n. 1) and Nolten (1775, 16–17) go no further than jealousy as a reason.

15. Calcagnini is the only source (rightly Puttin 1974, 115–16): Calcagnini 1544, 156–58; Nolten 1775, 15–16 speak of "your innocence, or (to call it the worst name) the lightness of your fault, and certainly provoked by many injuries."

16. Calcagnini 1544, 189 (Venice); 104 (Cesena).

17. *Del Significato de' Colori*. His Italian works went through numerous editions. Also a lost *De Socrate* (Calcagnini 1544, 168–69, 179). Olivieri (1992) is perhaps overeager to squeeze religious significance out of these works and other rather straightforward encomiastic poems of the period. See also Puttin 1974, 120–23, on Morato's works.

this time it is clear that his religious beliefs were changing or had changed. Near the end of 1532, Morato met Bartolomeo Testa, who had been a follower of the Swiss reformer Zwingli since 1529, and talked with him about baptism and the Mass. He lectured to his students on the ideas of Erasmus, Melanchthon, Zwingli, and Luther.[18] These pupils included Alessandro Trissino and his cousin Giulio Trissino; Alessandro, Niccolò, and Marco Thiene; and Count Carlos de Seso, all of whom were or would become prominent Protestants.[19] During this period he met Caelius Secundus Curio, who would remain a lifelong friend to him and his daughter (see below). Morato was in trouble with the Council of Ten in Venice in 1536,[20] and by 1539 he was lecturing publicly on Calvin's *Institutes of Christian Religion*.[21] Only a year before, the cardinals themselves had warned of the danger that such Italian teachers posed to the orthodoxy of youth.[22]

Morato also seems to have had some sort of mystical experience, though the one-sided nature of the correspondence does not allow us to learn specific details. Calcagnini replied rather cryptically to letters of Morato (dated 13 February 1538, when Morata was 11):

> I congratulate you that you have found a way, as your letter to me bears witness, that will carry you to that highest and perpetual happiness. It was in fact, I see, easy for you to do. First because you have always enrolled your name from the heart, not for deception, under the banner of Christian philosophy. And you've given proof of this in the way in which you have educated your family and your students with the

---

18. Olivieri 1992, 303, 307–8. Cf. the letter (text at Morsolin 1878, 410; also Puttin 1974, 201) of 29 May 1538 from the poet and dramatist Giangiorgio Trissino to his son Giulio complaining of Morato's infecting the young man with Lutheran doctrines; there is a similar letter dated 10 March 1542 (Puttin 1974, 204).

19. Cignoni 1982–84; Olivieri 1992, 307–8; Caponetto 1999, 199–203. Calcagnini (1544, 158) mentions Trissino.

20. Church (1932, 65) believed the case concerned heresy, but Puttin (1974, 199–200) rightly stresses that we cannot be sure. Savi (1815, 121–22 [non vidi; cited in Puttin 1974, 199]) cites the document of 10 May 1536.

21. Olivieri 1992, 317. The second edition of the *Institutio Christianae Religionis* appeared in that year. The first edition had been published in 1536.

22. In the *Consilium de Emendanda Ecclesia* (Kidd 1911, 315): "There is great and pernicious abuse in the public schools, especially in Italy, in which many professors of philosophy are teaching impiety. In fact, the most impious disputations occur even in church, and even if they were pious, divine matters are treated quite irreverently openly before the common people." A sloppy sentence, which Morata would have despised. For a similar and widespread attitude, however, cf. Calcagnini, below. On the spread of the ideas of Luther and Erasmus by these schoolmasters, see Seidel Menchi 1987, 122–42; 1993, 139–68; Bacchelli 1998, 337.

holiest of morals and teaching. Secondly, because if the things that are especially good are most suitable to our life, then we have to admit that there is nothing more in accordance with nature than that way of life which we teach, with Christ as our authority, in which all the greatest and most special good things are contained. And so nature draws us voluntarily to those things which are in fact the best. One is merely deceiving oneself by putting forward the difficulty of the matter as an excuse for laziness or bad habits.

I come now to your third letter in which you tell me that an incredible desire to see us had come over you, but it had been dispelled almost by divine providence. In this matter I cannot fail to approve strongly of your plan to submit not only all your acts but all your thoughts to the will of the highest power. Nevertheless, to tell the truth, I was sad to hear that the oracle cost you so much that it could only be compared to a fit of the ague. Otherwise, I think it's a good idea that you are not coming to us. . . . Be well and keep your desires within Christian limits. If you do this, I will think you happy.[23]

Despite the recalcitrance of the Venetian authorities, there had been active prosecution of heresy in Vicenza and with the arrival of papal legates for the proposed council the climate became increasingly dangerous.[24] Morato was able to return to Ferrara in June 1539, where Calcagnini had been working behind the scenes to influence the new duke, Ercole II, after the death of Alfonso I in 1534.[25] Morato was put in charge of the education of Alfonso's two youngest children by his mistress Laura Dianti, Alfonso (1527–87) and Alfonsino (1530–47).[26] He is found on the list of the professors at the University of Ferrara in 1546 and continued to teach till his final illness in 1548.[27]

---

23. Calcagnini 1544, 191–92.

24. This was the eventual Council of Trent. Morsolin 1878, 409–15; Brown 1933, 114; Olivieri 1992, 315–17. The pope personally intervened in 1540.

25. Calcagnini (1544, 169, dated 12 February 1537; 185, dated 8 November 1537) on his efforts on Morato's behalf. A letter from Bernardinus Trinagius (15 March 1539) hails his return to favor; cited in Bonnet 1856, 25.

26. Caretti 1940, 52 n. 2; Puttin 1974, 119.

27. Some indication of how valuable his services were considered is given by his salary, known for 1541–44—the rather respectable sum of 180 lire per year (above living expenses), raised in 1545–46 to 400: Puttin 1974, 119; Chiellini 1991, 237. Puttin (1974, 119) misidentifies Morato's second son Emilio (b. 1542) with his older son Alfonsino (b. 1540) and so miscalculates the date of Morato's death.

A HAVEN FOR HERETICS. The court in which Morata was raised was one of the most glittering in Europe. Under Alfonso I d'Este (b. 1476, r. 1505–34) and his wife, Lucrezia Borgia (b. 1480, m. 1502, d. 1515), Ferrara was home to—among many others—the poet Ariosto, the artists Dosso Dossi and Titian, and the eponymous musicians Antonio del Cornetto and Alfonso della Viola, who contributed to the birth of opera.[28] Alfonso's son, Ercole II (b. 1508, r. 1534–59), continued the tradition of magnificence.[29]

In the midst of her husband's court, the new duchess, Renée de France (1510–75), had established an island of French retainers and religious refugees. Renée was a deeply ambiguous and vacillating figure.[30] In 1528, at the age of eighteen, a little over a year after Morata was born, she had been married off to the twenty-year-old Ercole, in order to cement the political alliance between France and Ferrara.[31] The younger daughter of Louis XII (b. 1482, r. 1498–1515),[32] she was orphaned at the age of four and grew up in a milieu of evangelical thinking. She was raised at the royal court under the wing of the king's sister, Marguerite d'Angoulême, a strong supporter of reform within the church.[33] When Marguerite became queen of Navarre in 1527, she took Renée with her to Nérac. Other early influences included

---

28. Titian (c. 1480–1576) painted the Camerino d' Alabastro for Alfonso I between 1518 and 1523. For Ferrara under Ercole II's grandfather, Ercole I (b. 1431, r. 1471–1505), see Gundersheimer 1973.

29. For recent work on the arts at Ferrara, see Pade et al. 1990; Humfrey and Lucco 1998, esp. 27–54; Ciammitti et al. 1998. For a necessarily speculative look at the interactions of religion and music under Ercole II, see Nugent 1990.

30. Fundamental studies on Renée and Ferrara are Blaisdell 1969, 1972, 1975. Among older works, Fontana 1889–99 is deeply flawed in its desire to shield Renée from the charge of heresy, but should be consulted for its documentation; Rodocanachi 1896 [1970] is more balanced and useful but errs in the opposite direction. See Bainton 1971, 235–51, for a brief account.

31. For the marriage (28 June 1528) and spectacular festivities, see Catalano 1930, 1:579–82; Blaisdell 1969, 37; Tagmann 1978; Roffi 1984. For the political situation, including much shopping around by the fathers for suitable alliances, see the succinct statements in CMH 1:348, 361; NCMH 2:226; Blaisdell 1969, 39, 41–43; 1972, 201–2; Knecht 1994, 63, 274.

32. Renée was sister-in-law to François I (b. 1494, r. 1515–47), who succeeded as king of France, through her late elder sister, Claude (1499–1524). The oft-repeated claim that Renée said, "If I had a beard I would have been the king of France" (e.g. Bainton 1971, 235, without citation) is, of course, preposterous. With or without the Salic law, Renée was twelve years younger than Claude, who had long ago produced heirs to the throne. The origin of this myth seems to be a misunderstanding of a statement by Federico Gonzaga, for which see Fontana 1889–99, 1:77–78; Blaisdell 1969, 49.

33. Blaisdell 1969, 29–31. For the religious views of Marguerite, see Martineau and Veissière 1975 and Veissière 1986. Good brief discussions by Greengrass 1987, 18–20; Nicholls 1992, 123–25; Crouzet 1996, 331–44; see also NCMH 2:237–38; Roelker 1972, 172–73; Knecht 1994, 117, 147–48, 260–61, 308.

8   *Introduction*

Jacques Lefèvre d'Étaples, whom Marguerite took along as confessor. His emphasis on justification by faith ("sola gratia, sola fide") and on the Mass as a "remembrance and recollection" had a profound effect on Luther and led to Lefèvre's own works being condemned as Lutheran heresy by the Faculty of Paris in 1525.[34]

Renée loathed Italy — she steadfastly refused to learn Italian — and brought to Ferrara her own set of more than 160 French courtiers, including her guardian, Michelle de Saubonne, baronne de Soubise.[35] Mme de Soubise was an early follower of Calvin's and raised her children as Protestants.[36] When she was exiled in 1536, her daughter, Anne de Parthenay-Soubise, remained behind as Renée's companion until she too was exiled in 1544.[37] The duchess and her court, filled with "Lutheran bandits from France,"[38] remained a perpetual source of danger and embarrassment to Ercole, who struggled to maintain power in a duchy threatened with expansion by Venice on one side and reincorporation into the Papal States on the other.[39]

As early as 1530, Pope Clement VII had complained to the head of the Inquisition for Modena and Ferrara that Ferrara was rife with Lutherans.[40] Renée maintained a secret fund to aid those in flight from the prosecution in France.[41] Calvin himself passed through in 1536, and began a lifelong correspondence with the duchess.[42] So did the brilliant poet Clément Marot

34. Screech 1994, 62. For Jacques Lefèvre d'Étaples (c. 1455–1537), see Rummel 1994, 69–71 for a concise account; fuller studies by Screech 1964, Hughes 1984, Crouzet 1996, 88–103. François I appointed Lefèvre d'Étaples to oversee the education of the royal children (May 1526): Rodocanachi 1896 [1970], 10; Crouzet 1996, 195–96. Blaisdell (1969, 33) cautiously notes, however, that there is no direct evidence that Renée was one of the pupils at that time.

35. Blaisdell 1969, 34–35, 50; 1972, 200–201. For a list of Renée's court in 1529, see Rodocanachi 1896 [1970], 58–60.

36. See Blaisdell 1969, 25–28; Cignoni 1990–92. Her children and their descendants were to play prominent roles as Huguenots in the Wars of Religion. See Bonnet 1872, 17 (citing the memoirs of her son): "dès ce temps la dite dame de Soubise avoit congnoissance de la vraye religion et y instruisit ses enfants dès leur petitesse"; Roelker 1972, 174; see also Rodocanachi 1896 [1970], 10.

37. Cignoni 1990–92. Rodocanachi (1896 [1970], 84–92), Blaisdell (1969, 83), and C. Mayer (1972, 317) rightly give the date as 20 March 1536 (*pace* Bertoni 1936, 192). For the banishments, see Blaisdell 1969, 57–85. For the political background, see Blaisdell 1972, 203, 207. For Parthenay-Soubise, see Blaisdell 1969, 163–64 (misidentified by Flood and Shaw [1997, 88]).

38. Filippo Rodi, ambassador for Ferrara in Rome, to Ercole: Blaisdell 1969, 87, with archival documentation.

39. See Braun 1988 for a detailed political study.

40. Fontana 1889–99, 2:103; Flood and Shaw 1997, 89 (not citing source).

41. Blaisdell 1969, 166.

42. Blaisdell 1969, 127–45; 1972, 205–7, with bibliography and the few certain sources; see also Rodocanachi 1896 [1970], 127. For a convenient summary of background to the flights

(1496?—1544), whose French settings of the Psalms became the hymnal for the Huguenots.[43]

Other guests included Vittoria Colonna (1492–1547), the brilliant poet and correspondent of Michelangelo's.[44] She shared the growing concern with reform of the church and an emphasis on justification by faith with Bernardino Ochino, the most brilliant preacher of the age.[45] Colonna was undoubtedly responsible for summoning him to give his message in the Duomo of Ferrara in July and Advent of 1537.[46] After Ochino fled from the Inquisition in 1542, to Switzerland and eventually England, Colonna was herself investigated.

There were incidents of open defiance. On Holy Tuesday, 14 April 1536, one of the singers in the ducal chapel, Jehannet de Bouchefort, refused to adore the cross, considering it an act of idolatry, and stormed out of the Mass.[47] The resulting scandal eventually resulted in the torture of Bouchefort, various arrests, and a widening circle of appeals to Marguerite de Navarre in Nerác, the French ambassador in Venice, the Farrarese ambassador in Paris, and the pope in Rome.[48]

---

of Calvin and Marot, see Greengrass 1987, 24–26; also Kelley 1981, 13–19; Crouzet 1996, 224–39.

43. For Marot, see in primis Screech 1994; also Blaisdell 1972, 204–5; *BBK* 5 (1993): 864–72 (Grünberg-Dröge) Defaux 1990–93, 1:xii—xiii (a handy *chronologie*), cxxi—cxlv. For a loving (if eccentric) appreciation in English of Marot's poetry, see Hofstadter 1997.
Both Calvin and Marot first sought refuge at Nérac with Marguerite de Navarre, who had been the poet's first patron: C. Mayer 1972, 26–27. Renée made Marot her secretary. He had arrived by April 1535, when his salary is recorded; see Bertoni 1933; 1936, 189; Blaisdell 1969, 90; 1972, 204 n. 24; C. Mayer 1972, 28; also C. Mayer 1956. Marot left Ferrara in June 1536 and is in Venice by 10 June; by 31 July, he had written the third "De coq à la asne." For the poems composed for and about Renée, see Defaux 1990–93, 1:349–52 (with notes, 752–58), 2:77–116, 179–87 (with notes, 851–95, 953–58).

44. A portrait at Bainton 1971, 201–18; Gibaldi 1987; King 1991, 142–43; more detailed are Jung 1951 (now outdated); Firpo 1988 (= 1992, chap. 2); Bassanese 1994 (and literature there cited); Fragnito 1997. For her stay in Ferrara (8 May 1537–22 February 1538), see Blaisdell 1969, 167–77. Fontana 1889–99, 2:25–83; Rodocanachi 1896 [1970], 128–37 are both overly speculative.

45. For the central importance of Ochino to Italian evangelism, see in brief Caponetto 1999, 100–102; *BBK* 6 (1993): 1085–89 (Wenneker); Benrath 1877 (Eng. trans. of the 1st ed.) and [1892] 1968 (2d German ed.) remain fundamental. See below on Ochino's flights.

46. Fontana 1892, 2:74–75, Blaisdell 1969, 173, Fragnito 1997, 231.

47. Bertoni 1936, 188; C. Mayer 1972, 276, 313, 319–36. Bouchefort was eventually released and, like Marot, ultimately returned to Paris and the service of François I.

48. Blaisdell 1969, 91–115 (the date is mistakenly given as 1535 at p. 91); 1972, 203–4; 1975, 76–78; C. Mayer 1972, 276, 319–32; Flood and Shaw 1997, 116; Prosperi 1990, 273–74; for older accounts amidst much speculation: Fontana 1889–99, 1:318–20 (full text of the duke's

10 *Introduction*

EDUCATION AND JUVENILIA. It was to this "court within a court"[49] that Olympia Morata was summoned after her family's return to Ferrara, sometime between 1539 and 1541, when she was twelve to thirteen years old.[50] Renée had done her duty by producing, in rapid succession, Anna (16 November 1531), the heir Alfonso (22 November 1533: destined to be the last duke of Ferrara), Lucrezia (16 December 1535; later duchess of Urbino), Eleonora (19 June 1537), and finally Luigi (21 December 1538; the builder of the Villa d'Este at Tivoli). Anna was given a humanistic education, and Johannes Sinapius was engaged for this purpose. Sinapius (1505–60), a friend of Calvin's and a former professor of Greek at Heidelberg, had come to Ferrara to study medicine.[51] He had been a lecturer on the faculty and appointed as personal physician first to Jean de Langeac, bishop of Limoges and ambassador to Ferrara, and then to Renée herself.[52] Note that it was taken for granted that Anna, as the eldest daughter of a noble house, would be given a full humanistic education.[53]

It was decided that Anna needed a companion "in order for her to have someone with whom to compete in noble competition."[54] Renée's account books provide a glimpse into the schoolroom. In April 1542 (when Olympia was fifteen), the duchess ordered three copies of Aristotle's *Rhetoric,* one Ovid, one Erasmus, plus two copies each of Pomponius Mela and Ptolemy, one Euclid, four globes, and a map of the world—geography lessons were about to begin.[55]

And so Olympia Morata came to court. She had been educated by her father, who was by all accounts a genius at teaching, though his long and,

---

letter); Rodocanachi 1896 [1970], 110–27. For Marot's involvement, see C. Mayer 1956; 1972, 328–38; Screech 1994, 119–22.

49. The phrase is Bacchelli's (1998, 335).

50. Caretti (1940, 38, 51) gives the date as 1540; Rodocanachi 1896 [1970], 181, and Flood and Shaw 1997, 101 as 1541. It cannot be more accurately placed than between March 1539, when Morato returned to Ferrara (n. 26) and the death of Calcagnini on 24 April 1541 (see below).

51. At a salary of 36 livres a month: Rodocanachi 1896 [1970], 183.

52. Johann Senf or Senff ("mustard," latinized as *Sinapius*). See the detailed study by Flood and Shaw 1997, with additional details in Shaw 1998. He had arrived in Ferrara by 1533 and received his degree in 1535 (Chiellini 1991, 243; Flood and Shaw 1997, 82–85, 88); on the education of Anne, see Flood and Shaw 1997, 101, 105.

53. The younger daughter, Lucrezia, was also educated in Latin and Greek: Flood and Shaw 1997, 87 (letter of Palerio, extract and translation). Rodocanachi (1896 [1970], 181–82) claims that Morata was placed in charge of the education of Lucretia and Eleonora; there is no evidence for this.

54. Document 2 of the present text (Caelius Secundus Curio to Sixtus Betulius). For the value of emulation in education, see Vergerio, *De ingenuis moribus* 2 (Woodward [1897] 1963, 97).

55. At a cost of 79 livres; Rodocanachi 1896 [1970], 182–83.

frankly, rather tedious letter (or, more accurately, essay) to her shows little evidence of this (letter 1). It is a valuable document, however, for three reasons. The first—difficult to convey in translation—is that it shows how vastly superior a stylist the daughter was to her father, a man held in considerable esteem by his contemporaries (document 1 [Giraldus, *On the Poets of Our Time*]). Second, it gives us a glimpse of the authors with whom he wished his daughter to be acquainted. Third, and most important, it assumes she will be speaking Latin publicly.

Morata's other formal teachers included Johannes Sinapius's brother, Chilian (1506–63), for Greek (letters 2 and 3).[56] He, however, took no credit for her genius: "She was taught by German teachers no less than by those of her own country, but mostly, imitating the autodidacts, she used 'silent teachers,'" that is, books (letter 78).[57]

Further influence came from two sources. One was her father's old friend, Caelius Secundus Curio (1503–69), who would devote himself after her death to preserving her memory. Curio, from minor nobility, had been orphaned at the age of eight.[58] He was trained in law and literature at Turin, where, through the Augustinians, he read the works of Luther, Zwingli, and Melanchthon before he was twenty. Cardinal Bonifacio Ferreri had him arrested in order to prevent a trip to Wittenberg. While under house arrest in the convent of San Begnino, Curio took the bones of Saints Agapitus and Tibertius from their reliquary and substituted a Bible, with the message: "*This* is the Ark of the Covenant from which you may ask for true oracles and in which are the true relics of the saints." Following this famous public prank, Curio took up the life of a Protestant *picaro*, and later recounted his adventures with great zest. Once, after a debate in which he defended Luther by reading from the author's *Commentaries on Galatians*, Curio was again arrested by the inquisitors of the local bishop. He escaped—by tricking the guard into putting fetters on a fake leg[59] —to Padua, where he occupied the chair once held by Lorenzo Valla, and had to be protected by

---

56. Nolten 1775, 111–12; Blaisdell 1969; Flood and Shaw 1997, 101–2.

57. Nolten (1775, 46–47) claims that Anna d'Este (and therefore Morata) was taught Greek by Aonio Paleario (repeated by Smyth 1837, 148), but the cited letters merely express admiration for the learning of Renée and her daughters. See also Flood and Shaw 1997, 87.

58. For Curio, see Kutter 1955 for the basic study (esp. 9–48, 230–33); *DBI* 31:443–49 (for an excellent short summation of the facts). Church 1932 (esp. 61–71, 140–43) has a vivid account, based on original sources. See also Blaisdell 1969, 177–79; Williams 1992, 953–59; Flood and Shaw 1997, 90.

59. *Se non è vero*.... Details at Kutter 1955, 17–18; he later recounted the story in his *Probus* (later incorporated into the *Pasquillus Ecstaticus*).

an armed student guard. Under pressure from the Inquisition, he went to Venice, where he heard Ochino's Lenten sermons of 1539. While there he worked on the first draft of his *Pasquillus Ecstaticus*, which became a Protestant best-seller and was rapidly translated into Italian, German, and English—and just as rapidly banned.[60] In it, the Roman statue of the Pasquino, an antique fragment on which "pasquinades" are displayed to this day, comes to life and is carried off in a trance to see "The Paradise of the Popes," the heaven of fraud and deception, arranged like Dante's Purgatory.[61] This is one of the books that Morata asked Curio to send after her flight to Germany (letter 27).

Curio and Morato had met at some point after Morato's exile from Ferrara, and on 19 April 1541 he was able to offer Curio refuge in Ferrara.[62] Curio was then briefly employed as a tutor to Anna and the other children.[63] By October of the same year, Renée had sent him on to Lucca.[64] During these months in Ferrara he was able to hear Morata (age 14) deliver readings in Greek (almost certainly the "Praise of Scaevola") and the lectures on Cicero (document 2 [Caelius Secundo Curio to Sixtus Betulius]). Morata's poem "On True Virginity" may date from this period, since it shows affinity with Curio's language. He made a brief clandestine return from Lucca in September 1542 to rescue his wife and children, left behind in Tuscany. Passing through Ferrara, he gave Renée a copy of Bullinger's *Commentaries on Matthew* before departing on 24 October.[65]

Curio had a profound effect on Morato. In one letter he begged for Curio to send him

> whatever writings you can gather up that you think relate to the right way of living and which eagerly demolish the citadels of the faithless

---

60. Basel: Oporinus, 1544. The first edition was already circulating by 1543.
61. For its importance, see Biondi 1970 and Caponetto 1999, 32–34. The English title should give some idea of the contents: *Pasquine in a traunce: A Christian and learned dialogue (contanyning wonderfull and most strange newes out of heauen, purgatorie, and hell) wherein besydes Christes truth playnely set forth, ye shall also finde a numbre of pleasaunt hystories, discouering all the crafty conueyaunces of Antechrist. Wherunto are added certayne questions then put forth by Pasquine, to haue bene disputed in the Councell of Trent* (London: Seres, 1566).
62. Olivieri 1992, 317.
63. Blaisdell (1969, 178) dates their meeting to 1533, when Curio was teaching at Casale Monferrato and Morato in nearby Vicenza, but Kutter (1955, 26) shows that this rests on uncertain evidence.
64. For the chronology, see Kutter 1955, 42, and the letter below. He continued on to Switzerland in 1542, with a letter from Renée recommending him to Bullinger (Blaisdell 1969, 179). For Curio in Lucca, see Adorni-Braccesi 1994, 115–17.
65. Letter to Calvin: Calvin 1863–1900, 11, col. 479–82 [CR 39 = *Calvini Opera* 11]. *DBI* 31:444.

impostors and deceitful satraps. I strongly beg you again and again to do this. Farewell, best instrument and chosen vessel for the glory of God. Jesus Christ give you Tobias' guide [an angel] for your journey.[66]

After Curio left for Lucca (and ultimately Basel), Morato wrote a letter to him which is worth quoting in full (Curio 1553, 55–56; dated Ferrara, 30 October [1541]):[67]

> If human bodies, after their souls depart from them to be free and unbound, retained any sensation, instead of having nothing left inside them, I would now make this comparison and say that no human body has ever been so devastated at the departure of its soul, or felt so much pain after its departure, than it was for me (and is) sad and depressing to see that you have left and that I am without you, when I see that I am deprived of my divine teacher, sent to me by God Himself for my teaching and instruction. I do not think that Ananias, Paul's master, taught him with holier admonition and discipline, when he initiated him into Christ, than you did me.[68] However, it greatly relieves my grief to believe that I am in the bosom of our Christ and that He does not let me go.[69] For when I was in pain during the crisis, so that I saw myself abandoned on all sides, in great danger and colder than ice itself, lo, you were sent from God to break your journey with us, passing by many heroes who were begging for you to be their guest. Occasionally on my own, when I had any free time amid so many distractions (but I rarely have any free time), for a fraction of an hour beguiling my afflicted body and my rapidly approaching old age, I used to read, or I should say, skim, something by John or Paul or the other sacred writings. But your living voice and fiery spirit, with which the whole of you scintillates and by which you ignite others, so vivaciously and effectively moved, excited, and warmed me, that now I realize my darkness, and I now live, not I, but Christ in me and I in Christ.[70] What do I mean? You have turned me from a starveling to a vomiter and from very ice to very fire.[71] Now not only do I feel

---

66. C. S. Curio 1553, 54–55 (undated).
67. The literal translation reflects some of the infelicities of style.
68. Ananias (Acts 9:10–19), who removed the scales from Paul's eyes and brought about his baptism. There is an implication that Morato too has been an enemy of what he now sees as the true gospel.
69. Cf. Cic. *QF* 2.11.1.
70. Gal. 2:20.
71. A singularly repellent image.

14 *Introduction*

that I am being nourished to be flourishing and lively, but I can also make many other partakers by the abundance with which you have filled me.[72]

All that remains is for you to pray constantly to God that He may guard from all calamity the luxuriant crop sprung from your seed to a good harvest and glorious fruit for our Lord, to whom be eternal praise. In His grace, may you be well, together with all your family and our brothers.

The other influential figure in Morata's education was her father's old friend Celio Calcagnini (1479–1541).[73] Calcagnini was a protean figure: bastard of a noble house, student of Battista Guarini's, soldier, papal protonotary, professor at the University of Ferrara, upholder (on philosophical grounds) of the Copernican system, friend of Erasmus's and Marot's, read by Robert Burton, plundered by Rabelais.[74] There was indeed something Rabelaisian about Calcagnini. He was a bon vivant, ribald poet,[75] worldly churchman, moral relativist. He was obviously in sympathy with many of the aims of the reformers, yet a staunch anti-Lutheran, writing *On the Free Motion of the Soul* (De libero animi motu, 1525) to stand alongside Erasmus's *On Free Will* (De libero arbitrio, 1524) in answer to "the Lutheran cancer" of that author's *On*

---

72. Cf. Heb. 6:4.

73. In a letter of 14 February 1534, Calcagnini (1544, 182) asked Morato to "plant a kiss in my name on the forehead and ear of your daughter, Delia, who is already (as you write) chattering merrily away" [Deliae puellae iam festive, ut tu scribis, garrienti]. Nolten (1775, 27 [and Bonnet 1856, 27: "cette muse enfantine"]) saw this as a reference to Olympia, but *garrienti* is hardly appropriate to a girl aged eight; Delia must be the proper name of another daughter. Olympia had three sisters (letters 20, 27), of whom the third was named Vittoria (letters 27, 45, 46, 47). Smyth (1834, 130, 145) claims that Calcagnini was Olympia's godfather. However, this role was given to Bernardino Mazzolino (so the dedication to *Rimario di tutte le cadentie di Dante e Petrarca* of 1548, which reprinted a letter dated 15 April 1528: Tiraboschi 1822, 12 (= VII, pt. 3): 1747; Puttin 1974, 114. Calcagnini (1544, 157) said he stood godfather to a daughter born apparently just after Morato departed. This may be the Delia mentioned above. He also served as godfather to a son, Alfonsino, born in 1540 (Puttin 1974, 119 and 124 n. 24). Document 2 of the present text (Caelius Secundus Curio to Sixtus Betuleius) mentions Morata's "brothers."

74. Calcagnini was mentioned by Ariosto as one of the glories of Ferrara (*Orlando Furioso* 42.90, 46.14). A good taste of his works at Screech 1984; Bacchelli 1998; D'Ascia 1998, 317–20; also *DBI* 16:492–98; Moreschini 1991, 184–86. Calcagnini 1544 for prose works, poetry in Pigna 1553; for two poems, see Perosa and Sparrow 1979, 203–6. Bibliography at Chiellini 1991, 222; *DBI* 16:492–98.

75. *Description of a Cunt, Description of an Asshole, The Endurance of Priapus, Against a Pervert, Playing with the Girls* (Descriptio cunni, descriptio culi, priapi fortitudo, in impudicum, de lusu puellarum): Pigna 1553, 191–93).

the Bondage of the Will (De servo arbitrio, 1525).[76] In a letter (Ferrara, 23 July 1538), talking especially about predestination, he counseled Morato:

> There are certain things, as it were mysteries, about which it is better to be quiet and dissimulate than to bring out before the mob, such as, naturally, things which pertain to the first and primitive church. . . . I think there were and will be in days to come those who hold the author of this book more than a little inclined to the Manichaean heresy.[77] Of course, the same suspicion could fall on the Apostle to the Gentiles, Paul, if he fell into the hands of a rash and imprudent reader. . . . About things which it is dangerous to speak in the crowd and the gathering of the forum I have always thought this was healthiest: to speak as do many, to think as do few [loqui ut multi, sentire ut pauci], and to have this precept of Paul always on my tongue and in my memory: "Do you have faith? Keep it between yourself and God."[78]

This is less hypocrisy, or the sin of "Nicodemism" so railed against by Calvin,[79] than the genuine (if elitist) belief of a skeptical man of the professional class who profoundly distrusted the masses, and believed that interpretation of the Bible was best left in the hands of a hard core of professionals.[80]

Calcagnini was a great stylist and believed in Latin as a flexible international language. His attitude toward Cicero was highly sensible. Cicero was, of course, the greatest of authors, but only a fool would limit himself to the style of Cicero, much less to the words found in the corpus of his works. He had written observations on Cicero's *De Officiis* which prompted one *Defense*

---

76. See *DBI*, s.v. On Calcagnini and Luther, see his letter to Erasmus (Erasmus 1906–58, 6:117 [no. 1587]).

77. The title and author are never given, but the date and list of topics (justification by faith, predestination) seem to fit Calvin's recently published *Institutio*. Tiraboschi 1822, 12 (= VII, pt. 3): 1748 thought that it might refer to a book written (but apparently never published) by Morato himself. However, the language of the letter does not support that idea.

78. Rom. 14:22 (in Greek); Calcagnini 1544, 195–96.

79. After Nicodemus, who visited Jesus by night (John 3:2); it refers generally to a timid and secret adherent. John Calvin in his *Excuse à Messieurs les Nicodémites* (1544) applied it to Protestant converts in France who concealed their Protestant beliefs and outwardly practiced Roman Catholicism. See the bibliographical review by Tedeschi 2000, 969–72, and individual works by Rotondò 1967; Biondi 1974; Eire 1979; Turchetti 1987; Williams 1992, 892–96; Rummel 2000, 102–20.

80. Biondi 1974, 61–62; Prosperi 1990, 272; Bacchelli 1998, 338–39, 341. This was not far from Erasmus's view, especially about Luther and predestination. E.g. Erasmus 1906–58, 3:605 (no. 980).

of Cicero by Jacobus Grifolus (fl. 1546) and another by Marc Antonio Majoragio (1514–55).[81] Calcagnini clearly was the inspiration for Morata's lost "Defense of Cicero," which he praised.[82]

Calcagnini's influence on Morata may have been much deeper than has been realized. He seems to have been instrumental in leading Morata to an early belief in a distant Epicurean God. This will be considered below. Calcagnini died in 1541, when Morata was only fourteen, but it is hard not to see the influence of a profound scholar on a young one.[83]

A number of Morata's surviving works date from these first two or three years at court (1539–41, age 12–14). Most of her output was lost in the siege of Schweinfurt (see below), but Curio's copies of her juvenilia survived.[84] She was no more than fourteen when she wrote the defense of Cicero. The other lost works mentioned by Curio—dialogues in Greek and Latin in imitation of Plato, commentaries on Homer—also date to her period at court.[85] As her later metrical paraphrases of the Psalms show, her knowledge of Homeric poetry was profound.

---

81. Calcagnini 1544, 253–69 and his *De imitatione*, 269–86. See Screech 1984, 27–28; *DBI* 16:498.

82. Letter 5 and Curio's "Dedication to Isabella of Bresegna."

83. For the mysterious appearance of one of Calcagnini's works in the text of Morata, see notes to the "Dialogue with Lavinia della Rovere."

84. See the preface to Isabella Bresegna, below. Curio's 1562 edition of Morata added Latin translations of two stories from Boccaccio's *Decameron*. I do not believe they are correctly attributed to her but rather to her companion, Anna d'Este. Calcagnini (1544, 205) in two letters (one dated 22 January 1541) to Anna praised her "Milesian stories" [fabellae illae Milesiae] translated from Tuscan into Latin. There is no mention of Morata. One might speculate that these were perhaps a collaborative effort of the schoolroom (with Calcagnini tactfully mentioning only the ducal daughter?), or else Morata had been set a similar task earlier in her education. However, the translations were found by Chilian Sinapius among his brother's papers following Johannes's death, and he notes the difference in style from Olympia's other writings, which he attributes to youth (letter 81). This sort of exercise is certainly more appropriate to the ten-year-old Anna than the fourteen-year-old Olympia, already at an advanced stage of study. Nolten (1775, 115), Bonnett (1856, 102–3), Caretti (1954, 9 n. 14), Flood (1997, 179), and Pirovano 1998 saw some significance to the choice of the two stories, swipes at the cult of saints and monks respectively. However, anticlericalism was the common inheritance of Europe (see Dykema and Oberman 1993 for a full survey, esp. 271–313 on Italy), and the stories are also merely the first two in the *Decameron*. (Tedeschi [1974, 86 n. 33 and 1987, 104 n. 103] accidentally says there are three and makes them part of the diffusion of Italian humanist culture to the north, but they are merely homework). The choice of the *Decameron* itself, however, is certainly interesting. Dolce, for example, gave first place to Boccaccio in books to be avoided by girls (Dolce 1553, 19r; Grendler 1989, 88).

85. See the preface to Isabella Bresegna, where Curio gives her age as "not yet sixteen." Nolten rightly as 14 (1775, 115). The surviving dialogues (translated below) are later works.

Three poems, two in Greek, survive from this period. "On True Virginity" is a mild swipe at nunneries and echoes the language of her teacher Curio. The lament for Pietro Bembo (d. 1547) must date soon after his death. The third is one of the few works in which Morata deals explicitly with feminist issues. In it she takes the standard trope of the opposition of Parnassus and the Muses with women's work, "yarn, shuttle, loom-threads, and workbaskets." In this she seems very close to Cassandra Fedele in her rejection of "the lowly and execrable weapons of the little woman—the needle and the distaff."[86]

Morata had also written the *Praise of Scaevola* in Greek (letter 3, translated below). Most important, she had given public proofs of her talents in a series of preambles and explications of the text of Cicero's *Paradoxa*, which Curio heard her deliver before Renée's court. Morata's father had lectured on the *Paradoxa* and the choice was significant. The text, a brief explication of the major Stoic doctrines, was considered one for advanced students.[87]

The court served as a central location for the noble families to display both their women and the resources that they had to lavish on these women.[88] The display of the *learned* women, in particular, allowed the city to boast that it had the power not merely to educate its sons but its daughters as well. Morata's public exhibitions were part of this pattern of "conspicuous consumption,"[89] which is perhaps better understood under the Renaissance's own idea, and ideal, of "magnificence": the stunning expenditure of capital, cultural and otherwise.[90] Famous shows were the public Latin epideictic orations of Battista Malatesta, Costanza Varano (1426–47), Cassandra Fedele (c. 1470–1558), and others.[91] The stage too was used to display learned

---

86. Cf. Labé 1981, 17 on the same trope (trans. by Prine 1987, 149), Madeleine Des Roches (ode 1, "et nous donner le fuzeau pour la plume"). Contrast Catherine Des Roches's famous (and subtle and ambivalent) address to her distaff, "À mon quenoille": Des Roches and Des Roches 1993, 86–87, 292–93; trans. by Larsen 1987, 246, 249–50.

87. Jensen 1996, 73.

88. For the role of court in women's culture, see Wiesner 2000, 163–76.

89. On "conspicuous consumption" (the term coined by Veblen 1899, chap. 4, 68ff.) in the Renaissance, see Jardine 1996, esp. 379–424.

90. For example, *De magnificentia* (written c. 1486) and *De splendore* (c. 1498) by Giovanni Pontano (1422–1503); see Pontano 1965 (ed. Tateo). On "magnificence," see Cole 1995. The idea of "symbolic" or "cultural capital" was first formulated by Pierre Bourdieu, most famously in Bourdieu 1977, esp. 177–97, and 1986; see Guillory 1993.

91. For texts, see King and Rabil 1983; Fedele (ed. Robin) 2000; Parker (forthcoming). Fedele was asked to join the court of Isabella of Aragon in 1488; she begged off on grounds of love for her family. When the offer was repeated, her departure was prevented by a decree of the Doge, Agostino Barbarigo, "who forbade so singular an ornament to the fatherland to be removed"

daughters. So Alessandra Scala (1475–1506) performed Sophocles' *Electra* in Greek,[92] and Anna d'Este herself played a role in Terence's *Andria* in 1539, when she was seven years old, and later joined the other ducal children to perform Terence's *Adelphi*, under the direction of Johannes Sinapius, for the visit of Pope Paul III in 1543, when she was eleven and Olympia was seventeen.[93] Curio is explicit about Olympia's role in this sort of civic rivalry: "In a short time she was so proficient that she was a source of admiration to our citizens."[94]

LIFE IN COURT AND THE FALL FROM FAVOR. We can get only brief glimpses into the life at Renée's court during this period. The loss of so many of Morata's own letters was compounded by the seizure and destruction of most of Renée's correspondence after her death, and the subsequent loss in the burning of the archives of the Roman Inquisition in 1559, during the riots that followed the death of Pope Paul IV. The Office of the Inquisition at Rome had been established in 1542 and most of the d'Este territory was under its control. However, Renée, at the request of François I, had been removed from local jurisdiction, and had been placed directly under the protection of the Cardinal Inquisitors at Rome.[95] A list of her correspondents drawn up by the Inquisition reveals the names, among others, of Camillo Renato (fl. 1540–70); Giulio da Milano (Giulio della Rovere, d. 1571), in whose house in Venice Curio had been living before coming to Ferrara; and Pietro Paolo Vergerio (1497/98–1565), to whom Morata wrote in 1555 (letter 62).[96] An anonymous witness testified that, at some point in the early 1540s, Giulio da Milano had preached in secret during Lent before the ladies of the court and others, and had offered discussions of Scripture. He had declared the Mass an abomination and made Communion *a modo*

[qui publico Decreto tam singulare Patriae ornamentum traduci vetuit]: Fedele 1636, 30; King 1991, 199. Robin (Fedele 2000, 5) doubts the historicity of the decree, but it need have been no more than a public proclamation. For Fedele's likely date of birth, see Grafton and Jardine 1986, 45 n. 48.

92. Grafton and Jardine 1986, 53–55; Parker 1997, 267–69.

93. Frizzi [1847–48] 1982, 4:341–42; Mitchell 1979, 33; Flood and Shaw 1997, 104–5. For this display of noble children in acting roles, see Cruciani 1983, 35–36.

94. Document 2 of the present text (Caelius Secundus Curio to Sixtus Betulius). For similar displays by upper-class male students, see Grendler 1989, 31–32.

95. Blaisdell 1969, 184–86; 1975, 82.

96. Blaisdell 1969, 184, 194; 1975, 71. For Giulio da Milano (della Rovere), see *DBI* 37:353–56; *BBK* 19, s.v. and full bibliography there; also Caponetto 1999, 14–15, 100–101. On Vergerio, see Blaisdell 1969, 194–96; Schutte 1977; Caponetto 1999, 145–50.

solito, in other words, in both kinds.[97] Renato was arrested at the duke's behest and tried in Ferrara. The charges against him form a summary of Protestant teaching: that Scripture alone is the source of faith; that salvation depends on God's election; that the Mass, penance, and works are vain and a cheat. He abjured under the threat of death, was paraded through Ferrara, and sentenced to life imprisonment. He managed to escape, perhaps with Renée's help.[98]

Renée, however, was far from consistent. She attended Mass, made confession, and had François Richardot (whom Calvin hated) and later Jerôme Bolsec as her counselors and almoners.[99] In 1541, when Richardot defended taking the Mass, Johannes Sinapius's wife, Françoise de Boussiron de Grande Rys, refused to attend, thus angering Renée. Boussiron was one of Renée's ladies-in-waiting, famed for her beauty and piety (letter 23). Curio had fallen in love with her soon after coming to Ferrara, and had enlisted Calvin's help in interceding for him. Curio married her in 1538.[100]

Morata became increasingly isolated at court. Chilian Sinapius left Ferrara and his pupil in 1545, when she was eighteen, for a post as legal adviser in Speyer in Germany.[101] Later, Johannes Sinapius and his wife left for Würzburg by April 1548.[102] Morata soon thereafter asked Johannes Sinapius to present her poems to King Ferdinand I and to the great merchant Fugger, apparently in hope of securing some patronage (letters 10–11).[103] Then at some point after 1546, her father fell ill.[104] He had suffered from a severe stomach illness before, in January 1539, which he attempted to treat with litharge, the highly poisonous lead monoxide.[105] Morata left the court to

---

97. Anonymous *processo* of 1554: Casadei (1937, 54) and Blaisdell (1969, 202, 204), rightly see that the events referred to must have occurred in the early 1540s (contra *DBI* 37:355).

98. On Renato (a.k.a. Paolo Ricci), see Brown 1933, 91–93; Cantimori 1992, 82–97; Williams 1965 and 1992, 837–49, 874–76; Renato 1968; Blaisdell 1969, 180–85; 1975, 80, 84; Gleason 1981, 163–85.

99. Blaisdell 1969, 202–14.

100. Ibid., 130, 209, 215; Flood and Shaw 1997, 92–94, with documents there cited. Both Sinapius and Boussiron were longtime correspondents of Calvin's.

101. Flood and Shaw 1997, 122. See his remark on Olympia's being self-educated: n. 55 above (letter 78).

102. Letter 10. He arrived in Augsburg on 18 May 1548: Weiss-Stählin 1976, 91; Flood and Shaw 1997, 126. For Boussiron see above.

103. Flood and Shaw 1997, 126–27; however, Morata had not yet married Grunthler at this point.

104. Nolten 1775, 122

105. Puttin 1974, 203.

20 *Introduction*

take care of him, and after his death in 1548 continued at home to help run the household and educate her sisters and brothers.[106]

She returned to court but not to favor. Morata complained bitterly about the faithlessness of princes. It may be that in the closely watched world of the court, Morata's Protestantism was too open and too dangerous.[107] But she herself referred not to religion but the "hatred and slanders of certain evil people" (letter 19).[108] A more immediate cause for Renée's coldness presents itself. In one of the crueler ironies of dynastic marriage, on 15 September 1548 in Ferrara, as part of the ongoing political negotiations between France and Ferrara, Anna d'Este, the child of the evangelical Renée, was married by proxy to François de Lorraine, duc d'Aumale (1519–63), soon to be duc de Guise and infamous as the scourge of the Huguenots.[109] During the Wars of Religion, he would eventually wind up besieging his mother-in-law's château in Montargis as a Protestant stronghold (1562). The sixteen-year-old bride set off in procession for France to meet her husband. Letter 12 shows the coldness of the duchess toward Morata after the departure of her daughter. Morata had simply outlived her usefulness.

During this period, Morata had been studying philosophy.[110] Gasparo Sardi (1480–1564) dedicated his work *On the Three-Fold Philosophy* (De triplici philosophia, 1549) to her. In it he wrote:

> I understand from your letter written to me in Greek that you have thrown yourself on all the branches of philosophy "with sails and oars"

---

106. Document 2, letters 9–11 and 19, with notes. See above n. 27.

107. However, even in July 1550, while Morata was waiting to go to Germany with Grunthler, the ambassadors for Ferrara at Venice and Rome wrote the duke that the duchess was living as a Lutheran ("vive Lutheranamente"): Blaisdell 1969, 234.

108. Blaisdell (1969, 213) rightly criticizes as baseless Carretti's notion (1940, 52 n. 8) that Morata was the victim specifically of Jerôme Bolsec (she is more inclined to accept it on p. 266). The idea was floated by Fontana (1889–99, 2:297–300), and adopted by Flood and Shaw (1997, 106) and Flood (1997, 179). Sinapius makes a similar complaint against an unnamed *sycophanta*, usually taken to refer to Bolsec (letter to Calvin 5 December 1553: Calvin 1863–1900, 14: cols. 688–89, no. 1865 [CR 42 = *Calvini Opera* 14]; Flood and Shaw 1997, 204–5). Brown (1933, 105–6) tentatively suggested infighting among the Protestants, echoing Fontana (1892, 2:298–99), who anachronistically suggested a fight between the "calvinisti" of the court and the "luterano" Grunthler. However, Morata makes it plain that Grunthler fell in love with her only after her loss of favor.

109. Her uncle, Cardinal Ippolito d'Este, announced the forthcoming match on 21 July 1548. The decision was made by the new king, Henri II, and Ercole II on 19 August 1548 in a meeting in Turin, and the contract signed on 28 September. Louis de Bourbon, duc de Vendôme, stood proxy. The ceremony with both participants was finally held on 4 December 1548 in St. Germain-en-Laye. See *DBI* 43:316.

110. Nolten 1775, 117.

as they say, and that you have called your mind away from corporeal sensations and delights for that reason, so much that you'd like to seem to be alive only to yourself, as though everyone else were dead.[111]

This study may have included the worldview of Lucretius, which so deeply influenced her (see below).

LAVINIA DELLA ROVERE AND THE EXECUTION OF FANINI. Even in the period of her disfavor, Morata had one other friend in Lavinia della Rovere (1521–1601), five years older than she, the daughter of Niccolò Franciotti and Laura Orsini.[112] In 1541, Lavinia had married Paolo Orsini (d. 1581), a brilliant soldier in the service of the pope, the king of France, and later Venice. It was not a happy union, as Morata's dialogues and letters attest. Paolo was the son of Camillo Orsini, marquis of Tripalda (1492–1559), also a renowned soldier for the papacy and Venice, who had retired to Ferrara in 1543. Though a faithful servant of the church, the elder Orsini had been greatly influenced by Pietro Carnesecchi (1508–67) while at Venice and had given up fasting and penance, devoting himself instead to reading the Epistles of Paul, significantly without the intermediaries of the church fathers, relying only on the Holy Spirit.[113] Lavinia della Rovere was a frequent visitor to the court of Ferrara with her husband. Sansovino described her as "a lady of the most happy and fertile genius, who besides her other rare and noble qualities, is completely given to philosophy and the other humanities."[114] Morata and della Rovere shared a delight in studies and a sympathy in religious matters, which was put to the test by the arrest and execution of Fanino Fanini.[115]

Fanio Fanino (Fanio Camillo, c. 1520/22—August 1550), under the influence of "molti libri contagiosi" and the preaching of Bernardino Ochino, began himself to preach the central Protestant doctrines, first in his hometown of Faenza and throughout the Romagna, claiming that the Mass was not founded in Scripture, repudiating the intercession of saints, and empha-

---

111. Sardi 1549, cited from Tiraboschi 1822, 12 (= VII, pt. 3):1750–51. This Greek letter is lost.

112. See *DBI* 37:357–58.

113. Brown 1933, 178; Miccoli 1974, 1049–58; Caponetto 1999, 99, 238.

114. Sansovino 1565, 23v, cited in Bonnet 1856, 64 n. 3 and *DBI* 37:357. Blaisdell (1969, 188) identifies her as a companion to Anna d'Este.

115. Later in life della Rovere was won back to Catholicism by the preaching and example of St. Filippo Neri.

sizing the priesthood of all believers.[116] He was arrested first in 1547, and banished from Faenza and the papal territories, only to be rearrested two years later by the head of the Inquisition in the Romagna, the Dominican G. Antonio Delfini. Efforts to save Fanini began as early as March, when Camillo Orsini wrote to Ercole II from Parma and suggested that Fanini be released to him, and that this would be seen as a merciful act.[117] Instead, Ercole had Fanini transferred to the authority of Ferrara and on 25 September 1549 he was condemned to burn at the stake. Blaisdell rightly analyzed the political background: "With the Fanino case the Duke intended to prove to the authorities in Rome that in religious matters his state proceeded with extreme rigor, precluding the necessity of foreign intervention in the future, especially intervention by the Roman Inquisition."[118] Those sympathetic to the man and his message continued to try to save him. Renée provided money, and in a letter to her husband asked for Fanini's freedom, using the same arguments that Orsini had made (7 October 1549).[119] In the wake of the death of Pope Paul III (10 November 1549), Fanini's execution was postponed. Orsini repeated his request that Fanini be released into his custody.[120] Lavinia della Rovere tried to use her influence as well (letter 17). But to no avail. On 22 September 1550 he was executed. Foxe's *Book of Martyrs* described the event this way:

> Faninus, a learned layman, by reading controversial books, became of the reformed religion. An information being exhibited against him to the pope, he was apprehended, and cast into prison. His wife, children, relations, and friends visited him in his confinement, and so far wrought upon his mind, that he renounced his faith, and obtained his release. But he was no sooner free from confinement than his mind felt the heaviest of chains: the weight of a guilty conscience. His horrors were so great that he found them insupportable, until he had returned from his apostasy, and declared himself fully convinced of the errors of the Church of Rome. To make amends for his falling off, he now

---

116. See esp. Casadei 1934 (quote from p. 33) with original documents; Fontana 1889–99, 2:272–79 (extensive quotations); Blaisdell 1969, 186–89; 1975, 82; *DBI* 44:589–92; Caponetto 1999, 237–38.

117. 9 March 1549: text at Casadei 1934, 18; see Casadei 1934, 182–85, and Blaisdell 1969, 188, for Camillo Orsini's role.

118. Blaisdell 1969, 187; also 240. See Ercole's letter of 26 March 1549.

119. Blaisdell 1969, 188–89; 1975, 82 n. 49, citing the archival sources; also Fontana 1889–99, 2:273.

120. 6 January 1550; text at Casadei 1934, 199.

openly and strenuously did all he could to make converts to Protestantism, and was pretty successful in his endeavors. These proceedings occasioned his second imprisonment, but he had his life offered him if he would recant again. This proposal he rejected with disdain, saying that he scorned life upon such terms. Being asked why he would obstinately persist in his opinions, and leave his wife and children in distress, he replied, "I shall not leave them in distress; I have recommended them to the care of an excellent trustee." "What trustee?" said the person who had asked the question, with some surprise: to which Faninus answered, "Jesus Christ is the trustee I mean, and I think I could not commit them to the care of a better."

On the day of execution he appeared remarkably cheerful, which one observing, said, "It is strange you should appear so merry upon such an occasion, when Jesus Christ himself, just before his death, was in such agonies, that he sweated blood and water." To which Faninus replied: "Christ sustained all manner of pangs and conflicts, with hell and death, on our accounts; and thus, by his sufferings, freed those who really believe in him from the fear of them." He was then strangled, his body was burnt to ashes, and then scattered about by the wind.[121]

Nineteen days later, a fellow evangelical, Domenico Cabianca da Bassano, was executed at Piacenza.[122] Morata learned of Fanini's death only after she had escaped to Germany (letters 25 and 27) and the news spread throughout Europe.[123]

MARRIAGE AND ESCAPE. Thus far, Morata's life follows a pattern common to many of the learned women of early modern Europe: a brief burst of erudition, which enjoyed masculine encouragement only as long as the scholar remained a young girl. Once she became older, no longer merely a

---

121. Foxe 1926, 88–89 (chap. 6). A much fuller account in the later editions. See also Foxe 1837–41, 4:459–61.
122. Caponetto 1999, 225, for this and later executions.
123. Fanini's story was rapidly distributed, and later included in the earliest martyrologies, Francesco Negri's *A Brief Account of the Death of Fanio of Faenza and Domenico of Bassano, who were recently impiously murdered at the order of the Roman Pontiff* [De Fanini Faventini ac Dominici Bassananesis morte, qui nuper in Italia Rom. Pon. iussu occisi sunt, brevis historia, 1550], Giulio da Milano's *Esortatione al martirio* (2d ed. 1552), and Jean Crespin's pioneering French martyrology, *Actiones et monimenta martyrum* (1560, coll. 162–66).

curiosity for display but a potential disturbance to the order of things, she was married off, and her talents absorbed in child rearing and domesticity.[124]

Two things made Morata's story different. One is the extraordinary nature of her talents and her determination to pursue her study of "divine letters" despite circumstances far more horrific than mere disfavor at court. The other is the nature of her marriage and her husband. It was at this bleak period of her life, when she had lost her father, her childhood friend, and her position at court, that she found a partner in a marriage that seemed to both husband and wife to be literally made in heaven: "He has also given me as a bride to a man who greatly enjoys my studies" (letter 19). Andreas Grunthler (Grundler, Gründler, c. 1518–1555) was a relative of Johannes Sinapius's and a brilliant medical student, deeply learned in Greek.[125] He had studied at Leipzig, Heidelberg, and Paris, and took his laureate in medicine in Ferrara on 9 May 1549.[126] Lilio Gregorio Giraldi (1479–1552) in *The Poets of our Time* (De poetis nostrorum temporum, 1551) described him as a member of the household and an intimate of the duchess Renée.[127] He was already a famous poet in Latin and Greek, and in Giraldi's dialogue he is the guide to the modern German and French poets.[128] Morata presumably met him while still at court, and they seem to have started their love with "a kind of merry war" of teasing.[129] In him Morata found what the "silly women" and men of the first *Dialogue* had declared impossible, "a man who would prefer you to be educated than to be rich."

Morata and Grunthler were married sometime in late 1549 or early 1550, and Olympia composed a Greek poem for the occasion ("Wedding Prayer": Εὐχαὶ γαμικαί).[130] The letters and all the testimony of their friends paint a picture of a remarkable marriage. It was clearly a love match—Morata was destitute and her position in Ferrara had become untenable; Grunthler, though possessed of some small inheritance, was a young doctor just beginning a career. The couple planned to leave for Germany as soon as Grunthler

---

124. For this theme in the life of humanist women, see King 1976, 293–300; 1978, 814–15; 1980, 69; Grafton and Jardine 1986, 36–43. See below on the advice of d'Aubigné. The exceptions prove the rule: one thinks of Catherine Des Roches, who likely "rejected marriage because she did not wish to renounce her literary aspirations" (Larsen 1987, 239).

125. Giraldi 1894, 70. See Adamus 1615, 163; 1620, 81–83; Weiss-Stählin 1982.

126. Adamus 1620, 81; Pardi 1900, 136; Weiss-Stählin 1976, 87; Flood and Shaw 1997, 107.

127. Giraldi 1894, 3: "ambo [Grunthler and Francisco Porto] inter domesticos et familiares Renatae nostrae principis connumerati." For Giraldi, see document 1 of the present text.

128. For praise of Grunthler's own poetry in the dialogue, see Giraldi 1894, 70.

129. Letter 12: "If I ever change my mind, you'll be the first to know—just like I used to tell you openly that I had taken a dislike to you!" So Benedict and Beatrice in *Much Ado* I.i.27.

130. Weiss-Stählin 1976, 89 n. 23. Flood and Shaw (1997, 109) state "They were married according to the practices of the Reformed Church," but do not give a source.

had obtained a post. Her letters to him are deeply moving and remind us (if we need reminding) that in the Renaissance, Latin was a living language, so much so that a learned German married to a learned Italian might well conduct their loves and lives in it. Their marriage was conceived by the couple themselves as a match between equals, and looked upon by their friends as such. The lack of condescension in her contemporaries in speaking about the pair is striking.

In part, Morata's anomalous position as a married scholar was helped by the new Protestant understanding of marriage. The praise accorded Morata by men frequently touches on her "chastity."[131] The chastity of the learned woman had long been a morbid obsession with certain men. She was something unnatural, in need of confinement, ideally in a cloister (or, as in the case of Angela Nogarola, a reasonable facsimile thereof).[132] Morata's chastity, however, was that of a Protestant wife who was safely and properly fulfilling her one divinely ordained social role. The Protestant concept of marriage as women's only proper end, for all that it closed the limited educational opportunities that the nunneries had afforded, briefly provided a refuge for the learned woman.[133] Whatever the ultimate fate of women in Protestantism (and it is a battle still being fought), it is clear that the Reformation, for a period at least, feared learned women less than did the Counter Reformation.[134]

Ultimately, however, Morata was able to continue her studies not because of her role as a Protestant wife, nor as a humanist's daughter, but because of her own and her husband's individual determination.[135] One must not be anachronistic: Morata and Grunthler had in other respects a marriage typical of their time. All the household duties, including some of her husband's correspondence, fell to Morata. They were married for five years and had no children, the result of chance, separation, or illness (letter 27).

131. Letters 26, 51, 75, 79, and the poems by Marnix and Curio ("Apotheosis").

132. See, int. al., King 1976, 1980; Jardine 1983, 1985.

133. The literature is vast: Wiesner 1992 and Harrington 1995 make an excellent entry point for recent work. See also Davis 1975, 80, 82–86; Wiesner 1998, 65–66 for overviews. On Protestantism and elementary literacy for women, see the overviews by King 1991, 123, 170; Wiesner 2000, 146–49. For its lack of effect on higher humanist education for women, see Irwin 1979, 126–27. For a slightly later period, cf. the depressing advice given by the Protestant scholar Agrippa d'Aubigné (1552–1630) to his daughters: Aubigné 1969, 851–54.

134. Contrast the case of Caritas Pirckheimer: Pfanner 1966; Hess 1983; Bryant 1987; Barker 1995, for introductions and literature cited there.

135. Women humanists nearly always had the training and support of humanist fathers. See King 1976, 289, 294–95; 1980, 67; 1991, 184; King and Rabil 1983, 18–19; Jardine 1985; Parker 1997. Laura Cereta seems to have had exceptional fortune in finding a female teacher at her convent school who gave her such a solid grounding and love for learning that she was able to nurture it despite the misfortune of her later adolescence. See Cereta 1997, 4–5, 25–27 (ed. Robin).

SCHWEINFURT AND THE SIEGE. At this point the letters themselves give the best account of Morata's life. Grunthler left for Germany before the summer of 1550 (letter 12), meeting up with Johannes Sinapius in Würzburg (letter 13).[136] During his absence, Morata wrote one of her two surviving dialogues. Using Lavinia della Rovere as interlocutor, Morata reveals her intellectual history, from a view of a random universe (under the influence of Lucretius), through a spiritual crisis precipitated in part by her loss of worldly position, to a recognition of the providence of God and a decision to devote her powers to biblical study.

Grunthler had obtained the post of municipal physician in his hometown of Schweinfurt, which had been a declared Protestant town since 1541. He returned for Morata. Her sisters were settled in various households, but the couple decided to take Emilio, Olympia's eight-year-old brother, with them, in part to continue his education with Olympia.[137] She was glad to leave:

> In fact, I rejoice that all these things happened to me, for if I had remained any longer in that court, it would have been all over for me and my salvation. For while I was there, I was never able to undertake anything high or divine—not even to read the books of either the Old or New Testament. (Letter 19)

In exile, she referred to the court as the "fleshpots of Egypt" (letters 37 and 40), and hinted at danger from the Inquisition to those who had known her. She asked Dr. Valentio Carchesio to give her greetings to his wife and steward, but cautioned: "Whisper it in their ear, so that no one need fear for himself from Olympia's name. And the other people I love, if I weren't afraid that they might shudder at the sound of my name" (letter 37).

Morata and Grunthler traveled over the Alps, arriving in Germany on 12 June 1550. They came first to Schwaz, where they stayed with the royal councilor, Georg Hörmann, and then traveled with him to Kaufbeuren and Augsburg. They stayed for a period with Sinapius in Würzburg. Grunthler went on ahead to ready the house in Schweinfurt, where they were reunited

---

136. Grunthler left at some point after 11 March 1550, when he was present for the granting of a laureate at the University of Ferrara; see Pardi 1900, 154; Weiss-Stählin 1976, 90.

137. Document 4, letters 19, 25, 27, 40, 44, 45, 47. This Emilio was mistakenly identified by Teissier (1696, 98–101) not as Morata's brother, but as the scholar Emilio Porto (1550–1614), son of Francesco Porto (1511–81). Chiellini (1991, 237) bizarrely follows this idea (already corrected by Borsetti in 1735, 2:168, whom she cites in support!) and continues the legend of Morata's professorship (see below), claiming, "Emilio insegnò insieme a Olimpia lettere greche nell'Accademia di Heidelberg."

at the end of the year.[138] During all this time, Morata was continuing her biblical studies and working on what her contemporaries regarded as her most brilliant creations, a series of translations of the Psalms into Greek hexameters and sapphics, which her husband set to music (letters 15–23, 51).[139]

Settled in Schweinfurt, she rejoined her husband's relative, Johannes Cremer, whom she knew from Ferrara, and his fellow schoolmasters Andreas Rosa and Andreas Campanus.[140] She found there a preacher of the gospel whom she approved, and "many good men" (letter 37). She was also able to reestablish her correspondence with Curio and Lavinia della Rovere.[141] From Curio she requested copies of his *On the Education of Children* and the immensely popular *Pasquillus Ecstaticus* (letter 27). For della Rovere, Morata composed the *Dialogue between Theophila and Philotima*. In it she touched on many of her most important themes: Christian hope, faith in the promises of God, and the need for these to be strengthened by constant study of the Bible. In her emphasis on the transitory nature of this world, Morata seems to have found a way of integrating her early study of philosophy, especially Lucretius, with the transcendent promise of Christian salvation. She also looked specifically at women's roles in times of trial. With Lavinia's situation in mind, she presented Queen Esther as a model for the wise woman who must keep faith with God in the world of affairs.[142]

Morata entered into correspondence with many of the leading Protestant theologians of her day. She wrote Matthias Flacius Illyricus, requesting him to translate Luther's German works into Italian (letter 38). This had been a long-standing wish of the Italian reformers.[143] Most of her letters have been lost, but we know from later citations that her correspondents included Melanchthon (1497–1560) and Joachim Camerarius (1500–1574).[144]

---

138. Brückenstrasse 12, now demolished.

139. Letter 51. For Grunthler's printed music, see letter 77. See the preface to the psalms.

140. For Cremer, see letters 3, 38, 48–50, 65; for Rosa, letters 51, 58; for Campanus, letters 53, 55–60, 72, 74, 77. For this group and Morata's time in Schweinfurt, see Vorländer 1970; Saffert 1993, 518–23.

141. Letters 26 and 27; letters 25 and 28.

142. In this she shows a fine independence from both Luther, who hated the Book of Esther (*Tischreden*, no. 59), and Calvin, who ignored it.

143. So a letter from Ortensio Lando to Vadianus, 1543: Arbenz and Wartmann 1890–1913, 4:188–89; Tedeschi 1991, 33. On Luther in Italian, see Seidel Menchi 1977. On the trade in translations of Calvin and the continuing existence of Protestant groups in Italy, see Bozza 1985.

144. Titius 1684, 3: "Olympia Fulvia Morata, ein geborne Italiänerin, ein Gottsfürchtig und gelehrtes Weib, welche fertig die Lateinische Sprach geredet und geschrieben an den Hn.

28 *Introduction*

Georg Hörmann had not ceased his efforts on behalf of Grunthler, and had arranged for him to hold the post of personal physician to King Ferdinand I at Linz. The couple, however, turned it down for reasons of conscience. Linz was the capital of Lower Austria over the Enns in Habsburg territory. They feared the loss of freedom of worship and, with the warning of Fanini before them, persecution.[145] For the time being, Schweinfurt seemed safe enough for Sinapius to send his daughter there to be educated by Morata in 1552.[146] In 1553, Grunthler was apparently offered a post at Heidelberg (letters 35 and 41). The decision to stay in Schweinfurt, however, left them in the wrong place at the worst possible time.

It is soul-wearying to recount in detail the endless cycle of betrayals that made up the German wars of religion.[147] Morata had been keenly following events (letters 23 and 24). The emperor Charles V had defeated the Protestant leaders of the Schmalkaldic League at the battle of Mühlberg (1547). During the holding period of the Augsburg Interim (Diet of Augsburg, 1548), he stationed Spanish troops in Protestant towns. Grunthler had been appointed as the first city physician by the senate of Schweinfurt in part to deal with the fear of contagion from the two hundred soldiers stationed there in November 1549 (letter 25).[148] The unstable situation rapidly deteriorated. Albrecht II Alcibiades (1522–57), Margrave of Brandenburg-Kulmbach, had originally been in service to the emperor. He followed Maurice, elector of Saxony (1521–53), in his revolt against Charles V, and then, after the Treaty of Passau (2 August 1552), turned back to Charles. Albrecht used the opportunity to occupy large areas of Germany, including Schweinfurt. Maurice, his former friend and ally, now joined by the bishop of Würzburg (whom Johannes Sinapius served as physician; see letters 17 and

---

Philip. Melancht. Joach. Camerarium & Matthiam Flacium Illyricum, welche Sie insonderheit ganz fleissig gebeten, weil sonst in Deutschland kein so hochgelehrter Mann wäre, der gut Italianisch könte al er, daß er doch die heilige Schrifft wolte in welche Sprach bringen, auf daß die armen Italiäner nicht so jämmerlich durch das leidige Pabsthum möchten verführet werden." Morata's letter to Flacius (38), however, only mentions translating Luther's German books, not the Scriptures. Camerarius possessed an autograph copy of Morata's poem on Ps. 46: Bayerische Staatsbibliotek, Munich, Clm 10363, 103 r—v; reproduced at Kössling and Weiss-Stählin 1990, 174–75, with Camerarius's note "Olympia Morata Grunthlera faciebat."

145. Not without reason: Since the edict of 1527, "Lutherans" were subject to seizure of property, exile, and death for contumacy. Ferdinand, the major force behind the peace of Augsburg, had forbidden the persecution of the Hungarians who held to the Lutheran *Confessio Pentapolitana*, but was a fierce persecutor of the Anabaptists. The fate of Protestants varied greatly from town to town.

146. Document 4, letters 35 (she had been sent back by 15 January 1553), 41.

147. A good summary by Lindberg 1996, 242–48; NCMH 2:190–93.

148. Saffert 1993, 520.

24) and the bishop of Bamburg, together with the duke of Braunschweig and the citizens of Nuremberg, formed an alliance against him in the so-called Margraves' War (Markgrafenkrieg). Albrecht's troops barricaded themselves in Schweinfurt on 22 April 1553 and the siege began.[149]

Morata's letters are the most vivid witness to the intense suffering of the city (letters 40–41, 45–46). Albrecht's own soldiers pillaged the citizens; starvation and bombardment were followed by plague. All this Morata saw as just punishment for "our disdain for the word of God" (letter 40), but God in his mercy spared her and her husband. Albrecht's army made a breakout after fourteen months on 12 June 1554, leaving the city wide open to the enemy. Morata and Grunthler narrowly escaped being burned alive in the church in which they had taken shelter.[150] After harrowing adventures they made it safely to Heidelberg, with the help of the Protestant nobles Philipp, Graf von Reineck, and the Graffen von Erbach, Georg II (1506–69), and his brother Eberhard XIV (1511–64). They had lost everything, including Morata's precious books and most of her writings. The only thing to survive, miraculously enough, was her copy of Plutarch's *Lives* which Johannes Sinapius managed to find and return to them (letter 48). In the course of her escape Morata had contracted what was probably tuberculosis.[151] It would kill her only fifteen months later.

HER FINAL DAYS IN HEIDELBERG. Grunthler was soon appointed to the third Professorship of Medicine, a post he had been offered previously (letters 41, 43).[152] The religious settlement in Heidelberg, the principal court of the Rhine Palatine, was hanging fire. Church ordinances had made Lutheranism the official form of worship for only two years (1546–48), when they had been withdrawn as part of the Augsburg Interim.

Olympia, despite constant illness, continued her studies. She requested Calvin's recently published *Commentaries on the Lamentations of Jeremiah* (letters 41, 52) and studied deeply his *Commentary on Isaiah* (letter 46). Friends, including all the principal printers of the day, were eager to try and make up for the loss of her library (letters 44, 52, 54, 69). She in turn tried to provide texts to other scholars (letters 59–60).

---

149. For the background, see *CMH* 2:357; Saffert 1993, 520–22; Flood and Shaw 1997, 134–35.

150. Letter 45; this was the St. Johanniskirche. Saffert 1993, 522.

151. Letter 41. She identified it as a tertian fever in letter 46.

152. Contract of 12 July 1554: "al zu eim dritten Lectorem derselben Facultet"; Hautz 1862–64, 1:429; Weiss-Stählin 1976, 96 n. 49, with documentation.

30 *Introduction*

Morata also taught Greek to students (letter 64). This fact has given rise to a misunderstanding that she taught formally as a professor in the University of Heidelberg. The error seems to have originated with Hubert Thomas of Liege, secretary to Frederick II Elector Palatine, a friend of Johannes Sinapius's who lived in Heidelberg (see letters 41, 48). He mentioned

> Doctor Andreas Grunthler, whose wife Olympia, if one were to praise her correctly, would have to be called a Sappho of Lesbos [referring to her Greek poetry]. Both have been summoned by our prince to the honor of his University, he to be a professor of medicine, she to teach Greek literature, but she has put it off since she has caught an illness.[153]

Nonetheless, Morata did not mention any appointment for herself, though she described her life and Grunthler's post at length; nor is there any mention in the other letters, the records of Heidelberg University,[154] or any other contemporary source. It seems that Hubert had simply misunderstood (or overstated) Morata's situation.[155] However, more interesting than the mis-

---

153. Thomas 1664, 292 (bk. 14, anno 1554; text also at Bonnet 1856, 144 n. 2; Düchting 1998, 44): "Doctor Andreas Grunthlerus cuius uxorem Olympiam, si laudes recte dicere velis, Lesbiam Sappho vere diceres. Uterque a nostro principe in decus sui gymnasii ascitus est, ipse ut medecinam profiteatur, ipsa ut graecas litteras doceat, quod hactenus distulit morbo comprehensa." There seems to be a difference implied between *profiteatur* and *doceat*.

154. The archives do, however, mention her poetry (T. IX, F. 7, b: Hautz 1862–64, 1:431).

155. Already discussed by Bonnet 1856, 144; Hautz 1862–64, 1:430–31. The sources are not slow to praise either Morata for her learning or Frederick II for his generosity. Bèze ([1580] 1971) and Adamus (1615, 1620) know nothing about it. For other early sources, see the following: in discussing the praise accorded Cassandra Fedele's oration before the University of Padua, Tomasini wrote (1644, 352–53), "Quamquam non ignorem ex Italis Mulieribus publicè auditam in Germaniâ Fuluiam Olympiam, Bononiae Gozzadinam" [I am not unaware that women from Italy have lectured publicly: Fulvia Olympia in Germany, Gozzadini in Bolognia]. However, he was well aware that Fedele's oration was for a relative getting his baccalaureate, not for her own; Tomasini was not imagining a formal university position. (Bittizia Gozzadini [1209–61], who seems to have escaped the list makers, is claimed to have received a degree and even taught at Bologna: this, alas, is wishful thinking [for the sources, see Macchiavelli 1722; Fantuzzi 1781–94 (1782), 4:209; Bonafede 1845, 3–12; see the proper caution of G. Logan 1994, 791 n. 27]); the first women to obtain the Ph.D. were Elena Lucrezia Cornaro Piscopia (Padua, 1678) and Laura Marina Caterina Bassi (Bologna, 1732; taught at Bologna, 1732–78).

The error, in any case, was perpetuated by the bibliophile Paul Colomies (1638–92), who obtained a copy of Curio's 1580 edition, describing it as (1699, 45) "contient les Lettres & les Poësies d'une savante Italienne, que à l'âge de 29. ans faisoit des leçons publique en Grec dans la Chaire d'Heydelberg" [containing the letters and poems of a learned Italian woman, who at the age of 29 gave public lectures in Greek in the Chair at Heidelberg]. It has taken on a curious life of its own, repeated by Chiellini (1991, 237; see n. 126 above), and has spread (with advantages) to Cignoni (1982–84, 193), who has her *refusing* a chair in Greek, and popular reference works, e.g. Uglow 1998, 388: "She then went on to teach the other princesses, instructing

take is the fact that a contemporary thought it quite possible that this particular brilliant woman, under this particular generous patron, might have been offered some sort of formal appointment.[156]

Olympia was also having to deal with domestic worries: setting up a household, buying furniture, finding servants, hiring a cook, distributing alms, and dealing with some of Grunthler's correspondence (letters 49, 50, 53, 56–57). Plague broke out in Heidelberg and ultimately the university was closed (letters 54, 58, 71).[157] There were constant money worries (55–56).[158]

Morata resumed her wide correspondence. She wrote to Curio, and through him was in contact with Bernardino Ochino (letters 66, 69). She tried to reach Lavinia della Rovere, but no response seemed to be forthcoming (letters 44–47). She continued her attempts to enlist other Protestant divines in her plan to spread Luther's work in Italian.[159] Pietro Paolo Vergerio (1497/98–1565), now in exile in the Grisons, had initiated a correspondence with Morata at least as early as December 1554 (letter 62).[160] He sent her books and kept her informed about events in Italy. She gathered news about the persecutions in Ferrara and Italy (letters 41 and 58, Second Dialogue), and about Renée's recantation (letter 62).[161]

---

them in Classics, geometry and geography as well as literature.... She fled to Germany with a Bavarian student of theology and philosophy and began teaching Classics at Heidelberg. Her Greek and Latin dialogues were published in the year of her death."

156. Holzberg rightly points out that only "Privatunterricht" was involved (1987, 91) but seems to be concerned to prove that the state of Greek studies at Heidelberg was so dismal (despite the presence of Micyllus, who had been hired away from Frankfurt in 1547) that Morata would have been offered some sort of semiofficial post ("vielleicht in Form einer außerordentlichen Lektur" [93]) had she lived. Hardly flattering and at best speculative. Holzberg (91 n. 53) oddly seems to doubt that letter 63 was originally written in Greek (despite the text) and cites the Latin translation.

Unfortunately the University of Heidelberg would have to wait until 1906 for Anna Martha Kannegiesser to be appointed to the faculty of the Medical School and until 1929 for Gerta von Ubisch to be appointed Professorin für Botanik. Stockholm has the honor of having appointed the first female professor in Europe: the brilliant mathematician Sofya Vasilyevna Kovalevskaya (1884).

157. See also Grunthler's epitaph translated below on pp. 224–25. See also Hautz 1862–64, 1:475–76.

158. Though Grunthler's stipend was increased from 30 (Hautz 1862–64, 1:429: "von 30 fl. oder zum mindesten 25 fl.") to 120 florins a year (21 October 1554: Weiss-Stählin 1976, 96 n. 49, with documentation), payment was apparently slow in coming.

159. Similar works in the vernacular had made it through to Renée: Blaisdell 1969, 262.

160. It is extremely important that it was Vergerio who began the correspondence with Morata and sent her his work. For the dangers involved in a woman scholar initiating correspondence with a (senior) male, see King 1976, 284–85; 1978, 808–10; 1980, 72–73, 76–77; Grafton and Jardine 1986, 37–38, 40–41, 51–52.

161. See Blaisdell 1969, 232–68; also Fontana 1889–99, 2:337–401.

The duchess had been under intense pressure. In July 1551, Vergerio had rejoiced that she had definitively rejected the Mass.[162] There followed a long battle for her soul. The Jesuits sent Claudio Jay and Jean Pelletier; the French sent Matthieu Ory; Calvin sent François Morel. Under threat of denunciation and confiscation of her lands in France, on 3 September 1554, Renée capitulated and heard Mass. She was placed in the palace prison, and her two daughters were taken from her and put in a convent. The duke refused to return them unless she conformed.[163] Calvin upbraided her personally, and shared his disappointment with the Protestant world.[164] Morata, rather dismissively, expressed no surprise (letter 62). She did, however, still have hope for Renée's daughter, her former companion Anna d'Este, now duchesse de Guise (letter 63). Morata invoked memories of their shared studies, urged her to study the Bible, and begged her to use her influence with her husband and the king to intercede for the victims caught up in the broad swath of destruction cut by the Edict of Châteaubriant (1551).[165]

Morata had been seriously ill for over a year. Aware that she had only a few days of strength left, she wrote a farewell letter to Curio and copied out what poems she could remember (letter 71). She died 26 October 1555, something short of her thirtieth birthday. Grunthler movingly described her last days to Curio (letter 73). A talented musician, he composed a lament for her to the text "Quemadmodum desiderat cervus ad fontes aquarum" (As the hart panteth after the water brooks; Ps. 42:1).[166] Less than two months later, on 22 December, he and Olympia's brother Emilio died of the plague (document 4 [Johannes Sinapius to Jean Calvin]). All three lie buried in St. Peter's Church in Heidelberg.

RECEPTION AND PRESENTATION IN THE EARLY MODERN PERIOD

After Morata's death, Curio gathered up whatever works and letters he possessed. He added others passed on by Guillaume Rascalon, Grunthler's col-

---

162. Blaisdell 1969, 236; Caponetto 1999, 236.

163. Blaisdell 1969, 261–63.

164. Calvin to Jean Farel, November 1554; Calvin to Renée, 2 February 1555: Calvin 1863–1900, 15: cols. 297–98, no. 2037; col. 417–19, no. 2105 [CR 43 = *Calvini Opera* 15].

165. For a brief and judicious review of the nature and extent of the persecutions in France, see Greenglass 1987, 34–38, and Sutherland 1979, 44–47, 342–43; for a detailed consideration, see the section "La construction d'une conscience martyrologique" in Crouzet 1996, 398–438.

166. Curio to Crusius: Adamus 1620, 81; Weiss-Stählin 1976, 97.

Olympia Fulvia Morata (1526/27–55) 33

league who paid for their funerals, and Johannes Herold, and sent them to press in 1558 (see letters 77–81). Curio dedicated the volume to Isabella Manriquez Bresegna (Briceña/Briseña, 1510–67), wife of Garcia Manriquez, the govenor of Piacenza.[167] Bresegna was one of the aristocratic women who feature so prominently in the early history of Italian evangelism. She was part of the Neapolitan circle of Juan de Valdès, the *eminence grise* of the movement, and had been deeply influenced by the preaching of Ochino.[168] She wrote to Giulia Gonzaga and others in the circles of the *spirituali*, and had even attended a celebration of the Lord's Supper with Renée in Ferrara during the brief period before the duchess's capitulation. Bresegna, likewise under pressure from the Inquisition, left her husband behind and fled first to Milan, thence to Tübingen as a guest of Vergerio's, and on to Zurich. In 1559 she continued to Chiavenna. For the second edition, Curio found a more powerful and suitable dedicatee in Elizabeth I of England.

Curio was already addressing two audiences, as the first dedication (1558) made clear:

> Entire volumes exist devoted to famous women, and everyone reads them. And yet in these books how few women do we read of who to their erudition added chastity of morals, and even fewer who added true study of religion and a love of divine letters.

Curio's very success guaranteed that Morata was quickly entered in the lists of both those fighting the long continuation of the *querelle des femmes* and those seeking Protestant heroes. Among the former stand the jurist Heinrich Kornmann (1610), the brilliant philologist Gerardus Joannes Vossius (1650), and Johannes Sauerbrei (1676), an important early scholar of women's literature.[169] For the latter group, Simler praised Morata and Jane Grey for their learning in his life of Vermigli (1567)[170] and Bèze included her as the only woman in his *Icones* ("That is, True Images of Men Distinguished for Both Learning and Piety," 1580).[171] Caspar Titius deployed her in his

---

167. For Bresegna, see *DBI* 14:189–90; Church 1932, 54, 159, 171; Casadei 1937 (the most complete study); Rahner 1956 (drawing on Jesuit archives); Bainton 1971, 219–33 (a popular sketch); Williams 1992, 827, 861–62; Caponetto 1999, 67, 69, 217, 236.

168. On the importance of Valdès, see especially Firpo 1996 and Caponetto 1999, 63–75.

169. Kornmann 1669, 25 (1st ed. 1610, 57; non vidi); Vossius 1650, 9, English translation in Robinson 1799, 41–42; for Vossius, see Sandys 1903–8, 2:307–9; Thomasius and Sauerbrei 1676: 17–19.

170. Simler 1563, b iiij (non vidi, cited from M'Crie [1856] 1974, 233 and Bonnet 1856, 174).

171. "Id est verae imagines virorvm doctrina simvl et pietate illvstrivm," though without a facing image.

Theologisches Exempel-Buch (1684) in his opening chapter on the diffusion of the Bible.

Morata's reputation was wide enough for Jacques-Auguste de Thou, one of the authors of the Edict of Nantes, to include her in his *Universal History* (1604).[172] For this the loathsome Scioppius taunted him as "the praiser of Calvinist Amazons" and accused him of following Epicurus and "that younger Epicurus, Luther."[173] Thou was followed by the bibliophile Paul Colomies (1699, 45–47) and by Jean-Pierre Niceron (1729–45 [1731], 15:102–14). But Morata was an object of competitive national pride even within her lifetime and immediately after.[174] Later Italians were necessarily conflicted. They praised her learning and basked in the reflected glory, while deploring her heresy. Thus Tomasini, that pioneer of women's history, can bring himself to mention her only in passing (1644, 352–53) while devoting separate sections to Isotta Nogarola, Laura Cereta, Cassandra Fedele, Moderata Fonte, and the lesser-known Hypsicratea a Monte (d. 1584). Borsetti (1735, 2:167–68) was proud of her association with Ferrara, but wrote of her as having drunk "the Lutheran poison." Barotti (1793 [1970], 2:166) clearly admired her writings and studied to clear up the outline of her life, but could not avoid one comment, that "in her already corrupted mouth 'Christianity' meant the same as 'Calvinism' or 'Lutheranism', as this was the only Christianity she recognized as true."[175]

Protestant Germans had an easier time claiming her as one of their own. Melchior Adamus included her as the only woman among men such as Faust, Celtis, Erasmus, Copernicus, Melanchthon, and Neander, in his *Lives of the German Philosophers* (1615, 162–67).[176] Johann Peter Lotichius (1625, 94–96) included her in his library of poets (beside Weston), as did Georg Christian Lehms (1715 [1973], 172–80).[177] Johann Caspar Eberti listed her in his catalogue of distinguished women (1706, 255–59), which included the *Wun-*

---

172. Placed on the Index in 1609.

173. Thou 1733, 1:562 (Lib. XVI.xiv, anno 1555). Kaspar Schoppe (1576–1649) published an attack on Thou under the pseudonym Jo. Bapt. Gallus; reprinted in Thou 1733, 7:37. For Scioppius, see Sandys 1903–8, 2:362–63; Pfeiffer 1976, 49–50.

174. Document 2, "Dedication to Isabella Bresegna"; letters 78, 79.

175. So too Tiraboschi 1822, 12 (= Tom. VII, parte terza):1745. Frizzi (1847–48 [1982], 4:359–60) is especially amusing: "She distanced herself from court, some say in order to hide from the investigations which were being made there against the heretics, other say to help her father in his final illness. She lost, therefore, the duchess's favor . . ."

176. And again in his life of Grunthler (Adamus 1620, 81–83).

177. Lehns apparently had access to materials not included by Curio, since he printed the text of poem 5, which is not found elsewhere.

derkind Anna Maria Cramer (1613–27), hailed by contemporaries as "a second Olympia Fulvia Morata" (1706, 255–59 and 115). Georg Ludwig Nolten wrote the first full biography (1775).

Morata was pressed into service as a model of Protestant femininity by M'Crie (1827) and Smyth (1834), and after the publication of Bonnet's study (1856) pious lives of Morata became something of a cottage industry in England, America, and Germany. Nor has national pride ceased. There is an Olympia-Morata-Gymnasium in Schweinfurt (founded 1878, named for Morata in 1956) and an Olympia Morata Award for women scientists. There have even been two novels.[178]

However, of particular importance is the way in which Morata continued to serve as a model and inspiration to other learned women. So Catherine Des Roches (1583), in her "Dialogue de Placide et Severe," gave a roll call of learned women to the educationally advanced father, Placide, who echoes some of the poems in praise of Morata: "But what shall I say of Morata, who worthily received from heaven the name of Olympus?"[179] Elizabeth Jane Weston (1582–1612), notwithstanding religious differences, cites Morata as an exemplar in the *Parthenica*:

> May I not be said to be able to surpass Praxilla, Sappho,
>   and learned Corinna in my songs.
> May I not seek to be placed before you, learned Fulvia,
>   since my small vein flows from an arid little fount.[180]

Anna Maria van Schurman (1607–78) singled out Lady Jane Grey and Olympia Morata as models of learning in modern times.[181] Later, Morata was listed by Bathsua Makin (1673 [1980], 9–10, with some errors) and Mary Robinson (1799, 41–42, citing Vossius) in their campaigns for women's education.

MORATA'S WORKS AND THOUGHT

Olympia Fulvia Morata was unique—as a woman, as a scholar, as a Protestant. She lived that unique life, however, against a common background,

---

178. Mulazzi 1875 and Barton 1965 (non legi).
179. Des Roches 1998, 219, 238.
180. Weston 2000, 58–59 (trans. by Cheney and Hosington). Weston's praise was cited by Thomasius and Sauerbrei 1676, C2 v. Morata is the standard against which Weston is judged (and found superior) in several dedicatory epigrams: see Weston 2000, 245, 253, 311, 389, 417, 435.
181. Schurman 1998, 52.

and she participated in many of the most important intellectual movements and events of her age. I want to examine her background and her writings under the headings of Epicureanism, Biblical Humanism, Evangelism, and Protestantism.

EPICUREANISM. Morata made a statement of her own intellectual development in the first *Dialogue with Lavinia della Rovere*, written in 1550, when she was twenty-three:

> If only I hadn't wasted time in this great error and in ignorance of what's really important! I used to think that I was most learned because I read the writers and scholars of all the liberal arts and was wallowing in their works like mud. But even as I was exalted to the skies by everyone's praise, I realized that I lacked all learning and was ignorant. I had fallen, you see, into the error of thinking that everything happened by chance and of believing "that there was no God who cared for mortal things." So great was the darkness that had overwhelmed my soul. But God began to dispel it, and a little light of that unique and divine wisdom began to rise for me, and I proved in my own person that all human affairs are ruled by his wisdom. For when I was deserted and abject, as you know, he took such care of me that I found him to be a father and protector of orphans in a real sense. And believe me, no parents ever showed their children the indulgence that God showed to me. At last I realized how stupid I was.

It is easy to misunderstand what Morata said. She had not turned her back on classical literature and rejected the pagans in favor of reading only the Bible. The advice given by Gregorio Correr (1443) to Cecilia Gonzaga as she entered a nunnery provides an instructive contrast:

> So you must put aside your beloved Virgil, with Vittorino's pardon.[182] Take up instead the psalter [and] instead of Cicero, the Gospel. Believe me, I speak from experience: even if secular literature causes no harm beyond this, it leads the mind away form divine reading. You have in ecclesiastical writers, if you require it, the highest eloquence.[183]

---

182. Vittorino da Feltre (1378–1446), tutor to the Gonzaga family. One of the first humanists to advocate education for women.
183. Translated by King and Rabil 1983, 103. See also King 1976, 292. Cf. the advice of Caritas Pirckheimer to Conrad Celtis to abandon pagan myths for the church fathers: Pfanner 1966, 106, no. 47; English translation by Bryant 1987, 296.

There was never any question of Morata's following the example of Savonorola and abandoning Cicero. She would have disdained the Latin of most of the church fathers, whom Correr recommended, as crude at best. Morata continued throughout her life to read and imitate the classical pagan authors. Her letters were richly filled with quotation and allusion, as was this very dialogue (as a glance at the notes will show).

Rather, she claimed that, under the influence of her own pride and certain modern writers, she had fallen into a belief in a random universe. The phrase "that there was no God who cared for mortal things" (neque Deum . . . curare mortalia quenquam) is a quotation from Virgil and a summary of Lucretius's idea of gods who do indeed exist, but only at a distance, and are unconcerned with the human world.[184]

Among "the writers and scholars of all the liberal arts" whom Morata named, it is likely that her old teacher Calcagnini held first place. His influence on the young Morata, I believe, was profound. In a poem, understandably omitted from his posthumously collected works, entitled "Coelii Secta," (The sect of Celio), Celio Calcagnini at some point in his life launched an astonishing attack on Christianity and religion in general:

> Do not fear the empty dreams of terrifying death
> do not let the dog opening his mouth for three-fold barking
> be a reason for fear, and the gods' commands
> cruel and giving their not so happy orders,
> and the statues that do not respond to your words.
> Let not the houses of Lethe trouble your hearts
> with great cares, and the shadows which you say fly
> on the winds and infect your faces with their flying
> often making a horrifying sound with their rustling.
> It is empty superstition to call upon the mighty gods
> Let not even the lightning bolts sent through the ether deceive you! . . .
> Those who follow the dogma of Christ give a beginning to the world,
> which they think he created under the pretended name of Jesus
> out of nothing; so great is his power, they say.
> But you, greatest Plato, long ago sang the truth . . .
> Behold the Latin priests, who say of course there is a god
> to whom belongs the highest power over men and heaven
> but they worship him perversely, whom they do not deny exists,

---

184. V. *Ecl.* 8.35: "nec curare deum credis mortalia quemquam"; misunderstood by Bainton (1971, 254). Cf. Cic. *Div.* 2.104.

and say he is a man, to whom they give false names.
As they tell the story, he created the heavens, the earth and the stars,
they claim he was without material substance, but will alone,
which was highest, created it. Nothing stupider
has ever been heard. There is no one so rash
as to bring such words forth from his crazy mouth.[185]

This poem was collected in the notebook of Gasparo Sardi, the author of *On the Three-Fold Philosophy* (1549) dedicated to Morata. The poem is almost certainly a work of Calcagnini's youth, but as Bacchelli points out, a deep skepticism never left its author.[186] The whole piece is a dense series of allusions to Lucretius and his arguments against superstition, the fear of death, and belief in immanent gods. "Epicurean" was a broad brush with which to smear one's opponents during the Renaissance,[187] but Calcagnini's attack on Christianity is shockingly direct and unparalleled until early French libertine literature.[188] This is far beyond Valla's ultimately pious paradoxes in *On Pleasure* (De voluptate) or anything that Pomponazzi argued.[189]

What traces of "atheism" there were during the Renaissance can best be seen in the defenses made against it, which show less that people were making such arguments than that others were uncomfortably aware that such arguments could be made. Luther thought that Epicureanism had been dead a long time but now was reviving and spreading.[190] Aonio Paleario, the humanist and reformer, felt the need to devote three books of *On the Immortality of the*

---

185. Cod. Est. Lat. 174 Alpha 0.6.15, 117r—122v: Latin text first published by Bacchelli (1998, 351 n. 16 [my translation].

186. Bacchelli (1998, 342) cites Calcagnini 1544, 318 (for some reason in Italian): "One person says, 'It's good to be religious, but religiosity is not pleasing. Religion is a good thing, no one denies. But the more important it becomes, the more it sinks into superstition." [Bonum est, inquit ille, religentem esse: religiosum non placet. religio enim bona est, quis negat? sed quo fit auctior, eo propius in superstitionem declinat.] However, the point of this essay, "That enthusiasms need to be moderated" [Quod studia sunt moderanda], is that anything taken to excess, even scholarship, can become bad. Fontana (1892, 2:170–71) pointedly observed that Calcagnini had the good fortune to die the year before the foundation of the Roman Inquisition.

187. So Luther on Erasmus in *On the Bondage of the Will*, and cf. *Tischreden* nos. 675–76; for Erasmus's response in the *Letters*, see Erasmus 1906–58, 6:269–70 (no. 1670); and cf. 6:306, 310; 10:288; 2:123 (compared to Lucian). Even before Poggio's rediscovery of Lucretius (1417), *Epicurean* was a catch-all for luxurious living as well as denial of the immortality of the soul; e.g. Dante, *Inferno* 9 and 10. Morata used *Epicurean* similarly in letters 39 and 45.

188. Gauna 1992 for the earliest examples.

189. The comparison of Morata's early thought with Pomponazzi is common, but misleading (e.g. Cantimori 1990, 299; 1992, 528). The best overview of the reception of Epicurus in the Renaissance is Kraye 1988, 374–86. For Pomponazzi, see also Kristeller 1964, 72–90.

190. *Tischreden*, no. 4187.

Soul (*De animorum immortalitate*, 1536) to writing an anti-Lucretian epic. One of the most notable reminders of the influence that Lucretius might have was made by Calvin in *The Institutes* (1.2.2, 1.3.2)[191]:

> For, of what use is it to join Epicurus in acknowledging some God who has cast off the care of the world, and only delights himself in ease? What avails it, in short, to know a God with whom we have nothing to do?
>
> It is most absurd, therefore, to maintain, as some do, that religion was devised by the cunning and craft of a few individuals, as a means of keeping the body of the people in due subjection. . . . For though in old times there were some, and in the present day not a few are found, who deny the being of a God, yet, whether they will or not, they occasionally feel the truth which they are desirous not to know.[192]

Morata acknowledged the same power of Lucretius when she accuses herself of the sin of Epicureanism in her *Dialogue* with Lavinia della Rovere. Morata, of course, knew the poetry of Lucretius intimately, and she seems to have taken from it the same lesson that Calcagnini drew. She does not accuse herself of denying the existence of God, but rather of believing only in a cold and uncaring Creator.[193]

---

191. Calvin 1990 (Beveridge translation). Cf. 1.5.5: "We have a still clearer proof of this in the profane verses which the licentious Lucretius has written as a deduction from the same principle. The plain object is to form an unsubstantial deity, and thereby banish the true God whom we ought to fear and worship"; also 1.5.4, 1.5.12, and his *Commentary on Jeremiah* 38:15. Calvin's *On Scandals* (*De Scandalis*, Calvin 1926–59, 2:201 [Lat.], Calvin 1984, 136–40 [Fr. with notes]; Eng. trans. 1978, 59–62) offers a grab bag showing what and who qualified as "atheist" and "Lucianic men," naming three philosophers: Cornelius Agrippa, Michael Servetus, and Étienne Dolet, and three authors: Rabelais, Antonius Goveanus (de Gouveia), and Bonaventure Des Périers. While all were unorthodox, none qualifies as genuinely "atheist." For the probable author of the enigmatic "Cymbalum Mundi," see Des Périers 1983. See also Sidney's *Arcadia* III.10, where Crecopia argues that "these bugbears of opinions [are] brought by great clerks into the world to serve as shewels [scarecrows]" and "whereof they knew no cause, that grew straight a miracle" (Sidney 1977, 487, 488); she is roundly refuted by Pamela.

192. Lurking here unnamed is perhaps Machiavelli's disturbingly pragmatic discussion of religion (*Discourses* 1.1–15). Calvin devotes *Institutes* 1.16 to a refutation of Epicureanism and a defense of Providence.

193. This flirtation with what lay beyond heresy was a danger shared by several humanists in the forefront of Italian evangelical thinking. Camillo Renato was led unto the wilder shores of antinomianism and antitrinitarianism, while Fausto Sozzini would eventually deny the immortality of the soul and the divinity of Christ. See Cameron 1992, 209. On Sozzini (Socinus), see Cantimori 1992, 332–418 (passim; see index); Williams 1992, 978–89, 1128–29.

40 *Introduction*

BIBLICAL HUMANISM. This youthful concept of a distant God was shattered by Morata's personal crisis of loss of father and favor.[194] She continued her story in the *First Dialogue:*

> So great was the darkness that had overwhelmed my soul. But God began to dispel it, and a little light of that unique and divine wisdom began to rise for me, and I proved in my own person that all human affairs are ruled by his wisdom. For when I was deserted and abject, as you know, He took such care of me that I found him to be a father and protector of orphans in a real sense.

Morata saw divine intervention in her fall from grace into Grace. She wrote to Curio from what she thought would be the safety of Germany (letter 19):

> In fact, I rejoice that all these things happened to me, for if I had remained any longer in that court, it would have been all over for me and my salvation. For while I was there, I was never able to undertake anything high or divine—not even to read the books of either the Old or New Testament. But after the duchess was estranged from our family by the hatred and slanders of certain evil people, then these brief, fleeting, and transitory things no longer affected me with so great a longing. Instead, God has increased my desire to live in that heavenly home, in which it is more pleasant to live for just one day than to spend a thousand years in the courts of princes. And so I have returned to divine studies, in testimony of which there are some poems which I made last year.

She turned to the close reading of the Bible that would be her study for the rest of her life, and found therein a demonstration of God's providence. In devoting her genius to divine letters, Morata was not turning her back on classical antiquity but instead following the same intellectual path as Lefèvre d'Étaples, Erasmus, Calvin, Bèze, Zwingli, or Melanchthon: humanistic training putting itself at the service of Scripture. Her works show a familiarity with the Bible that was astonishing even in an age abounding in

---

194. Morata was, of course, baptized as a Christian and raised by her father within the evangelical faith. It is somewhat misleading, therefore, to describe her as "a case of conversion from humanism and a inclination toward rationalism in the style of Pomponazzi to a Calvinist rather than Catholic Christiany" [un caso di conversione dall'umanesimo e di tendenza razionalistica alla Pomponazzi al crisianesimo non cattolico, ma calvinista: Cantimori 1992, 528; also 1990, 299] and absurd to say she passed from "paganism" to religious belief (Cammelli 1941; Cignoni 1982–84, 195, who egregiously misreads the texts). Morata saw herself not as converting to Calvinism but returning to the Word of God. On the applicability of "Calvinist," see below.

exegetes. One notable feature is her total disregard of the church fathers. This, to make a necessary oversimplification, was part not only of the Reformation idea of *sola scriptura* but of a humanistic rejection of Scholasticism.[195]

EVANGELISM. Many historians have tended to view the Reformation in Italy reductively, as a matter of ideas and books coming down from the north and being sown on rocky soil. Earlier Italian scholars, in reaction, saw it mostly as a matter of the working out of indigenous ideas and calls for reform. However, the Reformation was a European event; the Alps were no barrier to ideas and people traveling in both directions.[196] Morata's life demonstrates this basic fact: raised by an Italian father, educated by Germans, living in a French court, writing to Swiss and Slovenes.

Morata's relation to the intellectual currents of what have been variously labeled as "philo-Protestant" or "crypto-Lutheran" groups in Italy can be defined first positively and then negatively: by what she espoused, and by what she rejected.[197] Positively she was "evangelical." This is a term much debated (and multiply defined) in modern historiography, but "evangelical" has two important points in its favor.[198] First, it was a label often used by their enemies and sometimes by evangelicals themselves.[199] This was Morata's own

---

195. Cameron 1991, 138–39. See Rummel 1995 for the relations of humanism and Scholasticism; for the Protestants and the church fathers, see Hendrix 1993.

196. Rightly Gleason 1978, 13 (with early literature); McNair 1981, 154; Pettegree 1992. For excellent brief surveys of the historiography of the Italian Reformation, see Prosperi 1996 and Firpo in Tedeschi 2000, xviii—lvi. For an overview of the field, see Gleason 1992. For the transmission south, see Seidel Menchi 1993; Rozzo and Seidel Menchi 1998; the articles in Perrone, ed. 1983; and Bussi, ed. 1987. For the transmission north, see Kristeller 1965 (Morato, however, never left Italy); Tedeschi 1974 and 1987.

197. The terms are Seidel Menchi's (1994, 183, etc.) and McNair's (1981, 149) respectively.

198. For the history and debate over the use and meaning of *evangelism* (and related terms), see Jung 1953; Gleason 1978; McNair 1967, 1–50 (esp. 4–9); Del Col 1980; McNair 1981; Peyronel Rambaldi 1982; Martin 1988 (esp. 208–9); Schutte 1989 (esp. 273–75); Seidel Menchi 1994.

199. Seidel Menchi 1994, 192, with n. 35 for important documentation from the archives of the Inquisition at Venice. To these one might add as various examples the following: the Summons to the Second Disputation at Zurich: "You are not unaware that evangelical teaching [Evangelica doctrina] and the truth of Holy Scripture are coming forth more clearly in this age of ours" (Kidd 1911, 427; 1523); Erasmus to Melanchthon (Erasmus 1906–58, 5:593; 1524); Erasmus to Bucer (7:231; 1527); George de Rive on the church desecrations at Neuchâtel by "le parti évangelique" (Kidd 1911, 485; 1530); the deposition of Badischon de la Maisonneuve in Lyon (Naphy 1996, 58; 1534); and the oath establishing the Reformation in Geneva, in which the citizens swore to live according to "this holy evangelical law and the Word of God [ceste saincte loye evangellique et parolle de Dieu]" (Kidd 1911, 519; 1536). In this way, *evangelical* resembles *Impressionist* or *Fauve*: a term used to collect members of a group whose common features or very existence the members might themselves have questioned. Fenlon (1972, 21–22) and

term; she referred to the Protestant towns of Germany as *città del evangelo* ("the cities of the Gospel": letter 45). Second, it serves to underline the central importance of the Gospel in the thinking of those who heeded Erasmus's call, "Ad fontes": "To the sources."[200] Rice has given the most general definition of *evangelical* as "a deliberate emphasis on the Word of God localized in Scripture."[201] However, McNair had already rightly objected to such a formulation:

> "Evangelism" at present is too loose a term to be patient of scientific application. . . . If it is taken to mean a return to the *Gospels*, this is so wide a definition that it would include every Franciscan and Capuchin. It is of precise use and meaning only if it is taken to signify a return to the *Gospel*, for to a Protestant the Gospel entails the doctrine of Justification by Faith.
>
> The crucial factor that defined the reformation in Italy was always the acceptance or rejection of the "Lutheran" doctrine of justification by faith alone.[202]

These are precisely the points that form the core of Morata's message. The First Dialogue concludes:

> Therefore seek Christ. Have no doubt: you will find Him in the books of the Old and New Testament, nor can he be found anywhere else. Pray to Him. Your labor will not be in vain. "He who calls on the name of the Lord will be saved."[203] Would so many very rich and great promises be in the sacred books unless God wanted to keep them? And so he promises to everyone in general, lest any one can doubt that these things were done for him. Or rather if you merely desire to get knowledge of faith, then know for certain that you will get it! This power cannot be found in our vicious nature, but it is the act of the Holy Spirit.

In a letter to her sister Vittoria (45), Morata quotes Romans 10:17 as her central text:[204]

Gleason (1978, 9) suggested *spirituali*, but this was confined to a small group of reform-minded ecclesiastics (Firpo 1988, Gleason 1993, 191). The most common term of attack, of course, was merely *luterano*, lumping together all forms of heterodoxy.

200. Fenlon 1972, 1–23.
201. Rice 1974, 473. For Erasmus and "ad fontes," see Huizinga 1952, 109–11.
202. McNair 1967, 6–7 and 1981, 150. Cf. Seidel Menchi 1994, 187.
203. Acts 2:21, Rom. 10:13.
204. And again in letter 47.

> He wants these to be the means to save you: the gospel and prayer. "Faith," says Paul, "comes through hearing and hearing through the Word of God." This is what he writes to the Galatians, that they have received the Holy Spirit by having heard the voice of the gospel, as is seen in the story of Cornelius, for while they were listening to the word of the Lord, the Holy Spirit fell upon them.[205] Make sure a day does not pass without reading with devotion, praying to God through Christ that He will illuminate things for you in the Holy Scripture with the interpretation.

Her constant theme was the need for daily, direct contact with the Word of God. To choose one example out of many, to Lavinia della Rovere during the siege of Schweinfurt, she wrote (letter 40):

> In all these evils, we have relied on one solace—the Word of God, by which we have sustained ourselves and because of which I have not looked back to the fleshpots of Egypt, but preferred to seek death here, rather than enjoy all the pleasures of the world somewhere else. . . . For we do not doubt but that all these things have happened to us because of our disdain for the word of God. . . . So with all your heart apply yourself to the sacred writings, which alone will unite you with God, and take all errors and false opinions from you.

Inextricably entwined with study of the Bible is the Protestant belief in salvation through faith. Consequently, Morata wrote to Andreas Campanus: "Children have sin from the contagion of Adam, but at the same time they lack the faith in Christ, which is given by prayers and the hearing of the word of God" (letter 60). The role of faith is given its clearest expression in her poetic setting for the text made central to the Lutheran concept of salvation, John 3:16:[206]

> So God always loved the human race
>   that he delivered his only-begotten son to death.
> So the Son in turn loved the human race
>   that he alone poured out his eternal soul,

---

205. Gal. 3.2–5 and Acts 10.44.

206. See, for example, Calvin's exegesis in *Institutes* 3.14.17: "The efficient cause of our eternal salvation the Scripture uniformly proclaims to be the mercy and free love of the heavenly Father towards us; the material cause to be Christ, with the obedience by which he purchased righteousness for us; and what can the formal or instrumental cause be but faith?" John includes the three-in-one sentence when he says, "God so loved the world, that he gave his only begotten Son, that whosoever believeth in him should not perish but have everlasting life" (John 3:16).

> So that whoever can believe in Christ the Bringer of Peace   5
> may live and not be able to perish in savage death.

PROTESTANTISM. *Evangelism,* however, is frequently used in a different sense, primarily to differentiate those with Lutheran leanings who nonetheless stayed in communion with Rome from those who made an open break.[207] But this is in some ways a misnomer. Ochino, Vermigli, Curio, Vergerio, and the others did not cease to be "evangelical" when they fled into exile. Rather, it was precisely this fact of "communion" in its most literal sense—whether people continued to observe the Mass or not—that made the difference between Protestant and Catholic.[208]

We can therefore define Morata's position negatively, by what she rejected. And those things were clear. The Mass was idolatry; the pope, the Antichrist.[209]

> And so in fear of this, over and over again I ask you, please let us know by your letters and those of your friends who live in Linz whether the Antichrist is raging there—which is the rumor that we have heard—and whether they are punishing those who are not present at their mass and worship God with pure religion. For this is our resolve: we will not worship in a perverse and impious religion but rather profess ourselves Christians. If, as is happening in other places, the spies of the Antichrist would spot us and try to force us to be present at their ceremonies, it is completely impossible for us to go there, for as I said, we would be sinning against God. (Letter 29)

---

207. So explicitly Imbart 1914, 3:viii (in coining the term); Jedin 1937, 2:135; Jedin 1949, 364–70; Jung 1953, 522: "Above all, Evangelism had no intention of denying the sacrament of Holy Orders, transubstantiation and the sacrifice of the mass"; McNair 1967, 1–50, esp. 4–10, Fenlon 1972, 20–21: "It is necessary to think of Italian Evangelism as a phenomenon which, drawing upon spiritual currents already existing not only in Italy, but in Europe as a whole, sought to adapt the insights of Luther . . . to the practice of a Christianity not externally different from that of Rome." So too Martin 1988, 208. If we wish to single out this group, it is here that *spirituali* is best applied. See Cameron 1992, 200: "The *spirituali* had long been convinced that, while the Protestant insight into the means of human justification was biblical and true, the truth of that insight must not be allowed to lead to the abandonment of traditional worship or to revolt from established hierarchical authority."

208. Cameron 1992, 199; cf. McNair 1981, 155. This is the very definition of what Calvin called the Nicodemites, who publicly conformed by attending Mass; Martin 1988, 230–31. See n. 79 above.

209. For the intellectual background to Luther's identification of the pope with the Antichrist, see Spitz 1988, 396. For Luther's statements, see Luther 1959, 1:29–37.

> We will hasten with oar and sail to the place where we are allowed
> to profess ourselves openly as Christians and not to have to use the
> ceremonies of the popes. (Letter 31)[210]

By fleeing to Germany, Morata was able to make a clear and open break with the Catholic Church.

> It has not escaped your notice how dangerous it is to profess oneself as
> Christian there [Italy] where the Antichrist has so much power, who
> even now I hear is raging against the saints and beginning to foam at
> the mouth. (Letter 27)

> As soon as I had left the idolatry of Italy, through the singular kindness
> of God, and went to Germany as the bride of Dr Andreas Grunthler,
> God changed my soul wondrously, so I who previously for so long had
> shied away from divine letters, now delight in them alone. On Him I
> concentrate all my study, work, care, and all my mind, as far as I can. I
> despise all the things which I used to admire so much: riches, honors,
> pleasures. (Letter 63)

We do not know exactly what form of worship Morata had been able to follow in the years 1548–50. Frustratingly we get glimpses into Renée's court almost exclusively before Morata's arrival or after her departure. During the imprisonment of Fanini, despite the testimony of the Ambassadors for Ferrara at Venice and Rome that the duchess was living as a Lutheran, she was still attending Mass.[211] In her banishment after 1548, Morata had lost whatever protection Renée's court may have afforded. Severe restrictions were placed on Morata's access to the Bible.[212] Once safely in Germany, she was able to practice "the pure religion of Christ" (letter 17), which she refers to only as "Christian" and "the church of God."[213] She thus went from what McNair called the "third degree of Reform" (exemplified by the early Zwingli,

---

210. See also letters 45 and 46 for "idolatry"; letters 29 and 31 for the "ceremonies" (*sacra*) of the pope; letters 27 (on the death of Fanini) and 29 for "Antichrist." Morata's disdain for the *sacra* reminds one of the views of Renato (Williams 1992, 843).

211. Blaisdell 1969, 234 (see note 100 above).

212. Letter 19, quoted above. So too document 3 of the present text (letter of Jakob Baldenburger): "She was trained in the liberal arts and was exceptionally studious in sacred literature from a early age. When she was not allowed by the courtiers to devote herself to these, the young lady married Andreas Grunthler, a German doctor, so that she could more easily devote herself to sacred literature."

213. Letters 23, 27, 29, 31, 42, 46, 50, 58, 63.

who passed from "Erasmianism to Biblicism") to the fourth degree of open revolt (exemplified by Luther).[214]

In Philip McNair's memorable phrase, "one can distinguish the Italian reformers according to whether they faced the threat of coercion by dying, flying, or lying."[215] In words that recall Morata's description of the "fleshpots" of courtly life, Giulio da Milano complained in his *Exhortation to Martyrdom* (1549), "But our Italians for the most part are willing neither to die nor to fly for Christ, and since the comforts of Italy are so very pleasant, in dissimulation they worship the Beast."[216] The condemnations of Camillo Renato and Fanini, the martyrdom of Girolamo da Pluvio and others throughout Italy,[217] the flights of Bernardino Ochino, Pietro Martire Vermigli, Camillo Renato, and Curio himself in 1542, and later of Filippo Valentini in 1545, Giulio da Milano in 1547, and Pietro Paolo Vergerio in 1549, had demonstrated to many that it was no longer possible to live a life based on the gospel in Italy.[218] The famous were followed by the anonymous, in such numbers that churches of Italian exiles made a significant presence in various communities over the Swiss border and even in London.[219]

"Evangelism simply did not protest," a scholar has declared.[220] But of course evangelicals protested. What else were Curio's pranks? Jehanette's refusal to genuflect? Boussiron's refusal to attend Mass? These were protests that led to imprisonment or banishment.[221] Flight was in itself one of the most effective acts of protest, as Vermigli himself had said in his *On Flight* (De fuga), written immediately after his own escape. Flight was necessary

---

214. McNair 1967, 3; 8–9: "It was their acceptance of the doctrine of Justification by Faith which distinguished them [the "third-degree reformers"] from Erasmians; it was their adherence to the Roman Obedience which distinguished them from Lutherans."

215. McNair 1981, 163.

216. "nè morir nè fuggir": cited from Comba 1895–97, 2:153. One must note that Giulio wrote his divisive call for others to become martyrs from the safety of the Grigioni in Switzerland.

217. In Venice: 4 in 1548, 5 in 1549, 4 in 1550; in other cities: 4 in 1547 (Brown 1933, 56). Grendler (1977, 57) gives the first execution specifically at the hands of the Venetian Inquisition in 1553.

218. Blaisdell 1975, 84 (on Valentini, with archival documentation); McNair 1981, 163–64; Prosperi 1996, 324. Marchese Galeazzo Caracciolo (di Vico), Conte Massimiliano Celso Martinengo, and Girolamo Zanchi (Curio's son-in-law) would all follow in 1551.

219. McNair 1981, 164–65; Williams 1992, 943–44; Firpo 1996, 117–94; Caponetto 1999, 225–30, 371–74.

220. Jung 1953, 523, cited with approval by McNair 1981, 152.

221. See Seidel Menchi 1994, 190–91, 193 for a list of open acts of protest.

to save not only one's life, but one's soul from Nicodemism.[222] Evangelicals protested and paid for their protests with exile or their lives. Morata was part of the slow spurting of exiles which deprived the Italian Reformation of its lifeblood.[223]

MORATA AND THE NATURE OF EVANGELISM. In 1953, Eva-Maria Jung wrote a seminal article entitled "On the Nature of Evangelism in Sixteenth-Century Italy"—seminal because it bravely nailed up three theses for debate: "Let us now explain the three essential characteristics of Evangelism: 1. It is undogmatic. 2. It is aristocratic. 3. It is transitory."[224] It has been difficult for scholars not to use her framework, since the targets she set up were so broad and enticing. Each of her points has been extensively and effectively challenged.[225] There remains, however, a certain amount of basic insight in each of them, and together they provide a good way of summarizing the main currents of Morata's life and thought.

UNDOGMATIC. By "undogmatic" Jung primarily meant that evangelism "was not so much interested in a dogmatic or ecclesiastical reform, as in the renewal of the interior man."[226] She was thinking exclusively of the *spirituali*, and even among them there was a more consistent dogma on faith and the gospel than she was perhaps prepared to admit.[227]

If, however, by undogmatic one means that evangelical thinking was indifferent to the sometimes vicious infighting over doctrinal formulations now breaking out among the Protestants, then this is an apt characterization of Morata's position. Some have attempted to divide Morata's religious thought into two stages, one "Calvinist," and the other more evolved and "Lutheran."[228] However, this is both false to Morata's own writings and anachronistic, dependent as it is on two monolithic constructions, one labeled "Lutheran" and the other "Calvinist." These terms can properly be applied, in discussing the first part of the sixteenth century, to designate certain

---

222. See Caponetto 1999, 217 for a summary. So too the Italian translator of Calvin's *On Avoiding Superstitions* (De vitandis superstitionibus, 1553): Cantimori 1992, 445–46.
223. Cameron 1992, 209; Caponetto 1999, 371–88.
224. Jung 1953, 520.
225. E.g. McNair 1967, 5–9; Gleason 1978; Peyronel Rambaldi 1982; Schutte 1989.
226. Jung 1953, 523, echoed by Gordon 2000, 278.
227. McNair 1967, 1–50; Gleason 1978, 5–12.
228. Cignoni 1982–84 (superficial and secondhand). The labels are variously scattered in writings about Morata.

broad concepts of doctrine, ritual, and church organization, but Morata resolutely refused to provide the cladistics that would allow her contemporaries (or modern scholars) to assign her to one particular genus within the species *Christiana*.[229]

Neither Morata nor any of her correspondents ever identify themselves, their beliefs, or their churches as "Lutheran" or "Reformed" or "Calvinist," or anything other than "Christian." The milieu in which she found herself, it is true, may properly be labeled Lutheran. The Rhine Palatinate (Rheinpfalz) was, generally speaking, more Lutheran in practice and dogma—at least until Friedrich III reformed the Reformation in a Calvinist direction. So too were the Counts von Erbach, who rescued Morata and her husband.[230] So too were the churches with which we can associate Morata: the St. Johanniskirche in Schweinfurt, where Luther's cousin Lindemann was preacher and where Morata and her husband were nearly burned alive; and the Peterskirche in Heidelberg, where she and her husband were buried.[231] But her presence in Lutheran lands was the result of circumstance, not choice. She went with her husband to Schweinfurt and Heidelberg because he was offered jobs there, not because he or she was fleeing areas tainted with Calvinism. Contrariwise, they did not attempt to join Curio and others in Geneva, that "most perfect school of Christ," as John Knox dubbed it.[232]

Just as there was no crude dichotomy in Morata's life between "Classical" and "Christian," so there can be no crude dichotomy between "Calvinist" and "Lutheran." Confessionalization—the gradual crystallization of parties and doctrine—meant nothing for Italy and little for Morata. As Cameron notes: "Italy, like other countries in Europe where no confessional standards or church structures existed, could not maintain strict fidelity to one strand of reforming thought. Lutheran, Zwinglian and Calvinist themes jostled for

---

229. See Grell and Heron 1996 for a clear introduction to what might constitute "Calvinism." See also Nischan 1999, esp. 142–58, for rites. Schilling (1986, 401) rightly refers to the 1540s to 1570s, even in Germany, as "Die vorkonfessionelle Phase"; so too Schilling 1992, 217. The best approach is to contrast the main statements of faith in effect in the last years of Morata's life, the Augsburg Confession (1530) and the Zurich Consensus (1549).

230. *NDB* 4:563; Georg II was the author of the Erbacher Kirchenordung (1560). See Press 1979.

231. The university had recently handed over the right of the patronage of the Peterskirche to the Lutheran Ottheinrich: Hautz 1862–64, 1:470–71. The full evangelical reform of the university under Ottheinrich began only in 1558 and included a subscription to the Augsburg Confession: Hautz 1862–64, 2:14–22.

232. "this place, whair I nether feir not eschame to say is the maist perfyt schoole of Chryst that ever was in the erth since the dayis of the Apostillis." Letter from Geneva to Mrs. Anna Locke, 9 December 1556. Knox 1846–64, 4:240.

attention."[233] Morata demonstrated this point clearly. She continued to study the works of Calvin (letters 43, 46) and the works of Luther (28, 38, 62). Her correspondents included Johannes Sinapius (who agreed with Calvin), Matthias Flacius Illyricus (who still agreed with Luther), and Vergerio (who agreed with nobody).

The Reformation in Italy was distant in all ways from the bitter fights of the north. Firpo writes of "the persistence of the Italian Reformation at an embryonic state, intent on defining itself essentially as the reappropriation of the sacred against the corruption and ignorance of the clergy and superstitious practices."[234] Once in Germany, Morata continued to demonstrate not an indifference to dogma but a desire to stress the gospel common to all. In this she much resembled Melanchthon and other irenicists. Her elevation of the Word of God over the definitions of men can best be seen in her discussion of two of the most divisive topics in Protestant Christianity: the nature of the Eucharist and the doctrine of predestination.

In 1555, she wrote to Pietro Paolo Vergerio:

> Furthermore, I am not ignorant that there is great controversy among Christians about the sacrament, which would have already been easily resolved, if men in council had consulted not their own glory but that of Christ and the health of the Church, which is preserved by concord. (Letter 62)

She refused to define a position on real presence versus commemoration, consubstantiation versus impanation, and all the rest. This stand was admirable but in some ways naive. It had been a quarter of a century since the failure to come to an agreement at the Colloquy of Marburg (1529). The Reformed churches in Switzerland had put together a holding position in the *Consensus Tigurinus* (1549), but the language had been left deliberately vague in places and left plenty of space for ill feeling among those within, and hatred among those without. Morata's insistence on the primacy of the gospel cannot help but remind one of John Donne's *summa*:

> He was the Word that spake it.
> He took the bread and brake it.
> And what that Word did make it,
> I do believe and take it.[235]

---

233. Cameron 1992, 200; Gleason 1992, 295–96.
234. Firpo 1996, 354.
235. Donne, "On the Sacrament" (1635, 388). Often attributed to Elizabeth I.

50 *Introduction*

Morata is an eloquent witness to the way that predestination could be received, even by the learned and theologically astute, as a doctrine of despair. She had clearly been discussing and wrestling with the problem long before she left Ferrara. The fear that she might not be of the elect had left her unable to pray. Soon after arriving in Germany, when she was finally able to get the books of theology forbidden in Italy,[236] she wrote to Lavinia della Rovere:

> So set aside the old error we were led astray by up till now, when we thought that before we pray to Him we ought to know whether He has elected us from time eternal. Rather, let us first, as He ordered, implore mercy from Him, and when we have done this, we shall know for certain that we are in the number of the elect. (Letter 28)

Morata's new understanding is very similar to what Luther *wished*, in any case, predestination to mean, and her view in this way resembles that of Bucer.[237] She refused to wallow in the tar pits of predestination versus foreknowledge, supralapsarianism versus infralapsarianism, and all the rest. Instead she presented a message of comfort and hope—partly because what survives from her hand are not works of systematic theology but responses to the immediate needs of friends and correspondents. Even her two dialogues were written with the specific situation of Lavinia della Rovere in mind. Morata's constant text is the faithfulness of God. He has promised to save us and he does not lie.[238] So in her letters to her sister Vittoria and to Cherubina Orsini:

---

236. She mentions that she will send works by Luther to della Rovere.

237. For Luther, e.g. *Table Talk* 263: "The sentences in Holy Scripture touching predestination, as, 'No man can come to me except the Father draweth him,' [John 6.44] seem to terrify and affright us; yet they but show that we can do nothing of our own strength and will that is good before God, and put the godly also in mind to pray. When people do this, they may conclude they are predestinated" (Hazlitt translation). Calvin assures us: "The doctrine of Election and Predestination. It is useful, necessary, and most sweet" (*Institutes* 3.21.1), but is not overly concerned about the human fears his doctrine may arouse: "Nor, indeed, have we elsewhere any sure ground of confidence. This we say on the authority of Christ, who, to deliver us from all fear, and render us invincible amid our many dangers, snares and mortal conflicts, promises safety to all that the Father has taken under his protection (John 10:26)." Bucer's doctrine found its way into the Thirty-Nine Articles of the Church of England (1563). Art. 17: "As the godly consideration of Predestination, and our Election in Christ, is full of sweet, pleasant, and unspeakable comfort to godly persons, and such as feel in themselves the working of the Spirit of Christ, mortifying the works of the flesh, and their earthly members, and drawing up their mind to high and heavenly things, as well because it doth greatly establish and confirm their faith of eternal Salvation to be enjoyed through Christ, as because it doth fervently kindle their love towards God."

238. Letters 28, 45, "Dialogue between Theophila and Philotima."

Know for certain that He will not lie, says Paul, and that He is generous to all who call on Him, and recompenses them (as he says in the Letter to the Hebrews) who search for Him. You must not try Him, saying, "If I am of the elect, I will still be saved." That is to despise the gospel with which God called you to salvation and to wish to test God. He wants these to be the means to save you: the gospel and prayer. (Letter 45)

Ignore the impious words of some who disparage the commandments of God and the means of salvation ordained by Him by saying, "If I am predestined I shall be saved, even if I don't study the scriptures or pray." He who is predestined and called by God will not speak such blasphemy, but will strive to obey God rather than test Him. God does us the favor and honor of talking to us through His scriptures. He teaches us, consoles us, and will we then disparage such a treasure? He invites us to pray, but we, abandoning all the means ordained by God, and being lazy, keep on disputing about the high counsels of the Lord, about what will happen. Let us use the remedies He left us, and that way we will show that we are the obedient children of God and so predestined. (Letter 47)

There is no trace of the full-grown doctrine of double predestination found in Calvin. Indeed, Morata only mentions damnation twice, once to assure Anna d'Este of our salvation from it (letter 63). The impious will be damned, to be sure, but because of their own sins, not a preordained reprobation (letter 45). Ultimately, God's election was a message of hope.

Morata expressed a clear dislike for the bitter fights that were tearing apart the churches, but this did not put her in the category of Cantimori's "heretical" migration.[239] When she was finally free to do so, she "participated fully and loyally in the life of Protestant churches" but not "in their internal polemics."[240] Her description of the life of the counts von Erbach, which she called "a great miracle," shows how keenly she was interested in questions of religious and civic governance (letter 46).

In many ways, letter 39, reproving a "certain German preacher" for his drunkenness and dissolute life, is her most remarkable work. It reveals not only her deep involvement in the life of the church but also an astonishing

---

239. Cantimori 1992, 9; Tedeschi 1974, 84.
240. Both parts of the definition of the "orthodox emigration" are in the formulation of Tedeschi (1974, 84), who rightly questions the rigidity of the distinction (90).

boldness of preaching. When women were forbidden to teach men, Morata spoke from a position of power, which seems to rest entirely on her known piety and admired erudition.[241] It is a woman's voice of authority within the Protestant church that would not be heard again.

ARISTOCRATIC. Somewhat dazzled by the famous names and the more obvious sources, Jung viewed evangelism rather condescendingly, as a delicate blossom that could flourish only in certain hothouses:

> Evangelism lacked all revolutionary character. It was an exclusive religion for the aristocratic élite. . . . Evangelism was basically a religion for the salons of distinguished ladies like Vittoria Colonna, Giulia Gonzaga, Caterina Cibo; for the studies of humanists like Valdés, Flaminio, Claudio Tolomeo; for the palaces of cardinals like Contarini, Bembo, Pole, Morone, Sadoleto, Seripando.[242]

Much research has gone into correcting this limited picture. Wills, notebooks, letters, and—on the few occasions when scholars were allowed to look at them—the records of the Inquisition, have all shown that evangelical beliefs had spread much more widely in society.[243] Cameron charts how evangelical ideas flowed from "the ecclesiastical elite of regular clergy, academics and senior churchmen" to "learned enthusiasts from the lay aristocracy" to "numerous literary and intellectual societies" and "artisans and petty bourgeois."[244] By 1553, the bishop of Verona was complaining that justification and other dangerous theological matters were being debated "even in the women's bath houses."[245]

Yet Seidel Menchi has estimated that "Philo-Protestants" never amounted to more than a generous two percent of the population.[246] This diffu-

---

241. 1 Tim. 2.12: "But I suffer not a woman to teach, nor to usurp authority over the man, but to be in silence." It is interesting to contrast this passage with the remarkable first-person testimony of Marie Dentière, chronicler of the Reformation at Geneva and wife of Froment, who wrote an open letter to Marguerite de Navarre (1539). In this she upholds the right of women to read and interpret the Bible, at least to each other. See Head 1987.

242. Jung 1953, 524.

243. Surveys in Gleason 1978; Schutte 1989; Cantimori 1990; Seidel Menchi 1994; see studies of specific genres and cities by O. M. T. Logan 1969 (Venetian wills); Schutte 1975 (vernacular letters); Marchetti 1975 (Siena); Grendler 1977 (Venice); Peyronel Rambaldi 1979 (Modena); Donvito 1983 (city religion); Martin 1988, 1989, 1993 (Venice); Adorni-Braccesi 1994, 1997 (Lucca).

244. Cameron 1992, 196, 197, 198. See also Peyronel Rambaldi 1979, 233–34, 246–54, 261; Seidel Menchi 1994, 189; Firpo 1996, 355.

245. "insino per i lavatori de le donne." One wonders how he knew. Prosperi 1968, 157–58. Cf. the remarks quoted by Martin (1988, 218–19).

246. Seidel Menchi 1994, 183.

sion of ideas was limited to the literate, and it never reached the masses, as it did so rapidly in the north. A partial reason is the Protestant emphasis on the written word. Even in what Seidel Menchi rightly called the "Era of the Preachers," 1518–42, "the primary evangelical activity was undoubtedly the production, distribution and reading of books."[247] But more obvious is the fact that after the establishment of the Inquisition in 1542, it was no longer possible to preach the gospel. Or rather, it was no longer possible to preach the gospel and live. The flight of the dangerously popular Ochino was proof enough even without the burning of Fanini. Evangelism in its root meaning, reading the gospel, was driven underground into "study circles."[248] In this process a central place was held by the lay confraternities that played so important a part in Italian civic life.[249]

Yet Jung was right to identify the aristocracy as taking a leading part in the spread of evangelism.[250] Morata provides a perfect exemplar of how evangelical ideas dispersed in the society of Italy. She came to the gospel through a humanist father, who had read the works of Luther and Calvin smuggled into Italy. She was raised, and for a while protected, in Renée's aristocratic court. She learned from northern Protestants and eventually escaped with one.

TRANSITORY. Where does Morata's life fit into the larger history of Italy and Europe? For Jung, evangelism "flourished for only ten years from 1532 to 1542" and Ochino's flight was the "death-blow."[251] Various chronological outlines have been proposed to improve on this limited vision of evangelism.[252] Cantimori divided its history into three stages: evangelism proper (ending in 1541/42 with the death of Juan de Valdés and the establishment of the Inquisition), "the crisis of evangelism" (1542—c. 1560), and "the second generation," represented by Carnesecchi (1560–80).[253] Most recently, Seidel Menchi has proposed her own four stages: "The theological call to arms (the era of the preachers, 1518–42)," "spontaneous diffusion (the era of the artisans, 1542–55)," "repression (the era of the conventicles, 1555–71)," and finally "extinction (1571–88)."[254] Her scheme is insightful,

---

247. Ibid., 186; quote from Cameron 1992, 195. See Prosperi 1968 on evangelical preaching.
248. Gleason 1978, 15.
249. Peyronel Rambaldi 1979, 230–33, 254–55; Cameron 1992, 191, 206.
250. Firpo 1996, 355, 357, 363. On aristocratic women in France, see Roelker 1972 and Blaisdell 1982; on bourgeoises, Davis 1975, 65–95.
251. Jung 1953, 525, 518.
252. Gleason 1978, 19–24; Schutte 1989.
253. Cantimori 1992, 434.
254. Seidel Menchi 1994, 186–95.

54 Introduction

yet there are clear troubles with these labels. She is right to emphasize the role of public preaching, but it did not cease completely in 1542, nor were books unimportant before. The diffusion of evangelical ideas, books, and sermons was hardly spontaneous, but rather a labor of immense difficulty and danger. Nor, of course, did repression begin only in 1555 or even in 1542, and the conventicles (secret associations) had been instrumental in spreading the message from the beginning.

Morata's life shows the falsity of limiting evangelism to a brief efflorescence of ten years, and the difficulties in other necessarily general divisions of time. Yet many aspects of her life exemplify many of the experiences common to the Reformation as it struggled to survive in Italy, especially those of study, flight, and exile.

Her youth coincided with the period of open evangelism. Her father lectured publicly on Luther, Zwingli, and Melanchthon. She was sixteen when the Inquisition was founded and Curio was forced to flee. Morata's adult life fell within the "crisis of evangelism." Even study of the gospel could survive only in small pockets, where the power of the Inquisition was opposed by reluctant nobles or recalcitrant cities.[255] Morata was special in that her refuge was the French-influenced court of Renée, but ultimately even a daughter of the king of France could not withstand the pressure. Morata's flight and exile were part of a large pattern of repression, diffusion, and ultimately extinction.

NOTE ON THE TEXT AND TRANSLATION

The basis of this translation is Curio's final and best edition of 1570. The first edition of 1558 had been hastily assembled. For the new edition of 1562, Curio had gathered several new documents. He was planning a new edition and was able to correct a number of small errors, but he died (1569) before he was able to supervise the printing of the last new edition, which appeared in 1570, seen through the press by Perna, yet another of the Italian refugees in Basel. A reprint of 1580 offers the same text, with miscellaneous works by other authors tacked on. The text of 1570 corrected a number of errors but also introduced a few. The edition of Caretti (1944) is invaluable, but the text is largely unaltered from that of 1570 and there are one or two additional mistakes. I have silently corrected some minor errors in the text in course of the translation. Others, which might affect the English, have been briefly indicated in footnotes or apparatus criticus.

255. Cameron 1992, 207–8.

Almost all of Morata's work was burned in the siege of Schweinfurt. There is almost no manuscript material, at least to judge by Kristeller (1963–) and other catalogues. However, a diligent search in the archives may well reveal more. Many of the letters of Camerarius and others of her correspondents are still incompletely published.

Other sources I have been able to locate, especially for the poetic tributes, not all of which were included by Curio, are indicated separately in the text.

Curio did light editorial work on a few letters. Some names have probably been suppressed (for example, that of the German preacher in letter 39). It is also not impossible that other phrases, such as "a certain pious and learned man" (letter 28), cover proper names, but given the need for caution in letters, such circumlocutions are most likely original. In three cases, we have slightly differing versions of the same letter. Curio published the text of two letters by Morata (20 and 27) during her lifetime (Curio 1553). Caretti (1940, 12–17) sets out the differences in the text. Most are purely orthographic or corrections of minor errors. However, in four places in these letters, Curio substituted elliptical phrases for Morata's more direct mention of her princess or simply omitted the potentially offending words. Thus Morata's "deserted by my princess" (1553) becomes "deserted by those from whom I least deserved it" (1558, 1562, 1570).[256]

Renée did not die until 1574 and in her later years returned to France to be a troublesome presence and an abettor of Huguenots. When the first edition appeared in 1558, Renée was in Ferrara and, though ostensibly a communicating Catholic, had not entirely ceased to write and give aid to heretics. Curio, Calvin, and others still had hopes of her.[257] For these two letters I have followed Caretti and the text of Curio's 1553 edition of his correspondence. Curio also published one of his own letters to Morata (26) in the 1553 edition without any changes. In addition, one of Curio's own letters (52) is preserved in autograph in the Basel University Library: its text (B) differs slightly from that of the published edition. A portion of it is reproduced in Kössling-Weiss-Stählin 1990, 121 and the additional text on p. 217. Here, of course, I have followed the autograph.

---

256. "a principe mea desertam" 1553 : "ab iis, a quibus minime debui desertam" 1558, 1562, 1570. The others are: Substitution. Letter 20: "Sed postquam princeps . . . (alienata fuit)" 1553 : "Sed postquam que nos tueri debuerit." Omission. Letter 20: "sed hos fructus omnes a nostris principibus retulimus" 1553 : "sed hos fructus omnes retulimus" 1558. Letter 27: "ullis principum precibus" 1553 : "ullis precibus" 1558.

257. See Blaisdell 1969, 1972, 1975, 1982. Calvin to Renée, 20 July 1558, Calvin 1863–1900, 18, cols. 260–62, no. 2575 (*Calvini Opera* 18 = *Corpus Reformatorum* 46).

There is, however, no question of Morata's text having been interfered with or "improved." The simple fact of the matter is that Morata was a better Latinist than even her editor, and he had a pious and respectful attitude toward her text. He was eager to preserve every scrap he could lay his hands on from Morata and her circle, so that he included quite ordinary letters from Grunthler on business matters.

In translating, I have tried to be as literal as possible while still conveying something of the variety of Morata's style. Her Latin is simply splendid. She ranks as one of the great stylists in an age of talent. Her prose is a flexible instrument, always correct but capable of ranging from the most formal (for example, in her letters to Vergerio) to the most conversational (for example, in her dialogues and her letters to her husband). Her writing is deep-dyed in classical literature. She lightly tossed off allusions, which she expected her equally learned readers to catch. I have attempted to note in passing only the more obvious ones. I have doubtless missed many others.

CHRONOLOGY

The chronology of Morata's life is based on a few fixed dates. The most important is given by Grunthler's letter to Curio (letter 73), dated 22 November 1555: "She died on 26 October, at four in the afternoon, not yet twenty-nine years old." The text of the editions differs only slightly.

1562, 206: "Mortua est vij. Cal. Nouemb. hora quarta pomeridiana, cùm nondu[m] nata esset annos xxix."

1570, 190: "Mortua est septimo Calend. Novembr. hora quarta pomeridiana, cum nondum nata esset annos xxix."

Curio's dedication page gives the same information: VIXIT ANNOS NON TOTOS XXIX (1558, 99; 1562, 275; 1570, 251). This gives a date of birth between late 1526 (after 27 October) and 1527. Bonnet (1856, 26) and all others subsequently state that she was born in 1526, but the date cannot be given so exactly.[258] Barotti (1792–93, 2:165) rightly states, "Olympia was born near the end of 1526 or the beginning of the following year." In calculating her approximate age in what follows, I have taken this fact into account. Thus I give her age (abbreviated *aet.*) as 1 for (most of) 1528 and so on.

The other near-contemporary sources simply state that she was twenty-nine at the time of her death. So the epitaph for Morata and Grunthler in

---

258. Puttin (1974, 115) bizarrely states that she was 16 in 1539, making 1523 the year of her birth.

Olympia Fulvia Morata (1526/27–55) 57

St. Peter's Church in Heidelberg: "Obijt mutato solo A<nno> S<alutis> DLV sup<er> milles<imum> aetat<is> XXIX," and the emblem page dated 1556, in the edition of 1558, by Johann Basilius Herold, repeated in the later editions: VIXIT ANNOS XXIX VICIT M. D. L. V. MENSE DECEMB., which should read *octob[ri]*, and was changed in 1562. Theodore de Bèze in his *Icones* (1580, fol. Ii.j.) repeats that she died at age twenty-nine.

On the other hand, letter 72 (Grunthler to Andreas Campanus dated 14 November 1555), first printed in the edition of 1570 (p. 200), reads: "Obijt xxvj. die Octobr. hora quarta pomeridiana, nondu nata esset annos xxviij." However, this is a simple printer's error for *annos xxvii<i>j*.[259]

The other date is given by Curio, who testified to having heard Morata declaim on Cicero's *Paradoxes* when she was "scarcely sixteen" ("sedecim vix annos nata confecit ipsa": dedication to edition 1558, fol. a2 verso). Curio was in Ferrara between April and October 1541 (see introduction). This would place her birth earlier in 1525, but it is more likely that Curio, recalling the event seventeen years later, was off by a year or so.

Of her later biographers, Nolten (1775, 14) mistook the date for Fanini's execution and states that she was born in 1528, and so ascribes her father's letter (1, dated 25 June 1540) to her twelfth year (22). However, this is inconsistent with his repetition of the fact that she died not yet twenty-nine years old (160).

Curio published the letters in a jumbled order and omitted or failed to supply many dates, which Niceron (1729–45, 15:113) rightly called "une négligence impardonnable." Bonnet (1856) was the first to work out the correct dates for most the events of her life and for her letters. Caretti provided a detailed discussion of the chronology (1940, 1–7) and added notes on the dating to each letter. I have seldom differed from him (usually by indicating a wider range of possible months) and in the main my numbering of the letters is identical with those of the German translation of Kössling and Weiss-Stählin (1990).

---

259. For example this edition (1570) prints the date of the letter as xiiij. Nouembr. 1555.

I
OLYMPIA MORATA: WORKS AND LETTERS

DOCUMENTS

1. LILIO GREGORIO GIRALDI, ON *THE POETS OF OUR TIME* (1551; WRITTEN C. 1549)[1]

There was also Pelegrino Morato, a scholar and critic from Mantua. He wrote many verses both Latin and vernacular, some of which have been published, others are still withheld. He spent many years at Ferrara as the teacher to the noble children. He was married there and had children. One of them was Olympia Morata, a girl clever beyond her sex. Not content with the vernacular speech, she is learned to the highest degree in Greek and Latin literature and seems almost a miracle to all who hear her. She recently married our Grunthler, who is planning to take her to Germany, to his home town of Würzburg.[2] [Wotke 1894, 94]

2. CAELIUS SECUNDUS CURIO TO SIXTUS BETULEIUS,[3] BASEL, 25 DEC. [1550][4]

You write to me that you wish to know more about our Olympia, a name which many think invented. I will do what you ask quite willingly and briefly, although Georg Hörmann[5] would also be able to testify to what sort of person she is.

---

1. Lilio (Giglio) Gregorio Giraldi (1478–1552) of Ferrara. See Wotke 1894; Horne 1962, 11–12; Flood and Shaw 1997, 96. The fictive date is the celebrations in Ferrara following the marriage by proxy of Anna d'Este to François de Lorraine, Duc de Guise, on 15 September 1548 in Ferrara. See his poem to Morata below.
2. Rather, Schweinfurt. Grunthler is one of characters in the dialogue.
3. See letter 26. Sixtus (Xystus) Betuleius (Birk), 1501–54, Latin schoolteacher in Augsburg and Basel.
4. For the date, see letters 19 and 26.
5. See letter 16.

Olympia had as her father Fulvio Morato of Mantua, a man outstanding in learning and morality, with whom I had a long-standing reciprocity and friendship. He was employed as an independent teacher in all the most famous cities of Italy, and he instructed and polished the sons of Duke Alfonso of Ferrara, the two brothers of Ercole, in literature and arts.[6] Since he knew that Olympia was endowed with the highest genius, he taught her at home with all the customary studies which train humans to the highest humanity. In a short time she was so proficient that she was a source of admiration to our citizens. And so when Anna, the daughter of Ercole Duke of Ferrara, was being instructed in the same learning by that excellent man Johannes Sinapius, in order for her to have someone with whom to compete in noble competition, it seemed good to her mother (whom I mention with the highest honor) to summon Olympia to court, where she lived for several years with great praise. There I personally heard her declaiming in Latin, speaking in Greek, expounding Cicero's *Paradoxa*, and responding to questions, so well that she seemed able to be compared to any girl of ancient times, who was outstanding for praise of her intellect.

While this was going on, her father contracted a fatal illness, and in order to take care of him, his daughter left the court and returned home. After the death of her father, because she was the eldest and thought that her mother was still too sick, she took over the running of the household and gave her brothers and sisters an honorable education.

There was at Ferrara at that time a certain Andreas Grunthler, a youth well educated in Greek and Latin, who was studying with the physicians and even earned the doctorate in medicine here. He admired Olympia's singular erudition and chaste morals; she in turn respected a man who had no bridal present other than talent. He chose her for his wife and they joined together in a beautiful marriage. He took her from here to Germany (for it was Germany that despoiled Italy of so learned a girl) where they lived at the home of Georg Hörmann, a counselor to the Holy Roman Emperor, at Augsburg.[7]

Therefore, there's no reason for doubt about that poem in sapphic meter, written in Greek, which celebrates the praise of God most high.[8] It is a work of a genuine Olympia, and one which does not seem remarkable to me who has known her from her earliest years and who has seen and possesses other works by her. She is more cultured in literature and the arts, Greek as well

---

6. Ippolito d'Este, the future cardinal (1509–72) and Francesco, prince of Massa (1516–78). See introduction.
7. Rather Kaufbeuern.
8. See below, her translation of Ps. 46.

as Latin, than anyone would think possible, and famous for her knowledge of theology.

So much about Olympia. You can get anything else from the excellent and exceptional Georg Hörmann.

3. FROM A LETTER BY MEDICAL STUDENT JAKOB BALDENBURGER, WRITING TO SWISS HUMANIST, PHYSICIAN, AND REFORMER JOACHIM VADIANUS (1484–1557), BASEL, 20 NOV. 1550

Finally—and even if it does sound ridiculous, it's got to be said—I am deeply moved by the erudition of Olympia Morata, a most learned woman, and spurred to the study of literature. For I am ashamed to be bested by a mere woman, and a young one at that.[9] This particular woman is descended from an important family and lived at the court of the Duke of Ferrara. She was trained in the liberal arts and was exceptionally studious in sacred literature from an early age. When she was not allowed by the courtiers to devote herself to these, the young lady married Andreas Grunthler, a German doctor, so that she could more easily devote herself to sacred literature. I cannot admire her learning enough. And since my letter contains nothing worth the reading by a most learned man, I'm appending some Greek verses, written by that same woman and sent to Caelius Curio, whose son I'm teaching Greek, so that you can see how devoutly she practices our religion, how much piety she possesses, and finally with how much learning she's imbued. If the mail carrier were not all set for the road, I'd send you the poems rendered into Latin verse by me.

[Arbenz-Wartmann 1890–1913, 6:890; Flood-Shaw 1997, 108]

4. FROM A LETTER BY JOHANNES SINAPIUS TO JEAN CALVIN, [WÜRZBURG,] 4 JAN. 1557

I am leading a solitary life like a hermit or a lonely swallow in the roof, an old widower and sick, still just barely dragging around my feeble limbs, or I should say a living corpse. Some time ago I entrusted my only daughter to

---

9. Louise Labé perceptively noted this very point (Labé 1981, 18; trans. by Prine 1987, 149): "And in addition to the recognition that our sex will gain by this, we will have furnished the public with a reason for men to devote more study and labor to the humanities lest they might be ashamed to see us surpass them when they have always pretended to be superior in nearly everything."

a certain noble lady to be educated, since I was probably going to have to leave for Speyer any day.[10] My brother Chilian Sinapius was acting as lawyer there, and his wife was the daughter of the Prefect of Wertheim, who had been brought up properly in the women's court of that pious woman, the dowager Countess.[11] I hoped my daughter would learn good habits as well as piety from her. However, she was unable to teach letters, which had always been the most important thing to her mother.[12] Some of fundamentals of the Latin language had already been laid down in her by the most learned *virago*, Olympia Morata, who had left the women's court at Ferrara, just as I had, along with Dr. Andreas Grunthler, her husband, for Germany and Schweinfurt, which was his hometown (and mine). But after the destruction of Schweinfurt (which I've already mentioned and in which I lost most of my relatives and my one surviving sister, who left behind three orphaned children, to add to my other misfortunes), she went to Heidelberg, where the Elector Palatine had summoned him to be Professor of Medicine at a quite good salary. There she died of a wasting illness on 26 October, last year.[13] A little while later, on 22 December, Grunthler himself died of the plague, together with Olympia's little brother, Emilio. And so I failed in my wife's last and most serious wish to teach my daughter Latin, although unwillingly, I swear, and there's no need of expiation, I think, but you be the judge.

[Calvin 1863–1900, 16, cols. 374–77, no. 2575 (*Calvini Opera* 16 = *Corpus Reformatorum* 44), Cod. Genev. 112, fol. 17. Flood-Shaw 1997, 213–15.]

10. Theodora Sinapius (b. 1543; Flood and Shaw 1997, 120 n. 26); see letters 43, 48, 49; also 10, 11, 14, 35.
11. Flood and Shaw 1997, 122.
12. Françoise de Boussiron de Grand-Ry; see introduction.
13. 1555, added in the margin.

DEDICATIONS

1. DEDICATION TO ISABELLA BRESEGNA.
FIRST EDITION OF 1558

Caelius Secundus Curio to the illustrious and religious woman Isabella Manriquez Bresegna, through Jesus Christ.

Socrates said that if women were carefully educated they would be no less fit and teachable in letters, the liberal arts, and in every virtue that is considered proper to men, including courage, than are males.[14] That this is true is clearly proved by many women not only in our lifetime but that of our fathers. I could offer examples from every age, but entire volumes exist devoted to famous women,[15] and everyone reads them. And yet in these books how few women do we read of who added chastity of morals to their erudition, and even fewer who added true study of religion and a love of divine letters. And of these scarcely any were outstanding in the command of both Greek and Latin together.

But our age, blessed in many things, is even more blessed than others in that it has produced several such women and among them one in particular, on whom God seems to have conferred all the endowments of genius. She was named Olympia Fulvia Morata, the daughter of that most learned man, Fulvius Moratus of Mantua. I would write her biography at this point, but it can be easily gathered and understood from the letters that follow. She was so learned in both Latin and Greek and the arts which these contain that she surpassed not only learned women but also many outstanding men. God added so great a love of His Son and divinity that she turned her attention to heaven. She produced many different testimonies to her divine genius.

---

14. Plato *Rep.* 5.451–56.
15. "de claris mulieribus": referring especially to Boccaccio's work of that name.

She undertook a defense of the Roman orator against certain of his new critics, an oration which Caelius Calcagnini, a most learned man, approved of highly (as can be seen from his letter, which we have added to the others).[16] She wrote remarks on the prince of poets, Homer.[17] She composed many poems in a variety of meters, especially on divine subjects, with great elegance. She produced dialogues, both Greek and Latin, in imitation of Plato and Cicero so perfectly that not even Zoilus himself would be able to find anything to criticize.[18] When she was scarcely sixteen years old, she wrote three Prefaces to Cicero's *Paradoxes*, which the Greeks call *prooimia* (which we publish here). With me and many other men and women in the audience, she elucidated the *Paradoxes* in the private Academy of the Queen of Ferrara, and lectured memorably and elegantly. She wrote these out afterwards at my request, in her own hand. I have saved them as though a new gift from the Graces to this very day.[19] All the others perished at the same time as her husband's hometown of Schweinfurt in Germany, as will be clear from one of her letters to me below.[20] We have managed to collect these few "leavings from the Danaans and hateful Achilles."[21] From these few, however, one may get a sample of the rest, even as one might recreate a lion from his claws.[22] There are also a few short orations, letters in Latin, and poems, some in Greek, some in Latin, all written in the sweetest and purest style. We have also added other peoples' letters and poems either to her or about her, so that the reader can see how much learned men thought of her. There may be more in other hands, since she wrote letters and poems to many people. I would like to request these, so that they may not lie uncollected. The owners may join theirs to these, so send them to us to be published. In this matter I must thank Guillaume Rascalon, the noble Frenchman, who after the death of Olympia and her husband (for once he saw that his dearest wife had ascended to heaven, he was not able to linger on this earth for very long), sent me everything he was able to find, and encouraged me to undertake this edition. Johannes Herold, a man of great reading and learned in antiquities, also showed me a few things.

16. This is the lost *Defense of Cicero*. See letter 5.
17. Also lost.
18. No Greek dialogue has survived. Zoilus (4th century BC), nicknamed *Homeromastix*, "The Homer Whipper." A proverbially harsh critic; cf. Ov. *Rem.* 366; Mart. 11.37.1.
19. This autograph manuscript still exists: Basel E III 34. A page of it is reproduced in Kössling and Weiss-Stählin 1990, 159.
20. Letter 42.
21. Verg. A. 1.30.
22. A common proverb: e.g. Erasmus, *Adages* 1.1.61.

Lest these things lie hidden any longer and we deprive the learned of such sweet and elegant reading, I have sent them to press. And I wanted them to appear under your most beautiful name, Isabella, most lovely and religious of women, so that by this small token you might realize how great is my respect for your well-known talent and remarkable piety. We all know how many devices have been used to test and assault your faith in Jesus Christ, and how with God's help it has remained firm and intact. For although I have not been a personal observer of the struggles of your people in our beloved Italy, I nevertheless have heard from those who were eyewitnesses, and often had conversations with them, full of pious and holy concern about you and your safety. Yet, what was more well known throughout the whole of Italy than the fact that Isabella Manriquez Bresegna, one of the most highborn of women, kept the integrity of her religion amid the dangers and losses which her confession of the Gospel of God brought in its wake? Just to mention one thing, I will not start from the time in which you began to be illuminated by the divine light in your home city of Naples, but speak about these most recent days, in which you showed yourself more than a woman, nay more than a man, no doubt mindful of His saying, he who begins and "endures to the end, will be saved."[23] You were at Piacenza, the wife of the prefect of that city, the noble Garcia Manriquez, in which city, as everywhere, you always gave famous examples of temperance, chastity, modesty, charity, patience. Therefore all the citizens of Piacenza bewailed your departure as that of a pious parent. You came next for compelling reasons to Milan, where you began to be attacked on a daily basis in order to turn you away from a sincere piety to a vain superstition. But whatever was thrown at you as a hindrance merely drove you in the direction you were headed, and whatever was meant to extinguish the light that God had kindled in you merely fanned the flames. Gusts of wind only serve to stir the fire, as the outcome showed. For when you realized what our Lord teaches, that it is not possible to serve two masters at war with one another,[24] you preferred to leave the one, in order to give yourself totally to the other, rather than satisfy neither. Therefore having followed Christ, the true and lovely Lord, you left the most demanding tyrant. You added yourself to the company of the saints in body, as you already had in mind, and despised the fragile goods with which you once were surrounded. But did your flight make you safe from battle and strife? In no way. For as soon as you crossed the Alps and settled there, messengers were sent with letters from your husband,

---

23. Matt. 10:22; not the Vulgate text.
24. Matt. 6:24, Luke 16:13.

brother, and others, to bring you back. Your two dearest sons followed, now men of great favor and authority. Others took their place, not immediately but in waves, so that if you did not fall to one assault, you would be forced to surrender, conquered at last by successive onslaughts. What did you do at this point, Isabella, a woman, born and raised in luxury and wealth? Did you yield, conquered by your love for your husband and child, and by a certain weakness? Not at all. Rather, like Mount Zion, which no power can move from its place, you remained immovable.[25] You took their weapons and blows on the shield of faith, you beat back and broke them all with the sword of the Spirit, which is the Word of God.[26] You responded that you sought nothing more in this mortal life than to live with your husband and sweetest children, but only if you could do so with a clear conscience; and that you were prepared to be with him wherever he wished, to go with him, and serve him, but on this condition and law: that you be able to serve Christ with a free conscience, and keep the faith granted you[27] (which was the most important thing of all) not only in right thought but also in pious action. In this you openly declared that you cared more for the approval of Christ than the perishable treasures of the Egyptians.[28] Far different than he who lately looking back to Egypt, wretchedly returned to Egypt.[29] And no wonder, for he had never really left Egypt, since he had brought the fleshpots of Egypt with him.[30] A rare example of modesty in a woman, and in such a woman, set not just before women, but also before men. O faith! O singular constancy!

These and other gifts of immortal God to you impel me to publish these divine memorials of our Olympia under your name and patronage. For to whom could I dedicate the works of so erudite and holy a woman, other than to a woman outstanding for nobility, genius, and religion? Especially to one who has not been ashamed (as have so many) to profess the name of Christ even in the middle of Italy.[31] Add the fact that in this way Olympia, whom Italy bore and Germany buried, will be restored to her native Italy.

Since this is so, Isabella, most noble and most dear to Christ, to you I dedicate these remains, not of the perishable body of our Olympia, but of her pious and immortal soul and talent, which I do not doubt you will

---

25. Ps. 125:1, which Morata translated.
26. Eph. 6:16–17; not the Vulgate text.
27. "ei" 1558 : "tibi" *correxi*.
28. Heb. 11:26.
29. One of Isabella's sons remained with her, the other returned.
30. Exod. 16:3; a favorite image with Morata: letters 26, 37, 40.
31. Cf. Rom. 1:16.

value more and keep in a holier place than certain bones and dust and other mortal remains of that type which the greed of priests and the credulity of the crowd think should be not only preserved but even kissed and worshiped with religious veneration.

To God the Father of our Lord Jesus Christ I pray that he may bring it about that you are able to aid the Church of Christ by your holy example.

2. PREFACE TO THE SECOND EDITION OF 1562 (REPEATED IN THE THIRD EDITION OF 1570)

To Elizabeth, Queen of England, France, and Ireland, True Patron of the Christian Church, Caelius Secundus Curio sends his greetings:

Many have inquired, most excellent Elizabeth, what is the reason why—since there is a single origin and nature of our souls by which we have understanding and are shaped to this our human form—there exists in the human race such a variety of manners and interests, so that we see that not only do men differ from women, but also that within each sex men differ from men and women from women in the variety of their interests in all senses. Different people offer different explanations for this. Some ascribe it to the stars, others say that we are driven to this or that by fate, others by the size of one's talent, and more secret and abstruse reasons are sought. I shall not undertake in this place either to refute or approve their opinions. However, given that there is in fact a single force and origin of our souls, there should also be one and the same reason for our interests; if there is a part of the soul born to follow and obey, it should follow the soul and reason, and so preserve the soul's excellence.[32] But that this does not always happen is occasioned by various notions which disagree with each other, and by which mortals are drawn to differing interests.[33] As the Poet said, "His own pleasure draws each one."[34] One is delighted by trade, another by agriculture, another by sport, another by the Muses and leisure, another by business. As another poet said, "The army camp pleases many, and the sound of the trumpet mixed with the bugle."[35]

---

32. Curio refers, not too clearly, to Aristotle's discussion of the soul in *Pol.* 1252a—1260b.
33. Referring to Aristotelean notion of *doxa* (belief) vs. *episteme* (knowledge), e.g. *EN* 1139b18ff. Thus according to Curio, the perfect soul (*animus*) has one basic form (*ratio:* reason, cause, principle), but within (fallen) individuals differing opinions (*opinio:* beliefs, ideas) give rise to the differing interests (*studium:* intellectual pursuit, study).
34. Verg. *E.* 2.65.
35. Hor. *Odes* 1.1.23–24.

However, when mortals pursue an interest in the mind and reason, such a great variety of manners and interests does not appear. Instead, they place thinking about and the study of the truth ahead of all else, and they pursue what fits the excellence of the soul and preserves its dignity. For we see that those who employ the mastery of the soul and the service of the body have left the common interests of men far behind, and beyond all the gambling of mortals have devoted themselves to heroic deeds, or to understanding the most excellent arts, and the knowledge of truth. So Alexander and Caesar, so Plato and Aristotle, so Demosthenes and Cicero, so Homer and Virgil. From whom come these sublime lines:

> May the Muses, sweet above all,
> whose sacrifices I perform, stricken with great love for them,
> accept me, and show me the paths of heaven and the stars.[36]

And these:

> The way must be tried, whereby I may be able
> to raise myself from the ground, and as victor fly through the mouths of men.[37]

How could this be, I say, unless they looked to the excellence of the soul, not the baseness of the body.

With a spirit even greater and far more divine acted our heroes Moses and Joshua, David and Solomon, John and Paul, who, having imitated the life of God on earth, were outstanding as truly blessed. Now if these things appear admirable in men because of their rarity, how much more worthy of even greater admiration must they appear in women? Some of whom have left the humble duties of women behind and, exhibiting a certain greatness of soul, have not hesitated to perform the activities of men. So much so that some have waged war and ruled kingdoms to the admiration of all, while others have excelled in the knowledge of philosophy and the most beautiful arts, and have not only equaled men, but certain women have even surpassed them in these same activities. Semiramis, Queen of Assyria, is not unknown, as is her courage and prudence in administering her kingdom. Nor she about whom the poet wrote:

> Raging Penthesilea leads forth her band of Amazons
> with their lunate shields, and burns in the midst of thousands.

---

36. Verg. G. 2.475–77.
37. Verg. G. 3.8–9.

> A bold strap bound beneath her outthrust breast,
> a warrioress, and a virgin dares to attack men.[38]

And these about another:

> Besides these, there came Camilla of the Volscan people
> leading a band of cavalry and troops flashing with bronze,
> a warrioress. She had not accustomed her feminine hands to the distaff
> and the weaving baskets of Minerva, rather the virgin was ready to endure
> hard battles, and to outstrip the winds with the speed of her feet.[39]

With Angla as leader, the Saxons once occupied Britain. What could be more glorious than that queen after whose name the noblest island of the ocean was later named?[40] What shall I say about Zenobia, whose genius, courage, and prudence were so great as to be admired by the Greeks and the Romans. For since letters are cultivated by genius, kingdoms are governed by counsel, and military affairs by courage, certainly she who has been educated in Greek and Latin letters, experienced in military courage, and instructed in the arts of ruling, has taught quite clearly that a manly soul is not wanting in the female sex, provided they do not refuse to cultivate it and follow its lead.

I will not mention Aspasia, Sappho, Praxilla, Corinna, Telesilla, Anyte, Cleobulina, and the daughters of Stesichorus, and all the others of that sort whose genius is celebrated in literature and history,[41] but I will not fail to mention holier women: Deborah the prophet and leader of the Israelites; Jael and Judith, by whose courage and wisdom the Israelites were freed from the greatest and gravest dangers. We read that Saba, Queen of the Ethiopians, came to Solomon; she had heard about his wisdom and consulted with him on difficult questions.[42] I could mention the Roman virgins Paula and

---

38. Verg. A. 1.491–94.
39. Verg. A. 7.803–7.
40. For the conveniently etymological Ang(e)la, cf. Christine de Pizan, *The Book of the City of Ladies* 2.61.3.
41. A standard list of poets. No classical source mentions the daughters of Stesichorus. However, a letter to them features in the pseudepigraphical "Letters of Phalaris," which were not exposed as a forgery until Bentley in 1687. Madelaine Des Roches ("Ode 1") cited the daughters of Stesichorus as well (Des Roches 1993, 89).
42. 1 Kings 10. *Regina Saba* in the Vulgate; often taken as a proper name. She is not, however, called queen of the Ethiopians in the Bible. The language, including the reference to the Ethiopians, is remarkably close to that of Laura Cereta (1640, 189; trans. at King and Rabil 1983, 82). This suggests either a common source, or that Curio, in his search for antecedents, had read Cereta's works in manuscript.

Eustochium,[43] and Cassandra Fedele, who flourished recently in Venice.[44] I could mention others of this and preceding ages, but there exist entire volumes on famous women and they prove that what Plato taught in the fifth book of the *Republic* and the seventh book of the *Laws* is true: that there should be the same training for women and for men both in arts and letters as well as in gymnastics and military science. He sets them in charge of the protection of the city, and assigns commands to them. And while he concedes that they are weaker in body than men, he makes them equals in soul.

Since that is so, what can be more admirable than those heroic women? What can be more holy? What better to imitate? These women, Queen Elizabeth, you have most wisely imitated. Or what is more true, you make the idea and image of your soul most beautiful and nearly divine by contemplating especially Christ, from whom all things flow into you, so that posterity will admire you no less than them. For the famous deeds you have done, so wisely and bravely, are celebrated not only in our literature and language but in those of other nations as well. No age will be silent about your praises. They will never be able to pass over silently your great forgiveness, your exceptional and unheard of clemency, your moderation in all matters of royal power, and finally your incredible and nearly divine wisdom. They will hail you virgin most learned and most chaste, woman most brave, queen most wise; by whose work God has restored the heavenly light of the Gospel not only to your England, but to peoples near and far has given peace and brought salvation. Therefore, your English subjects understand from your name that God has His house among them.[45] These things are above woman, above man; yet things that men could not do, Your Majesty, while a girl in age, a virgin in untouched purity, brought to perfection. Yet more and greater things are expected from such virtue, from such wisdom.

And since you are so good and so great, these memorials of Olympia Morata, a woman most famous for piety and letters, which she gathered and entrusted to me as the remnants of her talent as she was dying, I publish under your most fortunate name, and entrust them to your faith and protection. For to whom could the writings of a woman so learned and pious be better entrusted than to Elizabeth the Queen, the most learned and religious of all? With whose name could they better be published and come into people's hands?

---

43. Paula and her daughter Eustochium, to whom Jerome addressed several famous letters on sexual renunciation (*Ep*. 22, 30, 31, 33, 39, 108; a joint letter of theirs: 46).
44. 1465?—1558. See now Fedele 2000.
45. Curio etymologizes Elizabeth as *El-beth-*: "house of God."

Therefore accept this gift, unequal to Your Majesty and Highness, but, as I hope, the greatness of your name and your highest humane learning will elevate the littleness of my gift. How great her learning was, how great and how ardent her zeal for true religion, how great her endurance in the many adversities she suffered, how great her constancy, Your Majesty will easily see from this book. She had written many different testimonies of her genius and piety, nearly all of which perished together with her husband's hometown. From those that remain one may get a sample of the rest: like guessing at a lion from his claws, as they say. I have added some not inelegant writing by other people either to her or about her, to show not just my opinion about her learning but that of others, lest anyone think I am attributing more than is fair to an *Italian* woman. That I have dared to address you, a Queen endowed with such majesty, is due to your singular humane learning, celebrated by all, your clemency, letters, piety, and charity towards those who live their lives in exile for the sake of the truth. Add to this the fact that this is not the first time my love for you and your people is manifest. For I made most honorable mention of you in my supplement to Sabellico's *History*,[46] not as you deserve but in keeping with the brevity of a history, and I inscribed and sent my *Commentary on Cicero's Philippics* to your brother, King Edward.[47] Indeed, my son Horatius consecrated certain of his youthful writings to the same boy,[48] who if he had lived or if what he had ordered had been accomplished, things would have gone better for me. But his early and untimely death ruined and cut off not only my hopes but those of many good men. To all of these, if Your Majesty has forgotten, there are witnesses; I will mention only those two splendid knights, famed for every sort of virtue, Sir Anthony Cooke and Sir Wroth.[49] But all things are well and wisely ruled by God, whose providence destined for you that kingdom so long shaken and afflicted by the fates, so that all must confess that you rule the Britons not only humanely and by lawful inheritance but also by divine right and example, properly and in order.

---

46. Curio 1560; his edition of the universal history, *Enneades ab orbe condito* (Venice: Bernardinus Venetus, 1498; numerous editions and titles) by Sabellico (Marcus Antonius Coccius, called Sabellicus, 1436?–1506), the Venetian historian.

47. Curio 1551; no longer in the inventory to Edward VI's library (Nichols 1857 [1964], 1:cccxxxi).

48. Caeilus Hortatius Curio 1550; in the inventory to Edward VI's library (Nichols 1857 [1964], 1:cccxxx); see Cantimori 1992, 188 n. 1.

49. *Vrotus* 1562 1570. Sir Thomas Wroth 1516–73, intimate of Edward VI's, and afterwards in exile under Mary Tudor, a notable helper of the Protestants in Strassburg and Frankfurt. See *DNB*, s.v.

For all these reasons, I am sending to you these memorials of our Olympia together with a few things of my own. If they satisfy, as I hope, your exquisite taste, I am certain that they will satisfy others. Farewell, light of our age, and singular example of ruling well and holy.

Basel, 1 Sept. 1562

JUVENILIA: FERRARA, C. 1539–41, AGE 12–14

EDITOR'S INTRODUCTION

Curio preserved a number of Morata's juvenilia from his brief stay in Ferrara between April and October 1541. These include the prefaces to the public readings on Cicero's *Stoic Paradoxes*, and an epideictic oration in praise of the Roman hero Mucius Scaevola. See my introduction to this volume for the social setting of such public orations.

These are works of the schoolroom, but they show not only an astonishing command of Latin and Greek but a wide range of authors, including Cicero, Horace, Lucretius, and Juvenal in Latin; Homer, Isocrates, Xenophon, Lucian, and Plutarch in Greek. She translates Homer into Latin and then Propertius into Greek. Though she mixes in an Old Testament example with classical allusions, there is an interesting total absence of the church fathers, who are so frequent in the writings of earlier women humanists and so often recommended to them.

To this period also date the poems "To Eutychus Pontanus Gallus," "On True Virginity," and "To Bembo." See below for her poetry.

PROLEGOMENA TO CICERO'S **STOIC PARADOXES** [1541]

Introduction to the First Reading

Since we usually ask for pardon when we have erred accidentally or sinned impulsively, according to the famous saying from the works of Gellius attributed to Marcus Cato when he accused Aulus Albinus,[50] I need to ask and

---

50. Gell. 11.8. Albinus had written a history of Rome in Greek and asked for the reader's pardon for any grammatical or stylistic errors. Cato wondered why he had written in Greek in the first place.

beg pardon from you all under many headings. From you, my professors of humanity, and especially from you, Anna, a noblewoman as cultured as she is illustrious. And indeed I would have offered many things as an excuse for why I could have avoided my turn in this exchange of yours, by which you rightly judge one's cultured learning [ἐγκυκλοπαιδείαν]. Could I not have had a just case (as they say) of immunity, due to the fact that, as you know, I've been lying very seriously sick in bed for so long, and I've heard and read nothing worth remarking for so long? Not to mention that I really ought not as an unlettered little newcomer compete, like a mad Pentesilea, with such great men as these.[51]

Furthermore, since there will never be anything, no matter how arduous, that I would refuse to do if you impose it on me, princess Anna, I have chosen obedience over silence. The same thing has happened to me which I remember reading in a story about a soldier's servant who refuses a burden. It was a matter of indifference to him what baggage he picked up, as along as he did not go away empty-handed. He was frightened of the stacks of bundled hay and preferred to carry a chest full of the heaviest lead rather than straw, because he judged the weight not by weight but by its apparent size. So I thought that Cicero's *Paradoxes* would be easy because it is a short work. But after I had put my shoulders to the burden, I realized that it was heavier than Aetna, and that not even Hercules, or even Atlas could lift it. If I had been mindful of the precept of the poet, I would have tested well in advance what my shoulders could carry and what they refuse.[52] But at least it turned out well for me that I did not choose the *Dream of Scipio*, judging the work not from the greatness of the subject matter but the small number of its pages! What dreams you would have heard me recite then as I dreamed! And what snores! But perhaps we will fall asleep here too, and if it does not happen, that will be a miracle among other paradoxes.

But now let us see what Cicero himself has to say in this new philosophy, which does not differ much, in my opinion, from Christianity.

Introduction to the Second Lecture

Alexander the Great, the greatest in military discipline as he was in all other things, used to declare that just because someone had acted bravely in battle one time, or had been a bold swordsman in a single match, that did not immediately make him brave or famous; rather it was he who had acted nobly

---

51. Penthesilea, queen of the Amazons, who was killed by Achilles.
52. Hor. A.P. 38–40.

twice or three times or more that he believed and declared was a man of exceptional courage and whom he specifically included among the veterans who were dearest to him. He used to say that once was practically never, and that in his experience it very seldom happened that someone was able to do anything remarkable by chance rather than by his own efforts, since it was much easier to get a reputation than to keep one.[53]

Noticing this fact, that wise teacher of youth said not without reason, "Preserve your reputation."[54] That exceptional general had perhaps learned this from a certain outstanding archer, who was openly praised for shooting arrows at a great distance through a narrow ring that was barely larger than they were. However, he could never be persuaded, even though he was threatened with the death penalty if he did not obey the king's orders, to try such a feat before the king himself, fearing that he would not live up to the king's great expectation.[55]

Now I will tell you plainly that if your commands had allowed me, I would have gladly stayed silent, content merely not to have displeased you altogether in speaking that one time, and because I think I gained the sort of reputation where an increase is less to be sought than Fortune is to be feared, since my strength is not up to the task. So I would have given immortal thanks to God and thought that I had gotten away with it one time. But who knows whether I will be able to sustain and protect the difficult adversary set up for me, that is, the continuation of the reputation I have gained. In fact I will think that it has turned out wonderfully if I do not destroy my newborn glory through the faults of my tiny talent before it has been brought up. The orator Lysias once handed over the speech he had written for the defense to a man who had a trial date set. After the man had read it repeatedly, he went to Lysias all sad. "When I first read your speech," he said, "it seemed admirable. But after I read it over a number of times, it seemed dull and ineffective." Lysias smiled and said, "So what? Are you going to deliver it to the jury more than once?" as if to say, "It's enough not to displease the one time."[56] And so, under your orders, uncertain of the outcome, even though the task of reading and interpreting is "an act full of dangerous risk"[57] and the outcome of everything is uncertain, behold here

---

53. I have not been able to trace this anecdote.
54. Ps. Cato, *Disticha Catonis*, Brev. sent. 42 (25 Boas). The little moral handbook attributed to Cato was one of the most popular of Latin primers from the Middle Ages onwards.
55. Plut. *Reg. et Imp. Apoth.* Alexander 23 (*Mor.* 181B).
56. Plut. *De garrul.* 5 (*Mor.* 504C), a close translation.
57. Hor. *Odes* 2.1.6.

I have come into the arena once more, hoping for nothing more than to please you.

Now let us get down to business, so that my childishness, mixed with Cicero's eloquence, may seem less lisping and less inept.

Introduction to the Third Lecture

I am afraid, distinguished listeners, so help me God, quite afraid that deceitful Fortune will do to me what she usually does to many gamblers: she will favor them and flatter them once or twice so that they, thinking themselves blind, that is, the sons of the one great Queen, will expose once more boldly to chance whatever they can scrape up from anywhere. And now look: deprived of all fortune, they realize that Fortune is fortune, and they lash her heavily with many insults when they seem to be within sight of port, even when they are at the port. I am afraid, I say, that the same thing will happen to me that happens to many who are ignorant of the seductiveness of the sea,[58] and of how the sea always flatters[59] and lures them into sailing with its blandishments until caught out on the deepest waves it overwhelms them and tosses them out shipwrecked. Wisely did the ancient Romans, after a victory had been gained, give burnt offerings to their gods and decree supplications in thanks for success. In this way, unlike so many people, who, drunk with sweet fortune, become more insolent and argumentative, they, having been now made proud by their success, would not become overly audacious despisers of danger and foolishly rush into a place from which they could not retreat. Just so do we often see many, growing insolent from a lucky turn of events, crash unluckily when "power without counsel collapses under its own weight."[60] Homer in Book V of the *Odyssey* says of the proud man: "Happy he spreads his sails to the favorable winds."[61] The same Romans used to place at the foot of the chariot of the general celebrating his triumph "a man rough, dirty, . . . covered with rags and years,"[62] I mean filth and a horrible spectacle; and on the chariot there was a jester who would grab the edge of the triumphant general's toga and say, "Alas, look down from your chariot," as if to say, "Do you see that wretched and unhappy man? Beware

---

58. Cf. Lucr. 2.559, 5.1104.
59. "ficus quaerere"; see, e.g., Erasmus, *Adages* 2.3.3; cf. Zen. 5.91, Sud. G 1327.
60. Hor. *Odes* 3.4.65.
61. *Od.* 5.269. An allegorical interpretation.
62. Ter. *Eun.* 236. Morata's details are curiously wrong. There was no such old man, nor does the Terence verse allude to any such. It was a slave, not a jester (*scurra*) who said, "Look behind you" (Tert. *Apol.* 33.4). The ring was of iron (Pl. *NH* 33.11).

of becoming insolent because of your victory, for mortal affairs happen in a mortal way, and from this triumph you can become just like everyone else." The reverend senators wished these generals to wear a bronze ring on their finger when they celebrated their triumph as an amulet and a symbol that they too were born of the earth and, like iron and bronze, could get rusty, and so that they would not think that they were immortal gods, however glorious they were otherwise, and so become self-lovers [φίλαυτοι] and disdain others.

Therefore there are two things I must be especially afraid of from envious Fortune—which of the two I want less I don't know. Nevertheless, I am of the opinion that I should calculate that it will be less serious for me to be so deluded by her that, even though I seem to have accomplished something twice before, this third appearance by me will blacken my reputation and destroy completely my name and glory (whatever it was worth), than to fall into the vice of arrogance. But, I feel, since my mind is apprehensive of evil, though I am beyond the risk of this uncertain matter, I feel that I have fallen with my eyes wide open into another risk no less dangerous. But whatever will happen, I have not sought this assignment voluntarily, like Phaeton, but under orders; and whatever the ignominy, I prefer to be obedient to your orders than to be branded with the mark of obstinate rusticity. I am not ignorant that you know that "in great matters it's the thought that counts,"[63] and I know that you are most kind. Nevertheless, as I told you, because of my innate timidity and the thinness of my talent, I am all atremble and afraid, as though I were about to be summoned to the altar at Lyons.[64] Alas, at last I realize how stupid I am, and scarcely even now I look and survey how great is the audience around me. I am disconcerted and oppressed not only by today's gathering but by the two previous ones, like the blind man who, as long as he was blind, used to cross a huge terrible river on a narrow bridge at a fast pace; but as soon as his sight was restored and he was no longer blind, he saw how he had been making the crossing and was terrified; he would no longer set foot on the bridge which he used to commit himself to in ignorance. But, whatever happens, no sacrifice ever pleases God as much as obedience,[65] and in sacrifice Abraham did not make an acceptable offering by what he sacrificed but by his willing obedience.[66] So here I am, somewhat recovered and

---

63. ἐν μεγάλοις ἀρκεῖ καὶ θέλημα μόνον; apparently a Greek rendering (a pentameter) of Prop. 2.10.6: "in magnis et voluisse sat est."
64. Cf. Juv. 1.44: Caligula set up a rhetoric competion at the Altar to Rome and Augustus; the losers had to write praises to the winners or erase their writings with their tongues, or else be tossed into the Rhône or beaten (Suet. Gaius 20).
65. 1 Sam. 15:22; and cf. Hos. 6:6.
66. Gen. 22:1–18; the sacrifice of Isaac.

ready for a third time around, like an apprentice sculptor, still ignorant of the art which he professes, who has found a piece of Parian marble. No matter how small his skill, he will seem to have done something, even though he excels not because of his work but because of the material. *The Antiope* was most pleasing to the ears of the ancients no matter who the flute player was; *The Andromache* pleased because of its own elegance. An accomplished musician who performed for either of them would no doubt affect the audience even more. But if anyone other than Arbuscula or Roscius danced the Cyclops, the smell of saffron or the perfumes of Panchaia or the splendor of the scenery could not help him when he was driven from the stage by all the hisses.[67] So important is the material, so important is the artist that unless they come together, each will be defective, or if not defective, then less effective. There are, however, a few tunes so melodiously and rhythmically composed that they seem pleasant no matter what pipe or rustic voice they are performed by. So beautiful, so sweet, so lovely are the words of my dear Cicero that however they are pronounced they demonstrate the greatness of their inherent majesty. And that all may agree that this is plainly so, please listen to how much of their great majesty they retain even when spoken by me and how resplendently they still shine.

PRAISE OF Q. MUCIUS SCAEVOLA[68] (IN GREEK) [1541]

Editor's note: The main purpose of this composition is to show Morata's easy command of Greek vocabulary and idiom, which she drew principally from Xenophon. She has also clearly read Lucian and the orators.

That it is fitting to love our fatherland and to return a thank-offering to her for her nourishment[69] is clear to all, and it is in no way a secret that those

---

67. I.e. a great work of literature succeeds on its own, while a pantomime such as the Cyclops's dance needs the finest actors to make it palatable. Morata here gives a virtuoso display of learning. Cicero uses the *Antiope* (by Pacuvius) and *Andromache* (Ennius) to illustrate the superiority of the connoisseurs, "qui primo flatu tibicinis Antiopem esse aiunt aut Andromacham" [who at the first breath of the flute-player say, "That's *The Antiope*" or "That's *The Andromache*"] (*Acad.* 2.200). Horace mentions the Cyclops's dance (*Sat.* 1.5.63, *Ep.* 2.2.125) and quotes the mime actress Arbuscula, "'It is enough if the knights applaud me,' said bold Arbuscula, when hissed from the stage, despising the rest" (*Sat.* 1.10.76). Cicero mentions having seen the actor Antipho play Andromache; he was now past his prime, but Arbuscula was very successful (*Att.* 4.15.6). Q. Roscius Gallus was the most brilliant actor of his age (see, int. al., Hor. *Ep.* 2.1.82). Saffron was used as a perfume in the Roman theater (e.g., Lucr. 2.416, Hor. *Ep.* 2.1.79). For the perfumes of the semimythical Panachaia, see Lucr. 2.417, etc.

68. Morata's primary source is Livy's Latin account (1.12); and cf. DH 5.27–31, 35, Plut. *Popl.* 17.

69. Cf. Luc. *Patr. Enc.* 7.

who have dared to undergo dangers and labors on her behalf are rightly to be sung by all; no one would deny this. And among these, Mucius seems to me especially worthy of speech and praise, concerning whom I am now going to speak. Although he was a Roman of noble and illustrious family, when he was a youth, since he considered saving the fatherland as most important, he outstripped many even of the elders in courage and virtue. Once when there was a mighty famine in the city, Porsena, king of the Etruscans, being then an enemy of the Romans, confidently expected to bring them into subjection. Mucius, not enduring this, considered how he might free the city from the famine and the siege at the same time, and impose just penalties on the king for the things he had done. Therefore at first, with no one as ally in this, he thought to attack the camp of the enemy. Nevertheless, fearing lest the Senate in ignorance might think that he had run away as a fugitive, when the Senate was in assembly, he shared his plan with it, beginning with some such words as these:

"You see, men of Rome, in what state we are in and in what danger the city is about to come. Porsena, coming into our land, had become the cause of the greatest of evils for us, famine together with war. The famine, because of the want of necessities, has turned out to be unsolvable for us, and war on the other hand is not easy to solve. For if we, who are few, go in battle-array against many, the enemy will outflank us, and we will not withstand them since they are many times more numerous. But if we hand the city over to Porsena, and after taking the city he rules over us, we will never be able to get free of the slavery. For in tyrants there is an inextinguishable and innate desire to rule. Therefore shall we allow the fatherland to be in danger, judging our lives to be more important than freedom? It is the way of Romans rather to die nobly than to live with shame. For we know that the fate of death has been pronounced in sentence against us all.[70] But to die well nature has assigned to the good as her own. I neither reproach the others, nor blame those who now hesitate. For many have sunk in exhaustion from marching and running and bearing weapons. But what seems to me to be best to do, this I will explain.[71] I eagerly desire, men, in secrecy, to march against the enemy, attempting with the gods' help to take vengeance on the evil-doing king, either by killing him, or by doing some other noble deed of daring, which men born hereafter may praise. This, if it comes out well, will be good for you all and for the fatherland, but if it turns out ill, will be ill for none save me. Nevertheless it is necessary for you, settling the matter

---

70. Isoc. 1.43.
71. ἀλλὰ τὸ ἐμοὶ δοκοῦν κάλλιστον ἔσεσθαι δράσαντι. Morata seems be trying to create a Latin future perfect here.

in common, to examine this and, consulting together, to make a decree. If you also consider that this is for the good, I will march."

When he had said such things, they all praised his plan and sent him on his way. He went and ran off, bearing his sword hidden in a fold of his clothes. When he arrived at the plain where the Etruscans had encamped, he stood by the royal podium where he saw someone dispersing the pay to the army, who was sitting next to the king, with dress like his, and surrounded with many spear carriers, like the king himself. This was the secretary of the king. Mucius was at a loss whether he was this man or that one, but did not dare to ask, since he considered that this was not without danger; but not willing to return home without doing anything, assuming that this would not be good, he missed the king and instead of him killed the secretary. Then as he was turning around and planning his escape, bearing in his hands a sword dripping with blood—a witness to such a great deed of daring—as the army ran together towards the noise and shouting, he was seized by the bodyguards for execution, being dragged to the podium where the king was. But even then, neither turning pale nor trying everything to escape, causing fear more than being afraid, he boldly spoke these words:

"I am Mucius. I happen to be a Roman, an enemy to my enemies, and I have long been correctly persuaded that the fatherland must be helped in every way, and especially when it is in danger because it stands in difficulty. So now, when I saw her worn out to the final point of evil and besieged by you, I came hither from the Romans to meet you, taking no consideration for my soul and life, avoiding no labor, to pay you back evil for the harm you have done. For we Romans are prepared neither to harm nor be harmed. But since my hand has happened to err, I will not take it ill that I must pay the penalty for my failure. For the strengths of the Romans are both to act and to endure. You will not lack for others who share the same opinion. And since you preferred to wage war rather than peace, and to be called the enemy of the Romans rather than their friend, we must now take measures lest we fight against you while you are somewhat unprepared. We have learned that it is neither numbers nor power that in war produce victory, but whichever of the two goes against its enemies more strengthened in spirit; these men for the most part their enemies cannot withstand. Therefore we shall not lead forth troops nor divisions, but fight one on one, and not on the field, but within your tent and beside the very podium on which you happen to be sitting, even as just occurred. The youth of Rome declares such a war on you."

The king, clearly deeply disturbed and beside himself at the danger, ordered a fire to be kindled. But Mucius, turning towards him, said, "O king, behold how they despise death, those to whom honor and virtue and glory are dearer than the body." As he said this, he voluntarily and suddenly thrust his right hand into the fire, and as though being outside himself and removed from any sensation, he burned his hand up. The king seeing this sight, so hard to handle and hard to look at, seemed to be more pained than he who had been burned. He ordered the fire to be extinguished and spoke to the youth, "O youth, depart, having dared terrible deeds against yourself more than against me. I would praise you for having done these and other similar deeds, if you had dared them instead for my fatherland. But as things are now, because I have recognized that you are a noble and patriotic man, for those reasons I let you go." And Mucius, as though repaying the king for his gracious favor, revealed to him his plan. After the king let Mucius go, deciding to enter back into friendship with the Romans, he sent ambassadors, ordering them both to give and receive pledges of faith; to such an extent did the danger overhanging him from the conspirators trouble him. Thus the war was resolved. And Mucius thereafter, from his right hand having been mutilated, was nicknamed "Scaevola" [i.e. Lefty], to whom the fairest prize was granted by the Senate, a field directly opposite the city itself, situated next to the Tiber, which they say was ever after called "The Meadow of Mucius."

LETTERS: ITALY

LETTERS 1–8: FERRARA, 1540–1547, AGE 13–20
EDITOR'S INTRODUCTION

Few of these early letters are dated. Letter 1 is from Morato to his daughter on proper pronunciation of Latin. It is a strange, obscure, allusive, and overwrought effusion. Written in 1540 (when Olympia was thirteen), it shows the range of authors that he expected Morata to be familiar with, as well as the fact that he was already aware of her role in public demonstrations of her learning.

Letters 2–5 are to and from her teachers. Letter 3 was written in Greek and must date before Curio's departure from Ferrara about October 1541.

Letter 6 to her father was written apparently soon after she joined the court or at least when her relations with Duke Alfonso were friendly. The mention of her brother, Emilio, dates it some time after his birth in 1542. Letters 7 and 8 are short, undated notes to her teacher Johann Sinapius to cheer him up while he was ill.

Letter 1: Ferrara, 25 June 1540
Fulvio Pellegrino Morato to his daughter Olympia:

Although I am not unaware that there is nothing more difficult than (and indeed nothing even as difficult as) speaking (let alone teaching) about proper pronunciation, separate and apart from delivery, nevertheless, because I can deny you nothing (nor should I, because you are my daughter and eager not only to speak in a literary style but also to express your speech beautifully), I shall touch briefly on a few points.

First, to obtain a proper pronunciation is not just the first, second, and third parts of oratory, as Demosthenes said of delivery, but it is far nobler and of greater impressiveness.[72] Delivery, if it does not have all of its ornament in pronunciation, scarcely shines by any other means. Cicero tried to show that delivery and pronunciation were the same thing.[73] He said one ought to use the lips as the reins of the voice, sometimes lowering it, sometimes raising it, and adding splendor and melodiousness before it leaves the concavity of the palate, with the shape of the mouth now pursed, now relaxed.[74] Never imitate Arrius in Catullus,[75] and most important, appear to break nuts with your teeth or speak with both cheeks.

The matron, before she issues forth from her private women's quarters, consults her mirror and closest maid about what appearance, what face she should present. So should the voice. If it is harsh or overly melodious, it should be tempered with bars placed in its way and the opposition of tongue and teeth. If it is too thin, as far as possible, breath should be added with strong sides.[76] If it is too sharp and tinny, it should be darkened with pursed lips, so that it does not trip over long and bombastic words with too soft a palate. Let the lungs take a deep breath of air,[77] just like all the hooded Fustians, Stentors, Trachaluses, Greedy Gulls, Thrasoes, and Sir Oracles usually declaim (to make the occasional joke).[78]

Study so that your speech is fluent, i.e., pleasing in utterance. Demosthenes worked hard to pronounce his r's without any harsh hissing.[79] Theophrastus had a manner of speaking so well articulated with sweetness that Aristotle himself chose him as successor in his own Academy.[80] Thucydides was a sincere, even grand, speaker. The heart-changing Queen Peitho, the sweetness of Pericles, the bees of Plato, the chains of Hercules, the lyres of Orpheus and Amphion, the charm of Nestor, the loveliness of Christ Himself are nothing other than elegance: sweet, smooth, festive, soft, not

72. Cf. Cic. De Orat. 3.213, Or. 56; Quint. 11.3.6.
73. Cf. Cic. Inv. 1.9 (not exactly Cicero's meaning).
74. Not in Cicero.
75. Who had trouble with 'is haspirates: Cat. 84.
76. "inaminet": postclassical.
77. Cf. Pers. 1.14.
78. "ut multi cucullati bombali-bombaces . . . stentores, trachali, lari, thrasones, magniloqui." Thrachalus was an orator admired by Qunitilian (e.g. 12.5.5), with perhaps a glance back at the meaning of the Greek ("throat"). Thraso was the boastful soldier in Terence's Eunuchus. "Greedy Gulls" is a guess for the text's lari = λάρος (Lat. larus in Vulg. Lev. 11:16, etc.), used frequently by Aristophanes of Cleon (and cf. Luc. Tim. 12).
79. Quint. 1.11.5.
80. Gell. 13.5.3–12.

affected or overelaborate in speaking, but rather beautifully, wittily, cleverly, and quietly harmonious.[81]

To change the sound, not just in each sentence according to the meaning, but also in individual words is the mark of the most eloquent. Sometimes to prolong the breath, but never forced or sobbing, at other times to give the reins to the rush of the words, that is the mark of the greatest orator,[82] as is pressing on, exclaiming, and imploring according to the sense, and finally to imitate, but not like an ape.

The most powerful part of speaking is the art of making the speech wonderfully subservient to the matter in voice, not to mention sense. This cannot be taught or borrowed from anywhere, but only to the extent that the orator helps out his own nature by listening to others who seem to speak sweetly, or contrariwise ineptly.

Pronunciation is so valuable that Theophrastus got angry when an old woman recognized him as a foreigner by his pronunciation, and this the man who was renamed by his teacher Aristotle because of the sweetness of his speaking; he had been called Tyrtamus previously, according to Diogenes Laertius.[83] So valuable that the Greeks themselves would rather not know Greek than to make mistakes in pronunciation about their Aemilia, about Chrysostomus.[84] Many know Greek, but few pronounce it sweetly and well, as you can see anywhere. For if to know Greek did not consist of this especially, then even I would speak Greek!

Where does the praise of plays come from (not to talk about the sweetest orators now) except from pronunciation? Just so do flute players help their refrains with breath, and tongue, and fingers, now lifted up, now pressed down; likewise harpists modulate and tune their scales and harmonies by the tightening and relaxing of the strings. The gaze of our eyes, I say, and the stare of those declaiming does a great deal in acting. In the same way, the playing, now high, now low, of trumpets and flutes guides the motions, gestures, ferocity, of orators, actors, and soldiers. The tongues of the horn players with their vibrations help all the "Antiopes"

---

81. Peitho is the goddess of Persuasion, Pericles the great Athenian leader. Cicero (*Div.* 1.78, 2.66) and Pliny the Elder (*NH* 11.55) recount the story that bees settled on the lips of the infant Plato to foretell his honeyed words (a common legend). Lucian 5 (*Herc.*) 3, describes the Celtic image of Hercules/Ogmios, who leads a crowd of men by golden chains running from his tongue to their ears. The lumping in of Christ as another example of a rhetorician is extremely daring.

82. "oratoris" 1562 : "oratotis" 1570.

83. Cic. *Brut.* 172, DL 5.38; Theo-phrastus means "Told by God."

84. Text and reference uncertain: "et ut Graeci ipsi malint nihil Graece scire quam non belle pronunciare de sua illa Aemilia, de Chrysostomo."

and "Andromaches."[85] The flexibilities in the throat of singers, the most marvelous little bird, the nightingale with her sweetest and variable modulations, she alone, if anyone, can teach pronunciation.[86] This is the harmony of heaven, balanced against itself, yet aided and supported by the breath of the mouth.[87] "What if you had heard the thing itself?" as someone said.[88] Whence comes it, that the living voice affects us more? What is it? Do I not hear the poet in his trifles? And the whole theater exclaims if one syllable is off by being too long or too short.[89] Other than for us to know how to pronounce things best, is there any need to be familiar with the length of syllables and their attendant orthography? Indeed, you fight over the rules of music theory. And that saying, "I don't know how to speak but I can't keep silent."[90] What could not Roscius do with his articulate and speaking motions, as he expressed words with inappropriate limbs?[91] What could not the Sirens do? (I am now talking about words.) Ulysses felt within himself just how much the meretriciousness of others' speaking might affect and effect. Birds, not inglorious in flight, gesticulate as if led by an articulate voice.[92] Virgil, Caesar, Brutus, Cicero were most marvelous in pronunciation. Pallas, Mercury, the Nine Muses, the new order of the heavens, the number of the stars, Apollo leader of the Muses, recoverable Echo, do these not signify the manifold elegance of the voice and of human harmony?[93] What can the orator accomplish, unless he leaves his sting behind in the peroration?[94] The singer Phemius could cure illnesses with the modulations of his voice.[95] Who does not listen willingly and give ear to one who speaks sweetly? Cerberus let his ears droop, the wheels of Ixion stopped, when a

---

85. Typical Roman plays. See notes to Morata's "Introduction to the Third Lecture," above.

86. Obscure. Does "the flexibilities in the throat of singers" refer to the nightingale? To pronunciation?

87. A reminiscence of Ovid's description of the chaotic earth: *Met.* 1.12–13.

88. Apparently an allusion to the story in Plutarch (*Lyc.* 20) of the Spartan who declined to go listen to a man imitate the nightingale, replying, "I have heard the nightingale itself."

89. Possibly a reference to the famous story of the actor Hegelochos, who, in a performance of Euripides, meant to say, "From out of the waves again I see calm [γαλήν]" and instead mispronounced the accent and said, "I see a ferret [γαλῆν]: Schol. Ar. *Ran.* 303.

90. A common proverb: see Jerome, *Ep.* 69.2, 130.17.

91. For Roscius, see above, n. 65.

92. "aues non ingloriae volatu" 1562 : "aues non in gloriae volatu" 1570.

93. One can see here the baleful effect of the rhetorical manuals and emblem books. The new order of the heaven may be a reference to Copernicus.

94. Cf. Pliny 1.20.18, Cic. *de Orat.* 3.138.

95. Phemius is the bard in Odysseus's court who was forced to sing for the suitors. However, Morato seems to have attributed to him the episode in which the sons of Autolycus cure Odysseus's wound by singing over it: *Od.* 19.455–58.

88   *Olympia Morata: Works and Letters*

sweet voice was heard.[96] But if we chance to hear a bird giving back a human word, good gods, how amazed we are! How delighted we are.

In sum, to speak sweetly helps a case far more than all adornment, clothing, or gold helps women. Nor does the sun itself add more grace, elegance, and splendor to the sky, than a sweet voice does to pleasure, than a modulated pronunciation.[97] Indeed I never feel more titillated by a greater pleasure than when I hear someone chatting beautifully, learnedly, elegantly, and pleasantly, especially if they are speaking Latin. Not unjustifiably does the man say, "If you read, you sing; if you sing, you sing badly."[98] Nor would Quintilian have advised us in vain about the right way of teaching boys pronunciation, unless he had seen how much it is worth.[99] The fact that Augustus paid attention to Phonascus, who pronounced with a certain sweet and suitable sound of the mouth, having learned to tighten, relax, smooth, and harshen the voice, shows us of what great excellence is sweet pronunciation.[100] The *"Iulaea"* voice and —ἄπῳδος do not signify harshness of the voice, but rather a type of change or weakening, such as Doricism, iotacism, lambdacism, on other mistakes of that type.[101] There is nothing less pleasant or more absurd than an excessive pronunciation of words. Someone wishing to say, "His Imperial Majesty rejoices that you have arrived safely," would be laughed at by the audience if he said, "His Imperrrial Magesty regoyses that jew haf arriffed zavely."[102] Also to pronounce *m, n,* and *z* too exquisitely, with the opening of the lips too wide and gaping. Also dividing the first syllable of "sanctis" and "magnus" unpleasantly and too thickly, like the evil crow, when it calls for rain with full voice.[103]

96. When Orpheus played in Hades; cf. Ov. *Met.* 10.42.

97. "iucunditatis" 1562 1570 : "iucundiate" *corregi.*

98. Attributed to Julius Caesar in Quint. 1.8.2.

99. Quintilian (c. 35—c. 95 CE), author of *Institutio Oratoria*, the standard textbook on education after its rediscovery by Poggio in 1416 (first edition 1470).

100. Morato takes *phonascus*, "voice teacher," in Suet. *Aug.* 84.2 to be a proper name.

101. *Iulaeae voces* is the reading in the late and corrupt manuscripts of Lactanius's poem, "The Phoenix," best known perhaps from the version in Old English; the correct reading is *aedoniae voces* ("nightingale voices," line 47; see Migne *PL* 7, 279 for the old text). Though Lactantius was known (undeservedly) as the Christian Cicero, this is a rather postclassical reference for Morato to make. The adjective ἄπῳδος means merely "out of tune." The other words refer to various mistakes in the pronunciation of Greek. Morato is quoting from Quint. 1.5.32. Doricism (*plateasmus* = πλατειασμὸς) is pronouncing *b* as long *a*; iotacism is the reduction of diphthongs to /i/; lambacism is the opposite of rhotacism, pronouncing /l/ for /r/.

102. A series of mistakes and overcorrections: "Maiestas Caesarea gaudet vos advenisse incolumes" becomes "Magestas Caeffsarea caffdet fos fenisse incoglumes."

103. "ut" 1570 : "et" *correxi.* The mistake consists of dividing the syllables, so that they are pronounced /san-ktis/ and /mag-nus/ rather than /sang-ktis/ and /ma-ñus/. Morato recasts Verg. G. 1.388: "Tum cornix plena pluviam vocat inproba voce."

Cicero praised those who softened certain words,[104] which otherwise would be too harsh, with the sweetest pronunciation, articulating them deliberately, so that they would flow out very softly and sweetly, without the crackle and noise that a forest fire makes, and without the clash of vowels; also those who close or end their phrases so that no excessive beat or emphasis is heard.[105] For example, "Erat arx: Rex Xerses exercitum suum ad eam expugnandam ductabat."[106] Under those circumstances, you would not have heard any harshness from the excessive hissing of the repeated letter x. And no "dog letter" r sounded in the verse:

Africa terribili tremit horrida terra tumultu.

Just so they would have strengthened the fluency of other letters to make it as pleasant as possible. Such as:

O Tite tute Tati tibi tanta tyranne tulisti.[107]

The Greeks and Latins used accents, so that with these marks and lines, the voice of the speaker might be modulated, just like a singer or the blower of a flute. Cornelia taught the Gracchi to speak without solecism or hesitation but with seriousness.[108]

Infancy is nothing other than pronunciation without law. Today in Italy we have certain cities where they simply cannot pronounce certain letters, like r for the untrustworthy Ligurians, since they sprang from the ancient Eretrians.[109] Others turn the certain into the uncertain, like the Bolognese, who pronounce z instead of g in "ezerit," "virzinis," "rezina," "zero," "zente," and so on.[110] Nor am I unaware that those otherwise great writers, Erasmus and Rhodiginus, have written most confusedly about pronunciation, so that I

---

104. "Laudavit M. Tullius qui . . . molliebant": a mistake Morata would not have made!

105. Cf. Cic. *Part.* 21, *De Orat.* 3.40–41, 171, 185, and the longer discussion at 213–27. The metaphor may recall Vergil's description of a forest fire in *Georgics* 2.303–10.

106. A Latin tongue twister: "There was a citadel; King Xerxes was leading his army to attack it."

107. *R* was called the "dog letter," since the lip snarls (Pers. 1.109). These are two infamous examples of alliteration from the archaic Roman epic poet Ennius, known from the grammarians. "Africa, that horrible land, trembled with terrible tumult" (Festus 140.21); "O you, Titus Tatius the tyrant, took terrible troubles for yourself" (Donatus, *Schematis* 11, Prisc. GL II.492.25, 591.5 K, et al.).

108. Cornelia, "Mother of the Gracchi": a standard exemplum of feminine virtue. See Quintil. 1.1.6.

109. "ut vani Ligures r" 1562 : "ut vani Ligures" 1570. Cf. Verg. A. 11.715 for the epithet. The Ligurians are usually taken to be indigenous or of unknown origins in most classical authors; cf. Serv. ad loc.

110. I.e. palatalized.

do not hesitate to say that they have done a bad job.[111] For a good doctor not only describes and cures the causes of diseases but also teaches how one can counteract them in the future with an effective remedy.[112] They ought not only to have shown what everyone knows, but also taught how to produce the voice beautifully, pleasantly, sweetly. The voice, I say: she who gives form to the feelings of the soul, she who creates the meanings of human intelligence. If she does not come forth mostly solemnly, as ambassadors do, she brings shame on her masters.[113] I would rather be mute than to speak rustically, inarticulately, unpleasantly. Take care of your health.

Ferarra, 25 June 1540

Letter 2: [Ferrara, c. 1540]
Olympia Morata to Chilian Sinapius:

Although I usually gather many witnesses, dear Chilian, by acting as barker to my own goods,[114] nevertheless, because you are requesting a contribution from me, I will not act in such a way as to give you any reason by my refusal for not writing back.[115] Your letter was especially welcome to me, both because I saw in it your kindness to me, and because you seem to urge me powerfully to the study of a more refined learning, which indeed has brought me wonderful pleasure. I have always borne in mind that immortal God has given nothing better and more useful to the human race than these studies. Especially since our soul, which has been given to us by the best and greatest God from those eternal fires called stars and planets (for I am allowed to philosophize even before you),[116] is cultivated by nothing so much as the knowledge of literature, since in nothing else do we excel the other living creatures.[117] Therefore since letters surpass all human affairs, what women's spindles and needles (as you say) will be able to call me away from the gentle Muses? I have closed my ears against these women's spells just as Ulysses did at the Sirens' rocks. What? Will distaff and spindle be able to persuade

---

111. Erasmus, *De recta latini graecique sermonis pronuntiatione Des. Erasmi . . . dialogus* (Basel, 1528); Lodovicus Caelius Rhodiginus (1469–1525), *Lectionum antiquarum libri* XVI (Venice, 1517). See Sandys 1908, 2:232–34, for the battle over Erasmian pronunciation.

112. Morato is being unfair, since that is precisely what Erasmus did.

113. "Dominis fit ignominiae" 1562 : "Dominus fit ignominiae" 1570.

114. Cf. Cic. *De Orat.* 2.86: the context is that of a bad orator who gathers witnesses to his own stupidity by "crying his own wares." Read *multos*.

115. Cf. Cic. *De Orat.* 2.233.

116. Cf. Cic. *Rep.* 6.15.

117. Cf. Cic. *Fin.* 2.110.

me about a matter in which they have nothing to say? Or do perhaps these cheap gifts exhibit a certain enchantment in themselves? But my soul recoils so much from the ideas of women who wish me, as the saying is, to "lose the mainbrace to grab at the sheet,"[118] that I have decided to consider them to be the ones who are lost.

And so I shall have responded to what was the subject of your letter and at the same time put an end to my writing. About your pupils and how they are progressing in literature, I will only remind you of that cliché: "No good comes from the sheep, if the shepherd's away."[119] So there is no girl who does not urgently desire your arrival, I most of all. Farewell.

Letter 3: Ferrara, [c. 1541][120] (original in Greek)
Olympia Morata wishes good fortune to Chilian Sinapius:

How much each one ought to love his teacher I think has been made clear, as in a paradigm, by the famous Alexander, called the Great, who held his teacher in such esteem that he said he was indebted to him no less than to his father. For from his father he had received the start of life, but from his teacher the start of a good life.[121] I fall not the least bit short of Alexander, at least in love. I am only sorry that I am not able to return the same favor that he did. I am in a state of wonder when I recall your great kindness to me, that it was from you that I first received the letters and rudiments of the Greek language, which in every subject is not just "half of everything"[122] as many have thought, but "the greater part," in the opinion of Aristotle.[123]

But now I am afraid that someone might attack me with that saying of Agesilaos, that one ought to hate not the person who takes revenge when he suffers wrong, but the one who appears ungrateful when he has been done a

---

118. I.e. "ignore what is important for what is trivial." A Latin translation of a Greek proverb attributed to Hyperides: ἀφεὶς τὴν ὑπέραν τὸν πόδα διώκει. This is a remarkably learned, not to say obscure, reference. Morata's most likely source was *Apostolii Bisantii Paroemiae* (Basel, 1538), *Cent.* IV.52 (*Paroemiographi* Leutsch-Schneidewin II.319), the Proverb Collection of Michael Apostolius, which had just been printed, though she might have got it directly from the earlier editions of the *Suda* (A.4582, cf. A.4599, Y.213) or Harpocration (69.9 Bekker).

119. I.e. "When the cat's away, the mice will play." Also from Apostolius *Cent.* XIV.89 (*Paroemiographi* Leutsch-Schneidewin II.625).

120. The mention of the Praise of Scaevola dates the letter before Curio's departure in October 1541.

121. A recasting of Plut. *Alex.* 8.4.

122. For the proverb, see Plato *Leg.* 6.753e.

123. Arist. *NE* 1098b6.

favor.[124] However, no one, I think, will be able to accuse me of ingratitude if I attempt to advance in words to the extent of my ability. For the pupil does not seem ungrateful or senseless when he attempts, as much as he can, to imitate the life, virtue, and learning of his teacher. On the other hand, the teacher who offers virtue does not exact silver or money from the one who desires virtue, but rather offers the greatest profit to make the listener good and wise, whence comes no wealth but what is more honorable: fame and glory. Only by reaching for these things does man seem to differ from the other animals.[125]

There I set at nothing all the other things which the many call "good" and marvel at virtue alone. This alone I think the proper and inalienable possession of my soul. All else is too uncertain and ambiguous to guide my lot, but virtue is eternal and helps us with a divine fate, so that all who have it live well and do all things well. For virtue has its beginning and end not in knowing but in training and practice. And just as at the Olympic games it is not the most beautiful and the most powerful who win the crowns, but the competitors—for only from these come the winners—so too those who act right are the ones who possess what is noble in life,[126] for example, the noble Mucius who underwent such sufferings on behalf of his fatherland.[127] I am sending you an oration about him which I recently composed, for you first struck me as worthy of such a gift. You outshone all other men of our times in learning to such an extent that you are the only one of whom someone in praise might quote that line of Homer: "He alone thinks, but the others flit about like shadows."[128]

So when I think that everyone values highly the statues set up to the gods, even though they are worth nothing, I wish to address these remarks to you more than anyone else, so that my gift, small and dear to me, might appear worth something.

Farewell, and say hello to Cremer, the beautiful-haired puppy of the Muses, for me.[129]

---

124. Xen. *Agesil.* 11.3; and cf. Stob. 2.46 (a set of quotations), Xen. *Mem.* 4.4.24, Cyrop. 1.27 for the general sentiment.
125. οἷς 1562 1570 : ὧν *correxi.*
126. Cf. Arist. NE 1099a3–7. And see letter 46 below.
127. For Morata's "Oration on Mucius Scaevola," see above.
128. Cf. Hom. *Od.* 10.495.
129. Cf. *AP* 11.321. Johannes Cremer (Cramer, Crämer, c. 1522—c. 1555), schoolmaster in Schweinfurt, and a relative of Grunthler's; see letters 38, 48–50, 65. Saffert 1993, 518–19.

Letter 4: [Ferrara, c. 1541][130]
Celio Calcagnini to Olympia Morata:

Why should I pretend that I had wanted a letter from you, when I had not yet experienced its sweetness. Desire for something usually does not affect someone who has not developed a taste for it. But after you sent me your letter, which I think you wrote down while taking dictation from the Muses, I have to confess freely that I am now at last laboring under a desire for your letters. Not, of course, that they offer me material for criticism. Momus himself would find no fault in them, however closely he might pore over them with his keen eye.[131] How much less can I? In fact, I encourage your talent and its unique candor as a friend. So you have done an exceptional injury to yourself or certainly to me when you thought that I was the sort who criticizes another's writings. Or else you feared that you had written things that deserved to be crossed out or erased. If this suspicion has made you apprehensive, you seem to recognize your own talent too little, and not to have remembered that those pleasures of the Muses are clearly your birthright, which you took in with your nurse's milk, which your father, the true former of both your body and soul, obtained for you as if with a magic wand.[132]

Therefore, most distinguished maiden, I rightly congratulate you and urge you to continue making progress eagerly and make it better and stronger every day, so that our age too may know that the kindness of God never ceases and that the study of the arts has not abandoned womankind. Nature is not so worn out (as many advocates of her exhaustion think) that she cannot rouse up Aspasias and Diotimas even in our age, provided that one employs care and diligence.[133] You will provide easy proof of this, if you constantly apply yourself to the study you have begun, and employ the pen instead of the distaff, books instead of linen, and the stylus instead of the needle. And so that you might do this more easily, and that your praise might increase daily, behold, how opportunely Fortune has led you to the princely

---

130. A similar letter to Anna d'Este is dated 22 January 1541 (Calcagnini 1544, 205). In any case, before 17 April 1541, the day of Calcagnini's death: Barroti [1792–93] 1970, 1:287; Horne 1962, 10 n. 4.

131. Momus (Μῶμος), the personification of Blame. For Momus in the writings of Calcagnini, see D'Ascia 1998, 318.

132. Cf. Cic. *Off.* 1.158.

133. Aspasia, mistress of Pericles, and Diotima, the fictional interlocutor in Plato's *Symposium*, are conventional figures for the learned woman. For the pair, cf. Poliziano to Cassandra Fedele (Fedele 1636, 155; trans. King and Rabil 1983, 126, Fedele 2000, 90). Curio alludes to Aspasia in the "Dedication to Elizabeth I," as does Theodor Zwinger in his dedicatory epigram (see below).

court of the best and most helpful Duchess Renée and into the company of the Lady Anna, whose divine talent promises to add no less splendor to the happiness of her parents than it received from them. And you, since you have been well brought up by your parents, and gained chastity, modesty, and the beginnings of good studies at home, strive now also to pursue wisdom, elegance of manners, greatness of soul, and a contempt for all low things. Farewell.

Letter 5: [Ferrara, before 17 April 1541]
Celio Calcagnini to Olympia Morata:

I have read with the greatest pleasure the *Defense of Cicero* that you have just finished, first, because it comes from you, whose studies I have for some time especially encouraged, and second, because in it you have wondrously expressed your father's Venuses and Graces.[134] Then add this as a personal recommendation, that you wanted it to be a gift to me, and one so pleasant and delightful that it has been received into my innermost library, and placed among my most sacred treasures. And so I congratulate you on your most lively genius, full of charm, full of erudition, to which the happy and extraordinarily rich resources of vocabulary and the abundance of arguments, which you gathered with admirable artfulness therein, provided irrefutable testimony, so that you seemed to empty all the jars of oratory. What increases one's admiration is that, whereas it is the particular custom of other young girls to pluck the flowers of spring from here and there and so weave multicolored garlands for themselves, you have gathered not those blossoms which expire within the hour and quickly die together but rather the immortal amaranths from the fertile meadows of the Muses, with which, like the finest mosaics, you adorned and interspersed your entire oration. To them has an almost divine prerogative been given, that they shall never fade, but come to fruition with the benefit of age and reblossom every day.

May the Muses be angry with me if I am not absolutely convinced that Cicero, if the fame of so cultured a defense came to his shades, would personally give you thanks and even feel kind towards those scribes and accusers who thereby gave you the opportunity to burn the midnight oil over this most beautiful oration. Therefore, since you have pursued the adversaries of Cicero with so fierce a pen and defended the party of Cicero with so much zeal, you must see and be conscious of what great expectations you have stirred up about yourself and under what obligations you have placed

---

134. A lost work. See Curio's "Dedication to Isabella of Bresegna."

yourself, so that you are not allowed to change your oath of allegiance nor to abjure your military service, once you have pledged your sacred honor to it. So now you must be constantly and assiduously in Cicero's camp, until you have earned your just military pay and made it to the front ranks. And you ought to do it even more willingly and carefully so that you may more richly deserve the favor of the most excellent Lady Anna, in whose royal bodyguard you have enlisted. You should imitate her zeal for study: even though she encompasses all the highest virtues at her tender age, both Greek and Latin studies and eloquence most of all, yet she considers her delights to be but childish games. Farewell.

Letter 6: [Ferrara, n.d.][135]
To my father Fulvio Pelegrino Morato:

If I had the book of the doctor which you've begged for so often from me, I would have sent it by this messenger. But on all my bookcases I have nothing by a doctor, nothing on medicine, for I do not profess that science. Unless of course you count me as one of those who think they are learned if they've bought many books. Lucian's said enough about them.[136] This is not the place.

I rejoice that everything is turning out the way you want it. I'm so glad. Would that this joy might last forever. How suddenly I have entered into every joy, now that I know I have pleased the greatest and unconquered Duke Ercole II. There is no one of all the princes living today whom I'd rather please. For he is, as everyone says with one accord, "more just than justice."[137] Prudence and Learning hold no one to be his equal. But lest I slight his exceptional praises, for which he deserves to be carried to the skies, with my little talent I can do no better than to say with the poet:

> O may there remain a final portion of a long life
> and breath enough to speak your deeds.
> Thracian Orpheus will not conquer me in songs,
> nor Linus, although the one's mother and the other's father
> were Calliope for Orpheus and handsome Apollo for Linus.[138]

---

135. Not in the editions of Curio. Modena. Biblioteca Estense. Est. lat. 174 (Alpha O 6, 15); see Kristeller 1963—, 1:379a. Text at Caretti 1940, 61–62 (who provides a negative print facing p. 34).

136. Lucian. 31 *Adversus Indoctum,* "The Ignorant Book Collector."

137. *Apost.* VI.13 *(CPG* II.367).

138. Verg. *Ecl.* 4.53–57.

Our Chiron will be here presently.[139] The prince must be cured, on account of whose ill health he set out. When I have more free time I will write to Lady Lavinia, whose memory has never left my heart.[140] How I wish you would greet the most worthy and learned Vincenzo Maggi in my name.[141] Farewell. I ask you to pass on my greetings to my mother, my sisters, and my little brother.[142] A few words at random.[143] Your daughter Olympia.

Letter 7: [Ferrara, n.d.]
Olympia Morata to Johannes Sinapius:

Although I desire the chance for your help in everything, I grieve for your sake, not my own, that you are sick. This is most painful to me. But I hope that you will become better with due care. Just make sure that you don't worry about anything else right now (a mark of your kindness) than getting better as comfortably as possible. So I pray and ask my God for you to be well. For I earnestly place in Him every hope of your being cured. I will judge how much you care for me by how you care for your illness. Be well, dear master Sinapius. Be well, be well, and goodbye. Lady Logeria gives you her greetings.[144]

Letter 8: [Ferrara, n.d.]
Olympia Morata greets Dr. Johannes Sinapius:

If you are well, I have reason to be glad, but I'm sorry if you're not yet well enough. But please, my dear Sinapius, don't imitate those bad doctors who claim to possess the science of medicine in the case of other people's diseases but are not able to cure themselves.[145] Take special care of your illness.

---

139. Presumably referring to Johannes Sinapius, doctor to Renée.
140. Lavinia delle Rovere Orsini, who seems to be absent from court.
141. Vincentius Maius (Vincenzo Maggi). Friend of Boniface Amerbach and Henry Bullinger, diplomat in service to François I. See Church 1932, 74–78, 125–28, 187–71, 289 (who, however, at 74, confuses him with Vincenzo Maggi [V. Madius Brizanus], d. 1564, the literary critic and editor of Aristotle's *Poetics*); Fahy 1961; Tedeschi 2000, 339.
142. Emilio, b. 1542; the letter probably dates soon thereafter.
143. αὐτοσχέδια.
144. Unidentified.
145. Cf. Cic. *Fam.* 4.5.5.

LETTERS 9–11: AFTER MORATA LEFT THE COURT, 1548

Editor's note: Three letters date to 1548, apparently after Morata left the court to attend to her dying father and before her return and the subsequent rupture with Renée. Johannes Sinapius had left first for Augsburg by April 1548. In 9–10 Olympia asks Sinapius to present her poems to Ferdinand I and Fugger, apparently as recommendation for a humanist post with one of these great patrons.

Letter 9: [before April, 1548][146]
Johannes Sinapius to his sweetest Olympia:

I greatly rejoice that you are well and have no further need of my help as a doctor. About the return for you and your father, all is in hand, so that you will return here how and when you wish. When I asked about this matter, our most illustrious duchess told me that your return would be most pleasing to her, however you came, and that if you could not find any more comfortable way of return she would send you the litter in which you had been carried away. So talk with your father about what you think would be more pleasant or comfortable and pleasing for you. Be well. Greet both your parents in my name as courteously as you may.

Letter 10: Ferrara, 12 April [1548][147]
Olympia Morata to Johannes Sinapius:

I wrote you a rather lengthy letter a few days ago, so there is no need for me to sing the same old song all over again. You know what I want you to do for my sake in Germany. I'm not going to commend myself to you any more, nor nag you to present my poems to the king and to Fugger.[148] I know you're taking care of everything. Greet with my words your wife, little girl, and Oswald.[149] Lady Lavinia gives many greetings to them and to you.

---

146. Caretti 1940, 39 with n. 6 dates Morata's disease to c. 1545, after the visit of Pope Paul III to Ferrara, but there is no clear indication. The letter must date before the death of her father.
147. Sinapius has already left for Germany.
148. Ferdinand I (1503–64). Johann Jakob Fugger (1561–75), already a great patron of the arts.
149. Sinapius's nephew, Oswald Lurtzing.

Letter 11: Ferrara, 30 May [1548]
Olympia Morata to the most excellent Dr. Johannes Sinapius:

This long, more than Pythagorean, silence of yours makes me wonder, suspect, and fear. I wonder, since you swore by all that's holy, that you would never let anyone who was going to Italy escape without giving him letters. Not even one for us, and I've sent four letters to you and your wife! I suspect that you've forgotten all your friends, as if your journey led you through the Fields of Forgetfulness. And I fear not a little that something has held you up on the way. If only you had written how you all were doing, which we've wanted to know for so long, to say nothing of how anxiously we long to find out what you have done about our business before the king. We can't do anything about our affairs until we know what response he has made. So if you want us to be free of all care, worry, and fear, I beg you over and over again to undertake and deal with our business before the king and Fugger and to commend us to them, so that we may know that your commendation was no common one, and make sure that we know as soon as possible how things went. You could do nothing nicer for me. I commend my poems most earnestly to you. Be well and love me. Say hello in my name to your wife, nephew, brother, and little girl. The Lady Lavinia sends her greetings too.

LETTERS 12–14: MARRIAGE AND THE FLIGHT TO GERMANY, 1550, AGE 23

Editor's note: Morata married Grunthler sometime in late 1549/early 1550, and he set out soon thereafter to find a position as a doctor in Germany.

Letter 12: [Ferrara, April/May 1550]
Olympia Morata to her husband, Dr. Andreas Grunthler:

I am so sad that you've left me and will be away for so long. Nothing more painful or serious could have happened to me. Even though I can't see you, I'm never bothered by as many worries as when you are away. I'm always afraid that you'll fall or catch cold or break something. And when have I not been afraid of dangers worse than reality? You know the line: "Love is a thing full of worrisome fear."[150] If you want to remove the care I'm always afflicted with when you're gone, please, if you can do so without trouble, let me know what you're doing, how you are. I swear by all that's holy that

---

150. Ov. *Ep.* 1.12.

there is nothing dearer or sweeter to me than you. And I know you feel it too. If I ever change my mind, you'll be the first to know—just like I used to tell you openly that I had taken a dislike to you! I want, my husband, to be with you. Then you'd know clearly how great is my love for you. You can't believe how madly I love you. There's nothing so bitter, so difficult, that I wouldn't do it eagerly, if I could please you. So it's no surprise if this delay worries me, since "true love hates and cannot stand delay."[151] I could put up with anything for your sake more easily than this. So I beg you, I beseech you by your faith, that you do everything in your power to make sure that we're together in your country this summer, just as you promised. If you love me as much as I love you, you'll do it, I know. But I don't want to bother you, so I won't say any more. I just mentioned the matter, not to nag you, but to remind you of your promise, when you've already got enough to do.

About the clothes: there's no point in asking about them. The duchess let me know through one of her women that it's not true that the wife of the noble Camillo[152] said anything to her about visiting her daughter.[153] Nevertheless, she said, because her daughter wished it she had permitted it; her daughter had asked for a single dress for me, which she wasn't going to give her before she returned. She said this, I think, so that I would see that she was not doing it for my sake but for her daughter's, and (but it's better to be quiet, because everyone can see) to please Lysippa,[154] who I think was with her then. As things are, I scarcely believe I'll get them.

Letter 13: Ferrara, 19 May [1550]
Olympia Morata to the most learned Johannes Sinapius:

I ask you over and over again not to keep the man who is dearer to me than life there with you for more than a month, and send him back to his wife as fast as possible so that I don't waste away in misery from the pain. There was the boy in Terence who was barely able to be without *her* for two whole days.[155] How wretched do you think I feel, when I have to be without him for

---

151. Sen. *Herc. Fur.* 588.
152. The mother-in-law of Lavinia della Rovere.
153. Even the splendid Latin pronominal system cannot make it absolutely clear in indirect discourse who all these people are; but the "daughter" is apparently Lavinia della Rovere.
154. Probably a private nickname.
155. Ter. *Eun.* 181–87.

two months? "Those who desire grow older day by day."[156] So if you want to free me from many cares, send him back to me as fast as possible. And if he has need of your help, render it without delay. Quick favors are sweetest.[157]

Farewell. Give my greetings to your brother Chilian.

Letter 14: Ferrara, 1 June [1550]
Olympia Morata to Johannes Sinapius:

I beg you, most learned Sinapius, to pass this letter on as soon as possible to my husband Andreas Grunthler, so that he can know how I am doing. I have nothing at the moment to write you. I commend our business to you. Send my husband back to me as soon as possible. Farewell. Say hello to your wife, and little girl, signor Chilian, and Oswald in my name. Lady Lavinia gives many greetings.

DIALOGUE BETWEEN LAVINIA DELLA ROVERE AND OLYMPIA MORATA [1550, AGE 23]

Editor's note: Two dialogues are all that are left of Morata's mature prose works. The first was written in the period after Morata's marriage in the early summer of 1550 when her husband was away seeking a position in Germany. It gives us our clearest insight into Morata's intellectual development: from strictly classical reading and a worldview influenced by Lucretius and Epicureanism (possibly through her teacher Calcagnini) to an emphasis on scriptural studies. This change was precipitated in part by the material and spiritual crises of the death of her father and her own loss of favor at court.

Lavinia della Rovere and Olympia Morata talk together.

Lav. You are always poring over books, Olympia. Do you never take a break? The mind has got to relax occasionally, and then you can go back to your studies. Once your mind has collected and refreshed itself, it understands more quickly what's being taught.

---

156. Theoc. 12.2.
157. Rendered in Greek.

Olymp. That's true, Lavinia, but I agree with the man who said that every moment you don't spend in study is lost,[158] and I never waste the "costliest expense, that of time."[159] In fact, I feel like I'm sinning if I don't spend the time God has given me (for God has made leisure for us) in these literary studies, especially since I lack all other comforts which I could use to solace the desire I have because my husband is away.

Lav. You could do that more easily than Laertes did by tilling the fields.[160] For divine studies, I say, are fields: the healthiest and richest fields. From them the friends of God harvest ripe, rich, and immortal fruit. The rest of human literature is a pleasure to those for whom the eyes of the soul do not yet have the power to see the truth, so that they can view the heavens and contemplate heavenly things. And so they pluck what falls so quickly from these little flowers.

Olymp. If only I hadn't wasted time in this great error and in ignorance of what's really important! I used to think that I was most learned because I read the writers and scholars of all the liberal arts and was wallowing in their works like mud. But even as I was exalted to the skies by everyone's praise, I realized that I lacked all learning and was ignorant. I had fallen, you see, into the error of thinking that everything happened by chance and of believing "that there was no God who cared for mortal things," so great was the darkness that had overwhelmed my soul.[161] But God began to dispel it: a little light of that unique and divine wisdom began to rise for me, and I proved in my own person that all human affairs are ruled by his wisdom. For when I was deserted and abject, as you know, He took such care of me that I found Him to be a father and protector of orphans in a real sense. And believe me, no parents ever showed their children the indulgence that God showed to me. At last I realized how stupid I was.

Lav. But everyone said that you were endowed with remarkable piety and virtue.

Olymp. That was the story and what you heard. But if people would examine what is said about princes and their friends, they would not have such a great opinion about me. Flatterers, because they want to get close to princes, don't just flatter the princes but their friends too, or at least the ones

---

158. Pliny the Elder as described by Pliny the Younger, *Ep.* 3.5.16.
159. Plutarch, *Anthony* 28.
160. *Od.* 1.189, 16.137–41, 24.209ff.
161. Morata accuses herself of following the Epicureanism of Lucretius. Ver. *Ecl.* 8.35.

they think are especially close. You can give testimony about how far away I was from Christianity.

Lav. I remember. But even if everything they said wasn't true, I don't believe that this rumor about you was false: that you were learned in Greek and Latin.

Olymp. Rumor usually mixes lies with truth, in order to give some credence to its testimony. To be frank, I never shunned work or skipped my learned studies, even in the midst of other important obligations, but anyone who reads my writings could easily realize that I am not outstanding in erudition or learning.

Lav. I heard from your teachers how much work and labor you put into your studies, and in my opinion you acted wisely if you spent as much time on pursuing your studies as others waste on fixing their hair, getting dressed, or on other pleasures and the relaxation of mind and body.[162] But what I especially admire is that when you were a girl you never deviated from your resolve, despite the urgings of silly women and the attacks of men that you were going to waste all your other gifts and that you'd never find a man who would prefer you to be educated than to be rich.

Olymp. For my part, when I considered the matter over and over again as diligently as possible, I could find no other reason for me to work at these studies other than "it lay at the feet of God."[163] He gave me the mind and talent to be so on fire with love for learning that no one could keep me from it. For the Omnipotent One is the best of orators, Who does not use rhetoric to drive our minds towards what He wants and lead them away from what He wants. Everything is done according to His plan and purpose, and He does nothing rashly or thoughtlessly. So all these things perhaps will be for His glory and my betterment.

Lav. It's just as you say, Olympia: everything happens according to His plan and purpose. You couldn't find a better reason than this and I don't need to seek another. But let me urge you, in the midst of human life, to pursue divine studies. If you have gained some pleasure from these studies, in which there is no solid usefulness or delight except for children, then they render you imbued with a joy in which no illness is ever mixed: pleasure is appropriate to these studies. So if you will heed my advice you'll add these studies as maids or attendants to divine studies. "For we know that all things

---

162. A reminiscence of Cic. *Pro Archia* 13.
163. This is Morata's own reworking of a Homeric phrase: "It lies on the lap of the gods" (*Il.* 17.514, etc.)

work together for good for those who love God" [Rom. 8:28] and we pray God that it may be so for us.[164]

164. This is the end of the text. A new section, a paean to Wisdom, begins without break in all the editions. Bonnet (1856, 85–86) noted its oddness: "The dialogue between the two friends breaks off here, or rather it is transformed and ends in a sort of religious meditation mingling, as in a holy song, the enthusiasm of faith and the ardors of adoration and prayer." The text lurches abruptly into a style utterly unlike anything Morata wrote: "Et ego homo sum ex argilla quidem et luto fictus" (cf. Cic. *Pis.* 59) . . . [And I am a man, made of clay and mud]. The speaker is unquestionably male: "Eram vero ingeniosus puer bona indole praeditus . . ."

The solution to this puzzle is itself odd. This "Hymn to Wisdom" is almost certainly the "De Trinitate et sapientia divina sermo per ispum authorem in Cathedrali ecclesia Agriensi publice habitus" found in the Elenchus to Celio Calcagnini's (*Opera*, 1544), but curiously missing from the pages (listed as 492–94) where it is supposed to be (as is another brief work, "Somatia"). The effusion is very much in Calcagnini's style, who specialized in a brand of "impromptu sermon" (so his "In sacramentum Eucharistiae sermo tulmultuarius," delivered in the same church, which immediately follows the missing work: Calcagnini 1544, 494–96). The sermon shows many autobiographical references to his study of astronomy, botany, and so on. How it came to disappear from Calcagnini's works and reappear in Morata's is unknown, but I suspect that this too may have been found among Johannes Sinapius's papers (see the introduction in the present text, n. 84).

LETTERS: GERMANY

SCHWAZ-KAUFBEUREN-AUGSBURG [1550, AGE 23]

Editor's note: Grunthler returned to Italy and took Morata and her brother Emilio with him to his hometown of Schweinfurt. Letters 15–20 tell her friends of her safe arrival in Germany on 12 June 1550 (letter 16).

Letter 15: [Schwaz, soon after 12 June 1550][165]
Olympia Morata greets Gregorio Giraldi:

We arrived safe in Germany and were generously taken in by Georg Hörmann, a counselor to the king, at whose house we've been staying for several days.[166] He is sick and my husband is taking care of him. I am completely at liberty here. I spend the whole day taking pleasure with the Muses and no other business takes me away from them. Very often I devote myself to divine studies, deriving more profit and pleasure from the latter than the former. They think well of my husband. Our affairs are in good shape and it seems they'll get better before long. I wanted you to know these things, since I know you miss us and rejoice when we rejoice.

---

165. The Hörmann Chronicle reports that the Grunthlers were guests of Georg Hörmann for the month of June, 1550. Kössling and Weiss-Stählin 1990, 197.

166. Georg (Jörg) Hörmann von und zu Guttenberg (1491–1552), humanist, financier, administrator for the banking house of the Fuggers in Schwaz; see Flood and Shaw 1997, 109 n. 168 and literature there cited. See also document 2 in the present text. The Hörmann family chronicle (Hörmann 1770, 26, cited from Kössling and Weiss-Stahlin 1990, 197) notes their arrival in June 1550.

Letter 16: Kaufbeuren near Augsburg, 25 August 15[50]
Olympia Morata to Johannes Sinapius:

We got to Germany on 12 June and were hoping to go on to you as soon as possible. However, that most noble man, Georg Hörmann, has detained us longer than we thought and is planning to keep us here.[167] That's the reason I haven't sent any letters to you so far, and also because you said you were going to go with your lord to Augsburg.[168] After we have lost all hope of seeing you, I wanted to let you know about our arrival so that you could rejoice that we had arrived safely. Goodbye.

Letter 17: [Kaufbeuren near Augsburg, August/September 1550]
Olympia Morata to Lavinia della Rovere:

I've received such pleasure from your letters because, as I had hoped, I now know what you're doing and where you are. I had been worried that you would leave for Rome without letting me know, so that I would have no idea where to send my letters. And now that you've freed me from that worry, I thank you so much for promising me your support and help in aiding Fanino.[169] To tell the truth, that was as pleasing as anything could be. Your journey seems to offer me some hope, since I know how powerful your influence is at Rome. Besides, it occurs to me that even though you've left there it may offer him some aid. For no doubt the duke will promise all his support to you, now that you're leaving. So you'll be able to ask him, if he wants to do anything for your sake, to pardon a man who is without fault. This supplication ought to serve even for a very serious sin. In this case, you'll decide with your usual foresight what's best to do, and "not ignorant of evil, you will learn to help the unfortunate,"[170] especially those who are unfortunate and ruined not for any fault of their own but for the sake of Christ. You know well that whatever service and kindness you do to them, Christ will reckon as having been done for Him.[171] I won't write any more

---

167. The Hörmann family chronicle (Hörmann 1770, 49, cited from Kössling and Weiss-Stahlin 1990, 198), relates that Georg Hörmann traveled from Schwaz to Kaufbeuren on 8 July 1550. Curio's editions mistakenly printed the date as 1548.
168. Melchior Zobel of Guttenberg, bishop of Würzberg (1505–58), who attended the Council of Augsburg in 1548 and 1550. Sinapius served as his personal physician.
169. Fanino Fanini, Protestant preacher currently under sentence of death in Ferrara. See the introduction.
170. Verg. *Aen.* 1.630.
171. Matt. 25:40.

about this matter, because I know that his safety is as great a care to you as it is to me. I'm only encouraging you, lest you bow down the greatness of your soul under the most evil-minded appeals of men in matters which pertain to the pure religion of Christ.

I have no news to write you about what's been happening with me. We're here at the house of Georg Hörmann, but in a different town, about a day's journey from Augsburg. Here I'll try to lessen my grief over the death of my cousin and your desire for letters from me.[172] Now I have complete leisure to get back to divine studies as often as possible, which I think you ought to do, and I take more pleasure in them day by day. I'm glad you're going to Rome. I think it will be better for you there than where you are now and I'm sure the presence of your friends will lighten the cares which now are your cross—especially if you will bring that wonderful woman Cherubina with you, whom I greatly recommend.[173] I wish to commend to you highly my mother, sisters, and all my relatives. I won't let anyone who's going to Rome get past me without giving him a letter for you. I'm sure you'll do the same. My husband, to whom I'm always talking about you and who thinks a lot of you, thanks you for having written a P.S. to him in your letters. He gives you his greetings. Goodbye.

Letter 18: [Kaufbeuren, August/September 1550]
Olympia Morata to the most noble Magdalena Orsini:[174]

Although I am deeply affected with pain by the death of my cousin, when the news was brought to me of your having set out, I couldn't do anything other than write to you there. Not that there's anything which would be interesting for you to know or for me to write, but just so you'll know for certain that I'm thinking of you with the greatest love. Farewell, and greet your parents with my words. Farewell.

Letter 19: Augsburg, 7 October [1550][175]
Olympia Fulvia Morata Grunthler to Caelius Secundus Curio:

After being tossed about by many huge waves, I have arrived in Germany, as though in a harbor. My first priority, once I learned from that excellent

---

172. Unidentified; *consobrinus* makes him the child of a sister of Morata's mother.
173. Cherubina Orsini; see letter 46.
174. Sister to Paolo and sister-in-law to Lavinia della Rovere.
175. The text here follows that of Curio 1553, 13–16.

fellow, George Thrax, at Padua,[176] that you were there,[177] was to write to you, because you've been so concerned about us, and to let you, like a dearest relative, know what's been happening to us. Since you were the closest friend to my father while he was alive, I think I ought to continue that friendship: "For it is right for the children to receive a share of their father's friendships as well as his property."[178]

You should know that my father, after having undergone many labors, with remarkable faith in God, left the tumult and confusion of this world two years ago. After his death (which you will agree is better called his "lot," following the Greeks, than a "calamity," following the Romans), I was immediately abandoned by my lady and received only in the most humiliating manner.[179] This happened not just to me but to my sisters as well. This is the reward we got from our princes; for our labors we naturally got hatred. You can guess how grieved I was. There was no one to look after us and at the same time we were under siege by so many things that it seemed we could never emerge. But that best Father of orphans did not leave me in those evils for more than two years. He stirred up love for me in a certain German, a man outstanding in philosophy and medicine, named Andreas Grunthler. Not even the hatred of a prince or my wretched state could keep him from marrying me. He took me to Germany, where we stayed for a while with Georg Hörmann, a royal counselor, whom my husband cured of disease. We are soon to leave for my husband's city, which is located in the eastern part of Franconia and spend some time there with friends and relations. How great is my husband's honesty, how learned in Greek and Latin literature, I prefer you to learn from others rather than from my letters. But I do want you to know that even if I were in the greatest favor with my lady, if she granted me riches, I could not be placed in a better state than the one in which God has placed me, poor and despoiled as I am. He is educated, born in no low status, and his father has left him a small inheritance. So great is his love for me that nothing can be higher. I have faith that God will give the same help to my sisters. I left them with my mother at Ferrara. I have three sisters and all of marriageable age. I took my eight-year-old brother with me, whom I'm trying (as much as I can) to teach Latin and Greek.

I want to write all this to you, not to distress you with our troubles, but so that you can rejoice with us. God is our aid in our adversities. In fact, I

176. Unidentified.
177. Basel.
178. Isoc. 1.1 (in Greek).
179. Renée.

rejoice that all these things happened to me, for if I had remained any longer in that court, it would have been all over for me and my salvation. For while I was there, I was never able to undertake anything high or divine—not even to read the books of either the Old or New Testament. But after the duchess was estranged from our family by the hatred and slanders of certain evil people, these brief, fleeting, and transitory things no longer affected me with so great a longing. Instead, God has increased my desire to live in that heavenly home, in which it is more pleasant to live for just one day than to spend a thousand years in the courts of princes. And so I have returned to divine studies, in testimony of which there are some poems which I made last year.[180] I'm adding them below and sending them to you, so that you can see that God has given me, after I was overwhelmed by misfortunes, the leisure to give time to literature. He has also given me as a bride to a man who greatly enjoys my studies. And that's how things are with us. Please write me a friendly letter, when you have a spare moment, about how you and your wife are doing. Goodbye.

Letter 20: Würzburg, [October 1550]
Olympia Morata to Georg Hörmann, Royal Counselor:

I think that by now you have received the letter we gave to the rider for you a few days ago.[181] In it we told you about our health and our journey. We are still at Würzburg at Sinapius's house. We won't leave until our baggage, which is still at Bamberg, arrives. If you're wondering what I'm doing, I've given myself up to literature and often spend the whole day reading. Better relief I could not find. My husband is similarly engaged in his studies.

However, my little brother,[182] in order that we might know by experience that God has given his angels charge over his children, lest when they fall, they should dash against a stone,[183] fell from a window in a high place to the ground right on top of sharp stones a few days ago. But he took no more harm than if he had fallen on soft earth. He broke nothing and did himself no harm. He is alive and well to the considerable astonishment of us all. It is

---

180. These include her setting of Ps. 46; see letter 26. Curio added the text of Ps. 46 to his edition of his letters in 1553, 16–18, with a Latin translation by Sixtus Betuleius.

181. Lost.

182. Emilio (1542–55). See below, letter 27. Flood and Shaw (1997, 131) think this may have occurred at the Marienberg fortress in Würzburg.

183. Matt. 4:6, Luke 4:10–11, quoting Ps. 91:11–12; a paraphrase retaining the vocabulary of the Vulgate.

unbelievable and beyond nature that no harm came to him from so serious a fall. Thus God, Who is able to raise the dead from below, is accustomed to keep and protect His people unharmed, to Whom I commend and entrust us all.[184] Goodbye.

Editor's note: Lavinia della Rovere writes to Morata. She has received earlier letters saying that Grunthler had left for Germany but not Morata's letters announcing her own safe arrival.

Letter 21: Parma, 2 November [1550][185]
Lavinia della Rovere Orsini to Olympia Morata:

I received your letter and understand from it that your husband arrived there safely. O my Olympia, I'm so happy for you.

You write that you need my help, for me to ask my father-in-law and mother-in-law[186] to write to the duke and ask him to be willing to take care of those things which he promised he would do.[187] I want you to know there is nothing I wouldn't do for you, and our friendship wouldn't let it be otherwise. And so the second I got your letter, I asked him urgently to do what you asked. He said he would do so most willingly but that he did not have time for it at the moment due to all the business matters which did not even allow him a chance to breathe. Now that it's a little more convenient for him, I urged him to write to the duke and commend your affairs to him most diligently and also to Ferdinand, with whom I know his letters will carry more weight than mine.[188] So I hope (with God's help) that everything will go just as your heart desires. As for me, you should know that my situation is growing more desperate daily.

All that's left is to beg you to come to me with your husband and stay here until you have to leave, which will be pleasing to all and most pleasing to me.[189] But so that this inelegant letter doesn't bore you, I'll make an end of

---

184. Cf. Heb. 11:19 and 13:20. There is a glance here to the story of Eutychus, who fell from a window and was restored to life by Paul: Acts 20:9–12.

185. Paolo Orsini had been made governor of Parma in 1547 by Pope Paul III after the assassination of his son Pier Luigi.

186. Camillo Orsini (1491–1559).

187. The matter is uncertain. Morata may have been seeking permission and aid to go to Germany to join her husband. It may be a veiled reference to Fanini (see the introduction and letter 18 below).

188. King Ferdinand I.

189. Lavinia apparently had not yet received news that Olympia had left Italy and joined Grunthler in Germany.

writing. I would have written it in the mother tongue, except I know that you would rather read Latin. Nor am I afraid that you'll laugh at any infelicities, since you know I pay no attention to style.

Be well and greet your most learned husband in my name.

Editor's note: Morata stayed in Würzburg with Sinapius, while Grunthler went ahead to Schweinfurt.

Letter 22: *Würzburg, 22 November 1550*
Olympia Morata to Dr. Andreas Grunthler:

I hope you're well. First I want to know that you're all right, what you're doing, what's happening there, and how things are. I'm very anxious about what you think about your return or about sending for us. So, please, write to me diligently about everything: what's really happening. Don't invent anything false just to comfort me. If, God forbid, there's any danger, I desire so much to share it with you. If you do anything else, I'll think you've done me a great injury. But if there's no danger (may God make it so), take care of the business matters, if there's time, and write so that our baggage isn't sent on ahead if the road isn't safe, which is likely.

Above all, my husband, in the midst of these evils, I want you to know that we can have no firmer protection than God. I beg you to pray to Him with other pious men. There is nothing that the prayers of pious men cannot accomplish.[190] Our example is Elijah, who was "a man of like passion to ourselves," as James said, "and prayed fervently that it not rain, and it did not rain upon the earth for three years and six months."[191] So commend yourselves to God and hand yourselves over to Him completely. Immediately He will be with you. But I, who console others, am in need of consolation myself. I'm afflicted with a great deal of pain and I find no other relief for this illness, except when I pray for help from God. So I advise and urge you all to do the same. Write, I beg you, when I am going to see you, and be careful not to start the journey until you've checked things out. Goodbye.

Letter 23: *[Würzburg, December 1550?]*
Olympia Morata to Dr. Andreas Grunthler:

I got your letter and was so happy that you're planning to take me there. I was going to write you today in any case that you should. It's clear that the

---

190. Cf. James 5:16.
191. James 5:17, quoted in Greek.

prince will arrive, in order to wage war with men who have no fear, since they estimate that they are stronger than their enemies.[192] And the former seem to prefer waging war to giving a little money in order to pacify their enemies. But I, my husband, ask you over and over again not to leave me behind. Although others may feel secure, I am afraid, because I am certain that God is simply not on their side. So be sure to come to us by wagon as soon as possible, so that I can return. I believe Boussiron[193] is getting ready to go back, although she doesn't want to leave here until she's heard that they have gotten closer. "It's stupid to allow what you can avoid."[194] I'll expect you the day after tomorrow if the road is safe. I prefer to be in great poverty but in the church of God than to live life here and be rich in everything, especially when there's such danger. Please, I pray, don't forget us, and I beg you to take me from here. Let us give thanks to God, at whose command this has turned out all right for us. Say hello to everyone. Our hosts send you their warmest greetings. Goodbye.

LETTERS 24–28: SCHWEINFURT, 1550–51, AGE 24–25

Letter 24: [Schweinfurt, c. December 1550]
Olympia Morata to Thomas Lucius:[195]

Although I am quite sorry to bore you with my letters, nevertheless, when your piety came to my mind, I can only ask you for those things which faith and piety require. You know how much I owe my mother, both because she is my mother and has done all a mother's duty to me, and because she is a pious woman and bereft of her husband. You are not ignorant with what zeal God commended the widows to us.[196] So led by piety, I am sending some gold coins to her. I ask you to place the letters in her hands, so that the money will not be lost. You will do the favor not for her but for Christ.[197]

---

192. Albert (Albrecht) II Alcibiades (1522–57), margrave of Brandenburg-Kulmbach. See the introduction.
193. Françoise de Boussiron de Grand-Ry, lady-in-waiting to Renée, and wife of Johann Sinapius. See the introduction; Flood and Shaw 1997, 92–95.
194. Ter. *Eun.* 761.
195. Unidentified. In Italy, since he is to oversee the transfer of money to Olympia's mother. Perhaps a banker. Adorni-Braccesi (1994, 204, 244) identifies him as "Tommaso lucchese," but *Lucius* is not the usual form of the adjective.
196. E.g. 1 Tim. 5:3–16, James 1:27.
197. Cf. Matt. 25:34–40.

As for what you want to know from my husband about the state of things in Germany, since he does not have time to write, I will answer you in his place. Nothing in Germany is definite so far. The Emperor is at Augsburg and so are nearly all the other German leaders. But what they are planning to do there no one knows. He in any case said that he wishes the Council to assemble at Trent,[198] and in the meanwhile all the laws of religion of the Interim are to stay in effect, which no one had been forced to obey previously.[199] But as before, all are to live according to their own conscience.

You write that you have heard nothing from Sinapius for a long time. We haven't yet had a chance to see him because he has followed his bishop to Augsburg.[200] But we know from his letters that he's at Würzburg and doing well. That's all I had to write. Goodbye.

Letter 25: [Schweinfurt, summer 1551]
Olympia Morata greets Lavinia della Rovere:

I was greatly upset that I got your letter at a time when I could not respond. You know how difficult it is in winter to find someone you can give a letter to. And in addition to that evil, we're now separated by a greater distance of space than we were last summer. For when you went to Rome, we went to Schweinfurt, my husband's town. The Senate called my husband to his hometown to make use of his help on behalf of the Spaniards whom the Emperor had sent there to pass the winter. For these reasons I was unable to answer your lovely letter at once, as I wanted. Your news affected me partly with sadness, partly with joy. I couldn't help but be moved by the death of Fanini, a man endowed with great piety.[201] Later, however, his great faithfulness lightened my sadness. But I'm happy that you've brought my sister with you and I'm all the more overjoyed because this happened unforeseen and unhoped for. Truly, I can't say whether I've received more sorrow from the injuries with which my sisters were afflicted, or pleasure at the protection of God, Who, when we were in the greatest need of counsel, was there for us and saved us from suffering. I felt Him doing this for us, not only in Italy but often in Germany too. For you know the Devil lays traps for us everywhere,

---

198. The Council of Trent had moved to Bologna three years previously in 1547 and then been suspended.

199. The Augsburg Interim of 1548, an imperial decree that attempted to find a common ground between Protestants and Catholics. See *CMH* 2:183–84.

200. See letter 17 above.

201. See letter 27 below. Fanini was executed on 22 August 1550.

and unless God snatches us out of them we will not live for even one day. So I give Him immortal thanks that He watches over us, and I love you, because in this He has been willing to make use of your aid. I think I owe you all the more because you did me this favor voluntarily, even before you were asked. When a favor is done quickly, the favor is even more welcome.[202] Goodbye.

Letter 26: Basel, 5 September [1551][203]
C. S. Curio to Olympia Fulvia Morata:

When I received your letter written at Augsburg on 7 October last year, you had already set out for your husband's hometown.[204] I found this out when I tried to write back to you, but you were not to be found. No one was able to tell me the name of your town or village, if it weren't for the fact that at the last fair, when Johannes Sinapius asked to be remembered to me through Isingrin, the Basel printer, he mentioned you in the same letter.[205] From it I gathered that he knew for sure where you were living. So when Isingrin set out again for the fair, I decided to write to you and sent letters to Sinapius, who would be sure to send them on to you, which I don't doubt he will readily do for my sake as well as yours.

First, therefore, I give immortal thanks to you, Olympia, the glory and unique ornament of women, for the fact that after so many years and with so many lands lying between us, you have not forgotten me, and want to inherit the friendship your father had. In this you declare how much you value your father's opinion in the choice of friends and how much you value friends yourself and especially me. And so I want to persuade you of this, that I never valued anyone more than your father while he was alive, whose most honest arts and, what is more than all the rest, whose piety you imitate. And don't think that there is anyone living, with the sole exception of my wife and daughters, whom I value more than you, whom I love and cherish more than you alone. And so I congratulate you on your most outstanding husband just as I would if it had happened to one of my own daughters.

---

202. A common proverb. Cf. Publilius Syrus, *Sententiae*, letter I.6: "Inopi beneficium bis dat, qui dat celeriter."
203. Text also at Curio 1553, 20–22. See Note on Text.
204. Letter 19.
205. Michel Isingrin (1500–57). Flood and Shaw (1997, 202 n. 95) suggest that these were the book fairs of spring and fall 1551 at Leipzig (rather than Frankfurt, so Kössling and Weiss-Stahlin 1990, 200).

I give thanks to God most high that He has taken pity on you and rescued the flower of your youth and your virgin modesty from the fleshpots (that is, the court) and freed you for golden liberty.[206]

I greatly admire the hymn or ode composed in Greek, for in it you have recast David's Psalm 45.[207] If only you would do more of these, then we need not envy the Greeks their Pindar. So continue, my Olympia, in the way your Muse has long been calling you. She will place the sacred crown of laurel on your divine head.[208] For you have drawn your poetic inspiration from a more sacred fountain than did Pindar or Sappho. If you have given birth to anything new, which I do not doubt, whether from your head or from your most chaste belly, be sure to let me know, so that I may write new congratulations to you and enjoy that happiness with you. I also wish that you would write me more often. If you do that, you couldn't do anything that would make me happier. For I rejoice so much in the elegance, holiness, and sweetness of your letters. So that you'll know how enthusiastic I am about you, I'm sending you a copy of a letter I wrote a little after you left Augsburg to Sixtus Betuleius, a most learned man and a dear friend of mine.[209]

Be well, my dearest Olympia, together with your most excellent and learned husband, with whom may God cherish and protect you in quiet peace. If it should happen that you return to Italy, I ask that you make the trip through here, so that face to face we might be able to embrace and renew our old friendship with the joining of hands. My wife with all our children greet you. Again, be well, most happy and most holy couple.

Letter 27: Schweinfurt, 1 October [1551]
Olympia Morata Grunthler to Caelius Secundus Curio:

Your letter was most welcome to me, from which I understood that the long separation in time and space had taken away nothing from your kindness toward me. And that's just how the friendships of Christians ought to be. So I give thanks to my God, Who has thought me worthy of the honor of being loved by His people. For the impious, no matter how powerful, rich, noble, or even learned they be, I do not esteem, whether they hate me or whether they seem to love me. So your judgment about my poems was most pleasing to me. For since I value you most highly, if I had realized that it was

---

206. *sive ollis, sive aulis:* a pun with reference to the "fleshpots of Egypt": Exod. 16:3.
207. 46 in the common numeration (45 in the Septuagint and Vulgate).
208. *pone<t>:* poets should not crown themselves.
209. See document 2 above.

otherwise, you would have deterred me from this pursuit of writing. But now that it seems that is has not been disapproved of by pious men, and most of all not by you, I shall work at it as much as is in my power.

You ask that if ever we return to Italy we make the trip there to you. I cannot swear that we will never go there, but we are not now planning to return to Italy. It has not escaped your notice how dangerous it is to profess oneself a Christian there where the Antichrist has so much power, who even now I hear is raging against the saints and beginning to foam at the mouth so much that "you'd say the other one was just a game and joke compared to what this one's madness is doing."[210] He has sent his spies[211] to all the cities of Italy, and just like the last one he cannot be moved by any prayers. Last year (I don't know if you heard), he ordered a certain Fanini, a pious man of the most constant faith, after he had been in prison for two years (for he was never willing to abandon the truth not from fear of death, not from love of his wife and children), to be strangled and his body cremated. Not content with this, he then ordered his bones to be cast into the Po.[212] So although I am held by the deepest desire for my family, I would rather go to the ends of the earth than return to where that man has such power to be cruel. But if we have to leave here, there is nowhere else I'd rather go than to you. For I'd seem to be among my family, if it should happen that I spend my life with you. So if it's possible for my husband to follow his profession, either by curing the sick or by giving lectures, he would willingly accept a post for my sake. If this could happen, nothing would be more wonderful as far as I'm concerned. I'd be nearer Italy, and so I could send and receive letters more often from my mother and sisters, who are always before my eyes night and day. It's extremely difficult here, but I did get one this month after a long interval. And because I know you wish us all the best, it matters to me that I let you know all about them. My sisters are in service, one to Elena Rangoni Bentivoglio,[213] the other to her daughter, who was married in Milan, and who, when I wrote you, I thought had gone to Ferrara. But instead, when she was being forced to go on the road and everything was ready, a certain young man, his father's only son and quite wealthy, hearing this, did not allow her

---

210. Cf. Ter. *Eun.* 301. Pope Paul III (13 Oct. 1534–10 Nov. 1549) had recently been succeeded by Julius III (8 Feb. 1550–23 Mar. 1555).

211. *Corycaeos*; lit., inhabitant of Mt. Corycus in Cicilia, a lookout point for pirates, and so a byword for informers and spies; see Cic. *Att.* 10.18.1 (210 SB).

212. 22 August 1550; see Kössling and Weiss-Stählin 1990, 14; Flood and Shaw 1997, 117.

213. Relative of Lavinia della Rovere's, now at Modena: her huband's sister, Guilia Orsini, was married to Count Baldasarre Rangoni.

to leave, but asking no dowry, married her.[214] In May of this year she visited her mother at Ferrara with her husband and stayed for a number of days. Lavinia della Rovere, the daughter-in-law of Camillo Orsini, took my third sister with her to Rome.[215] I know no woman in Italy more learned than she and what is most important of all, she is pious. God deals so wonderfully with his saints. For instance, when we were staying with Sinapius at Würzburg, He was our aid in the greatest danger. My little brother, whom I have with me, fell out of an extremely high window onto stone. We thought he would surely die or, if he lived, it seemed "an impossibility"[216] to Sinapius and my husband that he would not suffer from epilepsy.

I would like to ask one thing of you: if you have the book you wrote, *On the Education of Children*, which I read at Sinapius's house, please send it to me when it's convenient. I want my sister, who is at Milan, to read it diligently. Also if you have the dialogue you wrote in Latin, *Pasquillus Ecstaticus*, we and a number of other good men who are here would like to read it.[217]

You now have a sufficiently wordy letter. But I'm not afraid to fill you full of writing, especially now that I understand that you do not despise my zeal in that genre. But I'll add just one more thing and stop. I think I have to give the answer to one question you asked me, whether I had given birth to anything. The children I bore on the very day and hour I received your letter, I am sending to you: these poems appended here.[218] There is also a Latin dialogue that I have just composed. When I've recopied it I'll send it to you. I have borne no other children, and so far I have no expectation of bearing any. But I ask you, most learned Caelius, to write to me diligently how your wife is doing, how many children you have there, what they are learning. All your doings are of the greatest concern to me. When you send me letters, you send them to our Sinapius at Würzburg. This town is only a day's journey away from Würzburg. Goodbye. My husband sends his greetings to you all.

Schweinfurt, 1 October, at night, in haste.

---

214. Another victim apparently of the purge in Renée's court.

215. Vittoria; see letter 45.

216. Quoted in Greek.

217. Curio's books are *De pueris sancte educandi* (Basel, 1549), with numerous titles and editions. For his best-selling satire *Pasquillus* (Basel: Oporinus, 1544), see the introduction.

218. Curio's edition of his letters (1553, 26) prints the text of poem 4, "Wedding Prayer," immediately after the text of this letter.

Letter 28: Schweinfurt [winter 1551/52]
Olympia Morata to Lavinia della Rovere Orsini:

I sent you a rather long letter this summer, to which I added the dialogue of a certain pious and learned man.[219] I don't know whether you got it. Letters are very rarely delivered in these turbulent times, in which everything seems to rage with war. We are parted by the greatest distance of space, as I wrote you before. So my dear Lavinia, if you get my letters less often (and I've only received one from you after we got here), please don't think it's happening because of my neglect or forgetfulness of you. If I had anyone to give them to, I wouldn't let anyone get past. I'd write to my mother also every day if I could. I always worry about her. I am so far from forgetting you that my anxiety about you increases every day. Indeed, if Germany did not give me the comfort of being allowed to have books of theology that we could not have there, I would not be able to bear my longing for my friends, especially you, who always "remain in the depths of my being"[220] and whom I always mention in my prayers. Your health is a great concern to me, and I'm afraid you're worrying night and day, as you usually do, and making yourself ill with care. So even though I am occupied with a lot of things to do, I put everything aside, because I wanted to write this dialogue for you so that at least while you're reading it you can take your mind off your troubles.[221] I suspect, with the war in France, that your husband has left you and that you are in pain (that's the way you are). So I've scattered some things, if not all, that relate to your circumstances in the dialogue, as you'll see. I'm also sending you some writings by Dr. Martin Luther, which I enjoyed reading. They may be able to move and restore you, too. Work hard at these studies, for God's sake; ask that He enlighten you with true religion. You will not lose. You don't think that God lies, do you?[222] Why would He have made so many promises, unless He wished to keep them? He invites and summons all the wretched to him.[223] He turns away no one. So set aside the old error we were led astray by up till now, when we thought that before we pray

---

219. Letter 25. The appended dialogue is uncertain, nor is it known to whom "cuiusdam docti ac pii viri" refers. The work cannot be Morata's own first "Dialogue with Lavinia della Rovere" (even if she were coyly referring to herself in this way), which was written in Ferrara before either of them left, nor the puzzling addition to that work, which can hardly be described as a dialogue.
220. Cic. *Fam.* 15.16.2.
221. Morata's "Dialogue between Theophila and Philotima."
222. Cf. Titus 1:2, Heb. 6:18.
223. Matt. 11:28.

to Him we ought to know whether he Has elected us from time eternal.[224] Rather, let us first, as He ordered, implore mercy from Him, and when we have done this, we shall know for certain that we are in the number of the elect. So far, there's been nothing done, but now arise, and consider not who is talking with you but what the words are and who they belong to. Goodbye.

DIALOGUE BETWEEN THEOPHILA AND PHILOTIMA [1551–52]

Editor's note: This second dialogue was written, as Morata said, as a form of the genre of *consolatio* for Lavinia della Rovere Orsini. The characters Theophila ("She who loves God," with a glance at Luke 1:1) and Philotima ("She who loves honor") are in part masks for Morata and della Rovere. However, Philotima is also anyone who plays the difficult role of court lady. Morata offers Esther as a model for those women who need to keep faith with God in the midst of worldly, marital, and political cares. The dialogue is at once an attempt to console an absent friend and a tribute to her learning.

Morata touches on several of her main themes: the need for direct contact with the Word of God, for Christian hope and endurance, for trust in the promises of salvation found in Scripture. "All things flow, collapse, and cannot stay long in one and the same place." In her insistence on the transitory nature of this world, Morata appears to have found a way of reinterpreting the pessimism of Lucretius, which had once so impressed her, within Christianity.

Theophila and Philotima converse.

Theo. Our life has been exposed to all the weapons of the Devil,[225] so that no matter where you turn in spirit or thought, you will always find something painful, especially in case of pious persons, who are troubled not only by their own difficulties but by those of others. And though I have my hands full of my own affairs,[226] pain is added to the rest of my miseries which I get from the bad fortune of my friend. So I have come here to console one who needs consolation.

---

224. The doctrine of predestination. See the introduction.
225. Cf. Cic. *Fam.* 5.16.
226. Cf. Ter. *Heaut.* 225.

Phil. I seem to hear the voice of my Theophila. Here she is. You've come just in time. I'm so sick with grief that I'm beside myself. Perhaps your presence and conversation can help.

Let's think about how we can talk together more easily. First, there's no need to explain to you the reason for my pain. Since so great a friendship exists between us and there is no woman dearer to me than you, I have long shared all my secrets with you.[227] Many good people know how much pain I have from my husband's frequent absences, and I suffer from it now. He has left me once again. He doesn't care that I miss him. I feel miserable here alone, but he feels fine.[228] I'm worn out by these and similar worries. When I was still a girl, there was nothing I wanted more than to meet a man with whose nature and manners I could agree, whose company I would always be allowed to enjoy. I thought there was no greater happiness in life than to have a husband who loved you greatly and with whom you could spend your life. That's the primary reason I got married, so that I might be happy with him. But when I see how differently it all turned out than I hoped, the more happiness I imagined there would be, the more pain I have now.

Theo. Since to give and take advice is part of true and Christian friendship—and to give it freely but not cruelly and to take it patiently and not grudgingly[229] —I must give you advice more boldly because you are more dear to me.

Phil. Say whatever you want to freely. I know that's only fair; in fact, we ought to take turns giving each other advice. Don't worry that I'll take it badly.

Theo. First, if you had read, as was proper, the books of the Old and New Testament diligently, you would have imbibed from these fountains a different opinion about human affairs, and you would have realized that everything turns out quite differently than we think it will. For as He says, "The heart of man thinks about his path, but the Lord moves his steps."[230] This way you would have learned to entrust and commit all things to God, and from the example of the saints you would have learned that many evils must be undergone. You never would have thought that you would be free of worries just because you got married, when you read about the many evils that came to even holy women who did not marry, like you, in order to live happily, but in order to serve God in this station of life by being good to

---

227. Cf. Ter. *Heaut.* 575.
228. Cf. Ter. *Ad.* 34 (of a philandering husband).
229. Cf. Cic. *Amic.* 91.
230. Prov. 16:9.

their husbands, educating their children in holiness and piety (or if not children, then those whom God had committed to them), imbuing them with the religion of Christ and divine letters.[231] So it's no wonder if everything hasn't turned out perfectly for you, especially since God was not the end you set before yourself, to which everything was referred and for whose sake everything was done. Finally, if we think about the matter correctly, we will understand that there is so great a multitude and magnitude of sufferings even* in the lives of those whose holiness shines above all the rest, that all the sufferings we have to endure in this life are no more a punishment than if a father should give a cuff occasionally to a son who is guilty of every crime and disgrace. So you shouldn't take it so hard if you have had some annoyance from the difficulties of life, since in your whole previous life you have despised God and His Word, placing everything ahead of Him; nor did you care for your own salvation or that of your family, who were entrusted to your faith. Instead, you relied on your nobility and the power of your relations. You placed more trust in them than in God, you gloried more in your riches than in God, and you never gave thanks for all the many benefits conferred upon you. But why waste words? Read the Ten Commandments diligently with their commentary, examine your life in them as in a mirror, and you will see that your life is heaped with every sin.

Phil. I cannot deny that I pay a far smaller penalty than my crime demands—none, really, if I consider my sins. But I see many women in a better position who certainly are not free from fault and live worse lives than I do.

Theo. I know you think they are happy, the women to whom they give a greater license and freedom of life, who live a life of leisure, are driven around in gilded carriages, indulge in clothes too much, as women usually do in Ferrara and other Italian towns, who dress not for their husbands but to please other men. If they don't repent their deeds, they will pay the right and proper penalties to God. Do you think they are happy and do you want to imitate them?

Phil. Well, to the extent that they adorn themselves and work to seem beautiful to others, I don't want to imitate them. As you know, I've always striven hardest for one thing, to be loved by my husband, content with him alone. But it does bother me that they have plenty of all the things I lack, things I ought to have lots of, as the daughter of such an important family, the things you just counted off. I don't want to have my husband grant me

---

231. This may be a glance at her own state. Though she and Grunthler had no children, she oversaw the education of her brother Emilio and Sinapius's daughter, Theodora, among others.

as much license in living as they have, but I would like to go out walking occasionally to recover myself, to ride in a horse and carriage as befits my station, to have beautifully made up couches, embroidered tapestries,[232] tables laid with the most exquisite foods,[233] so that I could sometimes invite women like myself to lunch or dinner, to have ready money so that I could give generously to others.

Theo. While you were counting off these things, I was reminded of my own silliness. I too was stuck in the same mud and still would be if God in His mercy hadn't pulled me out. What would you say was more stupid or absurd than if you saw a woman walking around in expensive clothing, with many jewels and gold, but her whole face covered in filth?

Phil. I wouldn't just say this was silly or absurd but positively insane.

Theo. Right, because she had neglected the one thing it was most important for her to adorn. Just so, we ought to think that we are no less crazy when we allow the soul, than which no more excellent or divine thing has been given us by God, to be utterly defiled with every crime, which smells worse to heaven than filth, whose foul odor God cannot bear. But in the meantime, we take care of the body, the prison of the soul, most eagerly and diligently. We want to have carriages, in which to be carried around the track of life, so narrow and so short, but we don't want to have the carriage in which we will be carried up to heaven, where the road is the longest, that is, faith. We want to live luxuriously and magnificently, but in the heavenly kingdom, than which there can be nothing more splendid or magnificent, we have no desire to live, though God has given us here an inn to stay for a while, not to inhabit. We dress our body beautifully, but we go out naked in what pertains to the soul. We want to have laden tables, but we have no desire for the Word of God, which is the only sweet food for souls. Human perversity is incredible. Now can you realize that the happiness of those you thought blessed is not really so great, and that you are happier than they?

Phil. Well, yes, if they don't have the heavenly goods, I'm convinced things are as you say. But there have been some women, holy and religious women, who had the goods of the body, who were beautiful and rich, and placed by God in the highest station of dignity; for example, Esther, whom a great king married, or Abigail, who was married to King David.[234] They cultivated piety, even though they flourished in riches and honors.

---

232. Pl. *Ps.* 147.
233. Cic. *Tusc.* 5.62.
234. See Esther and 1 Sam. 25, respectively.

Theo. God gives different gifts to different people and gives different burdens, and it is wrong to judge concerning His judgments. But we know for certain that He does nothing randomly but everything for our benefit. So if it were to our advantage to have those things, believe me, He would grant them generously and profusely—He Who gave Himself, than which there is no greater gift. And though you don't think that these things would get in your way when they didn't harm those women, why do you want them so desperately, why do they seem so wonderful to you, when those women considered them worth nothing? Since so great a desire for these things seizes you, is there any doubt that if you had them you would place them ahead of divine things and you wouldn't think about how you could get heavenly things? For you would have already gained what you wanted.

Queen Esther had a completely different attitude. She was so far from wanting to be queen that when she prayed to God she called Him to witness, the One before whom one dare not lie, that she recoiled from this station in life. And her whole life testified that she had spoken the truth, for neither riches, nor honors, nor the love of the king was able to draw her from God. Indeed we know that for the safety of her people she risked the loss of all those goods, and of her own head. For when the king, at the urging of the wicked Haman, had appointed the day for the destruction of the Jews and that saddest day had dawned, Mordecai, concerned for the safety of himself and his people, went to the queen. Begging and pleading with her, he besought her to try and save her people from death. And this could not be done in any other way than by winning over the king with supplication, even though it was forbidden for anyone to approach him without summons, for it was the custom in that kingdom that if anyone came to the king without summons he must surely die. Then she put herself in danger for the sake of her people and approached the king. Do you not believe that it was a greater grief for her, living with impious men in a court far from the people of God, to possess those things, than it is for you to lack them? Neither riches nor any goods of that kind cause loss or evil to those who are in *that* frame of mind. But they are a cause of destruction to those who seek for them, such as Queen Vashti, who, drunk with good fortune, became so insolent that she was unwilling to be obedient to her husband, the great king Ahasuerus. Therefore, favorable affairs tax the souls of even the wise, not to mention the impious who become insolent. And so God, lest they perish, deprives His people of these things, or, if He bestows them, afflicts His people with other griefs of the spirit. For if Esther had not had such great griefs of the spirit to endure, these good things would only have brought her as much pleasure as they usually bring people, and beyond any doubt she would have forgotten

God. For she was but flesh; as we read of the people of Israel, "My beloved has become fat, and kicked back."[235]

As to Abigail, since we know that David was involved in great difficulties, we have to consider that she suffered many evils also. If you look only at the splendor and outward form of their lives, you don't see the labor and worry as well. And whenever you think about your own difficulties, you are always placing before your eyes those for whom things are or seem to be going well. This is not what you should have done, but rather you should have placed before your eyes the miserable, the afflicted, the worried, the overwhelmed in this life; there are a greater number of them! I do not mention Christ Himself, the Son of God Almighty, Who drank the fill of greater and more bitter griefs than anyone else in the memory of man. I pass over the saints. Read their stories diligently and consider whether they did not endure greater disasters than we have, though they were far better than we are. I could give examples of many people who are alive at this time, but I'll just mention one woman of the highest rank and her noble husband, the duke of Saxony.[236] How great do you think their pain is, when they have been separated so long and since their love is strong and shared? Nor is he currently, as your husband is, in the highest honor, but an absent captive, deprived of all his possessions, all his titles lost, despised, humbled, in the power of his enemy, and yet of such piety and probity that I do not know if there is anything else like it on earth (to speak of princes). So great is the constancy of this man that a certain Spaniard of the imperial party has put down in his writings that not a single word of hopelessness has ever escaped his lips.[237] Their misfortune (if misfortune it can be called, for I rank his prison and ignominy ahead of all the triumphs and victories of others) is greater than yours. For there is no greater grief than when we realize or see that those whom we love and hold dear are suffering, especially those who once were flourishing. So these two obtained the greatest power, flourished greatly with honors, wealth, grace, and friends; now they are humbled and neglected.

235. Deut. 32:15.
236. Sibylle, duchess of Saxony, married to the duke and elector Johann Friedrich der Grossmütige (John Frederick the Magnanimous, 1503–54). He was captured and imprisoned at the Battle of Mühnberg (1547) and condemned to death. His sentence was commuted to life imprisonment by the emperor Charles V in exchange for the loss of land and titles; however, Johann Friedrich refused to compromise on religion and was widely hailed as a martyr to Protestantism. He was eventually released on 1 September 1552.
237. This would be Luis de Avila y Zuñiga (1500–64); see Avila y Zuñiga [1548] 1852, 448. His book was rapidly translated into all the major European languages. Morata would have read the Latin translation by Guillaume van Male (1550). See also Mentz 1908, 3:277 n. 3.

What can I say about others who daily, as you know, for Christ suffer injury, ignominy, exile, are killed, are burned? Look at it in this spirit and you will see that you are not as miserable as you think, but that you are the happiest. You are treated as a daughter by God; for whom He loves, He also chastises.[238] What greater happiness can there be than to be a daughter of God, most blessed to enjoy life eternal with Christ and to be a sharer of His kingdom.

Phil. You're preaching the truth, but I'm still so weak that my burden seems too heavy to me. So desire for the things I've mentioned still holds me. I would like to be relieved of this burden, if it were possible, but I don't see what can be done.

Theo. Patience will make lighter what you cannot change.[239] I can give you no better advice than if you are not able to bear adversities patiently to take yourself to Him Who calls all who labor and are heavy laden to Him to give them rest.[240] He cannot lie.[241] He Himself will strengthen you and give you, as He promised, the Holy Spirit, so that you will be able to taste all those heavenly goods, which beyond all doubt will ease your grief and fill your thirst for those things; for he will never thirst who has drunk from there.[242] You will sustain yourself easily with the hope of eternal goods, which are nevertheless more certain than these frail and fleeting things before our eyes. You will think the small inconveniences of your life are light when weighed in the balance against these.[243]

Phil. They seem light to you, but if you were in my place you'd feel differently.[244]

Theo. I haven't spoken about myself so far. Those who live closely with me know whether I am beyond the reach of arrows.[245] But any pious person can easily judge whether anyone who desires to serve God can live an easy life and whether the Devil will allow him to pass his life in peace and quiet. No, the Devil will do everything in his power to destroy that person utterly: now one thing, now another. If he does succeed one way, he tries another. He afflicts you with sickness, then ignominy, or he reduces you to poverty;

---

238. Prov. 3:12, Heb. 12:6.
239. Cf. Hor. *Odes* 1.24.19–20.
240. Matt. 11:28.
241. Cf. letters 28, 45; Titus 1:2; Heb. 6:18.
242. John 4:13–14.
243. Cf. Cic. *N.D.* 1.23.
244. Ter. *And.* 310.
245. Cf. Sen. *Dial.* 2.1.1.

he makes you hated even by your nearest and dearest; he brings dissension among the closest friends. I shall say nothing of the crucifixions of the spirit which are sometimes worse than the torments of the torturers. And who can enumerate the evils, troubles, and dangers which the pious must endure? There is no one who merely wishes to live piously in Christ who does not endure the bitterest griefs and miseries and daily bears his cross.[246] You only cast your eyes on your own evils.

Phil. It has been so ordained by nature "that we see and feel those things which happen to us, good or bad, more than those which happen to others, which we see only as it were at a distance. We judge differently about them and about ourselves."[247] My burden is the one that presses on me, and I would like to be free of it, if that were within my power. But if it can't happen that way, I'd prefer to bear the difficulties which this life brings and to possess the kingdom of Christ than to endure eternal punishment in the next life.

Theo. You are wise for thinking so. For everything, no matter how big, ought to be endurable if it is brief;[248] and what is briefer than this life? How many princes and famous men have died within our memory? The same mound that covers their bodies now buries their names, so that they seem never to have existed. So that old saw that everyone says is true: "Man is a bubble."[249] And Peter has said that the brevity of this life is aptly compared to a vapor,[250] so that long time ought to move us more than this brief one. And now is the time for us to be thinking about that perpetual life and not about this short one. You will never be able to be happy here. You will never have anything, though you have tried everything, in which you can rest except in God. Death must be faced. It threatens daily and because of the brevity of life cannot be far off. All things flow, collapse, and cannot stay long in one and the same place.[251]

Phil. You speak the truth and I plan to follow your advice. I desire to seek God, from whom all good things flow, or rather Who is the highest good. But I'm afraid that because of my many sins my way to Him is obstructed. You just said that He cannot bear the foul odor of sinners.

Theo. Don't be afraid. What I said is true, but you know how even a foul odor has all its force broken and weakened when a greater amount of a sweet

---

246. Luke 9:23; and cf. Matt. 10:38, 16:24; Mark 8:34, 10:21; Luke 14:27.
247. Cic. *Off.* 1.30.
248. Cic. *Amic.* 104.
249. Var. *RR* 1.1.1.
250. A misremembrance; James 4:14, and cf. letter 44.
251. Cf. Cic. *Orat.* 10 and Lucr. 2.69.

odor is present. Just so, no odor of sinners can be so foul that its force cannot be broken and weakened by the sweetest odor that flows from the death of Christ, which alone God can perfume.[252] Therefore seek Christ. Have no doubt: you will find Him in the books of the Old and New Testament, nor can He be found anywhere else. Pray to Him. Your labor will not be in vain.[253] "He who calls on the name of the Lord will be saved."[254] Would so many very rich and great promises be in the sacred books unless God wanted to keep them? And so He promises to everyone in general, lest anyone can doubt that these things were done for him. Or rather if you merely desire to get knowledge of faith, then know for certain that you will get it! This power cannot be found in our vicious nature, but it is the act of the Holy Spirit, Who cannot be overruled by God.[255] So it's clear to me that God has given you these thoughts and that if you do this you will grow more tranquil in your mind in the days to come.

Phil. Why do you want to leave so soon? Stay here just a little longer.

Theo. I've got to go home and take care of things there. For when the housewife's away, "what shouldn't happen happens faster than what should."[256] I'll visit you again soon.

Phil. That would be most pleasing.

LETTERS 29–40: SCHWEINFURT AND THE SIEGE [1552, AGE 27]

Letter 29: Schweinfurt, [1552]
Olympia Morata to Hörmann's son:[257]

Your father has very kindly written us and offered a post which we would gladly accept,[258] but we have run into a difficulty which seems will forever be an impediment to us; and since I think that it could be resolved by you, I thought that I ought to tell you in my letter what it is and how you might give us aid in this matter.

---

252. Eph. 5:2 and cf. 2 Cor. 2:11–16.
253. 1 Cor. 15:58.
254. Acts 2:21, Rom. 10:13.
255. "nullam repulsam ferre potest": the idiom humorously summons up the image of God and the Holy Spirit competing in an election.
256. Plaut. *Amph.* 505.
257. Anton; see letter 30.
258. As personal physician to Ferdinand I at Linz.

I think it is hardly unknown to you that we serve under Christ, and that we are bound with an oath to His military service, so that if we abandon it we will pay an endless penalty. Our General is so great that He has not only the power of life and death over His soldiers but is able to condemn them to eternal punishments, and He does not allow any of His men to sit in two chairs at once.[259] So this should be our greatest care: neither to throw away our shields out of fear of the enemy nor to throw ourselves rashly into danger, for that would be sinning against Him.

And so in fear of this, over and over again I ask you, please let us know by your letters and those of your friends who live in Linz whether the Antichrist is raging there—which is the rumor we have heard—and whether they are punishing those who are not present at their Mass and worship God with pure religion. For this is our resolve: we will not worship in a perverse and impious religion but rather profess ourselves Christians. If, as is happening in other places, the spies of the Antichrist would spot us and try to force us to be present at their ceremonies, it is completely impossible for us to go there, for as I said, we would be sinning against God. You can carry this out for us, that is, advise us. I ask and beg for you to do so. Goodbye.

Letter 30: Schweinfurt, [1552]
Olympia Morata to Anton Hörmann, Junior:

Noble sir: We have learned from your last letter with what diligence you have seen to our business and we know we owe you a debt of gratitude that will be difficult to repay. Your energy and kindness are such that we do not hesitate to avail ourselves of them, whenever we need your help. And so I want to press you to write to Milichius at least once—whenever it's convenient, don't trouble yourself—that he should take care to return whatever letters he has received from us.[260] Once you signify this to him, I will be able to send letters to my family and to receive theirs more easily. There's nothing sweeter to me in a foreign country than to learn about my family's doings and let them know about ours. If you can do this, it will the most pleasing of all your kind deeds towards us. If we are a trouble to you, put it down to your own kindness. Goodbye.

---

259. I.e. serve two masters. Cf. Macrobius 2:7.2–9, Sen. *Cont.* 7.3.9.

260. This Milichius has apparently failed to pass on Morata's letters. It is likely then that he was in Italy and so should not be identified with the only well-known bearer of that name, Jacob Milichius (Giorgio Melichio, 1501–59), an early supporter of Melanchthon's and a friend of Johannes Sinapius's. He was at one point professor of medicine at Wittenberg (*ADB* 21, 745). See Flood and Shaw 1997, 212 n. 127.

Letter 31: Schweinfurt, [1552]
Olympia Morata to Georg Hörmann, Counselor to King Ferdinand:

You have received only the occasional letter from me, not because I've forgotten you, but because there hasn't been anything so far that I thought interesting enough to write to you about. However, now that you want to know whether I have in mind to go where it appears God the best and greatest wishes to offer us a post, I'll tell you briefly what I feel. Now that God has joined me in steadfast marriage to the man I hold dearer than anything else in this life and after I followed him over "the passes of the Alps," I would follow him "with a brave heart even to the desolate Caucasus or the uttermost corner of the West."[261] Since he longs to go there, it pleases me too, for it is right for me to comfort myself to his will, and I am unable honorably to disagree with him. "Any earth is home for the brave,"[262] but we will hasten with oar and sail to the place where we are allowed to profess ourselves openly as Christians and not to have to use the ceremonies of the popes. In the meanwhile I have one favor to ask you: please let us know about this matter and, if it befalls us to go there, to commend us to any pious and learned men you know there. And although we can never do enough to repay the thanks we owe you for this favor, we will at least do all we can to remember it.

Letter 32: Schweinfurt, 20 November 1552
Olympia Morata to the young man Michael Weber:

Since we love your mother greatly for her exceptional piety, we cannot help but rejoice completely in her joy. So we take great pleasure and delight from the letters you have sent to my husband, both because they have provided an example of your piety and because they have given an indication of what progress you have made in letters. I congratulate your mother on this great good, that you have applied your soul to the study of letters and you do not (as most young men do) prefer "to hear the sound of a discus than that of a philosopher."[263] Believe me, a great gift has been given to you by God, if amid the evil morals of this age ("and they can reap a huge harvest of those," as the poet says)[264] you do not allow yourself to be corrupted. You may credit God with the fact that "you do not walk on the highway."[265]

261. Hor. *Epod.* 1.11–14: a singularly apt quotation.
262. Ov. *Fasti* 1.493.
263. Cic. *de Orat.* 2.21.
264. Pl. *Trim.* 32.
265. Quoted in Greek. A Pythagorean maxim, e.g. D.L. 8.17 [Pythagoras].

Therefore I rejoice and congratulate you and hope that the good opinion I have of you will grow more and more day by day, whereby you may render your mother overflowing with joy[266] and us, your supports, the friendliest of friends. Most important, do not impiously and ungratefully fail in your duty to God,[267] Who urged you to this way of thinking and gave you your talent: "The glorious gifts of God are not to be thrown away."[268] That you are being very careful that these sad times do not call you away from your course is nothing to feel anxious about. You will not lose anything by doing so. "It is no less a skill to preserve your gains than to seek them."[269] You will be able to read any book by your own prowess, though you lack a teacher. Not everything is passed on by teachers, who themselves, as it were, point a finger to the sources. If you listen to me, you will read diligently any book you think will be useful to you (I don't know your course of studies). You will pore over it and work on it alone, since it's better to do one thing well than many things moderately well, as Pliny the Younger said.[270] If you do this you will free your mother from any worry on that account.

But lest I seem to spur a willing horse,[271] I will do enough if I urge you to devote yourself to the study of sacred letters with all the power of your soul and with all your heart. They alone will teach you "what is beautiful, what is ugly, what is useful, what is not,"[272] and they will make you a better person and in these difficulties sustain you with their consolation. Be of good cheer, God will not desert you. He will protect and save His people even when they are embroiled in the greatest dangers. As He says: "Rule in the midst of your enemies!"[273] You will be able to draw more from this fountain. As we ought, we will offer you our help and zeal in everything we can.[274] My husband greets you. He would have responded to your letter if he had had the time. I have answered you on his behalf. Goodbye. May Christ watch over you.

---

266. Cf. Ter. *Ph.* 856.
267. "et tibi ingenium de sis impie ingratus" 1562 : "et tibi ingenium dedit impie ingratus" 1570 *Caretti*: "et tibi ingenium dedit <,sis> impie ingratus" : *supplevi*.
268. An adaptation of Hom. *Il.* 3.65: οὔ τοι ἀπόβλητ' ἐστὶ Θεῶν ἐρικυδέα δῶρα. οὐ γὰρ ἀπόβλητά γε Θεοῦ ἐρικουδέα δῶρα 1562 : ἐρικηδέα 1570: ἀποβλη τὰ γε Θεοῦ ἐρικηδέα *Caretti*.
269. It is somewhat surprising to find Morata quoting from Ovid's *Art of Love* (2.11)!
270. Cf. Pliny *Ep.* 9.29.1.
271. A common proverb, e.g. Cic. *de Orat.* 2.186, *Phil.* 3.19.
272. Hor. *Ep.* 1.2.3.
273. Ps. 110:2, cited from the Vulgate [Ps. 109:2].
274. Cf. Cic. *Fam.* 15.12.2.

Letter 33: Schweinfurt, [c. January 1553]
Olympia Morata to Anton Hörmann:

Our trunks with the books have arrived. Thanks so much: you've shown your devotion to us in this. I only hope we can repay you someday. We're sending this letter to Padua. Please, when you can do so conveniently, make sure our Laurenz, one of the most pious men, gets it. Goodbye.[275]

Letter 34: Schweinfurt, [c. January 1553]
Olympia Morata to Laurenz Schleenried:

We have finally received our books. Enormous thanks for having taken care of this so devotedly and diligently. The book of Avicenna was not in the trunk. If there's anything still owed you, let us know and we'll see to the money for you. We are still staying here in our hometown, and there's been no possibility of leaving because of the wars. I'm sure that you've been told that the duke of Saxony has been set free and obtained his former titles. "But enough about that."[276]

One thing above all I want to ask of you: to write to us, as soon as you have time, about events in Italy, especially about my ungrateful city of Ferrara. This is now the fourteenth month since I've heard anything about my mother. And although I've often written at length to her and to all my relatives and friends, no one writes me back. So I've decided to send you the letter, which (as you can see) I've appended to this one for you, so that you can take care of sending them on to my mother, and look around if there's any way for me to find out what they're doing. You couldn't do anything more pleasing to me. I beg you over and over again to do this and call on your piety. Goodbye.

---

275. Laurenz Schle(h)enried (see next letter); Bietenholz and Deutscher 1985–87, 3:224. A Protestant and a wandering scholar (d. 1556), at this point studying law in Padua. After gaining a doctorate in civil and canon law in Bologna, he became lecturer in canon law at Tübingen.

276. Maurice, duke and elector of Saxony (1521–53; created duke 1541, created elector 1547). Maurice had invaded southern Germany and Austria and driven out the armies of Charles V in the so-called Second Schmalkaldic War. The Treaty of Passau (2 August 1552) established a peace and his claims were recognized on 1 September 1552. "But enough about that" quoted in Greek.

Letter 35: Schweinfurt, 15 January 1553
Olympia Morata to Johannes Sinapius:

My husband recently sent letters to you together with your little girl.[277] I don't know whether you've received them or not. I'm sending these (as you can see) to Anton Hörmann, so that he can be sure to send my letters on to Laurenz at Padua. I have in mind, since I've received no letters after so long a lapse of time, to fish out from him what on earth's the problem that is producing such delay in the matter.

Your little girl is well and learning something new every day: "If you add a little to a little" . . . you know the rest.[278]

About the job: if you know anything for sure, please let us know as soon as possible.[279] We've heard that our Senate can help us a great deal in this matter, and we are confident it will do so.

My husband bids me give you and your wife his warmest greetings, and I ask you to greet her with my words. Goodbye.

Letter 36: Schweinfurt [c. April 1553]
Olympia Morata to Dr. Valentino Carchesio:[280]

We are greatly upset that you came to Germany at the very point when we could not get to see you. We are still in a state of suspense and worry, and eager to know what is going on in Italy, especially what my family is doing. I got almost nothing out of that thin little letter of the things that I would have been able to learn from you. And we would have congratulated you personally on your honor! But since we couldn't, I've decided to do it by letter. So we congratulate you, my Valentino, and hope that this will turn out successfully for you. Because of these most suspicious times, I am sending you these letters unsealed for you to send on to my mother, and to tell her that we are doing well. Don't say even a word about the terrible disasters,

---

277. Johannes Sinapius's daughter, Theodora, had been studying with Morata and had been sent back home during the siege of Schweinfurt. See the letter of Sinapius to Calvin, Calvin 1863–1990, CR 42 = *Calvini Opera* 14, 688–89; Flood and Shaw 1997, 204 (Latin text), 139 (Eng. trans.).

278. Cf. Hes. *Op.* 361.

279. This seems to be a different academic appointment than that at Linz. It is almost certainly Grunthler's eventual chair of medicine at Heidelberg (so Kössling and Weiss-Stahlin 1990, 201; see letter 41 below).

280. Unidentified. A medical friend, probably still in Ferrara.

because it might upset her with worry and anxiety.[281] God will watch over and protect us. He has been our aid so far, and there is no doubt that He will continue to give us His might and power. We'll write more if time allows. I would have liked to have sent you a psalm that I've recently rendered into Greek verse. Send our greeting in our words to your lady and to the others who miss us, if they're there. Goodbye.

Letter 37: Schweinfurt [c. April 1553]
Olympia Morata to Dr. Valentino Carchesio:

I have nothing to write you about at present. I don't think it's important for me to write my observations on the war that's currently hanging over Germany. Others will tell you the news, and rumor will bring even more. I don't think I should write about anything except what's certain. So in the last letter I wrote you, if I hadn't known for certain and seen with my own eyes that our preacher was a good man, I would never have praised him.[282] Indeed, how would I draw such a conclusion except from that touchstone with which the writings of the prophets and apostles have proclaimed that men are tested?[283] In other words, "from the two types" which He has weighed in the balance and it seems still will weigh, if the times demand it.[284] In these dangerous times he flatters no one, and inveighs as a preacher should against those who might easily increase his income, if he fawned on them. He lives a life in accordance with his words. Further, there are many good men here, "reborn not from perishable seed but through the incorruptible Word of the living God."[285] For their sake we are glad to be here and have most willingly left behind for you "the fleshpots of Egypt."[286]

But enough about that. It was so pleasing that you sent my mother's letters to me. And from your own letters I want to know what our most learned friend Lilio Gregorio is doing, "if he still lives and sees the light of the

---

281. Possibly the start of the seige of Schweinfurt in April 1553.

282. The letter referred to is lost. The preacher was almost certainly Johann Lindemann at the St. Johanniskirche, for whom Morata wrote a poem. See letter 51.

283. Cf. (int. al.), Prov. 17:3, Zech. 13:9, 1 Cor. 3:13, 1 Pet. 1:7.

284. Cf. Dan. 5:27.

285. 1 Pet. 1:23: ἀναγεγεν<ν>ημένοι ἐκ σπορᾶς <φθαρτῆς ἀλλὰ> ἀφθάρτου διὰ λόγου ζῶντος Θεοῦ: ἀναγεγενημένοι ἐκ σπορας ἀφθάρτον διὰ λόγου ζῶντος θεου 1562 1570 Caretti : et cf. "renati ex immortali semine per sermonem viventi Dei" 1562 1570 ("Graeca in hisce libris sparsim posita Latinis verbis, ne quis laboret, expressa").

286. Exod. 16:3; letter 26, n. 122 above.

sun?"[287] I ask you to give our greetings to him with our words, and also to that most learned youth, Joseph from Brixen, who is staying with Chavanus.[288] Write often about what you are doing, what's happening there. Most of all, pore over the sacred books. Beware of doing "work not worth doing."[289] Say hello to your wife, Agnese, and your steward.[290] But alas, whisper it in their ear, so that no one need fear for himself from Olympia's name. And the other people I love, if I weren't afraid that they might shudder at the sound of my name. Goodbye.

Letter 38: Schweinfurt, 26 May 1553
Olympia Morata gives greetings in Christ to the
pious and learned Matthias Flacius Illyricus:[291]

My dear sir: After I had thought long and hard about how I might enrich my own family and other Italians with the good things with which Germany overflows, but found no place of counsel or ability to help in myself, I realized that I might be able to obtain this easily through other learned men. And since your writings have made you well-known to me, you were the first to come into my mind as one who seemed able to help my fellow Italians, who are lost in so many errors and are in need of the good things of heaven. If you were to translate into Italian any of Luther's German books in which he argues against the general errors (for I do not yet understand German, although I have worked hard at it) or if you would write something in Italian on the same subject (you could do it far better than I, since you have unrolled the books of sacred Scripture, which I have barely touched with my lips),[292] I am sure that you would save many pious men from the errors by which they are misled. If you are willing to do this for the sake of the church, for which we ought to lay down our lives, you will bind them to you forever by your divine kindness. I think it would be even more useful for them if you were to write in Italian, since many of them are ignorant of

---

287. For Lilio Gregorio Giraldi, who had in fact died the previous year, see document 1 in the present text. Hom *Od.* 4.833: ἤ που ἔτι ζώει καὶ ὁρᾷ φάος ἠελίοιο : ἐι ἔτι ποῦ 1570 Caretti: ἠελίος 1562 Caretti.

288. Both unidentified.

289. ἔργον πάρεργον. A common saying, cf. Agathon frg. 11 ap. Athen. 5.185a. Morata might have known it from Galen 9.292, 15.422 K.

290. Unidentified. For *architriclinus*, cf. Vulg. John 2:8.

291. Famous and controversial Lutheran theologian (1520–75), a bitter opponent of the Augsburg Interim. See Olson 1981.

292. Cf. Cic. *Cael.* 28.

letters. I beg and beseech you again and again to do this through Christ, Who will account this a kindness done to Himself and from Whom, since I cannot thank you enough, "you will say you have made a huge profit."[293] I would try to obtain this from you with many words, if Johannes Cremer, my relative, had not discussed the same matter with you in letters and if piety did not speak on her own account. I only ask one thing of you, that if my letters are bothersome, please put it down not to my importunity but to your piety, which I relied on when I wrote. If you have any need of my aid, expect all the learning I have. I will not disappoint you. Goodbye.

Letter 39: Schweinfurt, [n.d.]
Olympia Morata to a certain German preacher:[294]

I have frequently hoped that an occasion would offer itself for me to talk with you, but since I have not yet been able to find one, I have decided to do through a letter what I would have done face to face if circumstances had allowed. But the teaching of Christ does not allow me to put off the matter any longer, and Him we must heed and obey. And so when I learned for certain that you are often sinning, it is absolutely necessary that I admonish you, if I want to be a hearer of the words of Christ. Likewise, if you reflect on the matter in the proper way, you ought not to blame me at all if I thought that you needed to be warned, because you act heedless of the most distinguished dignity of your office, heedless of your white hairs, when you give in to your appetites more than any Epicurus. Even men without a trace of the Christian religion know full well how base this is for a man of liberal education. All the more base for a Christian, then, whose life, if led in a holy and pure way, ought to invite and summon others to the worship of God and the undertaking of pure religion. Most base, then, for a preacher, who shows others the way but does not know the right way himself. For if a philosopher who sins in his way of life is the more base, in that he fails in the office of which he wishes to be the master, surely a preacher is the most base if he tells others how to lead their lives but leads his own most scandalously. Or is it not a great scandal to drink all the time, to be drunk, to abuse the wonderful gift of God, which was given to us that might enjoy it with an expression of thanks, not that we might abuse it?[295] "What

---

293. Ter. *Phorm.* 493.
294. Curio presumably suppressed the name.
295. 1 Tim. 4:3 (cited from the Vulgate); cf. Eph. 5:18, 1 Tim. 3:8, Titus 2:3.

doesn't drunkenness perpetrate?"[296] You know how the poem goes. But what was omitted by the poet is far more important: that drunkards usually speak obscenities, that they curse and swear by the most holy name of God (and he who violates it will never escape unpunished).[297] They pollute and defile their own bodies, which are the temples of God.[298] They grieve the Holy Spirit;[299] they expel and reject Him from them. They are called away from prayer. If God once inflicted so grave a punishment on the one who defiled the Temple at Jerusalem, what will He do to the one who defiles such a temple as this?[300]

In the meanwhile I say nothing "about the stumbling block" whereby the dignity of the minister is lessened, and Christ and the gospel are disgraced.[301] Ultimately the one who lives that way misteaches his followers by his corrupt morals more than he instructs them with learning. A man who accepts a fee to teach but misteaches, don't you think he's committing theft? You ought to be an example to your followers of modesty, sobriety, and temperance; instead by your evil life you sink them in scandal.

Please, I beg you, don't forget the words of Christ: "You are the salt of the earth. If the salt loses it flavor, how will it become salty? It is good for nothing except to be thrown out and trampled by men."[302] Think too about the saying of Paul: "I bruise my body and treat it like a slave, lest having preached to others I become unworthy myself."[303] What gall to urge your followers to imitate you, as Paul urged his to seek an example from him.[304] Or are they to imitate you in drinking and guzzling?

Nor can you defend this vice with the excuse of weakness of the flesh.[305] We know that all men fail and none can be found who lacks fault.[306] But those who have true faith "have crucified the flesh with its passions and desires."[307] The weak do not stay weak always, but sometimes become strong, so that sin

---

296. Hor. *Ep.* 1.5.15.
297. Exod. 20:7; cf. Matt. 5:34, James 5:12.
298. 1 Cor. 3:16–17.
299. Eph. 4:30.
300. 2 Macc. 9:5–28.
301. Cf. Rom. 14:13.
302. Matt. 5:13, quoted in Greek; possibly quoting from memory: ἡμεῖς ἐστε (ἐγὲ *Caretti*) τὸ ἅλας τῆς γῆς . . . εἰ μὴ βληθὲν (βληθῆναι 1562 1570 *Caretti*) ἔξω.
303. 1 Cor. 9:27, quoted in Greek.
304. 1 Cor. 4:16, 11:1.
305. Cf. Matt. 26:41.
306. Rom. 3:23.
307. Gal. 5:24.

no longer rules over them. And drunkenness is such a crime that even those who do not know Christ are able to abstain. So we're supposed to believe that a Christian, with the innumerable benefits of Christ conferred on him, can't keep sober, but the Turks, with nothing but that lost and profligate man Mohammed, live sparingly, containedly, soberly, to the extent of not even tasting wine? And if Paul thought that it was better for him never to eat meat than to cause offense to a brother, will you then not abstain, not I say from wine, but from this horrible crime?[308] And not just to keep your brother from being harmed or offended, but to keep a great multitude of men from perishing! We ought not to extenuate this sin in words, for God will not judge it by our opinion but according to His own pronounced sentence. He has placed drunkenness in the number of those crimes for which the offender will never possess the kingdom of God.[309]

Wherefore, over and over again I ask, beg, and beseech you through Christ, that at long last you change your ways, for the role of your office, for the "stumbling block," and even for your own salvation, lest on that final day you are in the number of those to whom it is said: "Depart from me, you evildoers."[310] God has closed His eyes so far,[311] and by His lenience is stirring you up to penitence. You are already of an advanced age. Come to your senses,[312] I beg you, so that glory and honor may come to God because of your holiness and changed ways, ways which up till now have afflicted Him with disgrace. Make sure you think about this with your whole soul, lest at last God demand the penalty of you and you perish forever. It has not escaped your notice that a base and scandalous life[313] shows that there is no faith in Christ, without which we shall surely perish. So I admonish and urge you to ask faith from God before death seizes you. Seek forgiveness, which He will give completely to the penitent, even He Who has sworn that He wishes not the death of the guilty.[314]

I have finished the things about which I thought I had to write to you. If you are a Christian, you will be far from taking them ill, but rather you ought to rejoice and be exceeding glad that you are warned. Farewell in Christ.

---

308. 1 Cor. 8:11–13.
309. 1 Cor. 6:10.
310. "stumbling block" quoted in Greek. Matt. 7:23, quoted in Greek.
311. "conivit" 1562 : "connivit" 1570: "convivit" *Caretti*.
312. "resipisce" 1562 : "respice" 1570 *Caretti*.
313. "flagitiosa" 1562 1570 : "flacitiosa" *Caretti*.
314. Ezek. 18:23, 32; 33:11; cf. 1 Tim. 2:4.

Letter 40 : Schweinfurt, 2 February 1554
Olympia Morata to the noble Lady Lavinia della Rovere Orsini in Jesus Christ:

I am wildly happy that in the midst of our great sufferings I have been granted an opportunity for writing to you, so that I can tell you, the nearest and dearest of all women to me (excepting my mother), what's been happening to us, not so that you'll grieve at our misfortune but rejoice in God's watching over us. You must know that our safety has been in the greatest danger for some time now and we are still in great danger and surrounded on all sides. We were besieged by the vast army of the two bishops of Würzburg and Bamberg and by the troops of the Elector Moritz and the Duke of Braunschweig and the men of Nuremberg as well, all because of the army of the Margrave of Brandenburg, which he quartered in this city.

But God has so covered us and guarded us that no one (incredible to say) has been killed by the missiles that are hurled at us night and day with such impact. He has driven off and warded off their attack from us. In all the evils and losses that war brings, He is still with us, and in our want of food, which is most severe, He kindly provides us with what is necessary for survival. He has even brought people back from the brink of death. Because of the close contact with the soldiers with whom the city is stuffed, a plague has invaded nearly all the citizens, so severe that nearly half the citizen body is dead from brain fever. My own most loving husband was infected with the disease and grew so seriously and dangerously sick that there seemed to be no hope for his life. But He who is accustomed to guide souls below brought him back by the great and ceaseless prayers offered by the church and by me. He took pity on me, who could not have borne such grief.

In all these evils, we have relied on one solace—the Word of God, by which we have sustained ourselves and because of which I have not looked back to the fleshpots of Egypt,[315] but preferred to seek death here, rather than enjoy all the pleasures of the world somewhere else. And although we have not yet been freed from these evils, nevertheless, because we have God so close to us, we have hope that we will be freed whenever it seems right and fitting to Him. Your part is to pray to Him with us, so that from this "pregnancy" (for we have been in confinement for nine months) we might give birth to happy offspring.

I had these things to write to you and to advise you about, so that you might take a warning from us which would be of some use to you. For we do not doubt but that all these things have happened to us because of our

---

315. Exod. 16:3; note 122, above.

disdain for the Word of God, which was the reason, as everyone knows, that Jerusalem was razed to the ground. So with all your heart apply yourself to the sacred writings, which alone will unite you with God and take all errors and false opinions from you. This will be the only provision for the road that you can take with you. All the rest, however dear, must be left behind.[316]

I beg you to urge my sister, whom I gave into your faith and protection, to do the same, for whom you will translate this letter for friendship's sake. I cannot write to her in these perilous times, and I am somewhat ashamed to load down with my letters this brave hero who is bringing them to you. Goodbye.

P.S. My husband and little brother add their greetings. Give my greetings in my words to all your family without exception. Goodbye again, my sweetest Lavinia, you who are always in my heart and whom I will never forget while there is breath in my body. Goodbye. Be well.

LETTERS 41–71: HEIDELBERG [1554–55, AGE 28–29]

Letter 41: Würzburg, 28 June 1554[317]
Johannes Sinapius to the most exceptional lady Olympia Morata:

Ever since the destruction of your hometown I have been hoping that you both would come to me and that soon my Theodora, who during the entire time of the siege has suffered a great loss of her studies, would have you again as her teacher. But as I understand from my brother Conrad, the Count of Rieneck, no less distinguished for his piety than for his noble birth, came to your aid in time with a comfortable carriage and provisions. The position at Heidelberg, which you were offered once, is still open, as Dr. Hartmann, our current legate from the Count Palatine, has informed us.[318] I have given him this letter to pass on to you. How I wish that you had heeded me when I earnestly urged you to go to Heidelberg, last year while your things were still intact. But whoever would have feared such a sudden and terrible destruction of your innocent and anyhow already sufficiently afflicted town? The wretched fate of your fatherland! Poor exiles and banished citizens, hearthless and homeless![319] How truly Homer wrote in book 15: "There is nothing

---

316. "clarissima" 1562 1570 : "carissima" *correxi*.

317. Sinapius still has not had confirmation of their arrival nearly a month later, 25 July 1554 (letter 48).

318. See letter 35.

319. ἀνεστίους καὶ ἀφηστίους 1562 1570 (cum ς pro στ) : ἀφηστίους καὶ ἀφησίους Flood and Shaw : ἀφεστίους *correxi* (cf. LXX Ecclus. 37:11, ed. Aldina 1518).

worse for mortals than wandering."³²⁰ But the hope of a different and true fatherland will console us as well as the knowledge that this world is not our home, but only granted us as a wayside inn,³²¹ and that He will repay us for this calamity with some richer kindness from Him. And enough about that.

I have quite recently received a fresh letter from Italy, dated 1 June, in which there was something of interest to you, though whether it will give you more information about the state of the court I don't know. It says that everything there is full of evils and dangers. Everywhere God is testing His people with the cross. When we consider their fate, we shall bear our own more mildly. Be well with your most faithful husband and let me know about how your affairs come out and if there's anything I can do for you.

At Würzburg, 28 June 1554, exactly a year to the day from the funeral of my sweetest wife.

Joining me in greeting you are Oswald, Theodora, Leonora, Brigida, Margareta, and Anna Schlosser with her daughters. In turn please greet Hubert and his son-in-law Andreas Gotwald, whose brother Matthäus was here with me yesterday.³²² Again, goodbye.

Letter 42: Heidelberg, 25 July 1554
Olympia Morata to Caelius Secundus Curio in Jesus Christ:

I think, dear Caelius, that I have no need to make use of any excuse to you for not having responded to the letters you gave me so long ago. The war lets me completely off. We've been under attack for fourteen months but have suffered no loss of life from it. As soon as Margrave Albrecht quartered his army at Schweinfurt because of its strategic location, his enemies, who were many, laid siege to the town. They began to assault it and to pound the walls on all sides day and night with siege engines. At the same time, inside the walls we were afflicted with many injuries at the hands of the Margrave's troops, and no one was safe in his own house. Besides, since the money they were owed was not being disbursed, they kept threatening that they would take everything from the citizens, as if we had invited or brought them here! The city was already completely exhausted from feeding so many soldiers,

---

320. *Od.* 15.343.
321. Heb. 11:15–16, cf. Heb. 11:10, 13:14. "diversorio" 1562 1570 : "diversio" *Flood and Shaw.*
322. Respectively Oswald Lurtzig, Sinapius's daughter, and two nieces. Margareta and Anna Schlosser are unidentified. Hubert Thomas of Liege, secretary to Frederick II, elector palatine (identified by Colomies 1699, 46). Andreas Gotwald (d. 1589/90), jurist in the Reichskammergericht.

and then from close contact with them a dire plague invaded nearly all the citizens, so severe that most were deranged from the pain. Death from the disease was the result for half the city. My most loving husband was affected by the disease, so that there seemed to be no hope for his life, but God, having pity on me in my utmost affliction, cured him without any medical intervention (there were no medicines in the town).

But as the poet says: "The departure of one ill is the approach of another to come."[323] Once the plague had been driven back by God, immediately we were besieged by an even bigger enemy army, which kept hurling fire into the city day and night. Often at night you would have thought the whole town was about to go up in flames, and at that time we were often forced to hide out in a wine cellar. At last, when we were hoping for a happy outcome to this war due to the Margrave's departure (he was going to march his army away on the following night), we fell in the greatest misery. For scarcely had he left the city with his army than on the next day the soldiers of the two bishops and of the men of Nuremberg invaded the city, and after pillaging it, had it burned.[324] Truly God snatched us from the midst of the flames, when one of the enemy soldiers himself warned us to get out of the city before it was burning in every quarter, because it was about to be burned to the ground. We obeyed him and left, stripped and denuded of everything—we were not allowed to take even a penny. In fact, our clothes were ripped off us in the middle of the town square and I was left with nothing to cover my body except a linen tunic. Then when we had escaped from the city, my husband was captured by the enemy. I was unable to ransom him even at the lowest price, and when I saw him being led away from my sight, I prayed with tears and "unutterable" groans to God,[325] Who immediately set him free and returned him to me.

But once we had left the city, we did not know where to turn. At last we made our way towards Hammelburg. I was barely able to crawl there. The village is three German miles from Schweinfurt, and the citizens of the town received us unwillingly, since they had been forbidden to offer shelter to any of us. Among the refugees I looked like the queen of the beggars. I entered the town with bare feet, unkempt hair, torn clothes (which weren't even mine but had been loaned me by some woman). I was so exhausted from the journey that I developed a fever, which I could not get rid of in

---

323. Sen. *Herc. Fur.* 208.
324. Albrecht's army abandoned the city on 12 June 1554 (see the introduction); see Saffert 1993, 522; Flood and Shaw 1997, 135.
325. Rom. 8:26, quoted in Greek.

all my wanderings. For since the citizens of Hammelburg were afraid for themselves, it was not possible for us to remain with them for long, but we had to leave within four days, even though I was sick. Then we were forced to pass through one of the bishop's towns again, and my husband was captured by the bishop's mayor, who said that he had been ordered by his most merciful lord to kill all the refugees who came there from Schweinfurt. We were captives, trapped between hope and fear, until we were let go by a letter from the bishop. Then at last God began to notice us. First someone led us to the most noble Count of Rieneck, then to the renowned Count of Erbach, who had often endangered his life and fortune for the sake of the Christian religion.[326] Both of them received us graciously and loaded us with many gifts. We stayed with them for many days until I was a little better and my husband was admitted to the college of the University of Heidelberg, where he will lecture on medicine.

You have an epitome of our sufferings; more later. Thanks so much for the books. They were most pleasing, but they perished with my other books, as did everything we owned. Greetings to your wife and children.

Letter 43: [Heidelberg, July 1554]
Olympia Morata to Caelius Secundus Curio:

A few days ago I sent you a rather lengthy letter, in which I informed you about our calamities. So now I'm being laconic and just asking as an additional request that you add the *Commentaries on the Lamentations of Jeremiah* by a certain learned man of our time to the books which we want shipped to us here.[327] You'll be doing me a great favor. Goodbye.

Letter 44: Heidelberg, 1 August [1554]
Olympia Morata to the most noble Lavinia della Rovere Orsini
in our Lord Jesus Christ:

I cannot imagine why, most noble Lavinia, you haven't sent me any letters except the one since you left Ferrara, unless this plague-ridden war that we've been ravaged by so long might seem to offer you an excuse. For I cannot doubt your kindness to me, which I know is mutual and the same as mine to you. For my part I have written to you very often and sent you a dialogue

---

326. Philip Graf von Rieneck; Georg II, Graf von Erbach (1506–69) and his brother Eberhard XIV (1511–64): *NDB* 4, 563; Press 1979.
327. I.e. Calvin's *Praelectiones in librum Prophetiarum Jeremiae et Lamentatione*. See letter 52.

that I composed.[328] From other learned men I've managed to extract entire books, but from you not even a letter. Nevertheless, I know from my friends, to whom I wrote to find out about you, that you're there.[329] So again and again I beg and plead with you, by our close friendship, as a special favor, release me by just one letter, for I've been terribly worried about you for nearly three whole years now. I believe you could do this more easily now, since we are in a more populous place than before, though we would not have come here if it hadn't been for the overwhelming catastrophe which befell us in the war and drove us out. How great that was and what we suffered you will learn from the letters I sent to Caelius. I don't think I need to write the same things in this letter to you, since you can learn everything clearly from them and at the same time learn that you have many comrades in misery. Believe me, there is no one, if he wishes to live his life piously in Christ, who does not draw a full measure of the bitterest pains and catastrophes. Personally we have often been forced into exile, but we've never been able to escape the world and the Devil. As the poet says, "Black Care does not get off the bronze-beak trireme / and sits behind the rider."[330] We always carry those domestic enemies with us—sin and the old Adam.[331] So we ought not to miss a moment to pray to God that we are not broken by such great evils. Otherwise, if we give in to sloth and laziness when we have so many battles to fight, we shall easily succumb and so perish forever. This is what even you have to watch out for, and you must have even greater diligence in sacred literature, and pray to God that you don't imitate the multitude of the impious (for everything is full of them) but rather that the Word of God may be your guide in living rightly and piously and a "lamp unto your feet."[332] That way you will not grow lazy. Most of all, see to it that you fear God, Who is able to cast both body and soul together into Hell,[333] more than mere men, whose lives the divine Scriptures compare to shadow, grass, flowers, and smoke.[334] Be of good cheer and brave heart. Every transitory thing, even if it is big, ought to be endurable. Here everything burns with

---

328. See letter 28.
329. Rome.
330. Hor. *Odes* 3.1.38–39.
331. Rom. 6:6.
332. Ps. 119:105 (cited from the Vulgate).
333. Matt. 10:28, Luke 12:5.
334. E.g. Ps. 109:23, 144:4, Eccles. 6:12, 8:13, and cf. 1 Chron. 29:15, Job 8:9, 14:2 (shadow); 1 Pet. 1:24, James 1:10–11, Ps. 103:15, Isa. 40:7–8, Matt. 6:30, Luke 12:28, and cf. Ps. 37:1, 92:7, Isa. 51:12 (grass); Job 14:12, Ps. 103:15, Isa. 40:6–7, James 1:10–11, 1 Pet. 1:24 (flower); Ps. 37:20, 68:2, 102:3, Isa. 51:6, Hos. 13:3 (smoke).

war and everywhere holy men are oppressed with sufferings. Many have fled even from England, so savage is the Devil. But all these things ought to be a great joy to us, since we know that they portend to us that the great and happy day will be soon, when we will begin to live a most blessed life together.

Meanwhile we greet you in letters and see you with the mind's eye. I could not commend my sister to you with greater zeal than I do now—not so that you should make her rich or lead her to your honorable station but that she may be enlightened with the knowledge of Christ. The form of this world is quickly passing.[335] My husband and little brother add their greetings to you.

Letter 45: Heidelberg, 8 August [1554] [In Italian][336]
Olympia Morata to her sister Vittoria:

To my dearest sister madonna Vittoria Morata, in care of the most noble signora Lavinia della Rovere Orsini.

Dearest sister,

By the grace of God we are safe, for which you too should thank God, Who got us out and freed us from such great dangers that if I wanted to write them all down I would fill a whole book. We have endured the disasters of the war and have been in continual distress for fourteen months, in the middle of the bombardment, both day and night, which often shot so many salvos against the city that it would be incredible to recount. But the Lord so defended us, while He wished to call the city to repentance, that only a very few people were killed and the city remained unvanquished. Despite all their forces they were never able to conquer it, even though it is small and not very well fortified.

But finally, through treachery, just when we thought that the enemy had left, as had been ordered by His Majesty and the other leaders, they entered and, having taken everything that was in the city, burned it. But the Lord miraculously freed us from the flame when one of the enemy soldiers himself advised us to go outside, when we had planned to stay in the church, where the smoke would have suffocated us, as it did others. Then my husband was captured twice. That was an intolerable pain, and I truly would have died

---

335. 1 Cor. 7:31 (Vulgate).
336. Curio supplied a Latin translation. The Italian original was first published by Bonnet 1878. Text from Caretti 1940, with corrections.

if the Lord had put off His help for too long. Through the grace of God I did not care about losing everything, and other than a dress nothing was left me.

But the Lord began to give us all that is necessary, and entrusted us to the hands of certain counts, lords of the highest degree, who clothed us honorably. The wife of one of these lords, who is the daughter of one the grand dukes and nobles of Germany, the counts Palatine, received me when I was sick and exhausted with so much charity that she even tended me while I was in bed.[337] She gave me a dress which is worth more than twenty-five scudi. Another lord, whom we had never seen before, whose name we did not even know, when we were on the road to come here gave us fifteen scudi for the trip. When we were about to leave, I came down with a fever and was sick for four whole weeks.

It's been eight days now since we came to the town called Heidelberg, belonging to the most excellent lord, the Elector Palatine,[338] where there is a University, to which my husband has been appointed by His Excellency as public lecturer, although during these wretched times people care more for arms than letters, since everything is upside down.

The bishops have a large army, which goes here and there harming the cities of the gospel, and after they had burned Schweinfurt and not left a house standing, they even burned the territory of the most pious prince there was in Germany.[339] There is great persecution in England and I hear that Father Bernardino[340] has fled to Geneva, so that in every place those who wish to be of Christ must carry the cross. But I am happier to suffer like this and be a true member of Christ than if I had the whole world, which I do not desire. I know full well that this is not the final persecution that we will have suffered, and if we live we will have to suffer many tribulations; nor are we without them at present. This city has good preachers but also priests and monks, and the situation is not clear. If only God gives me faith and steadfastness to the end, as I hope He will, since He has promised to listen to all that I ask of Him.[341] I pray to Him constantly for this and that He may grant me grace, for I, for the sake of His praise, in the face of the impious with whom all things are full, have so far never retreated a hair's breadth from religion. I do not agree in anything with the Epicureans, who in their

---

337. Elizabeth von Erbach, wife of Georg I.
338. Friedrich II of the house of Wittelsbach (r. 1544–56).
339. I.e., the count palatine.
340. Bernardino Ochino (1487–1564).
341. E.g. Matt. 7:7, 21:22, Mark 11:24, 1 John 3:22.

freedom of the flesh mistake the gospel.[342] But it is far better to suffer in this brief life than to remain forever in indescribable torment.

So I beg you, my dear sister, to take care of your salvation, and to fear Him Who created all things with a word, Him Who created you and showed you such kindness, more than a piece of flesh, which is like a wisp of straw— a little puff and how quickly it goes out.[343] If you feel that you are weak you must not excuse your weakness, for there is no greater sin than to excuse your sins. This is what David prayed for in Psalm 140: "Do not allow, O Lord, my heart to incline to excusing my sins."[344] The Psalm begins, "Lord, I have cried unto You." You must confess your weakness to God as to a doctor, and pray to Him that He will make you strong and give you grace to fear Him more than men. For this reason God is so often called in the Psalms "the God of our strength," because He makes us strong when we pray to Him.[345] He wants to be prayed to constantly. Know for certain that He will not lie, says Paul,[346] and that He is generous to all who call on Him, and recompenses them (as he says in the Letter to the Hebrews) who search for Him.[347] You must not try Him, saying "If I am of the elect I will still be saved." That is to despise the gospel with which God called you to salvation and to wish to test God. He wants these to be the means to save you: the gospel and prayer. "Faith," says Paul, "comes through hearing and hearing through the Word of God."[348] This is what he writes to the Galatians, that they have received the Holy Spirit by having heard the voice of the gospel, as is seen in the story of Cornelius, for while they were listening to the Word of the Lord the Holy Spirit fell upon them.[349]

Make sure a day does not pass without reading with devotion and praying to God through Christ that He will illuminate things for you in the Holy Scripture with the interpretation. Get up very early, a little earlier in the morning, for God wants you to seek first His kingdom,[350] and then do

---

342. Cf. 1 Cor. 8:9, 10:29. Here "Epicureans" refers primarily to those who would argue that predestination as God's elect gives them the freedom to indulge the flesh. See letters 28 and 41. Williams 1992, 414–15, 847. Curio had already written against them in 1541 (Kutter 1955, 44).
343. "ferro" *Caretti* : "fieno" *correxi*. Cf. Ps. 103:15 [102:15]: "hominis dies sunt similes faeno . . . vix ventus perstrinxit eum, non jam subsistit."
344. Cf. Ps. 141:4.
345. E.g. Ps. 18:1, 19:14, 22:19, 27:1, etc.
346. Cf. Titus 1:2, Heb. 6:18; cf. letter 28.
347. Heb. 11:6.
348. Rom. 10:17.
349. Gal. 3:2–5, Acts 10:44.
350. Matt. 6:33.

your job diligently, as God has commanded you. Serve your mistress wholeheartedly with all due honor and reverence and tell your lady that she should console herself with the Word of God, for soon we will arrive in port. Time flies as fast in afflictions as in the good times. She should console herself with the thought that she suffers together with the church, as with Christ Himself. Tell her that the lady whom I mentioned above in this letter has her own cross. She is the daughter of a duke from whose parentage and stock has come a number of Emperors, and she is content to be married to a count for nineteen years, during which there has never been an hour of health. For four weeks she has been in grave danger. I greatly feared that she would die. She is very pious and often talks of the life to come. And often, because of the Word of God, they have placed her property and life in danger.

Dear sister, pray to God as Moses did in Psalm 89: "Lord teach us that we have to die, so that we may walk wisely."[351] Seek to make God merciful. Seek God while He is to be found[352] and do not imitate the multitude of the impious unless you wish to have the reward that they will have: eternal damnation.

The Lord be with you and give you His Holy Spirit. Kiss your lady's hands for me, greet your companions and all the women and girls. I am writing to Lady Cherubina.[353] Write me a long letter so that I can learn how you are doing and how you are living. I eagerly desire letters from my dear Lady Lavinia, who is always in my heart. I have often written to her ladyship and to you but I have never had a reply. I sent her I know not how many little books. Let me know if her ladyship has received them and liked them, and don't be so slow to write. Please write me and don't be slow. It's amazing how many letters I write but no one writes me back. I sent some booklets to Lady Lavinia. Write me if she has received them. Keep yourself from idolatry. My husband and Emilio greet you.

Your sister,
Olympia Morata Grunthler.
Heidelberg, 8 August

---

351. Ps. 90:12.
352. Isa. 55:6.
353. The following letter.

Letter 46: Heidelberg, 8 August [1554] [In Italian][354]
Olympia Morata to Cherubina Orsini:

My dearest Cherubina,

You must thank God with us that He has in His great mercy freed us from the infinite dangers in which we stood for fourteen months on end. During a great famine the Lord fed us; we even had enough to give to others. He freed my husband from a pestilential fever which was in the entire city, and he was so sick for several weeks that if I had not had the eyes of faith—which look to those things which are not apparent[355] —I never would have been able to believe that he would be cured, because the symptoms of death were so clear. But the Lord, for Whom nothing is impossible,[356] and Who often works contrary to nature, cured him, and without any medicines, since due to the war no remedies could be found anymore in the pharmacy. God had mercy on me when I was in nearly intolerable pain. I have indeed proven many times what the Psalm says, that the Lord does the will of those who fear Him and listens to their prayers.[357]

As you know, my dear Cherubina, in the Scriptures fire stands for great afflictions, as is shown quite clearly by that passage in Isaiah where the Lord says that Israel should not fear, for He will be with them when they pass through the fire.[358] So it happened with us, for we passed literally through fire, not through a metaphor, rather we stood in the midst of fire. For the bishops and the others of that ilk who waged war against Schweinfurt hurled fire into the city day and night from all sides, and the artillery fired with such fury and power that the soldiers who were inside our city said that they had never heard of so many cannon shots being fired in the course of one day in any other war. In the first siege, calling the people to repentance by His goodness and His aid, God so protected His people that not even one person in the city was killed. In sum, God demonstrated His power in defending that city and freeing it from so many evils. In the end, however, through treachery, they got in unexpectedly, when it had been promised that they were going to leave at the command of the Emperor and the other princes. They

---

354. Curio supplied a Latin translation and later printed the Italian text of this and letter 47 in ed. of 1570.
355. Cf. Heb. 11:1.
356. Matt. 19:26, Mark 10:27, Luke 1:37, 18:27.
357. Ps. 115:11–13, cf. 147:11.
358. Isa. 43:2. The quotations and exegesis of Isaiah seem to show the influence of Calvin's recent *Ioannis Caluini Commentarii in Isaiam prophetam* (Basel), first published in 1551. Morata had requested the commentary on Jeremiah; see letters 42 and 52.

took everything there was in the city and set it on fire. The Lord delivered us from the flames, and through the advice of one of the enemy we escaped the fire. Then my husband was captured twice by the enemy, and I swear to you, if I ever felt pain I felt it then and if I ever prayed ardently, I prayed then. In my anguished heart I cried with inexpressible groans,[359] "Help me, help me, Lord, through Christ," and I did not cease until He helped me and freed him. I would like you to have seen how disheveled I was, covered in rags, after they tore the clothes off of us! While we were running away, I lost my shoes and had no stockings for my feet. I was forced to flee over rocks and stones—how I got there I don't know. Often I said, "Now I will fall down and die. I can't go on any longer." Then I said to God, "Lord, if You want me to live, command Your angels to lift me, for truly I cannot." I am still amazed when I think about how I covered those ten miles on the first day. I thought I had lost everything. I was so thin and ill and I fell sick the next day. Because of the exhaustion I caught a tertian fever, and I was ill throughout the journey. The Lord had not abandoned us, although everything had been taken from us, right down to the clothes on our bodies, for while we were still on the road He gave to us fifteen scudi by the hands of a gentleman we did not even know. He led us to other gentlemen, who clothed us honorably. Finally we came to be in this town, Heidelberg, where my husband had been made public lecturer in medicine and we now have as many household possessions as before.

I have written you this letter so that you may thank the Lord and realize that He does not abandon His people in their difficulties, so that you may be confirmed in faith that He will not leave you, although it might be necessary for you to suffer some things for the truth, since we must be, as Paul says, "conformed to the image of Christ" and suffer with Him, so that we may reign with Him.[360] The crown is not given except to those who compete,[361] and if you feel weak, my dear Lady Cherubina, as I still am—but the Lord strengthens me when I call on Him and pray to Him—then go to Christ, Who, as Isaiah says, will not break the shaken reed, that is, a weak and frightened conscience.[362] He will not frighten it further but rather console it, even as He calls to Himself all those who are heavy-laden with sins and weary.[363] Nor will He snuff out the wick that smokes, that is, he who is weak in faith;

---

359. Cf. 2 Cor. 2:4 and Rom. 8:26.
360. Rom. 8:29–30.
361. Cf. 1 Cor. 9:24–25, and also letter 3 above.
362. Isa. 42:3.
363. Matt. 11:28.

He will not cast him forth from Himself but make him strong.[364] Do you not know that Isaiah calls Him "mighty" and "gigantic,"[365] not only because He conquered the Devil, Sin, Hell, and Death, but also because he continues to conquer all His enemies in those who are His members and makes them strong. Why then do the Scriptures invite us so often to pray and promise us that we will be heard, unless we should go in all our ills and infirmities to our Great Physician? Why did David call Him "God of my strength," unless He made him strong.[366] So shall He be for you, but He wishes to be prayed to and that we study His Word, which is the food of the soul.[367] And if our body loses its strength when it does not have food, how will our soul be strong if it is not sustained by the Word of God?

So, my Lady Cherubina, be continually at prayer and read the Scriptures both by yourself and together with the Lady Lavinia and with Vittoria. Exhort her to piety. Pray together and you will see that God will give you enough strength to conquer the world, and you will do nothing against your conscience out of fear. Do you think He is lying when He says, "Truly, truly, I say unto you, if you ask anything of the Father in my name, He will give it to you" and "If two or three are gathered together on earth, and pray about something, I will do it"?[368] We feel His absence when we are weak, because we do not pray to Him.[369] As long as you are not too tired to pray, you will see that God will make you strong. And pray for us, as I pray for all the Christians who are in Italy, that the Lord make us constant, so that we may be able to confess Him in the midst of this perverse generation.[370] Here there is great contempt for the Word of God and very few care for it. We have idolatry and the Word of God both together, as they did in Samaria.[371] I've been hoping to have my dear mother with me, but everything is full of war. I must expect the consolation of being able to see her in the next life. The pious here do not lack the cross. May the Lord give us all faith and constancy, so that we may conquer the world.

Praise God, I want to write you about how I saw a great miracle during our persecution. We were in the court of certain lords of Germany, who had

---

364. Also Isa. 42:3.
365. Cf. Isa. 9:6; "forte e gigante": I have found no obvious source for the adjective "gigante."
366. See n. 345 above.
367. Cf. Deut. 8:3, Matt. 4:4, Luke 4:4.
368. John 14:13; and a paraphrase of Matt. 18:19.
369. "manca da voi" Caretti : "noi" correxi.
370. Deut. 32:5, Matt. 17:17, Luke 9:41, Phil. 2:15.
371. Acts 8:5–25: the story of Simon Magus.

placed their lives and fortunes at risk for the sake of the gospel, and who live lives so holy that I was amazed.[372] One lord has preachers in his city, and he is always the first to go to church. Then every morning before breakfast he calls together his whole household—not one of them must remain behind—and in his presence they read from the gospel and the letters of St. Paul. He gets down on his knees, and he and his entire court pray to the Lord. Then each of his subjects, house by house, must give him an account of their faith—the ladies of the house and everyone—so that he can see what progress they are making in religion. For as he says, he knows well[373] that if he did not do so, he would be the one obliged to give an account of all the souls of his subjects. I would that all the lords and princes were like that.

The Lord give you faith and increase you in your knowledge of Him,[374] because we ought to pray to Him constantly to increase in faith. For this the ways of the Lord summon us, for we ought not to stop as if we were perfect, but we should always walk onwards and increase in perfection.[375] Study the Scriptures diligently.

Emilio, by the grace of God, is safe and sound. I hope he will fear God—he listens to the sermons quite willingly and studies the Scriptures. I pray constantly for him and our whole household that they fear the Lord. My husband and I and Emilio greet you with all our heart. If Lady Lavinia is willing to write to me, her ladyship will be able to find ways and means. This city is very famous for its court and for its University.

Your Olympia

Letter 47: [Addendum to the above] [In Italian]

After I wrote my first letter, I wanted to add this second one to exhort you to pray to God to make you strong, so that you do not, through fear of those who can kill only the body, offend our sweet Lord, Who suffered everything for our sake. So, in order to be pleasing to Him you must confess Him, as He desires you to, before this perverse generation. Remember what David says: "I hate the congregation of the unrighteous and with the impious I shall not sit."[376]

---

372. The counts of Erbach.
373. "che fa bene" Caretti : "sa bene" correxi.
374. Cf. Heb. 6:1, Col. 1:10.
375. Cf. Phil. 3:12.
376. Ps. 26:5. See her metrical translation below.

Now, perhaps you'll say, "I'm weak, I can't do it." Do you think that all the saints and prophets, all the martyrs—of our time, too—were strong because of their own virtue and not because God made them strong? Think on those in the Scriptures who were weak but who did not stay weak forever. St. Peter denied Him. He is not given as an example for us to imitate, but so that we might recognize our fragility and not excuse it, and recognize the great mercy of Christ. He was not weak forever, but was made so strong that he later rejoiced to suffer for Christ. So we too, sensing our weakness, ought to approach the Great Physician with prayers and pray to Him to make us strong. For if we pray to Him, He will not fail in His promise. He does not want us to be lazy and idle but to be constantly at practice, armed with the weapons that St. Paul writes about in Ephesians, chapter 5.[377] We have a most powerful enemy who never ceases, but Christ has given us an example of how we can conquer him, that is, through prayer and through the Word of God.[378]

So by the love of Christ, Who has redeemed you with His precious blood, I beg you to study the Scriptures diligently, praying to the Lord that He enlighten you about them. Look at David, the great prophet, how often and with what ardor he prayed. "Lord, enlighten me. Teach me your ways. Create in me a clean heart."[379] Yet we, as if we were perfect, read and study nothing. No less a man than Paul writes to the Philippians that he has not yet obtained it but that he strives to obtain it.[380] We ought to increase day by day in knowledge of the Lord, and pray together with the apostles to increase in faith, and with David: "Keep my steps on your paths."[381] It is our fault that we are weak, because we excuse our weakness and do not use the remedies that Christ ordained, namely prayer and His Word. Do you think that He Who did and suffered everything because of His love for you will not listen to you when you pray to Him to make you strong, when you have all His sweet promises? If He were unwilling to listen to you, He would not have called you with so many promises. And so that you may not doubt, He has sworn that everything that you demand of the Father in His name He will give you. And he doesn't say that He's willing to give you just this

---

377. Eph. 6:11–17, in the modern numeration.
378. Caretti (1940, 110) and Kössling and Weiss-Stahlin (1990, 108) punctuate this sentence as a quotation. The references are to Christ's temptation in the wilderness (Matt. 4:1–11, Luke 4:1–13) and to Mark 9:29 (cf. Matt. 17:21).
379. Ps. 13:3, 25:4, 51:10.
380. Phil. 3:12–13.
381. Ps. 17:5.

or that, but everything that you ask for. And St. John says that if we ask something in accordance with God's will, He will listen to us.[382] Now to ask Him to give you faith and strength, so that you may confess Him, is that not in accordance with His will? Ah, how cold we are, and then we excuse ourselves! We ought to show our weaknesses to the Physician, and He will cure us. Is it not Christ's special role to save us from our sins and to conquer sin? "Knock, knock, and the door will be opened for you."[383] Remember that He is omnipotent, that if your hour has not come no one can harm a hair of your head.[384] What is in us is stronger than what is in the world. No longer consider what the vast majority does, but what the saints have done and continue to do right down to the present. Let the Word of the Lord be a lamp unto your feet; if you do not read or hear it, you will trip over the great stumbling blocks of the world.[385] I beg you to read this letter to Vittoria and to exhort her with your example and words to honor and confess God. Read the Scriptures with her. My dear Lady Lavinia, beg for her to read to you often something from the Scriptures, and you will feel the power of the Word of God. I have written you this, desiring your salvation. God knows, I pray that you will do so. I pray to the Lord that He will enlighten you and strengthen you through Christ, so that you may conquer Satan, the world, and your flesh, and gain the crown which will be given only to those who have conquered.[386] I know for certain that if you obey my admonitions, you will see that the Lord will strengthen you. Ignore the fact that I am a woman when I advise you. Rather be certain that God is graciously inviting you to Himself with words spoken through my mouth. All the false opinions, all the errors, all the disputes occur only because the Scriptures are not read diligently. David says, "You have made me wiser than my enemies with your laws."[387] Ignore the impious words of some who disparage the commandments of God and the means of salvation ordained by Him by saying, "If I am predestined I shall be saved, even if I don't study the Scriptures or pray." He who is predestined and called by God will not speak such blasphemy, but will strive to obey God rather than test Him. God does us the favor and honor of talking to us through His Scriptures. He teaches us, consoles us,

---

382. 1 John 5:14; cf. John 14:13–14, 15:7, 15:16, 16:23–26.
383. Matt. 7:7; Luke 11:9.
384. Luke 21:18; cf. Matt. 10:30, Luke 12:7, Acts 27:34.
385. Ps. 119:105; and cf. 1 Pet. 2:8.
386. 1 Cor. 9:25, 2 Tim. 4:8, James 1:12, 1 Pet. 5:4, Rev. 2:10; cf. Rom. 8:37.
387. Ps. 119:98.

and will we then disparage such a treasure? He invites us to pray,[388] but we, abandoning all the means ordained by God, and being lazy, keep on disputing about the high counsels of the Lord, about what will happen. Let us use the remedies He left us, and that way we will show that we are the obedient children of God and so predestined. Read how much God wants His Word to be honored: "Faith," says Paul, "comes through hearing and hearing through the Word of God."[389] I promise you that if we are lazy, faith and charity grow quickly cold again. And as Christ says, it does not mean anything to have begun, but one must persevere to the end.[390] "He who stands," says Paul, "let him take care lest he fall."[391] I pray you by the love of Christ to govern yourself according to the Word of God and not the opinion of men. Let it be a lamp to your feet; otherwise Satan will be able to ensnare you in various ways. Pass on my exhortations to my sister. Don't consider the person who talks to you; rather consider if she speaks her own words or those of God. If you do so, you will know what you must do if the Scriptures will be the rule of your life and not the authority of any mere person. Ask, search, knock, and it will be opened to you. Go to your dear bridegroom, think on Him in His Word. Truly it is a clear mirror in which shines all the knowledge you need. May God through Christ make it that I have not written in vain, even while suffering pain in my stomach. But may God grant that with my death I might to be able to help you and others to salvation.

Please write me one letter about how you are doing.
Your Olympia

Letter 48: Würzburg, 25 July 1554
Dr. Johannes Sinapius to Dr. Andreas Grunthler:

Although I am not certain whether you've reached Heidelberg yet, most learned Andreas, and my brother wrote me on 20 August from Speyer that he had heard nothing of your arrival, nevertheless, because I hope for what I pray for, and because Herr Hartmann thought it was true, I gave a letter for our Olympia to Herr Hartmann back on 4 July.[392] I included in it a letter which certain canons, our fellow countrymen, brought from Italy, and now

---

388. "ci invita e pregare" Coretti : "a" correxi.
389. Rom. 10:17; cf. letter 45 above.
390. Matt. 10:22, 24:13, Mark 13:13.
391. 1 Cor. 10:12. One of the proof-texts against the vulgar conception of predestination.
392. Harmann Hartmanni (1523–86), emissary from the count palatine.

I pass it on by means of Herr *Vitus* Grumbach, together with the *Vitae* or *Parallel Lives* of Plutarch, so that *Vitus* may restore these dead *Lives*, if you'll pardon the pun.[393] I know you are more intelligent and philosophical than those who are terrified or even prostrated by every loss or danger, although yours were great. No, if the world were to collapse, the ruins would strike you unafraid.[394] What do we have that we were not given? What did we bring into this world when we were born? Is it any wonder if God Who gave it asks back what is His? Let those grieve who lost their reason with their possessions. Your treasure is in heaven, which thieves cannot break through and steal nor fire burn.[395] Like that wise man of old, you take your goods with you whenever you set out: your piety, learning, reputation, and all good virtues and good letters.[396]

But what am I doing trying to teach fish how to swim or bringing wood to a forest? Back to the Plutarch. Word was brought to me a few days ago that some tombstones had been pried loose from the graves and walls of Schweinfurt and some of them had been brought here secretly. I looked for the epitaph of my father among them, which indeed I found and recovered. I also heard that a book from Schweinfurt was being sold. I immediately asked from whom, to whom, which book, and for how much! And so I recovered this copy of Plutarch's *Lives*. When I saw Olympia's name inscribed on the last page at the back, and that of a certain Paulus Silva (perhaps Magnolus Brixius?), I paid the price on the spot, and I'm sending it to you like a captive prisoner redeemed from the pirates. I asked around diligently to see if anything else was there of your clothes or books, offering the price and a reward in addition. But I didn't find anything. I would give it to you most willingly if I could somehow undo in any small way part of the enormous loss you have suffered. I take this disaster so bitterly, for your sake, for the sake of my sister's children, and for my own sake, both because of what's happened to the country and what's happened privately.

I can only hope that our Olympia may pity her most innocent city and think it worthy to avenge her own and her city's disaster with the pen, since greater vengeance belongs to God. I want it as much as possible but I cannot do it, so distracted am I by all sorts of cares and worries. And due to

---

393. *Vitus* as the Latinization of Veit Grumbach.
394. Cf. Hor. *Odes* 3.3.7–8.
395. Matt. 6:19–20; cf. Luke 12:33.
396. Cf. Cic. *Para.* 1.1.8–9, referring to Bias of Priene, one of the traditional Seven Wise Men. It is interesting to see here near the end of Morata's life a reference from an old friend to the book on which she gave orations when she was a girl.

advancing old age, I'm tired not only of things of this sort, of elegies and threnodies, but of myself, so much so that with this weariness of the spirit I am too tired even to teach my daughter, who had so happily laid the foundations of grammar with Olympia, and whom her mother, even as she was dying, wanted more than anything else to learn Latin.[397] It was naturally always my intention, once the siege of Schweinfurt was lifted, to send her back to you so that she could resume her interrupted studies. But alas, how uncertain, vain, and blind are the counsels of men. However, I have not lost heart if you have made your way to Heidelberg, and I shall even, if I can ask this favor of you, send her to you in a while. Johannes Cremer is returning to Schweinfurt and offers all his help in restoring learning to the young. His wife and son were my guests for a couple of days, and they went back home a few days ago with their relative, Herr Johannes Bellermann. A little house survived which they have the use of for tutoring certain pupils, and they are planning to spend the winter in it. But I am afraid that since they are going to have such accommodations, they will not be able to take my daughter. I will not mention the fact that I can't believe that anyone could build on the foundation that has been laid with the same dexterity that Olympia has shown. Many of my friends are advising me to send her away to some court or other for this purpose. But where can this happen better than in Heidelberg, where she'd be in a court, and with the best teacher and the one she's used to? If you are still in Fürstenau or are going to stay there longer, I hope that a place can be obtained for her with the help of my patron, the excellent Daniel Stibar.[398]

I urgently ask you to let me know not only what the state of your affairs has been, but what it is now, and what you hope it will be. Four days ago a letter carrier from Basel was at my house. I used him to write to my close friend Michael Isingrin, the bookseller at Basel, about the destruction of Schweinfurt and how pitiably our cities had been treated.[399] I added a little about you both so that he could pass it on to his neighbor and friend, Caelius Secundus, who loves you both dearly. That way, if he has any words of consolation, since he is a pious man and extremely fond of Olympia, he can write to you at Heidelberg and send letters to my brother Dr. Chilian Sinapius at Speyer.

My bother Conrad sends his greetings, as do my daughter Theodora and my niece Brigida, also Leonora, who is teaching them both to embroider.

---

397. See document 4.
398. Daniel Stibar (Stieber) (1503–55), canon of Würzberg.
399. "tractati sint" 1570 : "sunt" *Flood and Shaw*.

Greetings also from the licentiate Faius, formerly a monk at Banz and now master of the household to the countess of Holech. Be well, together with Emilio and all your friends. If you have made it to Heidelberg, give the most respectful greetings in my words to the noble Hubert, the son-in-law of the noble Andreas Gottwald, who is naturally very fond of you both, and the most excellent Hartmann.[400]

Würzburg, 25 July 1554.

P.S. Theodora hadn't gotten up yet when I was writing this at dawn; otherwise she would have added her own letter. I'll add it later, when we're more certain about your situation.

Letter 49: [Heidelberg, c. August 1554]
Olympia Morata to Dr. Johannes Sinapius:

We've received your letter, which master Veit passed on to us. I could not reply to your earlier one, which was given to me while I was lying in bed, held up by sickness at Fürstenau. Now I'll reply briefly to both. First I give you great thanks, because you show how much you wish us well from the bottom of your heart.[401] So you should know that we have been treated with great kindness and gifts,[402] first by the illustrious count of Rieneck, and then by his most noble relatives, the counts of Erbach. A few days ago we made it to Heidelberg. My husband is preparing his lectures. I was totally occupied today in buying furniture so that we can move into our house. Up to this point we've been staying at the home of a certain good man. I have written to our Cremer and asked him urgently to send me an old woman to be a cook, one of the wretched, poor, and wandering citizens of Schweinfurt, and I eagerly expect her any day. As for your wanting your daughter to stay with me, I want you to know that she would be most welcome, both so that she might alleviate my sickness in these foreign parts and also that I might do a favor for your wife, even though she is dead. As far as it is in me I will never fail her, and I will embrace her with more kindness even than before, now that she has lost her mother. So if you want to send her to me and not to a court (for I plan to spend my life far from courts), I ask you to do it as soon as possible. Please arrange it with Cremer to send her along with the maid (I entrusted to him the business of asking for one several days ago) and a bed of her own, since I can't at present buy so many beds, and they are

---

400. See letter 43 above.
401. "nobis te <bene> velle significas" : *supplevi*.
402. "magnis" 1562 1570 : "magis" *Caretti, Flood and Shaw*.

very expensive here. And could they bring the knapsack with the remains of what has been recovered of our things? I could take her often with me to the illustrious counts of Erbach, whose probity and holiness I can vouch for. Count Erbach has three daughters, beautiful and piously educated, with whom she can enjoy friendship and intimacy. Do what is best for her, and if you want to send her to me, don't wait for the maid, although you can guess how inconvenient it is to be without one. More later.

I thank you so much for the Plutarch. Greet everyone in your family and the licentiate Faius, since he is no longer a monk. My husband greets you all and my brother, who would write to Theodora if he weren't so taken up with household business. Good-by to you all.

Letter 50: [Schweinfurt, after August 1554]
[Johannes Cremer] to Olympia Grunthler:

I will reply briefly to your letter sent to me from Heidelberg on 1 August.[403] Of course, I spare no labor or effort to send you as soon as possible an old woman or a maidservant who will be eager to carry out her orders, but I have made little progress so far. What can I do when so many people of either sex are still sick and a great number have made their departure from this life, and many are dying day after day? Every time I cross the square here, I always run into people who are either sick, or can scarcely drag around their weak bodies, or look like they will soon be confined to bed. In the last few days Leonard Zeul has fallen asleep in Christ. I was at his house the day before, encouraging him to console himself with the gentle and sweet words of our Redeemer and high priest Jesus Christ, Who bids all to come to Him who want to enjoy eternal life. And I am sure that he was submissive to me, or rather not to me, but to Christ Himself, whose words these are. Laurenz Rosa has also died, and also Ludovic Scheffer of the same disease or one very similar to it which you told me your husband had suffered.[404] He was just buried on the twelfth of August. He was confined to bed for about two days, during which time he was unable to say a single word. Jaundice followed. Sinapius, summoned by a letter from me, offered what help he could, but the medicine that might have been able to bring him back from death's door arrived here too late. My stepfather is suffering from tertian fever. But why

---

403. The letter is lost. The name of the writer is not given in the 1570 ed. However, cf. letter 49, where Morata asks that Cremer be in charge of this matter. See Kössling and Weiss-Stählin 1990, 206.
404. Laurenz Rosa, father of Andreas (see letter 51).

write so much? The majority of our dwindling number of citizens still are not terrified by the heavy wrath of God. What the future will be you can easily guess.

But to return to the point from which I digressed. I am working as hard as I can every day for you to have a cook, but I'm not getting anywhere. Your maidservant's mother, whose name is Kunigunde, has promised that she will be your servant, but a fever prevents her, so that what you hoped for can't happen for a couple of days. If you can wait just until she gets better the matter will be taken care of. If the delay will cause you difficulty let me know. I don't doubt that your Barbara, who was at my house yesterday with Conrad's wife, will do for you if you can put up with her habits.[405] Let me know personally what you think and how you feel. There'll be no delay on my part. However, you should know that there are few or no maids I know of who would be suitable for you. So take a look at what you want to do, for there's no advice or help to be found in me.

As soon as your money is brought here it will be distributed according to your wishes, and it will leave nothing for you to desire. The poor people in the hospital whom you know and have been worried about have all been scattered in the recent flight from town, and no one knows where on earth they are. I have decided to spend the winter here with my wife and parents, if our God wills it, to whom I give and shall give thanks as long as I live, for everything that I had buried in the ground because of the madness of our soldiers I found still untouched, so that I can keep myself reasonably alive. If I lack anything I know that He Who has looked out for me so far will alleviate my want. Since I commit to Him my very soul, the most important thing of all, why not this insubstantial little body?[406] Be well, together with your husband and all Christians. Remember us in your prayers to our high priest.

Letter 51: [Schweinfurt, 1554?]
Andreas Rosa to Olympia Morata, distinguished for her piety and learning.[407]

Since congratulations, even when tardy, are usually not unwelcome, (although yours, O chaste Olympia, the glory of womankind both for piety and for wisdom, were almost the first to come to me), I hope that this response, delayed not by negligence nor by forgetfulness of our earlier friendship, but

---

405. Morata's maid, apparently.
406. "quid in corpusculum" 1570 : "quid ni" *correxi*.
407. Schoolteacher in Schweinfurt. Saffert 1993, 519–20.

rather by the distance between us and the lack of letter carriers, cannot but be favorably regarded by you.[408] My regard for you and your husband, that most illustrious and excellent man, who has been most friendly to me, and though separated by distance yet how closely joined by kindness, I trust is obvious from it. How clearer than the evening star your regard for me shone out from your last letter in two things: first, in the pain and great grief which I saw you had felt for my misfortunes; second, in giving me friendly advice, that I should devote myself entirely to the study of letters so that I might better administer a gift sent from God. So even if I had thought that I should do this another time, or if I had thought differently, your earnest and friendly advice would have changed my mind and encouraged me towards studies. Please dismiss any grief I may have caused you from your mind and help me (now that I have emerged so recently from these waves of fortune) and my studies. That is, please write out for me the psalms which I hear and understand you are rendering into Greek verse, a work you began at Schweinfurt, or after your most beloved husband, Dr. Andreas, who is so friendly to me, has set them to music. You could do nothing that would please me more.

Next: I was glad to send your letter to the wife, or rather the widow, of Johannes Lindemann of pious memory, and to his son, just as I had promised.[409] If I can do anything for you in the future, I promise that I, my aid, and my labor will not be lacking. Goodbye.

Letter 52: Basel, 1 September 1554
Caelius Secundus Curio to Olympia Morata:[410]

Dear Olympia,

You have an all too just excuse for not having replied to my letter, which, if it can be said just short of impropriety, I would have preferred that you had not. But what can you do? "So it seemed to the gods," as the poet said, about things unknown to us,[411] but not unknown to God. And so we must submit our judgment to His divine judgment, and venerate His counsels as hidden but nonetheless just. In your letter you have given me clear examples of both

---

408. Morata's early letter to this young man is lost, but seems to have contained an exhortation to learning similar to that given Michael Weber in letter 32.

409. Morata wrote a Greek poem in his honor. See below.

410. The response to letters 41 and 42. This letter is preserved in autograph in the Basel University Library: its text (B) differs slightly from that of the published edition. A portion of it is reproduced in Kössling and Weiss-Stählin 1990, 121 and the additional text on 217. The deletions from the autograph are enclosed with angled brackets: < >.

411. Ver. A. 3.2; and cf. 2.428.

divine severity and divine mercy: of His severity in the destruction of your hometown, of His mercy and pity in your salvation from the flames and your continued safety through so many threatening dangers. I do not doubt that, at that time especially as at others, you felt how great is the power of faith within a religious spirit and how great is the power of divine providence, which is always there for those in danger and distress. And especially when God, the Father of Jesus Christ and our Father, pitied you when you were most wretched and restored your best and most loving husband to health, even though he was afflicted with a mortal illness and no remedies could be used. And then He freed him from the enemy, though he had been captured twice, as a favor to your inexpressible groans ("unutterable," as you wrote in Greek).[412] And then He guided you to those best and pious heroes by whom your calamity was somewhat alleviated. And finally, your most learned husband was elected to the University of Heidelberg to explicate the books of the physicians at the summons of the most wise Duke Palatine.

Despoiled and stripped of all your goods, you barely avoided the fire. But that's not so, for you and your husband carried off all your possessions with you, just like Bias of Priene: your talent, learning, wisdom, innocence, piety, faith, and all the other things counted as true "goods."[413] You left behind playthings, not *your* goods but those of Fortune, which are scarcely worth being numbered as goods; that's what the enemy took. If they had been truly yours, the enemy could never have taken them away from you. Since that's the way things are, as long as you are safe I think I have no reason to grieve. I think you should do the same; give thanks to God your preserver that just as you were partners in calamities and afflictions, so now you are partners in the piety of a grateful soul.

About the books, I wrote to your husband about what had to be done. I have instructed my printer that the Homer you are looking for, along with some of my own books, should be sent to you as a gift with my compliments from Frankfurt. If the commentary on the Lamentations of Jeremiah[414] can be found at Frankfurt, I'll make sure you get it, for I see that you are thinking about the grief of your husband's city. So come, give us a "little Heracles" of a work, so that we can crown you with the laurels which you have long deserved.[415]

---

412. n. 325.
413. n. 396.
414. θρήνους.
415. "Sophocleum" 1562 1570 : ἡρακλείδιον B.

The man who is delivering this letter to you is named Johannes Herold, <a good fellow, and especially well-educated.>[416] He is very eager to get a look at you and asked me to use my letter to open the doors to a friendship with you, so that he might be allowed to venerate the sacred prophetess. I ask you <for both of you> to receive him <as you would receive me personally>, and let him know that he owes some part of it not only to your kindness but also to my commendation.[417] I want to have some news about Fulvio's brother,[418] and if you have any news about your mother and sisters. Farewell, my Olympia; be well, O glory of our Italy.

Basel, 1 September 1554

<My wife gives you many greetings, as do my children. I have joined my eldest daughter to an Italian doctor in Strassburg.[419] He gives public lectures alternately on divine letters and on Aristotle's *Physics*. My eldest son, Orazio, nineteen, returned last June from Italy as a doctor of medicine. Again, goodbye. Signed by my own hand. C.S.>[420]

Letter 53: [Heidelberg, 1554]
Olympia Fulvia Morata to Andreas Campanus:[421]

Because of my ill health, the day before yesterday I was forced to hire whatever cook I could find here, who asked a florin a month, and only on condition that she be allowed to do work for herself. The people here have no shame! But since necessity is a cruel weapon,[422] I hired her for one month at that wage. But because I couldn't manage these expenses even if I were a satrap, I earnestly ask you and your parish priest to give me help in the meanwhile so that after this month there's a prospect of a different servant, either an old woman (which I'd prefer), or a young girl. I promise that I

---

416. "vir bonus, et comprimis [i.e. cum primis] eruditus" B. Basilius Johannes Herold (1511—post 1566), humanist and editor in Basel.

417. "ut sic illum accipias" 1562 1570 : "ut ambo sic illum accipiatis, ut me praesentem acciperetis" B || "aliquid debere" 1562 1570 : "aliquam debere partem" B.

418. "De Aemilio fratre" 1562 1570 : "De Fulvi fratre" B.

419. The theologian Hieronymus Zanchius (Girolamo Zanchi), professor at Neustadt an der Haardt and leading architect of reformed orthodoxy within Lutheranism (Bonnet 1856, 162; Kutter 1955, 257–59). See letter 69.

420. 1562 1570: "My wife and children, whom you asked me to greet, greet you and yours in turn. They wish you from the heart all the best and all honor."

421. Campanus (Glock), fellow citizen of Schweinfurt with Grunthler, now schoolteacher in Mosbach am Neckar. Saffert 1993, 519.

422. Livy 4.28.5.

will give a woman five florins. I ask you to give me your help in this matter; you will find me mindful and grateful. The little girl I talked to you about—immediately after you left, a man brought her to us in a box; she was sick herself.

Be well, together with your wife and family. My husband greets you. I ask you to pass on my greetings in my words to your wife and parish priest, and apologize to him if he was not received by us as he deserved: the fever had already attacked me. Goodbye.

Letter 54: Heidelberg, 1 December [1554]
Olympia Fulvia Morata to Caelius Secundus Curio:

You shouldn't wonder why, most learned Caelius, I haven't sent you any letters for a while: an illness has held me up. You'll be able to guess how strong it was by the fact that yesterday it deprived me of my senses. I swear to you with every oath that I was called back from the dead by God, "And I declared that I would see the dead and the house of Hades / On this day."[423] Now that I've recovered from a great and deadly illness (though I haven't completely recovered my strength), I don't think I should do anything before leaving a sworn statement in your mind[424] with this little letter about how hard I take it that there's no way I can pay back proper thanks to you for your kindness. Please say the same to our friend Johannes Herold, and give enormous thanks to him and those most learned and cultured men, Isingrin, Oporin, Herwagen, Froben, and Episcopius, who gave me so many splendid authors.[425] No forgetfulness will ever erase our memory of such meritorious acts.

Here many people are afraid for themselves because of the plague and are getting ready to escape. However, it has taken only a few from our midst, and has affected us not a bit. But we commend and entrust ourselves totally to God. My husband asks me to add his greetings. Greet your wife and children. Be sure to stay well.

Heidelberg, 1 Dec.

---

423. *Il.* 15.251. τῷ 1570 : πῷ Caretti.
424. Cic. *Fam.* 2.3.1.
425. The honor roll of printers in Basel: Michael Isingrin (1500–57), Johannes Oporin (1507–68), Johannes Herwagen (c. 1497–1558), Hieronymus Froben (1501–63), Episcopius (Nikolaus Bischoff) (1501–64).

Letter 55: Heidelberg, 24 December [1554]
Andreas Grunthler to Andreas Campanus:

I have read what you wrote me about those boys, your sister's children. It was the same as the licentiate Melchior had indicated to me. If he had been able to return to you, there would have been no need of this letter. I pointed out to him, as was the case, that I know nothing of the people and places here, and so can't know where or with whom he could best make provision. Further, I too was tossed out by that same shipwreck and I have scarcely recovered as yet, and since I have more than enough to do at home, I cannot take care of anyone else's business, and I don't have enough time to do so.

However, because of our common hometown, or rather because of the ashes of our common hometown, I earnestly desire that provision be made for them, nor will I cease to inquire until I find something certain that I can tell you about this matter. That way in the meanwhile I can be of aid, if not to all, then at least to one person and to his studies. If I knew more about the progress of the elder of the boys, perhaps even now I would be able to write you something definite. If he had progressed to the point where he could listen to public lectures with profit, I would take him into my house so that he could visit the public schools in the company of Emilio, who is my wife's brother, a boy twelve years old. However, I won't be able to do that before January 13. I already have two other boys at my house who moved here after the flight from Schweinfurt, and whom I have taken care of without payment for four months now with, to be frank, the greatest difficulty. I have nothing to live on except hope. Our most illustrious count invited me here with a respectable stipend, to which the University contributed not a little, but so far nothing has been paid (for the date for payment has not arrived). Whatever money I have I brought with me, some rescued from the ruins, some given by certain heroes. It has all been spent on books, clothing, beds, and other furniture, so that frankly there's not a penny left. I still have a few gold necklaces and rings, which I would be glad to sell or preferably pawn to someone for a reasonable amount of money. However, there is no one here who will loan money without usury, much less merely interest. In this matter then, please see what aid you can be to me! If there is anyone where you are who can lend me twenty florins, I can send him a gold necklace as collateral and set a day for repayment. I could perhaps do this here, but I don't want the story to get out. So take a look, please, and let me know.

What I said about January 13: the reason is that one of the boys who is with me now will leave on that date.

Be well and remember me as I remember you.

Letter 56: Heidelberg, 5 Jan. 1555
Andreas Grunthler to Andreas Campanus, the schoolteacher:

I have received the twenty gold pieces which you sent me. I realize they had been gathered by you previously, since the number squares up exactly, with each one containing twenty groschen. It only remains to come to an agreement about repayment. You should know that on 24 Feb., sixty gold pieces from my salary are owed me. As soon as they are counted out, twenty will be sent to you so that you'll know that I've been not only a faithful but indeed a grateful debtor.

About the boy, do whatever you think about his case. Please do not hesitate to call on me if you need anything in the matter. My wife would like to have a girl about ten or twelve years old with her, who might do some light household tasks and occasionally follow her to church. If you have any advice in this matter, we ask you to let us know.

We hope to talk with you as soon as you get here. So whenever you have a free moment, fly here. My wife greets you along with everyone.

Heidelberg, 5 January, in the year of our Lord (which I hope will a happy and prosperous one to you all) 1555.

Letter 57: Heidelberg, 25 January 1555
Olympia Fulvia Morata to Andreas Campanus:

Since my husband is not home, I have nothing to write about in answer to your letter, except that I still need a girl badly. So if you could send your niece or some other suitable girl to me as soon as possible, you'd be doing something I'd be very grateful for. Because it's my husband's hometown, I am very well disposed towards the people of Schweinfurt. Whomever you send to me will get no injuries from us and will be piously educated. Be sure to stay well and either send a girl to us, or, what would be even more pleasing, bring her yourself, if it can be done with no inconvenience. Greet your wife in my name.

Letter 58: Heidelberg, 26 January [1555]
Olympia Fulvia Morata to Chilian Sinapius, in Jesus Christ:

I haven't replied to your letter, because we thought that our boy who had set out for your house to deliver the citrons[426] had told you, as we explicitly

---

426. Widely regarded as an antidote.

ordered him to, that we could give no help to your relative you wrote to us about, even though we have worked very hard to make it possible to provide for another of those whom we have been feeding for so many months now; but we were unable to accomplish anything.[427] Andreas Campanus still urges us to accept his nephew. Believe me, if we could help all the citizens of Schweinfurt, nothing would be more pleasing and welcome to us. Even Andreas Rosa, the schoolmaster, has written us that he is spending his life in dire poverty and would like to put his efforts into educating boys here, but the plague prevents him. If you can do anything (for you can do more than we), help those miserable people and bend all your thoughts, you and Gotwald, on helping your hometown. We are trying as much as is within us.

From the letter which I just got from Italy, I gather that the Christians at Ferrara are being punished cruelly; they are sparing neither high nor low. Some are being put in chains, others are being exiled, others are planning on flight. Be sure to let me know anything about your brother. My husband greets you and says hello to your wife and to Andreas Gotwald.

Heidelberg, 26 Jan.

Letter 59: [Mosbach am Neckar], 31 January 1555
Andreas Campanus to Olympia Morata, most
modest as well as famed for her remarkable erudition:

I would have sent my girl with the letter carrier, Olympia, most learned of all, except that she has suddenly fallen ill. She has developed two sores under her armpit this week of a type which I have never seen before. In addition, my mother has at long last begun to lose her mind and various types of illnesses are starting to attack my nephews, so that on all sides I have to work very hard. Therefore, in this matter, in so brief a period of time, I am not able to give you as much help as the matter calls for, since I too am disappointed. I wanted to let you know by letter as soon as possible so that you would not let any more suitable women go because you were relying on this hope.

I need commentaries on Cicero's *Letters to Atticus*. If there are any for sale I ask that they be bought for me; if not that, at least someone would loan them to me for a few days or the space of a week. I would gratefully promise to return them unharmed. Farewell, three times and four times, with your most distinguished husband.

Given 31 Jan. 1555.

---

427. "cum non mediocriter laboraverimus, ut alteri ex istis, quos iam tot menses aluimus hîc, prospici posset: sed nihil effecimus" 1562: "aluimus; hic prospici posset, sed *sic interpunx.*" Caretti, Flood and Shaw.

Letter 60: Heidelberg, 2 February 1555
Olympia Morata to Andreas Campanus:

I am sorry that your daughter and others in your family are sick. If she gets better, let me know at once. I prefer to be a maid than to have the maids of the sort to be found here. In the meanwhile, console the sick among you with the Word of God and so teach them that, if God wishes them to leave this life, they may meet Him prepared. Children have sin from the contagion of Adam, but at the same time they lack the faith in Christ, which is given by prayers and the hearing of the Word of God. I write to you, not as a pig teaching Minerva, but out of goodwill.

I've been looking diligently for the commentaries on the *Letters to Atticus* in the bookstores and among my friends, but I've not been able to find one. There is a great lack of good authors here. If I had had any, nothing would have pleased me more than to help you in this as in all other things. My husband sends you many greetings.

Letter 61: Heidelberg, 10 February [1555][428]
To the noble Valentin Wehner, Senator of Schweinfurt:

I was touched with great pain when I learned that you were seriously ill and had lost your children. Yet when we consider the misery of the times, we take less pain from the death of children; in fact we think we ought rather to be glad for than grieve at their death. As for them, I do not think you are without consolation, and as for the other troubles I do not doubt that you are sustained by the consolation that God reproves those whom He loves,[429] that He first wounds in order to heal,[430] leads to the dead that He may lead back up,[431] and always consoles those whom He has afflicted.[432] He is near to those who are sick at heart; if we suffer with Him, we shall also reign with Him.[433]

We, of course, are greatly troubled by your afflictions, and we would gladly help you no matter what it might cost, if it were possible. But even

---

428. Text at Beck 1842, 179–80, Weiss-Stählin 1976, 96–97. My thanks to Dr. Prof. Rainer Kössling for having sent me a copy of this document.
429. Prov. 3:12, Heb. 12:6.
430. Job 5:18.
431. 1 Sam. 2:6 (cf. Tob. 13:2).
432. 2 Cor. 1:7.
433. 2 Tim. 2:12.

if we cannot heal ourselves of these ills, we have a God well-pleased with us through His Son, a God Who created everything from nothing and for whom nothing is impossible.[434] So as He bade us, we will pray together to Him, and He will keep His promises. If we can do anything for you, please call on our help.

Greet your wife in my name. My husband and Emilio join in giving you many greetings.

Letter 62: [Heidelberg, spring 1555]
Olympia Fulvia Morata greets Pietro Paolo Vergerio:[435]

Dear Sir:

I would have answered your letter a long time ago if I had not been prevented by a severe illness, from which I am only now recovering. But now I can put it off no longer. A great desire to write to you has held me ever since I read your books and saw that your soul was ready and eager to help the church. So I was convinced that you would do what I asked of you for the sake of the church. Modesty has so far kept me from writing you, and I was also afraid that I might give others the idea that I was showing off if I wrote to you first.[436] Now, however, I am exceedingly glad that you have given me an opportunity. And so first, I give you great thanks for your book which you gave me.[437] Next, I demand that which before I did not dare to ask. It is this: since you strive with all your heart to advance the cause of the church, for that very reason please translate into Italian the Latin version by Vincent Opsopaeus of Martin Luther's book titled the *Greater Catechism*.[438] If you read the book diligently, you know how much benefit it will give to us Italians, especially the young. Therefore, over and over I beg you and beseech you through Christ that you please undertake this work for the sake

---

434. Matt. 19:26, Mark 10:27.

435. Pietro Paolo Vergerio the Younger (1497/8–1565), Old Catholic bishop of the Grisons (Graubünden) in Switzerland, sympathetic to the Reformation. After witnessing the deathbed agonies of Francis Spira, who had recanted his Protestant faith, Vergerio formally resigned his office, was excommunicated, and fled. He continued to urge the cause of reformation in Italy by a steady stream of pamphlets. See Schutte 1977.

436. See the introduction on the significance of Vergerio being the one to initiate the correspondence.

437. Vergerio had recently published many pamphlets, including *Concilium non modo Tridentinum sed omne Papisticum perpetuo fugiendum esse omnibus pijs* [Not just the Council of Trent but any Papal Council must be avoided by all pious people; 1553].

438. Published in 1529.

of your brothers, for whom we ought even to seek death. Furthermore, I am not ignorant that there is great controversy among Christians about the sacrament, which would have already been easily resolved if men in council had consulted not their own glory but that of Christ and the health of the church, which is preserved by concord.[439] And so to return to my previous point, I think that book would be of the greatest usefulness to our fellows if you were willing to render assistance to them in this matter. I cannot urge you enough to do it.

About what has been happening at Ferrara, we have learned from the letters of a certain pious man the same things which you wrote back in December. It does not seem odd to those of us who know her "down to her skin."[440] We are more amazed that certain others have defected from Christ. That my mother has been constant amid all these storms I give thanks to God and ascribe it all to Him. I have begged her to come to us with my sisters out of that Babylon.

My husband thanks you for the kindness you have shown him. His love for you is all it should be. We both heartily beg that you come soon as a welcome guest and not miss the opportunity for visiting that has been given you. Goodbye.

Letter 63: Heidelberg, 1 July 155[5]
Olympia Morata greets Anna d'Este, Duchess of Guise, in Jesus Christ:

Although we have been separated for some time now by a great distance, most Illustrious Lady Anna, nevertheless your memory has never left my heart. If I had dared (and I had many good reasons), I would have sent my letters to you. But now an opportunity has presented itself, and when a certain learned and pious man visited us here on his journey from Lorraine, the first thing I did was to find out from him what and how you were doing.[441] Since he promised that he would take care to get my letters to you, I did not think that you would be so hard-hearted as to fail to read with kindness

---

439. Vergerio had written extensively on the debates of the Council of Trent, especially those surrounding transubstantiation.

440. Pers. 3.30. Referring to the imprisonment and forced recantation of Renée de France in 1554.

441. Probably Guillaume (Guilielmus) Rascalon, a doctor and envoy from the Guise to the Palatine Court at Heidelberg, who later put up memorials for Olympia Morata and Andreas Grunthler. See Kössling and Weiss-Stählin 1990, 207; Flood and Shaw 1997, 137 n. 94.

letters sent to you from one who was educated with you from the tenderest years. You know how closely we lived together for all those years, even though you were my lady and mistress, and how we shared the study of letters, which rightly ought to increase more and more a mutual kindness between us, uniting us closer day by day.

Noble lady, I call God to witness, I love you and wish you well from the bottom of my heart. If I can serve you in any way (not that I would wish to live at court again—that I could do here—but), if while I am apart from you I can be of help to you, in consolation or any other way, know that I would do it with a willing heart and a singular zeal.

But the one thing I most desire is for you to apply yourself seriously to the study of the sacred writings, which alone can unite you with God and console you in all the miseries of this life. I myself have no other solace or delight. As soon as I had left the idolatry of Italy through the singular kindness of God, and went to Germany as the bride of Dr. Andreas Grunthler, God changed my soul wondrously, so I who previously for so long had shied away from divine letters now delight in them alone. On Him I concentrate all my study, work, care, and all my mind, as far as I can. I despise all the things which I used to admire so much: riches, honors, pleasures. I wish over and over for you, greatest lady, to think on them too. Nothing, believe me, is stable here below and everyone, as the poet said, "must walk the road of death,"[442] and soon. "For life is fleeting."[443] Riches profit nothing, honors nothing, the favor of kings nothing. Only that true faith, in which we embrace Christ, can save us from eternal death and damnation. Since this is the gift of God, you ought to pray for it from Him with the greatest prayers. It is not enough to know the story of Christ (even the Devil knows it), but one ought to have the faith that works through love,[444] that makes it possible to dare to confess Christ, even among His enemies. Otherwise, as He said, "He who is ashamed of me, of him will I be ashamed before my Father."[445] Nor would there have been any martyrs if they had hidden their faith.

Therefore, my sweetest lady, since God has blessed you with such kindness in order to open His truth to you, and since you know that all the men

---

442. Hor. *Odes* 1.28.16.
443. Cic. *Tusc.* 1.76.
444. Gal. 5:6: Morata translates ἀγάπη as *dilectio* rather than the Vulgate's *charitas*.
445. Mark 8:38.

who are being burned there are innocent and are undergoing so many tortures for the sake of the gospel of Christ, it is your clear duty to show how you feel, either by pleading for them to the king or by praying for them.[446] If you are silent or connive, allow your people to be tortured and let them be burned, and fail to show at least with words that this displeases you, you will seem by your silence to conspire in their slaughter and to agree with the enemies of Christ.

Perhaps you will say, "If I do that, I may make the king or my husband angry with me and make many new enemies." Think that it is better to be hated by men than by God, Who is able to torture not just the body but also the soul in perpetual fire.[447] But if you have Him as a friend, no one will be able to harm you, unless He permits it, in whose hands all things are. See to it that you think on these things. If only I knew that you were seriously cultivating piety and fearing God! Apply yourself, I beg you, to sacred writings and to prayers. Christ said, "Whatever you ask from the Father in my name, he gives to you."[448] Remember that you were born in an immortal state[449] and do not listen to those who say, "Brief is this life. Therefore let us indulge ourselves and enjoy the pleasures of this world."[450] Rather, listen to Paul, who says, "If you live according to the flesh," that is, if you give yourself over to the pleasures of the flesh, "you will perish forever."[451]

I will write more to you later on this matter if I learn that my letters were pleasing to you, and I will make sure that Christian books are sent to you if you wish to learn Christ. I have written this to you prompted by the deepest love. For when God calls me to the highest heavenly kingdom, my greatest wish is that you will be a sharer in the same eternal joys. If I learn that it has happened as I wish, I will take the greatest pleasure from it and give great thanks to God. Goodbye.

Heidelberg, 1 July 155[5][452]

---

446. The Edict of Châteaubriant (1551) had created harsher penalties against heresy.
447. Matt. 10:28.
448. John 14:13.
449. "te <im>mortali conditione generatam esse" 1562 1570 : *supplevi*.
450. 1 Cor. 15:32, cf. Isa. 22:13.
451. Rom. 8:13.
452. "Calend. Iulij 1554" 1562 1570. See Kössling and Weiss-Stählin 1990, 208 for the correct year (where, however, "Juni" is printed by mistake).

Letters: Germany

Letter 64: [Heidelberg, 1555][453]
Jerôme Angenoust to the sweetest Olympia Morata, greetings:

Truly, Olympia, the old proverb says, "We only realize the usefulness of something, when we have nearly lost it." So I, realizing my departure, begin to understand the pleasure and enjoyment I was able to gain from your conversation, and the profit I was able to derive from your speeches. But the happiness which I hoped to have has been destroyed by the need which befell me to go back to France. I am unwillingly summoned to my fatherland, and this country, in which I was accustomed to rejoice and be glad so eagerly, I am compelled to leave as if carried away by force. I am blinded now and deprived of the good of your company and sight because my return was announced to me sooner than I expected. Every day I was getting further in Greek conversation, so that I spoke with you more easily, but I seemed to be too weak to be able to converse with you randomly on any topic at all. Therefore if you decide that I have erred because I saw you only rarely, attribute this to fear. Nevertheless I greatly regret it. But I encourage myself that the more difficult it is to be away from you, the sweeter will be the remembrance of you while you are away, and all the more pleasantly will I enjoy summoning Morata to mind.

Farewell and be lucky throughout your life and love me even as I love you.

Letter 65: Ehrenfriedersdorf, 25 June 1555

Wolfgang Rupprecht, once pastor to the Margrave, now the pastor of the church of God assembled at Ehrenfriedersdorf.[454] To the most excellent Olympia Morata, outstanding in piety and probity, grace and peace.

God bestows family love[455] on the human race so that it may be a reminder of His great love towards His Son and towards us, and so that it may

---

453. Original in Greek. Hieronymus Angenosios, i.e. Jerôme Angenoust (d. 1596), of a distinguished family of Champagne, was a Greek student of Olympia Morata's who had been sent by François I to search for Greek manuscripts in Italian libraries. He was recalled to become procureur of the city of Paris and was viewed as sympathetic to the Hugenots; see *DBF* 2.1103–4. See also his two (disheartening) poems about her below.

454. 1522–64. Army chaplain (Feldpfarrer) to Albrecht II Alcibiades in 1550; later Lutheran minister in Ehrenfriedersdorf 1554–56, and at the St. Johanniskirke in Schweinfurt 1556–63 (Simon 1962, 41, 53). Read "olim Marchio<nis>." Correct the dates at Kössling and Weiss-Stählin 1990, 231.

455. στοργὰς.

form the bonds of human society. He wishes us to be moved by a longing for our families and in grief to test our piety. Family love is the more distinct in the best natures. Therefore I do not doubt that you are grieved by the loss of your relative, master Cremer, especially in the case of such a man in whom piety was praised and who was also cultivated in the learning of every art and inclined to virtue not only by his own nature but also because he was ruled by the Holy Sprit, and who had entered into that study wherein his talent would have been of help to the propagation of the arts and the salvation of the church. Wherefore I do not accuse you of softness of spirit but rather recognize and approve of your piety and grieve greatly with you, as well as for the sake of your hometown, especially since I see that with our current lack of correct teachers the church will be deprived of seminaries of learned men.

Nevertheless, because of your wisdom and learning you know that we have been ordered by God both that we should grieve and that there should be a limit to sadness.[456] First let us decide, since we are certain that these events are ruled by divine counsel, to bend our minds to the obedience we owe to God, so that even in hard times we may submit to Him sweetly. For these are the sincerest and truest reasons for moderating our grief: that we know we must obey God when He calls us or our loved ones, next that we leave here for the companionship of Christ and the church, and that after a brief interval of time each will embrace his loved ones again. When we think on these reasons, pain is eased.

There are other things that do not ease grief but somehow dull it, for example, the sight of our present miseries, the dissipation of the republic, the madness of the leaders, which increases daily. When I contemplate these things, I burn with such indignation that I long to leave this life. Nevertheless, we must pray to God that He will preserve some of the ministers of the doctrine and of the churches. And if He calls some away, if He first snatches pious men from the impending ruins, we must think that He has done well with them. Even as Isaiah says: "The just man is taken away from the sight of evil, he goes down in peace, and grows quiet on his on bed."[457]

I write this while thinking about your grief, hoping in some way to ease it, and I ask you to let it in as some sort of consolation. Forgive the fact that up till now I have not sent you any letters, especially since before my departure I promised that I would write more often. I pray to God, the eternal Father of

---

456. E.g. Eccles. 3:4.
457. Cf. Isa. 57:1–2.

our Lord Jesus Christ, that He will keep you safe, and that excellent doctor, your husband, together with your brother. Farewell.

At my house in Ehrenfriedersdorf, 25 June, in the year 1555 after the birth of Christ.

Letter 66: Heidelberg, 7 July 1555
Olympia Morata to Caelius Secundus Curio:

Although I am still sick, since I've got so good an opportunity to write to you, most learned Caelius, I didn't want to give in to my illness in this matter, but I wanted to greet you with a little letter. After I heard from our friend Herold that you were sick too, I've been extremely worried about your illness. So I beg you to relieve my worry, which you can do by writing me that you've gotten better.

You need to know that I am daily more and more consumed by the force of the illness, and there is not an hour in which I am free of fever. Thus I am being snatched away by God, lest I perish with this world. If you can in any way recompense the pious man who is bringing you this letter, please do it.

Farewell in Christ, my excellent Caelius. My husband greets you. Give greetings in my words to your family and to Bernardino Ochino, whom I love greatly in Christ, and to Herold.

Letter 67: Worms, 14 July 1555
Charles du Moulin, the lawyer, greets Olympia Morata:[458]

Most learned and Christian lady, at first glance you will wonder that a man quite unknown to you would write to you. However, the enclosed note from P. P. Vergerio will soon remove your concern.[459] I received it from him at the end of July in Stuttgart to pass on to you. I had already decided even before the month was over to go to Heidelberg, both for other reasons but especially to greet you, the glory of women. But hindered by some business, I am forced to take a different route, so I have included Vergerio's letter in mine. And so on this occasion I have had the boldness to write to you. I congratulate you, since I see that you are as endowed with true piety as with letters (even Greek poems) and lately celebrated throughout Italy by the

---

458. c. 1500–66, canon lawyer who converted to Protestantism.
459. See letter 62.

poets.[460] The Lord preserve, increase, and always prosper your most dear husband.

Letter 68: [Heidelberg, summer 1555]
Olympia Morata greets Ioannes Infantius of Barr:[461]

After Philotheus[462] had asked you to greet me for him with your words, now that I've come to know your kindness, even though the illness with which I was afflicted after your departure is still severe, I could not fail to write you. I was most grateful for the books and letters, for which I give you much thanks. I would have done it sooner, if my illness, as I said, had not prevented me. Your letters were given to me when I was confined to bed, and I still have not been able to emerge from that bout of poor health. What will happen with me I don't know. I commit myself and hand myself over completely to God, and I desire to be dissolved and to be with Christ.[463] I can't write any more. The fever, from which I'm never free even for a moment, prevents me. So goodbye, and pray to God on my behalf. My husband greets you. Greet the Italians who have added their greetings to your letter.

Letter 69: Basel, 28 August 1555
Caelius Secundus Curio greets Olympia F. Morata:

I have received from you, my dearest Olympia, who are like a daughter to me, two letters written and sent at various times.[464] What you asked me for in the first, namely that I give your thanks to our printers here for their kindness to you, I will see to most diligently. Or rather, you will do it personally most effectively, for when your letters have been read out loud and viewed, they will see you breathing and speaking: your hand, your elegance, the force in your letters.

I am extremely sorry that you were unable to write to me because you were burdened with a very severe illness. Since I was sick myself at the same

---

460. This I take to be his sense. Des Moulin, in attempting a Tacitean *variatio*, has rendered himself obscure: "Gratulor tibi <quam> cum vera pietate tantam quantam vidi literarum peritiam, Graecis etiam carminibus, in media Italia a Poetis nuper celebratam: <quam>" *supplevi* : "peritam" *subieci*.
461. Unidentified.
462. "Lover of God"; in German, *Gottlieb*; unidentified.
463. Phil. 1:23; see letter 71 and the poem "Olympia's Vow."
464. Letters 54 and 66.

time and had been for many days, my disease was doubled by the news of your ill-health. Nor was it enough that I was shot with two arrows, but a third was added which nearly killed me, already weakened by the first two, and laid me low. For my daughter Violanthis, who is at Strassburg with her husband,[465] after the saddest miscarriage fell into such misery that for seven entire months she has been struggling with death. Nevertheless, a few days ago she seemed to recover a little, and I hope through God's clemency that she will get better, even as I have gotten better. So if you too have recovered, my light (or rather, the light of our age!), I shall think everything has been put back right for me. For from the letters which you gave to Gallus, that good man,[466] for me on 9 July, I understand that the fever had not yet left you, which was most upsetting to me. That saying is true, my Olympia, and in agreement with your well-known piety, that we are punished here by God, lest we be condemned with the world, as the blessed Paul writes.[467] Let us struggle therefore, and with constancy bear whatever befalls us, certain that nothing happens to us by accident or randomly but by divine providence and for our good.[468]

I have greeted my wife and children, all of whom love you, in your name; also Bernardino Ochino, that most learned and holy old man, and Herold, and some others, especially Boniface Amerbach, that expert in the law and most excellent man, to whom I wish you would write.[469] He is one who has worked hard so that you all could be here among us: a man to be extolled for his kindness, piety, learning, and all that is praiseworthy. Do so; for he admires and kisses all your letters which I have shared with him.

You will be receiving from the Frankfurt fair certain little books of mine. Once you've read them (if there's time in your illness to read my lucubrations), write me what you think of them. Your husband, Doctor Andreas, whom especially I love for his erudition and piety, will do the same.

Please write me about your brother: what he's doing, whether he's learning and wishes to imitate his father and you. Greet them both in my name. The same to all the rest.

Farewell, dearest Olympia. Look after your health carefully so that you may continue to adorn our age. We quite envy that town of yours. Send

---

465. See letter 52. For Violantis Curio, see Kutter 1955, 257–59.
466. Perhaps the Eutychus Pontanus Gallus addressed in poem 1; otherwise unidentified.
467. 1 Cor. 11:32.
468. Cf. Rom. 8.28; this may also be an allusion to Morata's own flirtation with Epicureanism; see the "Dialogue between Lavinia della Rovere and Olympia Morata."
469. (1494–1562). Jurist in Basel; for a portrait, see Gilmore 1963 and the vast *Amerbachkorrespondenz*, ed. Hartmann 1942– .

any polished works you have so that we can publish them here, especially your poems. And when you write me back, send me a copy of this letter (get someone to copy it), because I didn't have time to make a copy and I want to keep a copy for some reason.

Again, farewell and live in our Lord Jesus Christ, to whom you are wholly dedicated.

Letter 70: Speyer, 25 September [1555]
Chilian Sinapius greets Andreas Grunthler:

Although you can find out whatever you want about my affairs quite easily from my relatives (your countrymen), nevertheless I wanted—because I've got a bit of leisure here with my boots on[470] (I'm about to head off to Worms)—to write you briefly. Our own Amphictyonic League has already transferred the whole *dicasterium* to Esslingen.[471] Almost everyone's set out for there on account of the plague that's running amok; such, in any case, is the rumor about you that's been scattered among us.

Sinapius, my brother, is now spending time at the baths in Wiesbaden, near Mainz, where I recently visited him. He is in very weak and uncertain health and anxious about the success of the baths, which, when I spent three days there, did next to nothing for me. If you want to send any letters to the hometown, you've got people who can carry them easily. I ask, if any letters addressed to me are sent to you, that you send them via the coachman; he knows my house. Unless I change my mind, I've decided to spend the whole winter here.

Be well, you and your beloved and learned wife, Olympia. Give her friendly greetings from me.

Speyer, in haste, 25 Sept.

Her final letter
Letter 71: [Heidelberg, shortly before 26 October 1555]
Olympia Fulvia Morata greets Caelius Secundus Curio:

You may guess, my Caelius, my sweetest father, what a tender sprit they have, those who are joined together by true (that is, Christian) friendship, by the fact that I was unable to keep from tears when I read your letter.

---

470. *ocreatus:* Hor. 2.3.234.
471. I.e. the Imperial Diet is set to meet in Esslingen. Chilian is making a pedantic joke.

When I heard that you had been called back from death's door, I wept for very joy. I pray God to watch over you, so that you may long be able to serve your church by your kind deeds and usefulness. I am very sorry about your daughter's illness. But I lessen my sorrow because there is hope, as you write, that she may be able to get better.

As for me, my Caelius, you must know that I have lost any hope for a longer life. As far at it lies in the power of medicines (and I have used so many), there is nothing that can help. They expect that in a few days or hours I will depart from here. In fact, I don't know whether this may not be the last letter you will get from me. My bodily strength is gone. I have no appetite for food. Congestion tries to suffocate me day and night. The fever is high and constant. There are pains throughout my body that keep me from sleeping. Nothing remains but to pour out my breath. But there is still a spirit in my body that remembers all my friends and the kindness they have done. So to you and to those kind men who have blessed me with so many lovely gifts, I wanted to give great thanks if the fates had allowed. I think I am going to depart soon. I commend the church to you, that whatever you do be of use to her. Be well, my dearest Caelius, and don't grieve when my death is reported to you, for I know that then at last I shall live, and I desire to be dissolved and to be with Christ.[472]

You asked about my brother: he has gotten to the point where he needs spurs more than a bridle.[473] Heidelberg seems deserted, first by the flight of so many from the plague and then by the deaths of many.

My husband adds his greetings. Salute your family in my name.

The poems which I was able to remember after the destruction of Schweinfurt I am sending to you as you ask. All my other writings were lost. I ask that you please be my Aristarchus and polish them.[474]

Again, goodbye.

---

472. See n. 255.
473. Cf. Sen. *Ep.* 94.23.
474. c. 216–144 BCE. Head of the Library at Alexandria, who edited Homer and the Greek lyric poets. An example of the perfect critic (cf. Cic. *Att.* 1.14.3).

POETRY

Editor's note: Nearly all of Morata's literary works were lost in the burning of Schweinfurt. Curio had preserved her juvenalia, and she copied out some poems for him on her deathbed (letter 71). Poem 5 is not found in the contemporary sources and comes from a collection of 1715.[475] Other works may yet be found.

Few of the poems, therefore, can be dated with precision. Three certainly come from her early years at court. Poem 1, on her studies, is best placed during her early years of study at Ferrara (cf. letter 2 with the same sentiments). "On True Virginity" is a satiric epigram on nuns and supposed celibacy. Though anticlerical themes were common to Catholic and Protestant alike, Morata's language is very close to that of Curio in a letter to her father (10 June 1542); the poem may reflect Curio's influence and may date to about the time of his visit to Ferrara.[476] The elegant poem on the death of the great Venetian humanist Pietro Bembo (1470–1547) must date soon thereafter.

---

475. Lehms [1715] 1973, 176, citing Spangenberg 1591, 415 (bk. 13, chap. vii, non vidi).

476. Curio 1544, 161: "Those who force their children into monasticism and approve of that impure celibacy should know that they are initiating and consecrating them not to God (who neither orders not approves such things), but to either Vesta or Venus. That is, to the perpetual flames and fires of lust and (as Jeremiah said) to Moloch or Cupid the god of lust. I'll tell you bluntly: it's just the same whether they've prostituted their children to some man's lust or to the monks and priests." Morato had written to Curio to announce the birth of his son, Emilio. The letter was printed as an appendix to Curio's *De liberis pie Christianeque educandis;* see Kutter 1955, 44; Adorni-Braccesi 1994, 116 n. 218. Caretti (1954, 49), however, dates the poem, inappropriately, to 1549 just before Morata's marriage.

1. Ὀλυμπίας τῆς Μωράτης εἰς Εὐτυχὸν Ποντανὸν Κέλτην

οὔποτε μὲν ξυμπᾶσιν ἐνὶ φρεσὶν ἥνδανε ταὐτὸ
κοὔποτε πᾶσιν ἴσον Ζεὺς παρέδωκε νόον.
ἱππόδαμος Κάστωρ, πὺξ δ' ἦν ἀγαθὸς Πολυδεύκης,[477]
ἔκγονος ἐξ ταὐτῆς ὄρνιθος ἀμφότερος.
κἀγὼ μὲν θῆλυς γεγαυῖα τὰ θηλυκὰ λεῖπον   5
νήματα, κερκίδιον, στήμονα, καὶ καλάθους.
Μουσάων δν ἄγαμαι λειμῶνα τὸν ἀνθεμόεντα
Παρνάσσου θ' ἱλαροὺς τοῦ διλόφοιο[478] χορούς.
ἄλλαι τέρπονται μὲν ἴσως ἄλλοισι γυναῖκες.
ταῦτα δέ μοι κῦδος. ταῦτα δὲ χαρμοσύνη.[479]   10

[4 ταὐτῆς αὐτῆς 1570 Bonnet]

TO EUTYCHUS PONTANUS GALLUS[480]

Never did the same thing please the hearts of all,
and never did Zeus grant the same mind to all.
Castor is a horse-tamer, but Polydeuces is good with his fist,
both the offspring of the same bird.
And I, though born female, have left feminine things,   5
yarn, shuttle, loom-threads, and work-baskets.
I admire the flowery meadow of the Muses,
and the pleasant choruses of twin-peaked Parnassus.
Other women perhaps delight in other things.
These are my glory, these my delight.   10

2. DE VERA VIRGINITATE

Quae virgo est, nisi mente quoque est et corpore virgo
  haec laudem nullam virginitatis habet.
quae virgo est uni Christo ni tota dicata est,
  haec Veneris virgo est totaque mancipium.

477. A reworking of Il. 3.237.
478. A reference to Soph. Ant. 1126.
479. A biblical use: LXX 1 Kings 18:6, etc.
480. I have not been able to trace him; Κέλτης/Gallus may be an ethnic. Curione mentions a Gallus (letter 69, 1555).

ON TRUE VIRGINITY

A virgin, unless she is a virgin in mind as well as body,
   has no share in the praise for virginity.
A virgin, unless she is totally dedicated to Christ,
   is a virgin of Venus and completely her slave.

3. Ὀλθμπίας τῆς Μωράτης εἰς Βεμβόν

κάτθανεν Ἀονίδων κῦδος μέγα παρθενικάων
   Βεμβός, ὁ τῶν Ἐνετῶν φωσφόρος εἰναλίων,
ᾧπερ ἐνὶ βροτέοισι τό νῦν ἐναλίγκιός ἐστι
   οὐδεὶς οὔτ' ἔργοις οὔτ' ἐπέεσσιν ἀνήρ.
οὗ θανέοντος,[481] ἔδοξεν ἀμ' εὐεπίῃ πάλιν αὐτὸς   5
   εἰσιέναι στυγερὸν Τούλλιος εἰς Ἀΐδην.

[3 ᾧπερ : οὗπερ 1562 1570]

TO BEMBO

He has died, the great glory of the Maiden Aonides,
   Bembo, the morning star of the sea-going Venetians.
Among mortals now there is no man resembling him
   neither in words nor in deeds.
When he died, it seemed that together with eloquence   5
   Cicero himself went a second time unto hated Hades.

Editor's note: Around the time of her marriage in 1550, Morata composed a "Wedding Prayer." Curio printed it first in his edition of his correspondence (1553, 26) immediately after letter 27 (dated Schweinfurt, 1 October [1551]). The poem is cleverly constructed as a single sentence, with the Christian doctrine of marriage (Eph. 5:22–33) placed in the form of a classical aretology. A couplet on the pain of separation is almost certainly from a lost letter to Grunthler during his absence in Germany in 1549. It recalls Plato's famous myth of the divided lovers in the *Symposium*.[482]

---

481. By analogy to the Homeric θανέειν; the participle is regularly θανών.
482. Text from Lehms [1715] 1973, pt. 2, 176, citing Spangenberg 1591, 425 (c. VII, lib. XIII; non vidi).

4. Εὐχαὶ γαμικαί.

Εὐρυκρεῖον ἄναξ, πάντων ὕπατε κρειόντων,
　ἄρσεν' ὃς ἔπλασσας θηλύτερόν τε γένος,
ὃς κἀνδρὶ πρωτίστῳ ἑὴν παράκοιτιν ἔδωκας.
　ὄφρα τάγ' ἀνθρώπων μή ποτ' ὄλοιυο γένη,
καὶ θνητῶν ψυχὰς νυμφὴν τεῷ ἔμμ εναι υἱῷ,　　　　5
　τὸν δ' ἔθελες θανέειν εἵνεχ ἑῆς ἀλόχου,
ὄλβον ὁμοφροσύνην τε δίδου πόσει ἠδὲ δάμαρτι.
　θεσμὸς γὰρ πέλεται λέκτρα γάμοι τε τεός.

WEDDING PRAYER

Wide-ruling Lord, highest of all rulers,
　Who formed the male and the female sex,
You Who gave to the first man a wife for his own,
　lest the race of man die out,
and wished the souls of mortals to be the bride of Your Son　　　　5
　and that He die on behalf of His spouse,
give happiness and harmony to husband and to wife,
　for the ordinance, the marriage bed, and weddings are yours.

5.

Quam miserum est tanto seiungi tempore amantes,
　altera cum nescit alter pars ubi sit.

How miserable it is for lovers to be separated for so long a time,
　when one half does not know where its other half is.

Editor's note: The few fragments of Morata's religious poetry that we possess, apart from her Psalms, are most likely the ones she copied out for Curio from memory during her final days. Only one can be dated. Morata wrote an elegy for Johannes Lindemann (1488–1546), Martin Luther's cousin and a preacher in Schweinfurt.[483] Andreas Rosa in a letter of 1554 (letter 51) mentions having sent it on to Lindemann's widow. The language of the poem is purely Homeric and the well-fitted epicisms add a quiet solemnity to a Christian poem.

---

483. c. 1493—before 13 June 1554; head preacher (Oberpfarrer) at the St. Johanniskirche in Schweinfurt 1547–54: Simon 1962, 39, 53.

6. Ἐπιτάφιον εἰς Ἰωάννην Λινδεμαννόν ἐκκλησιαστήν.

ἔνθα κατευνηθέντα βροτὸν κατὰ γαῖα καλύπτει,
  ὃς ποιμαίνεσκεν πώεα καλὰ θεοῦ.
ὃς τ' ὀίων ἕνεκα πλείστους ἐμόγησεν ἀέθλους,
  τὰς μὲν ῥυόμενος μαρνάμενος δὲ λύκοις.
Νῦν δέ μιν ἀργαλέου καμάτοιο μίνυνθ' ἀπολήγειν,   5
  εὕδειν τ' ἐν τύμβῳ Χριστὸς ἄνωγε θεός.
ὄφρα μὴ ὅσσα γε κήδε' ἅπασι βροτοῖσιν ἐφῆπται,
  ὀφθαλμοῖσιν ἴδῃ, μηδὲ κακόν τι πάθῃ,
ἀνστήσει δὲ Χριστὸς ἑὸν τάχα μηλοβοτῆρα
  σήματος ἐξαγαγὼν ἤματι τῷ πυμάτῳ.   10

EPITAPH FOR JOHANNES LINDEMANN, PREACHER.

There the earth hides the mortal lulled to sleep,
  who shepherded the beautiful flocks of God,
who on behalf of his sheep suffered the greatest pains,
  rescuing them, while he fought with wolves.
But now Christ our God orders him to cease for a little   5
  from his hard labors and rest in a tomb,
lest he see with his eyes how many griefs hang over
  all mankind, or lest he should suffer any ill.
But Christ will soon raise His own shepherd,
  leading him out of that tomb on the final day.   10

Editor's note: As in the Psalms, she shows a strong talent for recasting biblical themes. "On Christ Crucified" refers to John 3:14.

7. Περὶ Ξριστοῦ σταυροθένυος

ὡς ὀφέων ποτὲ τοὺ κεκακωμένον ἕλκεϊ λυγρῷ
  χώρῳ ἐν οἰοπόλῳ χάλκεος ἆθλεν ὄφις,
ὡς ὃν μὲν βροτολοιγὸς ὄφις δάκεν, ἄλθεται αἶψα
  εἰς θεοῦ υἱὸν ἰδὼν ὑψόσ' ἀειρόμενον.

ON CHRIST CRUCIFIED

As once the brazen serpent cured those harmed
    by the painful bite of the serpents in the deserted region,[484]
so the one bitten by the serpent who is the plague of man is cured quickly,
    when he looks upon the Son of God lifted up on high.

Similarly, she recasts John 3:16 in the following:

8. OLYMPIAE FIDES

Sic deus humanam gentem vel semper amavit
    filium ut unigenam traderet ille neci.
sic genus humanum dilexit filius ipse,
    solus ut aeternam fuderit ille animam,
ut qui pacifero possit confidere Christo   5
    vivat nec saeva morte perire queat.

OLYMPIA'S DECLARATION OF FAITH

So God always loved the human race
    that He delivered His only-begotten Son to death.
So the Son in turn loved the human race
    that He alone poured out His eternal soul,
so that whoever can believe in Christ the Bringer of Peace   5
    may live and not be able to perish in savage death.

    Editor's note: So too in her final illness, Morata recalled Phil. 2:23 and repeats the phrase in her letters.[485]

9. OLYMPIAE VOTUM

Dissolvi cupio, tanta est fiducia menti,
    esseque cum Christo quo mea vita viget.

THE PRAYER OF OLYMPIA

I long to be dissolved, so great is the confidence of my mind,
    and to be with Christ in whom my life flourishes.

---

484. John 3:14 recalls the brazen serpent of Num. 21:4–9, Wisd. of Sol. 16:5–8.
485. Letter 68 to Johannes Infantius and letter 71 to Curio in the summer of 1555.

PSALMS

EDITOR'S INTRODUCTION

An English prose translation of a Greek verse translation of a Greek prose translation of ancient Hebrew verse is a curious object, and it is difficult for us modern readers to recapture why these poems were regarded by Morata's contemporaries as her most glorious achievement.

The Book of Psalms lay at the heart of the worship of the new Protestant churches.[486] The services being forged across Europe demanded a new song to the Lord. Luther called for poets to write fresh hymns and hunted all over Saxony for poets to create metrical versions of the Psalms.[487] Müntzer made the service largely sung and insisted on the Psalm for the day being sung in its entirety.[488] Bucer in Strassburg created complete psalters in German, while Marot translated the Psalms into French verse. Calvin published a psalter in 1539, which included eight of Marot's Psalms and five of his own, all intended for congregational singing. Marot published thirty Psalms in 1541, expanded to fifty in 1543, and called forth the talent of many musicians. His metrical psalms became the centerpiece of Huguenot worship.[489] Psalms of this form became part of the liturgy of the Old World and the first book to be printed in the New.

Morata's Psalms represent a unique moment in the cultural history of Europe. They are an exemplary product of both halves of biblical human-

---

486. Overview at Cameron 1991, 256. A selection of primary sources in translation by Music 1996, 37–70.

487. 1527: Luther 1883–1948 (WA), 12:218; Luther 1955–76, 53:36; Blume 1974, 58. Luther paraphrased Ps. 130 as the hymn "Aus tieffer Not."

488. Williams 1992, 128.

489. Kidd 1911, 566 (other sources at 560, 583, 616, 628). For Marot's Psalter, see Pidoux 1962. Various settings have been recorded.

ism.[490] There had been a flourishing tradition, among the evangelically minded, of turning the Psalms into classical Latin meters, with examples by Obsopoeus (1531), Franciscus Bonadus (1531), Eobanus (1538), Marcantonio Flaminio (1546), Jean de Gagny (1547), Salmon Macrin, and George Buchanan (1548).[491] Flaminio with his usual modesty claimed to be the first.[492] Morata, however, was the first to use Greek.[493] She was followed in this endeavor by the brilliant George Buchanan with certain others (1566) and Jean de Serres (1575).[494] There is no evidence that Morata knew Hebrew; her inclusion of the noncanonical Psalm 151 shows clearly that she was working directly from the Greek text of the Septuagint.[495]

Morata's Psalms are superb demonstrations of their author's command of ancient Greek and of Homer's poetry. In this way, they functioned no differently than other display pieces of humanist Greek poetry. However, even the earlier translations were more than mere exercises in verse composition. Flaminio said specifically that he wrote his versions because he wanted to inculcate good morals by making sacred poetry acceptable to the scholar and accessible to the young.[496]

Set to music by her husband, Morata's songs of praise were intended to have a genuine devotional purpose. She wrote them to be read, to be sung, and even perhaps to be used in the worship of the church.[497] The worshipers she imagined, of course, were not the general vernacular congregation but that smaller set of those "learned in the languages." This set, however, was larger than we today might imagine, and the Reformers wished it to grow larger still. Group study of the Bible, even in Greek, was an important part of

---

490. So Krause ([1879] 1963, 2:205–6) on Eobanus's translation: "Was in jener Zeit für den höchsten triumph der humanistischen Wissenschaft galt, erkennen wir jetzt als ein in Prinzip verfehltes, den unreigentümlichen Geist der hebräischen Poesie vernichtendes Werk."

491. Later, Paul Dolscius in 1555, the year of Morata's death.

492. See Maddison 1965, 159–68.

493. She may have been inspired by the classical example of Apollinaris, bishop of Laodicea, d. c. 390. However, the editio princeps was not published until 1552, after Morata had been at work on her Psalms for some time.

494. *Psalmorum Dauidis paraphrasis poetica: nunc primum edita . . . Psalmi aliquot in versus Graecos nuper à diuersis translati* ([Geneva]: Apud Henricum Stephanum, 1566). The *diversi* appear to include Frédéric Jamot, Florent Chrestien, and Henri Estienne himself. The tradition was continued by Theophilus Cangiserus (1611), Denis Petau, S.J. (1637), and James Duport (1667).

495. Pace Bainton 1980, 120; Cignoni 1982–84, 194, who makes the same claim for her father, Morato. Ps. 151 is not found in the Hebrew text, nor was it admitted to the Vulgate.

496. Maddison 1965, 160.

497. For the psalms and singing in the worship of the church in hiding at Venice, see Martin 1988, 219. For Morata's own musical skills, see letter 77.

Italian evangelism.[498] In the reformed cities, provisions were made not just for study in the three languages but for worship as well.[499] This is not yet the stage of post-Tridentine sanctification of Latin as the language of the Vulgate and the Mass.[500] Even after the First Act of Uniformity (1549; 2 & 3 Edw. VI, c. 1), prayers in Latin, Greek, and Hebrew had always been allowed "for the further encouraging of learning in the tongues in the Universities of Cambridge and Oxford," and the Book of Common Prayer was actually translated into Latin (1560), since this was the vernacular of the universities, Winchester, and Eton. So too in Germany, where not only were the old Latin texts gathered for liturgical use in the new church by Lucas Lossius (1553) but new Latin psalters were created by Johann Spangenberg (1544).[501] Eobanus's elegiacs appeared with the blessings of Luther and Melanchthon and were wildly successful, reprinted some fifty times.[502]

Morata's choice of Psalms is in itself significant. We know that she had begun to turn some of them into classical Greek verse even before she left Ferrara.[503] However, others were written in Schweinfurt and in Heidelberg.[504] They are all appropriate to her own situation of exile: from court, from friends, from family, from country. Morata chose Psalms of endurance, of suffering tempered by hope. Her final choice, Psalm 151, particularly seems to hold a personal exhortation. God, who she had once thought cared for nothing, turns out to be the one "who cares for all things .... who sees all things for all ages." He is the God who watches over the poet, who rejoices her soul with the beautiful lyre.

PSALM 1 (IN HEXAMETERS)

O blessed one, who leads his life, not persuaded
by the evil-weavings of the profane, nor tarries on the path

---

498. Seidel Menchi 1987, 73; 1994, 192; Cameron 1992, 199.

499. Besides the famous *Prophezei* (for which see Kidd 1911, 448–50; Büsser 1994), public lectures in Greek and Hebrew were given at the Great Minster in Zurich (Kidd 1911, 422). America inherited this goal: at the College of William and Mary (est. 1693), during the daily chapel service, the Gospels were read in Greek and the Psalms sung in Hebrew.

500. Fourth Session of the Council of Trent, 1546.

501. *Psalterium carmine elegiaco redditum* (Frankfurt: C. Egenolph, 1544) and the famous *Cantiones ecclesiastictae* (Magdeburg: M. Lotter, 1545). Blume 1974, 48.

502. Krause [1879] 1963, 2:199–207.

503. Document 2 (mentioning Ps. 46). Letter 19 to Curio, written after Morata's safe arrival in Augsburg (7 October 1550), included some poems, one of which was Ps. 46 (cf. letter 26), which she said she made "last year."

504. Letters 36, 51.

of the sinner, nor sits upon the couch of the destructive
man, but the law of God night and day
wholly is a care to him in his heart unceasingly ever. 5
Like a flourishing tree, planted beside
the streams of an ever-flowing river, it is weighed down
with ripe fruit. The wind does not bring its leaves to the ground.
So the man who delights his heart in the laws of God
will flower forever upon the much-nourishing earth, 10
and in all the works that he works happiness follows.
But the lawless man is driven hither and thither
like chaff, which the rolling force of the winds bears along.
Neither will the hostile in the crowd of those who do good
rise up, nor ever in the assembly that brings fame to men. 15
For God completes the road of the good man
but the profane walk along a vain road.

PSALM 2 (IN HEXAMETERS)

Why has so great a din of mortal men arisen?
Why do the peoples rage vexing over vain things?
Scepter-holding kings and leaders all have gathered
together, plotting in their minds
not against a mortal man, but God and the Anointed Lord, 5
saying, "The mighty bonds from our body
let us rip, and let us throw off their yokes from us."
Hearing these things, He who is king in heaven laughs,
but then becoming angry, He will speak a mighty
word, which will show and disturb their hearts, 10
for this Anointed He commanded to be the most kingly
of all, and to govern holy Zion.
He says that which God commands Him to say: "I am the son
of God, and He begat Me today, looking like Him
in deeds and form. And He spoke a word to Me: 15
'Ask Me so that you may obtain as your share the nations of men.
For I shall give you a scepter so that you may rule with might
all the men of the east or of the west.
Them you will grind with the flashing iron of your staff
easily, like a vessel the potter has made with his hands.'" 20
Therefore now all kings and law-giving men,
no longer is it right to be without sense, but to be mindful,
and to fear God, trembling and delighting,

for the child to bend down, lest steep destruction
fall upon you suddenly, when He has become angry. 25
But thrice-blessed are those trusting in this king.

[22 ἀπυνυσσέμεν 1570, i.e. ἀπινυςς-]

PSALM 23 (IN HEXAMETERS)

The king of great Olympus and the much-bearing earth
shepherds me. What shall I want? For in a soft
meadow He seated me, where flows beautiful-streaming water
with which He refreshes me, whenever labor has overcome my heart.
He Himself leads me to the straight path of justice 5
for the sake of great mercy and His glory.
And if I go through the misty gloom of monstrous Hades,
nevertheless the mind in my breast will be untrembling.
For You have always gone beside me as a helper,
And Your rod and staff support me when I have fallen. 10
You send forth for me a beautiful and well-polished table
which gave me great and mighty strength, when I am overpowered
by hostile hands in mighty combat.
You anointed my head richly with oil, and a cup
You gave me, preparing it full of honey-sweet wine. 15
You always pity me in your heart, so that all the days
I may dwell in your high-roofed great and beautiful house.

[12 δαμάσσω 1570 : δαμάσθω correxi 15 ἐνίπλεον 1570 : sed ἐνίπλειος more
homerico 16 κοίρα 1570 : κῆρι correxi 17 ὑψιρεφὲς 1558 1562 : ὑψιρδφὲς 1570
: ὑψερεφὲς correxi]

PSALM 34 (IN HEXAMETERS)

I shall hymn You, Father, all days and nights,
in You shall I end, from You shall I begin, while I am among
the living and see the shining light of the sun.
Only in You shall I exult, O glorious Lord of Lords,
You alone are my highest glory. 5
You whose stout heart is chilled in your breast,
rejoice and sing with me the God who lives forever.
For He alone pities those who are worn down by painful evils
and listens to all the prayers of those
who call upon Him when they are upon the razor's edge. 10
When I sought Him, I quickly found Him.

And He saved me, and took all the fear from my limbs.
Whoever is in grief and calls upon this King,
his cheeks will never blush for shame.
Whoever cried aloud, lamenting and grieving, 15
He has heard his shout, and freed him from evil.
And angels are marshaled around the pious man,
in all his troubles they are his helpers.
O mortals, consider in your mind and soul
how God is great-hearted and gentle to you. 20
O blessed man, who has trusted in Him, and respects Him.
For such a man will never be without You, but
enough livelihood and great happiness will attend him.
Even rich men have still desired livelihood,
but those who fear God the Father have wealth unharmed. 25
But come, O children, and I shall give you wide counsel,
be persuaded by me and I shall teach you to fear God.
If any of you wishes to live joyfully,
he must keep his tongue from saying any evil word,
nor speak having guile in his heart, but do good. 30
Make peace with God and with men.
For never does God hide His eyes from the righteous man,
but standing by him, He rescues and guards him.
But looking darkly at the enemy, He watches him,
so that he becomes unknown to all mortals. 35
When the good lift up their hands in prayer to Him,
He Himself hears them pray and wards off evil from them,
and standing near He guards the man who has been wronged.
And to the man who has suffered at heart He is a helper.
The righteous are greatly distressed, but God will put a stop 40
To all their weeping and tearful groans.
Guarding them steadfastly and all their bones.
No one will ever break nor split any of them.
The man who plots lawless things against this one,
or whoever hates the godly righteous man, 45
never will he be guiltless but guilty always.
But those who trust in God will be always guiltless.
He will deliver those who serve Him, having given his Son as ransom.

[10 ἤδη 1570 : ἀκμῇ *correxi* 10 ἅπαντα μοι ἐκ δέος εἵλετο γυίων 1558 1562 :
ἅπαντας μοι ἐκ δέως εἵλετο γυίων 1570 : ἅπαν τε μοι ἐκ δέος εἵλετο γυίων
correxi 12 κακέει 1570 : καλέει *correxi* στρατιοῦνται 1570 : στρατόωνται *correxi*
25 πατέρ 1570 : παατέρ *correxi* 39 ἐπάρροθος 1570 : ἐπίρροθος *correxi*]

PSALM 46 (IN SAPPHICS)[505]

For wretched mortals
a helper and unbreakable shelter is my God,
Who alone came as an aid to those who are
    greatly distressed.

Therefore, my heart, you shall fear nothing 5
even if before your eyes you see the whole earth
and shadowy mountains pushed into
    the ocean.

Even if the full sea should attack the high peaks
of the lofty-leafed mountains with its hateful waves 10
and the very earth herself
    of the wide ways.

Nevertheless the spring of the city that does the will of God
is holy, pouring forth a clear stream.
It will enchant the house gleaming with gold 15
    of God Who is forever.

For this city He rules with strength,
the King of men Himself, and Lord
of gods, and no labor, no grief
    comes to her. 20

Many tribes of wide-ruling nations
and many kings are roused against us,
the echoing earth is in confusion
    with their noise.

---

505. This poem is mentioned in letter 26 (and cf. 19). A manuscript, apparently autograph, of this psalm has survived in the papers of Joachim Camerarius: Bayerische Staatsbibliotek, Munich, Clm 10363, 103 r-v; reproduced at Kössling and Weiss-Stählin 1990, 174–75, with Camerarius's note "Olympia Morata Grunthlera faciebat".

But the Ruler, the mighty Lord of Hosts, 25
the glorious leader of every command,
appears as our and our people's helper
   and guardian.

O race of men learn all of His works
how beautiful, how wondrous they are. 30
both on the earth and the homes
   of starry heaven.

The dread battle of mortals He has destroyed,
He has shattered the bent bow, He has broken
the sword, and again burnt their shields 35
   in shining fire.

"Look upon me," said our Lord
the war leader, "How great is My power, what sort
are my weapons. I alone rule both mortals
and the heavenly ones." 40

But the Ruler, the mighty Lord of Hosts,
the glorious leader of every command,
appears as our and our people's helper
   and guardian.

[4 μογοῦσι MS 1562 : μοδοῦσι 1570 15 θέλξει MS 1562 : θέλουξει 1570 35 κῆε ῥίνους MS : κῆ ἐρίνους 1562 1570 : ῥίνους *correxi*]

PSALM 70 (IN HEXAMETERS)

Hasten, my God, to ward off ruin from me as fast as possible.
Confuse the heart in the breasts of all the sinners
who attempt to send my soul to Hades.
Disgrace them, Lord, and make them fall back,
and set in dishonor those who think evil against me. 5
Let them flee headlong from me with downcast eyes,
those who call me with heart-cutting words.
But let them rejoice who seek after You, Shepherd of the people,
let them praise You and greatly honor You for ever,
those who love with all their heart Your Son, Who helps in our trials. 10
But I am poor, and deeply grieved at heart.

Hasten, my God, to ward off ruin from me as fast as possible.
Hasten, Lord God, unto me. Master, do not delay.

PSALM 125 (IN HEXAMETERS)

As steep Mount Zion remains in place unshakable always,
so are those who trust in God. They do not fall into the hands of their enemies.
And as the city of Jerusalem is closed in by the mountains,
so God is the unbreakable shelter around His people.
Therefore those who plot wicked things against the good
will not always rule and be strong, while the good trust
in the promises of God and guard their faith.
Lord, give good to the good, and make the citizens of Jerusalem
flourish with all the good things in peace. But destroy
the wicked, as You promised, and the fickle men.

[3 κεκλεισμένον 1562 : κεκλησμένον 1570 10 ἄλλο προσάλλους 1570 : ἀλλοπροσάλλους *correxi*]

PSALM 151 (IN ELEGIACS)
A PSALM OF DAVID, OUTSIDE
THE ONE HUNDRED AND FIFTY.

I was the smallest in my parents' house
    and younger in birth than my brothers.
I shepherded the woolly sheep in the great mountains
    and rejoiced my soul with the beautiful lyre.
My brothers were large and best in form.
    But splendor of body did not help them,
for He Who cares for all things, gave the scepter to me,
    God, Who sees all things for all ages.

II
WRITINGS ABOUT OLYMPIA MORATA OR IN HONOR OF HER

LETTERS AFTER THE DEATH
OF OLYMPIA MORATA

LETTER 72: HEIDELBERG, 14 NOVEMBER 1555
ANDREAS GRUNTHLER GREETS THE SCHOOLMASTER
ANDREAS CAMPANUS:

You have perhaps been wondering, dearest Andreas, that I stopped writing for so long a time, as if I had forgotten both myself and you. But the number of my preoccupations due to my wife's serious and lengthy illness, with which you know she was afflicted, was so great that I have not had time for anything else.

She died on the 26th of October, at four in the afternoon, not yet twenty-nine years old.[1] Now that all is well with her—for she is alive, even as she swore just before she died that she would be, with Christ in the most beautiful light—I for my part, because of my grief, can't do anything other than make my friends fellow sufferers in my pain. So if I'm only now responding to some twenty such letters, please put it down to my grief.

Nevertheless, I want to make sure that you know that I am not unmindful of your great kindness, for of course the length of the illness cost me a great amount of money. You would be doing me a great favor if you would deal with the people whose money it is, and get them to allow me to keep it until June of next year, so that I can spend it for her, as is the custom. If not, please let me know, and I'll make sure that it's repaid this December. Though it will be difficult, I don't want you to go to any difficulty on my account.[2]

The man who brings you this letter is a fellow townsman of mine, and worked for me last year, a good youth and not unlearned. If you can help him with any advice so that he can stay with someone for a while, until the

---

1. "nondu nata esset annos xxviij" 1570 : "xxvii<i>j" *correxi,* see Note on Chronology.
2. The 20 florins referred to in letters 55, 56.

scattered members of our university come back together, you'll be doing me a favor. If you can, please let me know.

I've nothing to add except that I hope you, your wife, and children are well.

LETTER 73: HEIDELBERG, 22 NOVEMBER 1555
ANDREAS GRUNTHLER GREETS
HIS FRIEND CAELIUS S. CURIO:

I ask you, my most distinguished friend, to see how God afflicts me in every way: after my country was destroyed, my goods stolen, my friends and most of my relatives killed, He has at last even taken away my dearest and sweetest wife. Had she alone survived, I think I could bear all the rest with restraint. But this is the greatest disaster to overwhelm me, like the enormous tenth wave that comes after the others, and I can't find any way to lessen my pain.[3]

She left this life with a great eagerness, and I might almost say, a certain enthusiasm for dying, since she was convinced that she was being called hence from long torturing pains, from this wretched light to endless happiness. But the memory of the sweetest and most pleasant life we lived together somehow just does not bring any consolation. She lived with me for less than five years, and I have never seen another soul more sincere and pure, or conduct more moral and holy. What can I say about her singular piety and learning? I don't think there's any need to praise her to you, since you knew her first, and I don't want to seem to be bragging about what was mine. So I turn this whole matter over to you learned and educated men, and I am sure that some of your group will think her death worth adorning in poem or oration. Let me add my tears to these, when on account of grief I finally can. For there is a type of grief like mine, that is, the deepest, in which not even tears can be shed, because the soul, already wounded and destroyed by the greatest losses, when some new bitterness occurs simply grows numb. And so for now I just can't do anything.

But for the time being—for I think this is what you want, although I barely can—I'll tell you briefly how she died. She was close to death, and after she had awakened from a nap, she seemed to me to be joyful with some sort of happiness, and she smiled to herself. I went towards her and asked why she had smiled so sweetly. She said, "In my sleep I saw a place shining with the clearest and most beautiful light." She couldn't say any more

---

3. For this Roman belief, see Ov. *Met.* 11.530, Sen. *Ag.* 502, etc.

because of her weakness, so I said, "Cheer up, my dear wife, you will live in that beautiful light." She smiled softly again and nodded her head and a little later she said, "I am totally happy." She didn't say anything else, except as her eyes grew dim, "I can barely make you out anymore, but everything else seems to me to be full of the most beautiful flowers." And those were her last words. A little while later, as though overcome by a sweet sleep, she breathed her last.

For several days, she had been emphatically stating that there was nothing she desired more than to be dissolved and to be with Christ, Whose great kindness to her she never ceased to praise, as much as the force of the disease let her. He had enlightened her with the knowledge of His Word. He had turned her soul from all the pleasures of this world. He had kindled in her a desire for the eternal life. She never hesitated in every conversation to call herself a child of God. Nothing meant less to her than when someone, in order to console her, would say that she would eventually recover from this illness. She would say that God had measured out a certain course of life for her, brief but full of work and woe, and she did not want to turn "from the finish-line back to the starting-gate."[4] She was asked at that time by a certain good man whether she had any little thing on her conscience which might make her unhappy. But she said, "For seven whole years now, the Devil has not stopped trying in every way to force me from the true faith; but now, as if he had lost all his weapons, he's disappeared. I feel nothing in my soul except the deepest tranquility and the peace of Christ." But it would take too long to recount all the things which she said to our great admiration, so holy, piously, steadfastly, and most bravely. She died on the 26th of October, at four in the afternoon, when she was not yet twenty-nine years old.

She had received a letter from you from the last Frankfurt fair, to which she very much wanted to respond and send you a reply written in her own hand, although she was grievously ill. But after she had changed a few things and was unable to recopy it due to her weakness, she handed it over to me. So I'm sending on to you, as you'll see, a letter which presages this saddest event, together with a few psalms which she composed in Greek and a few short epigrams. When she had written the letter, I reminded her about the illustrious Boniface Amerbach. She said, "You know I wrote to him once through Herold, but I still haven't got a reply. And now I have nothing to write, and if I had, I'm not able. So, when you write to our dear Caelius, ask him to greet him in my name too."

---

4. Cic. *Senec.* 83.

I keep her brother at my house but I don't think he's making any progress, since I can't be with him and he doesn't have any other boys to emulate. All the schools here have been deserted. If you think he would be better off with you, I'll give him what help I can, and would only want him to emulate the praise of his sister, who had been educating him by herself up till now. But I await your advice on the matter.

What concerns me now is how to tell this news to my mother-in-law. I know that this wonderful woman, who has many other afflictions, will be greatly distressed. So it seems best to me, if you, with your piety and eloquence, and since you've sent her letters before, would prepare some addition to my letter and, as it were, prepare her mind for this unhappy report. I don't want to burden you, but what am I to do? I can't see what ought to be done and I have no one else to turn to. If I can ever do anything for you in turn, I will do it for sure (I'm not exaggerating), willingly as a friend. I have not yet read your books, nor anything else, during the entire time I saw my dearest wife lying so sick in bed. As soon as I can do anything else, I will read them closely, especially those about the Kingdom of God, which I hope will be some remedy for this sickness of mine.[5]

In the meantime, my dear Caelius, with your dearest wife and sweetest children, be well, better than I am.

LETTER 74: MOSBACH, 24 NOVEMBER 1555
ANDREAS CAMPANUS GREETS
PROF. ANDREAS GRUNTHLER, M.D.:

After I read your letter, written with your usual talent, most splendid of all my friends, I was stricken by the untimely passing from this life of your most learned and pious wife. But a mind that lived in Christ and now sits above the stars "should not be adorned with tears nor funeral weeping. Why? She flies learned through the mouths of men."[6]

Nor is there any reason for you to be worried about the money. It belongs to the children of my late sister and is still under my control. So if there were anything more I could do, I'd do it "eagerly, hands and feet."[7]

---

5. *Coelii Secundi Curionis De Amplitudine Beati Regni Dei, dialogi sive libri duo.* [Basel: Ioannes Oporinus], 1554.

6. An adaptation of the famous epitaph of Ennius, the father of Latin poetry: "Nemo me lacrimis decoret nec funera fletu / Faxit. cur? volito vivos per ora virum." Cited by Cic. *Tusc.* 1.34 (cf. *Tusc.* 1.117, *Senec.* 73).

7. Ter. *An.* 161.

I've not seen the boy, but he made sure that other people sent the letter on to me. If you'd like him to live with me for a few days, that's no problem. And so goodbye.

Given at Mosbach, 24 Nov. in the year 1555 after the Virgin gave birth.

LETTER 75: [BASEL], 1 JANUARY 1556
CAELIUS S. CURIO GREETS LUCRETIA MORATA:[39]

Although I have not written to you very often, my dearest Lucretia, who are like a sister to me, this has not been because of any forgetfulness of your kindness towards me, but the unfairness of the times. I remember, I well remember, how friendly you were to me when I was at your home back when your husband Fulvio was still alive.[10] Because of our relationship, although I was always away, I heard with great rejoicing of the heart that your affairs were going well, and when they went ill I received the news not without great pain. And so after grieving for the death of Fulvio, my closest friend, when I heard the news about Olympia's marriage to Andreas Grunthler, a most scholarly young man and a doctor, I felt the greatest joy, because I saw that a most beloved and learned girl had found her equal by divine providence. And afterwards, when she was taken away by her husband to Germany, unexpectedly reminded by her in a letter to cultivate that most holy friendship which had always existed between me and her father Fulvio, I did not cease, for I did not think that those friendships were true or solid which did not pass to one's heirs and were not eternal.[11] And so we both immediately persevered in it. She wrote to me as to a father, I to her as to a dearest daughter; the letters sent back and forth bear witness to that.

Meanwhile disaster befell the noble town of Schweinfurt. When I heard about it, my mind was filled with incredible pain, since I was afraid that they both, as well as your son Emilio, had perished at the same time as her husband's town. And although no matter what sort of death one may die—death is always death—the mind nevertheless recoils from a death which does not allow the natural and allotted course of life to be completed but violently breaks it by the application of some external force. With one exception: if it befalls one to suffer death for the sake of our most holy religion and the truth. That form of death I judge most fortunate. With that one exception, if it befalls someone to leave this life among his friends and family, peacefully,

---

8. Curio printed this Latin translation of his letter, written originally in Italian (see letter 76).
10. In 1540, when Curio was fleeing the Inquisition. See introduction.
11. Cf. letter 20.

quietly, in comparison to that death by violence, I don't think it a death, but a sweet departure and a safe journey.

I can easily imagine, when your Olympia departed from you with her little brother and husband in order to make so long and difficult a journey, to be led off in the remotest lands as if torn away from you, that that departure was the equivalent of a death to you, when you thought that you were perhaps never going to see her again in this life. Indeed, you might have thought that she was so far from your sight that it was not much different than if she had left this life. Then, after you heard about the cruel and wretched destruction of the hometown of your son-in-law, I do not doubt that you mourned them as if dead.

So I think I can understand, if it happened that one of them was called from this life full of miseries and disasters to that better life, that you would feel no greater pain than those great and many pains which you have already felt for them. And now let us speak the truth, my sister Lucretia. What is stable and firm in the turmoil of this world? Or what do we think ought to be sought earnestly by a Christian soul? Those things don't move me at all, especially the things which nearly everyone admires the most: wealth, honors, pleasures. I am far more eager to pass from here, so that I may be with my Lord Jesus Christ, my Savior, in that eternal and blessed life. And I can swear to you plainly that this was always the desire of your Olympia, as I heard her say many times and as the letters written by her husband to me bear witness.

And so at last God has granted her wish. He has taken her, not just from you, from whom long ago she had been plucked like a ripe fruit from its tree, but also from the arms of her dearest husband, and from the bonds of the body, to enjoy the goods which are truly good, which she hoped for and eagerly desired. And I confess, if we only look to ourselves, we must be in anguish with missing her, but if we look to her good and her happiness, and then at the misery of this life, there is a way to console ourselves and to be happy for her. For to be anguished only about one's own misfortunes is not the part of one who loves a friend but loves only himself.

If we wish to examine the matter a little more deeply, Olympia is not dead, but she lives with Christ, blessed and immortal, and after so much suffering and labor has been received into a sweet and longed-for rest. She lives, your Olympia lives, I say, Lucretia, even in this world, and she will live as long as there are men in the world, in the living and immortal memory of her works, of her divine memorials, and of all the best talents. And the life that is contained by body and soul is not the only thing to be considered life, but much more that which flourishes in the memory of all ages, which posterity increases, which eternity itself will always watch over.

And since this is so, you too, Lucretia, with that prudence, faith, and piety of yours that I've already mentioned, ought to submit your will to the will of God, then concede to nature her rights, who made all of us in part mortal; and finally respect the just and holy desire of your Olympia, through whom you and your whole family, indeed all Italy, will always more and more be commended. Her talent, learning, piety, and chastity will be celebrated in the opinion of all mortals.

Having thought and pondered over these things in your heart, you will eventually be able to put a limit to your grief, and you will give only those tears to your daughter that a pious and religious way of life seems to demand. Farewell.

LETTER 76: [BASEL], 15 MARCH 1556
CAELIUS S. CURIO TO ANDREAS GRUNTHLER:

You cannot imagine that there is any way I can express in mere words how much sadness your letter brought me. When you told me of the death of the woman whom I both loved uniquely because of the memory of her excellent and most learned father, and whom I esteemed religiously because of her own singular piety towards God and her deep learning. And though I know how much you loved her, that you will continue to love her even in death, and how miserable you feel about her departure from this life, I still want you to grant me that in a different way of love I may not be inferior to you. You weep for your dearest Olympia as a wife. I cry for her as a daughter, not because of nature, but because of what is nobler, piety and charity. But since she left life in such eagerness of spirit and in faith in God, as you write, let us grieve for our loss and misfortune, but let us greet her happiness with good wishes rather than sadness, so that whenever we recall her divine virtues we may be seen to love her rather than ourselves. For if we grieve that we cannot enjoy her company, then the evil is ours and we ought to bear it philosophically, so that we don't seem to be thinking only of what is useful for us personally. If we grieve as though something bitter had happened to her, besides the fact that we are acting contrary to our profession of faith, we who know that those who leave this life in the faith of Christ and eagerness for Him, as she did, are subject to no penalty, we are certainly not interpreting her great happiness with a sufficiently grateful mind. I have never found a medicine better for easing the grief of my mind, and I am sure that you, her husband, have availed yourself of that wisdom.

I have written to your mother-in-law as you requested and I consoled her in what way I could. You'll have to be the judge of how well. I'm sending the letter to you, translated later from Italian into Latin so it could be published.

I've decided to publish as soon as I can all of the remains of our Olympia which I have with me, together with the judgments and praises of learned men about her. I would have published them already, except that all our printers have been fully occupied. I've written not an epitaph exactly but an apotheosis of her in a few verses, and I'm going to add my letters to hers, and yours to me about her death. These will stand in the place of a formal Life and have the authority of first-person testimony. I would like to ask you to send me as soon as possible whatever writings by her you can find either in your possession or that of others so that they can be added to the rest.

About Emilio, your wife's brother. I think your school either has been rebuilt or is shortly about to be rebuilt and reopened, especially now that you have a prince so exceptionally well-disposed towards letters and religion.[12] But if it isn't yet, or you don't expect that it soon will be,[13] I urge, indeed I ask, that you send him to me. I will never fail him for my part.

So copy out everything as soon as possible and let me know what you think will happen to you. And what you didn't seem to want to write about Olympia in your last letter to me, go ahead and write. Your letters will be carried to me quite safely and faithfully. I don't know when we shall be together again, though I hope for it very much. For on seeing you, I will seem to see not only you, but Olympia herself.

Goodbye. Basel, 15 March 1556

My wife greets you and little Fulvio Emilio.

Editor's note: Curio added to the later editions a few letters about Morata and about the process of gathering her works.

LETTER 77: MOSBACH, 13 MARCH 1559
(1570: 209–11; NOT IN 1562 EDITION)
ANDREAS CAMPANUS GREETS CAELIUS SECUNDUS CURIO:

Caelius, jewel of the theologians:

The preacher for the Counts of Erbach, a close friend of mine, has just given me a present of Morata's book, printed at Basel.[14] As I was reading the preface, I understood that you were very eager for any still-remaining letters written by her, and so I am sending you two sent by her and three sent by the doctor.[15] I leave it up to you to decide what to do with them.

---

12. Ottheinrich.
13. "sperarem" 1562 1570 : "sperares" *scripsi*
14. Curio's first ed. 1558.
15. Letters 57 and 60; letters 56, 72, 74.

I read all the letters in the book with the utmost care, all the more willingly since she wrote for the most part to my countrymen (you're an exception), especially the one in which she mentions so honorably the generous Counts of Erbach, and I could not let it go in silence without telling you the truth.[16] There are three of them.[17] The eldest married the sister of the most illustrious Elector Palatine who will now be installed in the Palatinate, a man endowed no less with erudition than with a singular piety and constancy.[18] What seems especially wonderful to me is that the brothers can still all live together, which is something truly good and pleasant.

Ten years ago, there were four of us, who came to them by chance. They received us most politely and, after lunch was over, bade us go into the courtyard to a building constructed out over the water. They then began to discuss the so-called "Emperor's new reformation" from twelve till three.[19] They also wanted our advice, and to hear what our opinion might be on so difficult a matter. Once the debate was over I questioned one of the preachers and he said, "In my whole life I have never found cross-examiners of such sharp intelligence as these counts." Another preacher, master Nicolaus N. of Michelstadt, swore that he had learned more from his count than from six whole years at Wittenburg.

But to return to Olympia. She and her husband were escorted by guides provided by the counts as far as Hirschhorn am Neckar. At the inn there it chanced that the schoolmaster was trying out his pupils in the art of music. They weren't doing their job very well or with any spirit and were quickly falling into mistakes in their singing. So when she saw that they were deeply embarrassed, she didn't hesitate to come up and help the boys, to the great admiration of both pupils and teacher. I was present on many occasions when he told the boys that they should never forget this and urged them to keep it fresh in their memories, saying, "What? Isn't it a wonder that once a woman sang so sweetly with you. And without even a rehearsal!"

As for Andreas Grunthler, he and the schoolmaster Georg Treuthugerus, a learned man and very well-read, were talking of various things, and Grunthler happened to mention his name. Since he recognized the name, he ran

---

16. Letter 45, also 41 and 49.
17. George II (1506–69); Eberhard XIV (1511–64), who shared the inheritance; and their younger brother, Valentin II (1517–63). Press 1979.
18. Elizabeth von Erbach, wife of Georg I, sister of Friedrich III der Fromme ("The Pious"), of house of Wittelsbach (b. 1515, r. 1559–76).
19. The Augsburg Interim.

home and fetched back books printed with songs composed by Andreas Grunthler, which greatly astonished both the doctor and Olympia.[20]

Afterwards, when I first returned to Hirschhorn, to arrange for a stipend for my sister's children, who had lost their parents and nearly all their possessions at Schweinfurt, the school principal told me the whole story and that the doctor and Olympia were at Heidelberg. I then loaned them twenty florins.[21] For this sum of money, after their deaths, I was sent their clothing and furniture, so that I might never grow forgetful of them at any hour: the object moves the senses.

Be well, most learned Caelius, and forgive the wordiness and roughness of this letter.

Given at Mosbach, 13 March 1559

LETTER 78: SPEYER, 28 JULY 1560
CHILIAN SINAPIUS TO CAELIUS SECUNDUS CURIO:

I have not yet responded to the letters you sent me some months ago, my most learned as well as most cultured fellow, however much they pleased me, because I've not been able to fulfill your most reasonable request as much as I'd like for some time now. For constant business and my wife's ill health have kept me from gathering up those surviving works of Olympia Morata which had been left behind with me but then had been dispersed—some loaned to friends and not returned—and then sending them on to you. But I'm sure that my excuses have been made to you long ago, as much by his own good will as at my request, by that most highly educated and literary young man, Basil, the son of the most excellent lawyer Boniface Amerbach, who was entrusted by you to me and who looks on me as a friend. I'd like you to know for sure that the fact that you have kept a memory of me for so long has been extremely pleasing and pleasant to me, especially since it's been twenty years or so since we used to see each other in the court of Ferrara.

Now about our friend Olympia, that most excellent and learned woman, whom you've written to me about, I think it's better to say nothing than too little. For what could be said in praise of her that wasn't exceeded by her own piety, scholarship, and sweetness of morals? How far she excelled in both languages and the interpretation of sacred Scripture is quite splendidly indicated and proven by her letters and other writings which were published

---

20. Alas, I can find no trace of these.
21. See letters 55 and 56.

thanks to you. I envy you and your Italians such a famous glory, and I wish that this highest ornament among the women of any nation anywhere had been born in Germany, where she died. But I know that you aren't unaware that she was taught by German teachers no less than by those of her own country, but imitating the autodidacts she mostly used "silent teachers."[22]

I'm sending you a few little verses of mine, written with a crude talent, more for the sake of showing how I feel about her than because I think they're worth reading. You know that the lawsuit I've been involved in for the last ten years has kept me from the gentler arts. So take my good intentions into account if you are unsatisfied. Be well, most excellent man, and think well of me.

LETTER 79: BASEL, 1 SEPTEMBER 1560
CAELIUS SECUNDUS CURIO TO CHILIAN SINAPIUS:

One ought not to blame a response that comes late if it was missed not because of negligence or lack of attention but was held up by business or necessity. I know how great is the storm of Imperial affairs, how big the crowd of lawyers, and you need not fear that I am insufficiently experienced in these things not to accept the delay in your response in any way other than is right, especially from you, whom I know to be the most polite and diligent of men. So if your reply was late, it was not any the less welcome, especially since it brought with it news about our Olympia, which could not help but be pleasing and welcome to me. Add to this the excuse of the most elegant young man, Basil, who already diligently reminded me of your important business and absence in his letters to me. And so not only is the most polite Chilian excused in my eyes, but I myself am rather accused, for interrupting a man so overwhelmed by such great affairs with these lesser matters. This you will attribute to my love for that famous woman and my zeal for her praise, with which I am all aflame. As you write, you would even envy us her, unless a little of her praise redounded to the credit of her German teachers, by whom she was educated and not just Italians. For we have to confess, most learned Chilian, that she made use of the Sinapius brothers while she was in the court of Ferrara with the princess. Nevertheless, her father Fulvius gave her to the princess when she was already well-adorned, for a young girl, with literature by himself. And while he was with you at court, he did not cease to teach and instruct her, as you know. In this, the Germans are more blessed

---

22. Gell. 4.2.1.

than the Italians, since it was among you that that most learned woman of all left both her final thoughts and her own most chaste body. It was from there that she flew to heaven, and returned to God and Christ the Lord the spirit which she had breathed first in Italy.

That is the reason I am asking you for her final monuments, and also why I have given you a letter for your brother, which I ask you to give to him as soon as possible. The things you've sent me are most pleasing. If you can make any other recoveries, I beg you over and over to do the same thing. I also ask you, as I have done and will do, to remember me and never let it be obliterated for any reason. Goodbye.

Basel 1 September 1560

LETTER 80: BASEL, 1 SEPTEMBER 1560
CAELIUS SECUNDUS CURIO TO JOHANNES SINAPIUS:

Since I have published whatever monuments of our Olympia I could find, my most excellent friend Sinapius, and I see that they have been received by everyone with open arms, like the shields that fell from heaven,[23] it seemed a good idea to me, for the greater glory of Olympia, to prepare a new edition, one better and more polished in every way.

To bring this about I have written to your brother, that most learned of men, at Speyer, not to refuse to contribute anything he has to this edition. He sent me everything he could, together with some epitaphs on Olympia and advised me to write to you, who without a doubt had other exceptional things. So I beg you, by the shades of Olympia and by our mutual friendship confirmed over so many years, to hasten to send me whatever monuments of her you have as soon as possible, so that the praises of your great pupil may grow more and more illustrious. If you do this, as I hope, you will perform the funeral rites for the shades of a divine woman, and not only will you do something pleasing to those who are eager for her praise (who are everywhere beyond number) but also something useful and enjoyable to all. At the same time you will make sure that I know all about your affairs, how things are with you and your children, as is only right for a friend to know. Goodbye, best and exceptional man.

Basel, 1 Sept. 1560

---

23. Verg. A. 8.664: the *ancilia* were small figure-eight shields sacred to Mars, which were said to have fallen from heaven in the reign of Numa. They were kept in the Regia and carried by the Salii in a processional dance.

LETTER 81: SPEYER, 15 JULY 1562
CHILIAN SINAPIUS, JURIS CONSULTUS, GREETS CAELIUS SECONDUS CURIO:

I have no doubt, most learned and cultured man, that my long silence has raised the suspicion that I have not been as mindful as I should have of both our Olympia and our friendship. I can offer an easy explanation for both. You've heard long ago from our friend Basil[24] about my constant business and ceaseless demands on my time. Further, I think it is superfluous to refer to the death of my dear brother,[25] but I do want you to know that, beside the bitter grief, the guardianship and administration of the estate of his only daughter fell primarily on me. But now that she has lately been given in marriage to the imperial counselor Christopher Elephant, I have been freed from most of the responsibility. So at the first opportunity I didn't neglect to hunt diligently for any remaining memorials of Olympia in my brother's library. I've transcribed what was found there and sent to me from Würzburg and I wanted to send it on to you by this messenger, to make up perhaps for my hesitation and delay by diligence and abundance of material. But I want you to consider carefully that Olympia wrote the translations from Boccaccio in her adolescence, lest they seem not as well made or to differ from her other writings in style. I've been told that the citizens of Heidelberg are also busy searching for Olympia's memorials with the same idea as you, but not as rightly and properly. I especially want to be careful that people don't think I'm to blame for her not being given her proper praise and celebrated, and so I'm all the more eager to satisfy your hopes or at least the restoration of the way things were. I'm also sending some epitaphs for my brother. Best wishes, best of men.

---

24. Basil Amerbach; see letter 78.
25. 13 Dec. 1560; see Flood and Shaw 1997, 149.

POEMS IN HONOR OF OLYMPIA MORATA
WRITTEN DURING HER LIFETIME

Editor's note: As was the custom, Curio included a number of dedicatory epigrams in his edition. I have supplemented these with a few others from various sources. The poets include friends who knew her at Ferrara (Lilio Gregorio Giraldi, Didacus Pyrrhus, Curio, and Sinapius) and Heidelberg (the professor Jacob Micyllus and her student Jerôme Angenoust), along with others who knew her only through her correspondence, poetry, and reputation.

POEMS BY VARIOUS LEARNED MEN WHO WROTE
EITHER ABOUT OLYMPIA HERSELF OR HER PRAISES[26]
LILIO GREGORIO GIRALDI[27]

You are altogether splendid and you sparkle with the light
of virtue, tender girl educated at court
among the virginal chorus of Renée
among the chorus of the Pierian sisters.
Happy he whom this girl serves.
Happy the parents who bore her
and called you by the name Olympia.
Happiest he, if ever it befalls you

---

26. From Curio (1570). The first group of poems was written to Olympia herself during her lifetime; the second is posthumous.
27. Not in the editions of Curio. The text is taken from Bonnet 1856, 40 n. 1, citing "Gyraldi *Poemata inedita*, Bibl. de Ferrare." This is Ferrara. Biblioteca Communale Ariostea. I 70. "Ferrariensium et Exterorum ad Farrarienses carmina mss a Jo. Andrea Barotti Ferrarien(si) collecta 1764." See Kristeller 1963–, 5:539. The date would seem to be close to Giraldi's description of himself and Morata in *De poetis nostrorum temporum*, c. 1549. See document 1.

to be enjoyed as a wife to a husband.
Here I myself am most blessed
even in my arthritic pain
an old man to whom such a girl is kind.

DIDACUS PYRRHUS TO OLYMPIA MORATA[28]

If I think on your face, Olympia, in it
   stand both Venus and Pasithea the companion of Venus.
If your morals, they are such as Brutus's most beautiful wife had
   or the goddess who has the Gorgon on her breast.[29]
If your poetry, when I hear your words, Sappho of Lesbos
   sings to me with a voice a little sweeter than usual.
Hail girl with outstanding soul, with outstanding talent.
   The only one to bring the earlier ages back to Latium.
You are the only hope of your learned father, the apple of your mother's eye,
   the glory and delight of your fatherland.
And if it is given to me happily to bind with a garland
   these late poems which the day admires,
your fame will go not just through Italian towns,
   however far the kingdoms of Italy spread,
but it will penetrate to the Portuguese and the Indians
   and where the Arcadian cowherd drives his plough,
and where the sun runs overhead, and on the citadel of the Thunderer
   (if there is any faith in Pyrrhus) she will claim her place.

---

28. Not in the editions of Curio. Didacus Pyrrhus Lusitanus (Jacobus Flavius Eborensis, Diogo Pires, 1517–99), Portuguese Marrano humanist and poet; one of the interlocutors in Giraldus's *De poetis nostrorum temporum*. For this interesting figure, see Roth 1959, 109–10; Tucker 1992; some of the Latin poems in Pires 1983. The poem seems to date before the death of Morato in 1548. (Not to be confused with Diogo Pires, also known as Solomon Molcho, c. 1500–32, the bizarre messianic kabbalist).

    The text as printed by Weiss [Stählin] (1976, 86) from the MS is a mess. I have made the following emendations: 2 come : comes; 9 patria : patris; 12 carmine : carmina; 16 lychaomius laus tua : Lycaonius plaustra (cf. Ov. *Tr.* 3.12.30); 20 cingit Ulysses moenia facta munu : Ulyssea . . . manu; 22 lauri : lauro; 25 venturas : venturae. The MS (I 70) is correctly cited by Tucker (1992, 195). See note 1 above.

29. Porcia (Portia): a famous exemplar of feminine virtue. On hearing the news of Brutus's death she committed suicide by swallowing live coals (Valerius Maximus 4.6.5, Dio 47.49.3). The goddess is Athena.

And perhaps where the western sea with its vast whirlpool
  girds the walls made by the hand of Ulysses,[30]
boys ignorant of Venus and chaste girls,
  and the crowd of Muses, their hair bound with laurel,
will sing the wonderful name and morals of Morata.
  You yourself will give material for such praises.
And unless I am deceived by the sweetness of future fame,
  I will have a share of such great fame.
I will have a share of the fame, for I have always honored you,
  Morata, and your father with wonderful love.
And now where your virtue calls you, begin, O maiden,
  to add a great name to your "Peregrine" fathers.[31]

JACOB MICYLLUS TO THE LADY OLYMPIA MORATA, WIFE OF ANDREAS GRUNTHLER, A MOST VIRTUOUS AND LEARNED WOMAN.[32]

You who conquer the Latin nymphs and the Greek,
  you born from the sacred seed of the Pierian chorus,
accept these verses drawn from a lesser distaff,
  and badly woven on a German loom.
If they please you, I think they could please Apollo,
  and that I have received a great reward for my labor.
But if I ever seem to you to have wandered from the truth,
  a little more or a little less than I should have done,
let the novelty of the subject matter pardon the fault;
  grant this pardon to the beginners and show us the new road.
For no small part among the winging arrows
  fly far off, driven from the set target.
Nor does the right hand which aims at the enemy from afar with whistling spear
  always go away with its vow accomplished.

---

30. Lisbon, ancient Olisipo, sometimes Ulisipo by folk etymology. There was a tradition that the town had been founded by Ulysses (Solinus 23, by confusion with the Odysseia mentioned by Strabo 3.149, 157).

31. "grande peregrinis iungere nomen avis": with a pun on the name of Pelegrino Morato.

32. Jacobus Micyllus (Jacob Molsheym of Strassburg), 1503–58, a student of Eobanus Hessus's and later Melanchthon's at Wittenberg. He lectured on Greek at Heidelberg. See Sandys 1908, 2:267, Kühlmann and Wiegand 1989, 278–80.

PETRUS CORTONAEUS TO OLYMPIA MORATA[33]
[GREEK, WITH TWO LATIN TRANSLATIONS
BY GILBERTUS COGNATUS NOZERENUS][34]

The olden days wondered at women who composed poems,
    Praxilla, Sappho, and Corinna,
But now is for us rather to be amazed before Olympia,
    the ornament of well-founded Ferrara,
Not only is she learned in twofold eloquence,
    but she takes the prizes for twofold speech.
Therefore let each consider his own race blessed, we
    shall always praise our own as better!

GILBERTUS COGNATUS TO OLYMPIA MORATA

Resplendent virtue gave you your first name, Olympia,
    and your *morals* and inborn modesty your second.
Famous Olympia will take you for the merits of your genius
    and your fame will always survive.

THEODOR ZWINGER OF BASEL TO OLYMPIA MORATA[35]
[HENDECASYLLABLES]

Let the poets of old praise
the Lesbian maiden, famous for vice,
and willingly call her the Tenth Muse.
Let us rather praise our own girl, pious and modest,
the protection, glory, and master
of Latin and Greek together,
to whom Minerva has given the intelligence of Aspasia,
Hermes gave eloquence, Venus beauty,
the tuneful Muses mellifluous song,
and Grace willing and yet modest

---

33. Petrus Cortonaeus, author of *Varia Carmina Graeca* (Venice: Gryphius, 1555).

34. Gilbertus Cognatus (Gilbert Cousin), 1506–67, of Nozeroy in France (var. as Nucillanus, Nozarenus, Nozeranus, Nozorenus). Secretary to Erasmus, editor of Aristotle, Ovid, Lucian, and St. Caesarius of Arles; placed on Index Librorum Prohibitorum of 1559. See DBF 9:1061–2; Screech 1978.

35. Theodor Zwinger of Basel (133–88) professor of medicine, editor of Aristotle and commentator on Galen and other medical texts.

morals. The Father of the gods
wanted you to be called
Olympia Morata, God most high,
who rules all things through His power.

THE SAME TO THE SAME

In order that Calliope, long tired of Latin Muses
   and too harassed by Tuscan measures,
might have a companion in studies and a comrade in labor,
   Morata is chosen by the judgment of Pallas.
Calliope sees to the Greek Muses, but Olympia rules
   over ours, in morals and in eloquence.

PHILIPS VAN MARNIX [36]

Sappho was famous once, Corinna praised,
   and even Praxilla was held in great honor.
But why? Only because the ancients scarcely believed
   that the gentle sex could be inspired by Phoebus's power.
But what if that age had seen you, Olympia,
   so outstanding with Nature's dowry!
Whatever Phoebus has, or Cyllenius,[37] or Pallas,
   God has brought together in you alone.
If you should attempt to enclose something in Greek measures,
   the Maeonian goddess is made visible in your verses.[38]
Or if you prefer to sing verses in Latin poetry,
   Vergil's Muse is there to help you.
Or, leaving Helicon and the Muses completely,
   you wish to write free words in prose rhythm,
lo, immediately Mercury gives you flowing words
   and pours Nestor's song from your sweet mouth.

---

36. Marnix, Philips van, Heer van Sint Aldegonde (1540–98), Dutch Protestant theologian. His satire, *Den byencorf der H. Roomsche Kercke* [The beehive of the Roman Catholic Church] (1569), and his Dutch poetic translation of the Psalms (1580, 2d ed. 1591) were highly influential.

37. Mercury, as god of eloquence.

38. *Maeonis* as a fem. adj. to *Maeonius* (not a classical usage), here as metonymy for "Homeric" (cf. Ov. *AA*, 2.4, *Pont.* 3.3.31).

Add to this a piety pleasing to a chaste genius,
   and a pleasing love and fear of God the Highest.
In vain do the ancients vaunt their own age
   with puffed-out cheeks and praise it to the stars above.
Our age is more blessed, and God favors our age more
   from His highest citadel.

THE SAME TO THE SAME

The former age once bore poets and learned girls
Praxilla, Sappho, and you, Corinna.
Now comes to us the great glory of Ferrara
Olympia, rightly more to be admired.

JERÔME ANGENOUST TO OLYMPIA
[GREEK]

God has sent from Olympus to mortals the heavenly
   as a paradigm to the wise.

SAME TO THE SAME

Nature denied you nothing of all her gifts
   with one exception: that you were a woman.[39]

---

39. Dotibus ex cuntis tibi nil natura negavit:
       hoc uno excepto, foemina quod fueris.
   It makes one want to weep.

EPITAPHS BY LEARNED MEN

CAELIUS SECUNDUS CURIO
HENDECASYLLABLES ON THE APOTHEOSIS OF OLYMPIA FULVIA MORATA[40]

O traveler, you who stop to smell the earth
strewn with violets and everything everywhere
fragrant with the odor of Arabia, listen kindly.
You know the three Graces, the nine Muses,
famed in the writings of the men of old:
Women who have any share
in more elegant art or sophisticated erudition,
the poets by general agreement attribute
to them these goddesses' hearts, nourished by that spirit[41]
which the chorus of sacred poets tells
came from the ethereal shores.
She, whom perhaps you think is covered by this tomb
is the tenth Muse and the fourth Grace.
Pallas called her Olympia
because they say she was born as a poet from Olympus.
But why was the name Fulvia given to her?
Perhaps because she was like yellow gold[42]

---

40. Carlus Utenhovius (Charles Utenhove, 1536–1600) of Ghent, scholar and champion of Dutch independence. He appended a free translation of this poem in Greek anacreontics. Utenhove was tutor to Camille de Morel (b. 1547), a Latin poet and scholar of the next generation; see Stevenson 1998, 90–92.

41. "Harum pectora nutriente Phoebo, flatu" 1562, 1570; 1562 errata: "dele flatu," but "Phoebo" is clearly a miscorrection. It is difficult to convey in translation how vastly superior a poet Curio was to the others here represented. The Latin is elegant and tight.

42. A pun on *fulvus*, "yellow."

refined by evil trials
and tested by harsh fates
and found purer than gold.
Or because like the golden eagle
accustomed to live among the blessed in heaven
she has left the low-lying lands too swiftly.
And because powerful with wise talent
with rare gifts of talent she shone among the girls for her learning,
endowed with chaste and good morals,
that is why she was called Morata in the common tongue.
Christ the Lord gave her to be seen
on earth, but as soon as He saw how on fire she was
with love for Him, suddenly
He snatched her away to heaven, and joined her to Himself
tied with the firm bond of marriage.
With Him she now takes her quiet rest
a sharer in perpetual happiness.
And you, traveler, be well and live long.
Cultivate virtue in a soul proved excellent
which alone can make you blessed in heaven.

To my long-standing friendship with her father Fulvius Moratus and her mother Lucretia Morata, and to the divine genius, writings, and true piety of Olympia Morata and to the grief of her husband Andreas Grunthler, Caius Secundus Curio dedicates these hendecasyllables. She lived less than xxix years. She went to Christ on the 26th of October in the Year of Christian salvation 1555 at Heidelberg.

JACOB MICYLLUS
AN EPITAPH ON THE LADY OLYMPIA FULVIA MORATA, WHO DIED ON THE 26TH OF OCTOBER 1555.

The Italian girl Olympia is covered by this pile of earth
the leading woman among the Pierian choruses,
who once left the country of her fathers with her husband
and settled by your waves, O blond German,
here where the vineyard keeps the distant Franks busy
and nearby the river Main overflows with clear waters.
When the bestial soldiers raged in the burning town
and carried off the holy objects profaned by the enemy hand

twice robbed of her possessions, twice near to cruel death
she came to the rivers of the Neckar joined to the fords.
She had added the writings of the Greeks to the Latin Muses
and was equally learned in either tongue.
A rare specimen of happy Nature, and the only woman
to be set ahead of all men for genius.
But neither the honor of praise nor grace holds back the Fates.
She died, and lies buried in the long night.
Pray for rest and quiet sleep for her ashes,
visitor. All else is free from death.

OFEMIANUS, JURIS CONSULTUS[43]
TO THE MEMORY OF OLYMPIA MORATA,
A MOST LEARNED WOMAN

The most learned Olympia has left this mortal life
but because she left it with great profit
it is not right to mourn. For she has climbed to
the "Olympian homes" of the gods, which she religiously cherished.[44]
She is now in heaven "mingling dear to the blessed gods"[45]
one to whom the world was always unfair.

THE SAME
[GREEK]

If Sappho is the tenth of the singing Muses
then most divine Olympia is inscribed as the eleventh.

TO THE MEMORY OF DOCTOR ANDREAS GRUNTHLER,
HUSBAND OF OLYMPIA, OUR COLLEAGUE.[46]

Having lost the companion of your studies and the wife of your bed,
who is now to be numbered among the Muses,

---

43. I.e., a lawyer. I have been unable to trace Ofemianus.

44. Both 1562 and 1570 read "δώματα, quae coluit, religiosa deum." However, the adj. corresponds to nothing in Homer and is colorless unless taken as fem. nom. sing.

45. ὀλύμπια . . . δώματα (a common Homeric phrase; cf. *Il.* 1.18, etc.) and μακάροισι φίλη μιχθεῖσα θεοῖσι (built from various Homeric blocks; cf. *Il.* 20.347, *Od.* 1.82), two Homeric phrases.

46. No author is given.

Grunthler you have now given your soul to heaven, your bones
to this tomb, because to live longer was no longer sweet.

CHILIAN SINAPIUS, JURIS CONSULTUS
EPITAPHS TO OLYMPIA

You who once excelled with every gift of genius,
   the light of the virgin and female chorus,
have died not yet having lived for thirty years,
   than whom there was no woman more learned in Latin.
Her name was Morata, but Olympia was her famous first name,
   if Olympus holds any fame.
Hating the impious dogmas of the Pontiffs, she acknowledged
   the true faith of Christ with piety.
The Margrave laid waste the region of Franconia,
   a region which was the cause of his own death.[47]
The citizens were taken away, Olympia was stripped,
   her husband Andreas, a doctor in the medical arts, fled,
and coming at last to Heidelberg under an evil omen
   both ascended to those above in a short space of time.

Those whom a sincere love had joined together throughout their entire life
   could not be torn apart finally even in death.
Here lies Andreas Grunthler and his wife Olympia.
   The earth lies on their bodies; their souls hold the stars.

Through various misfortunes,[48] splendid Olympia
   has climbed to Olympus; now she has the gift of eternal light.
She celebrates the teaching of Christ the Redeemer;
   for her there will be an endless life with Christ.

If piety, morals, candor, learning, and modesty
   could allow one to enjoy lifelong prosperity
then Olympia would have lived as long as the Cumaean Sibyl.
   But she lies snatched away by a premature death.

---

47. Albrecht II Alcibiades, margrave of Brandenburg-Kulmbach (1522–57). See letters 40 and 41. The poem therefore dates after 1557.
48. Cf. Verg. A. 1.204.

If among the girls of ancient times there was any one
   who was outstanding for learning, who loved religion,
Olympia Morata outdid her in cultivated genius
   more learned than learned men.
Among the leading lights, experienced in Latin and Greek language,
   she worked on her studies day and night.
Poring over the divine volumes of sacred law
   she gave to herself an exceptional name.
But alas, too soon Olympia yielded to the fates,
   she who alone was worthy to live all the days of the Sibyl.
And yet she still lives with the better part of herself
   and has the joys of eternal light.

As once when the virgin Constantia burned[49]
with love for Christ and sincere religion
and boldly defeated the crowd of the ancients with learned speech
and overturned the false teachings of the "wise,"
such flames did Olympia conceive in her mind
setting no joys of world ahead of Christ.
Olympia was loyal to Christ as long as she lived,
unsurpassed in defending the true faith of Christ.

ANOTHER. FOR CAELIUS SECUNDUS CURIO

The pious enjoy a brief span
of life. They leave us behind in a swifter
course, while for worse people the number
of days is drawn out, by God's will,
for those whom He loves go fast
having the joys of eternal light.
Those above give room to the evil, so that
they may imbue their hearts with good morals.
Therefore Morata for a few years on earth
was worthy of a better life.

---

49. "Costeria" 1562, 1570; "Costieia" 1562 errata. Despite the confusion of the name, apparently a reference to the legend of St. Catherine of Alexandria (e.g. *The Golden Legend*). However, *Catharina* simply cannot be made to fit the meter. The only alternative seems to be *Constantia*, which does scan. However, the evidence for a legend of this type for Constantia (also called Costantina; a daughter of Constantine; the Italian Santa Costanza) is slight. Cf. *De laude virginum*, attributed to St. Aldhelm: "plures name Christo convertit dogmate turmas" (P.L. 89.274B–275B; *Acta Sanctorum*, ed. Bollandus-Henschenius, Feb., Tom. III [Feb. 18], 70b).

Thus since "Caelia" has been received in Heaven
it is fitting for us, Caelius, to ease our grief.[50]

CASPAR STIBLIN
OLYMPIA: AN ECLOGUE

Cloudy night had poured its black wings over the earth
as I took the most grateful gifts of sweet sleep,
when, lo, through the dark shadows came Apollo,
unkempt, with funeral clothing. His face did not shine
with its usual radiance, nor was his head adorned
with a crown woven from green ivy leaves—his custom before—
instead he was grieving, wrapped in the shadow of a somber cloak.
Groaning piteously, he watered his face wet with tears;
he began sad words and said these things:
"Mourn, O Pierides for the pitiable funeral of your girl,
brought on too soon by the wool-weaving goddesses.[51]
Mourn, you eloquent offspring of divine Helicon,
whom Minerva's care, sprung from Jove, nurtured in her bosom.
Celestial Olympia has died by an unworthy fate
Olympia has deserted the grieving earth.
The most brilliant star has left our chorus."
Now the nymphs mourn, and all the Oreads.
In the deep valley, Venus herself makes the cliffs
resound with weeping, and the rural gods, the she-satyrs
redouble their lament: "Our Olympia has left us!
She who often held back the rushing streams of the Eridanus[52]
with her divine song, and made it stand still in midstream
and enthralled us in the deepest waves.
She who made the vales of the cloud-bearing Apennines re-echo
and soothed the green woods and the echoing groves.
What fate has overwhelmed you, Olympia?"
    Although a sudden trembling went through my frightened limbs,
yet I said: "O Phoebus, you wish to inquire deeply

---

50. A pun on Caelius's name and *caelum*, "heaven"; "Caelia" is thus a punning translation of "Olympia ," which also serves to indicate Caelius's fatherly love for Olympia. It is a pity this is not a very good poem.
51. The Parcae or Fates, who spin the yarn of life.
52. The river Po.

into the cause of this bitter complaint?" Immediately he began:
"Once there shown far a man most famous in the Italian city
which takes its high name from rigid iron,[53]
a man worthy to be venerated by all for his liberal arts.
His name was MORATUS, for he was outstanding
in holy morals, and offered a model
of an honorable life. From his chaste wife he received
three girls, and nourished them in holy honor
from their earliest years. He engendered love for virtue
in them and bade them give their first offerings
at once to the sacred Muses. But one excelled the others,
the one we weep for, far ahead in judgment,
learning, genius, virtue, talent, and intelligence.
She applied her young heart to books of sacred Wisdom
and sighed for the high peaks of Mount Parnassus
when she had lived but twelve years.
We all encouraged the wonderful efforts of the Muse.
As did I: for she bathed her shining lips in the sacred waters
of the Medusan spring,[54] and learned faith
moved her to play with her fingers a song, which Thalia
herself would wish to hear, and Thracian Orpheus would desire,
for which you would scarcely trade the songs of Homer's lyre
or praise the Muse of him who made Ascra famous.[55]
"Eagerly she traced the forensic podium of Argolic treasure,[56]
then the long speeches of the Ausonian tongue,[57]
expert she would play in the Boetian manner
and no less bring forth a noble song on the Latin strings.[58]
Thus her fame touched the shining stars of heaven,
and she began to be famous, spoken of in the mouths of men.
Thus the lady garnered great glory for the delights

---

53. Ferrara, as if from *ferum*, "iron."

54. The fountain of Hippocrene, on Mt. Helicon, which offers poetic inspiration. It was opened by a blow from the hoof of Pegasus, also called Medusaeus, since his rider Bellophon carried the Medusa's head. Cf. Ov. M. 5.312.

55. Hesiod.

56. I.e. the Greek orators.

57. I.e. Latin oratory; cf. Ov. Tr. 5.7.61.

58. Greek and Latin poetry.

of the court on the Po, and was held in high honor.
So great was the admiration, Olympia, for your song.

"But at length, hating the noise and the great turmoil.
this young lady, who loved quiet, left the noble court,
accustomed as she was to live her life in calm retirement.
But when she was ready to strike her sweet songs
to the lyre string, as a companion in her studies and her life,
she chose Grunthler, embraced in his loving arms,
whom Franconia gave birth to, from a noble father.
He was already famed in Machaon's art,[59]
a youth outstanding for his talent, handsome in appearance,
learned in elegance and both languages,
in short the one who was worthy to be Morata's mate.
With an equal consort he returned to his fathers' home,
and entered his city with everyone applauding.

"But when Schweinfurt fell in the great disaster,
and the Margrave raged, the devastator in wild war,
even her husband was fleeing the crisis of present Mars,
alas wretched Olympia wandered through the middle of the crowds,
uncertain—not even the Muses protected her.
Where could she go, where turn her steps,
tossed with so many evils. Her husband thrown out of the city:
the only one who could offer solace to her
afflicted by these wretched events, and ease such grief!
But when she escaped from the savage enemies,
the hero, the Elector Palatine, took her into his own calm halls,
and cherished her, exhausted and full of hardships, together with her husband.

"Mourn, O Pierides for the pitiable funeral of your girl,
brought on too soon by the wool-weaving goddesses.
And you, cruel Mars, stupidest of the profane gods,
and despiser of the sacred Muse, who refreshes all,
whom slaughter and book delights, and the massacre of men.
Whence comes your madness, this insanity for the sword,
so that only you delight to cut down innocent poets?
Poets have even moved the tyrant of the underworld with their singing
and the cruel Eumenides and the other monsters of the Tartarean

---

59. Son of Aesclepius; i.e. medicine.

swamp, but you alone are not softened by any art.
Destruction, wailing, slaughter, your only delights!
May heavenly Jupiter consume you with burning fire.
May he place Pelorus upon you with its rocky weight,[60]
or hang you up in fetters in the mountains of the Caucasus,
so that as you endure for ever arctic snows and the frosts of Scythia,
they may watch, Themis and Peace, the best of all things.

"Mourn, O Pierides for the pitiable funeral of your girl,
brought on too soon by the wool-weaving goddesses.
While she sang the sweetest songs to an Aeolic plectrum,[61]
while she touched highest heaven with her sweet singing,
while she enchanted men and wild beasts, came horrible Violence
and stopped her pouring forth sweet melody from her lyre.
Just as the swan on the banks of the Ionian Caystrus
sends forth a pure voice from its throat when death is near,
she sang, even as fainting she breathed her life into the air.

"Mourn, O Pierides for the pitiable funeral of your girl,
brought on too soon by the wool-weaving goddesses.
What goddess envied you your Muses, Olympia?
What disaster stole the great glory of the Ausonian shore,
which famous Ferrara bore in lucky birth
and handed to the Germans, when only a few years had rolled on?
The land of Italy may well roar against in complaint.
Who is able to commemorate your praises, Olympia?
Who can equal your sad funeral with the rivers of his tears?
While Olympia was alive, the loss of Sappho would appear less
ill-omened; even your fate could be endured,
learned Alcaeus, and the sad chorus would not urge
even your merits, Alcman. All these, sweet Olympia
made up for by herself while she lived with her Lesbian verse.

"Mourn, O Pierides for the pitiable funeral of your girl,
brought on too soon by the wool-weaving goddesses.
Lesbos will praise the divine modulations of Alcaeus,
and Paros will praise Archilochus, the Boetian rivers
melodies of Pindar's lyre, Mytilene
Pelasgian Sappho. Both the German fields
and the Hesperian woods will long praise you in song."

---

60. Capo di Faro, the mountain at the southeastern tip of Sicily.
61. *Aeolic* is an allusion to Sappho.

As Phoebus was lamenting these things to my ears
I awoke from sleep, and Phoebus said one last thing:
"May you live forever, sweet Olympia, blessed
may you live. Poets will please your shades with song.
Your glory will live throughout the whole world."

THE TOMBSTONES

E*ditor's note:* Morata's tombstone stands today in the north entrance hall of the Peterskirche in Heidelberg. Grunthler's tombstone had been lost by 1620[62] but was copied by contemporaries.[63] For Rascalon, see notes to letter 63.

SACRED TO GOD IMMORTAL

To the virtue and memory of Olympia Morata, daughter of the philosopher Fulvius Morato of Ferrara, beloved wife of Dr. Andreas Grunthler, a woman whose genius and singular knowledge of both languages, whose probity in morals and highest zeal for piety were always held above the common level. Men's judgment of her life was confirmed with divine testimony by the most holy and peaceful death which she died. She died in exile in the year of Salvation 1555 age 29. Buried here with her husband and brother Emilio. Guillaume Rascalon, M.D., for those who well deserve it placed this in piety.

SACRED TO GOD BEST AND GREATEST, THREE IN ONE

To Andreas Grunthler of Schweinfurt, a man of great learning, doctor and philosopher. As soon as the university, in which he had barely begun to teach

---

62. Adamus 1620, 82.

63. Inscriften-Kommision der Heidelberger Akademie der Wissenschaften DI 12 Nr. 276. Photograph and text of Morata's tombstone at Neumüllers-Klauser 1970, 150; Raff 1983, 94–95; Kössling and Weiss-Stählin 1990, 157. Texts at Morata 1562, 271–72; 1570, 223; Adamus 1615, 70; 1620, 82–83 (with errors); Niceron 1729–45, 15:111–12; Weiss-Stählin 1976, 99 (a number of typographical errors and the loss of several lines); Flood and Shaw 1997, 137–38 (following Adamus and with flawed English translation).

the art of medicine in exile, had scattered from here in fear of the plague,[64] he desired to be freed from the body, and in accord with his prayer, he was freed, not only from weariness at the loss of his friend and wife, that incomparable example, his Minerva (he was most forbearing in every change of fortune), but also so that, having been taken out of this dense ignorance of heavenly matters into the light, he might no longer offend God with his errors. For one who lies here in hope of the resurrection, a friend for a friend, a doctor for a doctor, Guillaume Rascalon placed this.

---

64. "schola, in qua vixdum ab exilio profiteri artem coeperat" Morata 1562 (262), 1570 (223), Niceron : "in qua vixit dum" Adamus, Flood and Shaw : "autem" Flood and Shaw.

VOLUME EDITOR'S BIBLIOGRAPHY

PRIMARY SOURCES

Adamus (Adam), Melchior. 1615. *Vitae Germanorum philosophorum, qui seculo superiori etquod excurrit, philosophicis ac humanioribus literis clari floruerunt.* Heidelberg: Rosa.

———. 1620. *Vitae Germanorum medicorum, qui seculo superiori, et quod excurrit, claruerunt.* Heidelberg: Rosa.

Arbenz, Emil, and Hermann Wartmann, eds. 1890–1913. *Die Vadianische Breifsammlung der Stadtbibliothek St. Gallen.* Mitteilungen zur vaterländischen Geschichte, 24, 25, 27, 28, 29, 30, 30a. 7 vols. in 2. St. Gallen.

Aubigné, Agrippa d'. 1969. *Oeuvres.* Edited by Henri Weber, Jacques Bailbé, and Marguerite Soulié. Paris: Gallimard [ed. Pléiade].

Avila y Zuñiga, Luis de. 1548. *Comentario de la guerra de Alemaña hecha de Carlo V. Maximo Emperador Romano Rey de España en el año de M.D.XLVI y M.D.XLVII.* Cited from the 1852 ed., *Comentario de la guerra de Alemaña* (Biblioteca de autores españoles XXI, Madrid).

———. 1550. *Commentariorum de bello germanico, a Carolo V. Caesare Maximo gesto, libri duo a Gulielmo Malineo Brugensi latine redditi & iconibus ad historiam accomodis illustrati.* Translated by Guillaume van Male (d. 1560). Antverpiae: I. Steelsii.

Bembo, Pietro. 1729. *Opere del cardinale Pietro Bembo; ora per la prima volta tutte in un corpo unite.* 4 vols. Venice: Francesco Hertzhauser.

Bèze, Theodore de. [1580] 1971. *Icones. Id est verae imagines virorvm doctrina simvl et pietate illvstrivm.* Geneva, Apud I. Laonium. Reprint, with introductory note by R. M. Cummings, Menston, England: Scolar Press.

Bollandus, Joannes, and Godefridus Henschenius, eds., 1643–. *Acta sanctorum quotquot toto orbe coluntur,* etc. Antwerp: Apud Ioannem Meursium.

Calcagnini, Celio. 1544. *Caelii Calcagnini Ferrarienis pronotarii apostolici opera aliquot.* Basel: Froben.

Calvin, Jean. 1863–1900. *Opera Quae Supersunt Omnia.* Edited by Eduard Cunitz, Eduard Reuss, Paul Lobstein, Alfred Erichson, Wilhelm Baldensperger, and Ludwig Horst. *Corpus reformatorum,* vols. 29–87. Brunsvigae: C. A. Schwetschke.

———. 1926–1959. *Joannis Calvini Opera Selecta.* Edited by Petrus Barth. 5 vols. Munich: C. Kaiser.

———. 1978. *Concerning Scandals.* Translated by John W. Fraser. Grand Rapids, Mich.: Eerdmans.

———. 1984. *Des scandales*. Edited by Olivier Fatio and C. Rapin. Genève: Droz.
———. 1990. *Institutes of the Christian Religion*. Translated by Henry Beveridge. 2d ed. Chicago: Encyclopaedia Britannica.
Caretti, Lanfranco, ed. 1940. *Olimpia Morata. Epistolario (1540–1555)*. Ferrara.
———. 1954. *Opere di Olympia Morata*. Ferrara.
Cereta, Laura. 1640. *Laurae Ceretae Brixiensis Feminae Clarissimae Epistolae; iam primum e m[anu]s[criptis] in lucem productae a Iacobo Philippo Tomasino, qui eius vitam et notas addidit*. Patavii: Sardi. Available on-line at <www.uni-mannheim.de/mateo/desbillons/cereta>.
———. 1997. *Laura Cereta. Collected Letters of a Renaissance Feminist*. Edited and translated by Diana Robin. Chicago: University of Chicago Press.
Colomies, Paul. 1699. *Bibliothéque choisie*. 2d ed. Amsterdam: George Gallet.
Crespin, Jean. 1560. *Actiones et monimenta martyrum. Qui a Wicleffo et Husso ad nostram hanc aetate in Germania, Gallia, Anglia, Flandria, Italia, & ipsa demum Hispania, veritatem euangelicam sanguine suo constanter obsignauerunt*. [Geneva]: Joannes Crispinus. [The Latin ed. of Crespin's *Livre des martyrs depuis le temps de Wiclif et de Jean Hus jusqu'à present*, 1554 (various titles)]
Curio, Caelius Horatius. 1550. *De Amplitudine misericordiae absolutisssima oratio, a Marsilio Andreasio Manuano Italico sermone primum conscriptua, nunc in Latinum conversa, Caelio Horatio Curione, C. S. F. interprete*, etc. Basel: Ioan. Oporini.
Curio, Caelius Secundus. 1544. *Coelii Secundi Araneus, seu de providentia Dei*. Basel: Oporinus. [Includes text of *De liberis pie Christianeque educandis epistola*]
———. 1551. *M. Tullii Ciceronis Philippicae orationes XIIII in M. Antonium: a Caelio Secundo Curione post omnes omnium castigationes diligentius emendatae*. Basel: [Apud Hier. Frobenium et Nic. Episcopium].
———. 1553. *Caelij Secundi Curionis Selectarum epistolarum libri duo*. Basel: Ioannes Oporinus.
———. 1554. *Coelii Secundi Curionis De amplitudine beati regni Dei, dialogi sive libri duo*. Basel: Ioannes Oporinus.
———. 1560. *M. Antonii Coccii Sabellici Opera omnia, ab infinitis quibvs scatebant mendis, repurgata et castigata: cum supplemento Rapsodiae historiarum ab orbe condito, ad haec usque tempora, pulcherrimo ac diligentissimo, in tomos quatuor digesta: qui, quid contineant, aduersa pagina indicabit: atque haec omnia per Caelium Secundum Curionem, non sine magno labore iudicioque confecta*. Basel: Per Ioannem Heruagium.
Defaux, Gerard, ed. 1990–93. *Clément Marot. Oeuvres poétiques completes*. 2 vols. Paris: Bordas (Classiques Garnier).
Des Périers, Bonaventure. 1983. *Cymbalum Mundi. Bonaventure Des Periers?* Edited by Peter Hampshire Nurse. 3d ed. Genève: Droz, 1983.
Des Roches, Madeleine Neveu, and Catherine Fredonnoit Des Roches. 1993. *Les oeuvres: Madeleine Des Roches, Catherine Des Roches*. Edited by Anne R. Larsen. Genève: Droz.
———. 1998. *Les second oeuvres: Madeleine Des Roches, Catherine Des Roches*. Edited by Anne R. Larsen. Genève: Droz.
Dolce, Lodovico. 1553. *Dialogo della institution delle donne*. 4th ed. In Vinegia [Venice]: Gabriel Giolito de Ferrari e Fratelli. Reproduced on microfilm, "History of Women," reel 26, no. 166 (New Haven, Conn.: Research Publications, 1975).
Eberti, Johann Caspar. 1706. *Eröffnetes Cabinet dess gelehrten Frauen-Zimmers*. Frankfurt

and Leipzig: Michael Rohrlach. Reproduced as *Archiv für philosophie- und theologiegeschichtliche Frauenforschung*, bd. 3. Munich: Iudicium, 1986.

Erasmus. 1906–58. *Opus Epistolarum Des[iderii] Erasmi Roterdami*. Edited by P. S. Allen, H. M. Allen, and H. W. Garrod. 12 vols. Oxford: Oxford University Press.

Fedele, Cassandra. 1636. *Clarissimae feminae Cassandrae Fidelis Venetae Epistolae et Orationes Posthumae*. Edited by Philippus Tomasinus. Patavii: Bolzetta. Reproduced on microfilm, "History of Women," reel 32, no. 199 (New Haven, Conn.: Research Publications, 1975). Also available on-line at <www.uni-mannheim.de/mateo/desbillons/fedele.html>.

———. 2000. *Cassandra Fedele: Letters and Orations*. Edited and translated by Diana Robin. Chicago: University of Chicago Press.

Foxe, John. 1837–41. *The Acts and Monuments of John Foxe: A New and Complete Edition*. Edited by Stephen Reed Cattley. London: R. B. Seeley and W. Burnside.

———. 1926. *Fox's Book of Martyrs. A History of the Lives, Sufferings and Triumphant Deaths of the Early Christian and the Protestant Martyrs*. Edited by William Byron Forbush. Philadelphia: John C. Winston.

Giraldi, Lilio Gregorio. 1894. *Lilius Gregorius Gyraldus. De poetis nostrorum temporum*. Edited by Karl Wotke. Berlin: Weidmann.

Giulio da Milano. 1552. *Esortatione al martirio*. [Poschiavo?]. [non vidi] The text is reproduced in *La Rivista Cristiana* 8 (1880) 1:3–10 and *Opuscoli e lettere di riformatori italiani del '500*, edited by G. Paladino. Bari: Laterza, 1913–27. 2:178–80, 182–86.

Hartmann, Alfred. 1942–. *Die Amerbachkorrespondenz*. 8 vols. Basel: Verlag der Universitatsbibliothek.

Hörmann, Wolfgang Ludwig, Freiherr von und zu Gutenberg. 1770. *Ehren Denckmal und Stammen Register des adeligen Geschlechtes derer Hörmann von und zu Gutenberg. Aus alten Briefschaften und sicheren Nachrichten mit Beyfügung der Wappen von ihren Befreundungen, zusammengeschrieben von Wolfgang Ludwig Hörmann von und zu Gutenberg. Anno 1770*. Manuscript B 89, Stadarchiv Kaufbeuren. [non vidi]

Kidd, B. J. (Beresford James). 1911. *Documents Illustrative of the Continental Reformation*. Oxford: Clarendon Press.

King, Margaret L., and Albert Rabil Jr. 1983, rev. ed. 1992. *Her Immaculate Hand. Selected Works by and about the Women Humanists of Quattrocento Italy*. Binghamton, N.Y.: Center for Medieval and Early Renaissance Studies.

Knox, John. 1846–64. *Works*. Edited by David Laing. 6 vols. Edinburgh: Wodrow Society.

Kornmann, Heinrich. 1669. *Sibylla trig-andriana, seu, De virginitate: Virginum statu et jure tractatus novus et iucundus*, etc. Oxford: Ed. Forrest Bibliop. Reproduced on microfilm, "Early English Books, 1641–1700," reel 845:9 (Ann Arbor: University Microfilms, 1978).

Labé, Louise. 1981. *Oeuvres completes*. Edited by Enzo Giudici. Genève: Droz.

Lehms, Georg Christian. [1715] 1973. *Teutschlands galante Poetinnen mit ihren sinnreichen und netten Proben: nebst einem Anhang auslandischer Dames*. Frankfurt: Anton Heinscheidt. Reprint, Leipzig: Zentralantiquariat der DDR.

Lotichius, Johann Peter. 1625–28. *Io. Petri Lotichii, D. Medici & C.P. Cas., bibliothecae poeticae pars prima et secunda* [-pars quarta et ultima]. Francofurti: Sumptibus Lucae Jennisii. Reproduced on microfilm, "German Baroque Literature," reel 8, no. 40 (New Haven, Conn.: Research Publications, 1969).

Luther, Martin. 1883–1948. *D. Martin Luthers Werke. Kritische Gesamtausgabe*. Weimar: H. Bohlaus Nachfolger. [*WA*, the Weimar edition; vol. 15, 1899]
———. 1902. *The Table Talk of Martin Luther*. Translated and edited by William Hazlitt. London: G. Bell and Sons.
———. 1955–76. *Luther's Works*. Edited by Jaroslav Pelikan and Helmut T. Lehman. St. Louis: Concordia.
———. 1959. *What Luther Says: An Anthology compiled by Ewald M. Plass*. 3 vols. St. Louis: Concordia.
Makin, Bathsua. [1673] 1980. *An Essay to Revive the Antient Education of Gentlewomen*. London: J. D. to be sold by Tho. Parkhurst. Reprint, with introduction by Paula L. Barbour, Los Angeles: Augustan Reprint Society, no. 202.
Martineau, Christine, and Michel Veissière, eds. 1975–. *Correspondance, 1521–1524. Guillaume Briçonnet, Marguerite d'Angoulême*. Genève: Droz.
Morata, Olympia Fulvia. 1558. *Olympiae Fulviae Moratae mulieris omnium eruditissimae Latina et Graeca, quae haberi potuerunt, monumenta*. Edited by Caius Secundus Curio. Basel: Petrum Pernam. [The 1st ed., dedicated to Isabella Besegna]
———. 1562. *Olympiae Fulviae Moratae foeminae doctissimae ac plane divinae Orationes, Dialogi, Epistolae, Carmina tam Latina quam Graeca*. Edited by Caius Secundus Curio. 2d ed. Basel: Petrum Pernam. Reproduced on microfilm, "History of Women," reel 62, no. 396 (New Haven, Conn.: Research Publications, 1975). Available on-line at <www.uni-mannheim.de/mateo/desbillons/olimp.html>.
———. 1570. *Olympiae Fulviae Moratae foeminae doctissimae ac plane divinae opera omnia quae hactenus inueniri potuerunt*. 3d ed. Basel: Petrum Pernam. Reproduced on microfilm, "History of Women," reel 62, no. 397 (New Haven, Conn.: Research Publications, 1975). [The 4th ed. is merely a reprint of this with miscellaneous additions.]
Naphy, William G., ed. 1996. *Documents on the Continental Reformation*. Houndmills, England: Macmillan.
Negri, Francesco. 1550. *De Fanini Faventini ac Dominici Bassananesis morte, qui nuper in Italia Rom. Pon. iussu occisi sunt, brevis historia*. [Wittenberg: Josef Klug]. Reproduced on microfiche, Wolfenbüttel: Herzog August Bibliothek, 1988.
Niceron, Jean-Pierre. 1729–45. *Memoires pour servir a l'histoire des hommes illustres dans la republique des lettres, avec un catalogue raisonné de leurs ouvrages*. Paris: Briasson. [Vol. 15 published in 1731]
Pfanner, Josef. 1966. *Breife von, an und über Caritas Pirckheimer auf den Jahren 1498–1530*. Landshut: Solanus.
Pigna, Giovan Battista. 1553. *Io. Baptistae Pignae Carminvm lib. qvatvor: ad Alphonsvm Ferrariae principem. His adiunximus Caelii Calcagnini Carm. lib. III., Lvdovici Areosti Carm. lib. II*. Venetiis: Ex officina Erasmiana, Vincentii Valgrisii.
Pires, Diogo. 1983. *Diogo Pires. Antologia Poética*. Edited by Carlos Ascenso André. Textos Humanísticos Portugueses 1. Coimbra: Centro de Estudos Clássicos e Humanísticos da Universidade de Coimbra.
Pontano, Giovanni Gioviano. 1965. *I trattati delle virtu sociali: De liberalitate, De beneficentia, De magnificentia, De splendore, De conviventia*. Text and translation by Francesco Tateo. Rome: Ateneo.
Renato, Camillo. 1968. *Camillo Renato. Opere, documenti e testimonianze*. Edited by Antonio Rotondò. Corpus reformatorum Italicorum. DeKalb: Northern Illinois University Press.

Robinson, Mary. 1799. *A Letter to the Women of England: On the injustice of mental subordination*. With anecdotes. London: T. N. Longman and O. Rees.
Sansovino, F. 1565. *De gli huomini illustri della casa Orsina*. Venezia: Stagnini. [Often treated as a second volume of *L'historia di casa Orsina*]
Sardi, Gasparo. 1549. *Epistolarum liber, varia reconditaque historiarum cognitione refertus. De triplici philosophia commentariolus*. Florentiae: L. Torrentinus.
Schurman, Anna Maria van. 1998. *Anna Maria van Schurman. Whether a Christian Woman Should Be Educated and Other Writings from her Intellectual Circle*. Edited and translated by Joyce L. Irwin. Chicago: University of Chicago Press.
Sidney, Sir Philip. 1977. *The Countess of Pembroke's Arcadia*. Edited by Maurice Evans. Harmondsworth, England: Penguin.
Simler, Iosia. 1563. *Oratio de vita et obitv clarissimi viri et praestantissimi theologi d. Petri Martyris Vermilii*. Tigvri: Christophorvm Froschouerum Iuniorem.
Spangenberg, Cyriacus. 1591. *Adels Spiegel. Historischer, aussfürlicher Bericht, was Adel sey und heisse, woher er kom(m)e*, etc. Schmalkalden: Michel Schmück. [non vidi; copies at Harvard and Folger]
Thomas, Hubert (Leodius). 1664. *Annalium de vita et rebus gestis illustrissimi principis Friderici II Electoris Palatini Libri XIV*. Frankfort: Johann Ammon.
Thomasius, Jacob and Johannes Sauerbrei. 1676. *Diatriben academicam de foeminarum eruditione priorem . . . proponit Johannes Sauerbrei*, etc. Lipsiae: sumptibus Johannis Erici Hahnii. Available on-line at <http://www.uni-mannheim.de/mateo/desbillons//foemi.html>.
Thou, Jacques-Auguste de. 1733. *Jac. Augusti Thuani Historiarum sui temporis tomus primus [-septimus]*. 7 vols. London: S. Buckley.
Titius, Caspar. 1684. *Loci theologici historici, oder, Theologisches Exempel-Buch*. Leipzig: Christoph Gunther. Reproduced on microfilm, "German Baroque Literature," Harold Jantz Collection no. 2506, reel 514 (New Haven, Conn.: Research Publications, 1973).
Tomasini, Giacomo Filippo. 1644. *Iacobi Philippi Tomasini episcopi Aemoniensis Elogia Virorum Literis & Sapientia Illustrium*. Padova: Sardi. Available on-line at <http://www.uni-mannheim.de/mateo/desbillons/elogia>.
Vossius, Gerardus Joannes. 1650. *De quatuor artibus popularibus. Gerardi Ioannis Vossii De quatuor artibus popularibus, de philologia, et scientiis mathematicis*. Amstelaedami: Ex typographeio Ioannis Blaeu.
Weston, Elizabeth Jane [Westonia]. *Collected Writings: Elizabeth Jane Weston*. Edited and translated by Donald Cheney and Brenda M. Hosington. Toronto: University of Toronto Press, 2000.

SECONDARY SOURCES

Adorni-Braccesi, Simonetta. 1994. *"Una città infetta." La Repubblica di Lucca nella crisi religiosa del Cinquecento*. Florence: Olschki.
———. 1997. "Religious Refugees from Lucca in the Sixteenth Century: Political Strategies and Religious Proselytism." *Archiv für Reformationsgeschichte* 88:338–379.
Bacchelli, Franco. 1998. "Science, Cosmology, and Religion in Ferrara, 1520–1550." In Ciammitti et al. 1998, 333–54.

Bainton, Roland H. 1971. *Women of the Reformation in Germany and Italy.* Minneapolis: Augsburg Publishing House, 253–68.

———. 1980. "Learned Women in the Europe of the Sixteenth Century." In Labalme 1980, 117–28.

Barker, Paula S. Datsko. 1995. "Caritas Pirckheimer: A Female Humanist Confronts the Reformation." *Sixteenth Century Journal* 26:259–72.

Barotti, Giovanni Andrea. [1792–93] 1970. *Memorie istoriche di letterati ferraresi.* 3 vols. Ferrara: Rinaldi. Reprint, Bologna: Forni.

Barton, Florence Whitfield. 1965, *Olympia: A Novel of the Reformation.* Philadelphia: Fortress.

Bassanese, Fiora A. 1994. "Vittoria Colonna (1492–1547)." In Russell 1994, 85–94.

Beck, Heinrich Christian. 1842. *M. Johannes Sutellius. Reformator und erster Superintendent der Kirchen zu Göttingen und Schweinfurt.* Schweinfurt: Christian Wetzstein.

Benrath, Karl. 1877. *Bernardino Ochino, of Siena: A Contribution towards the History of the Reformation.* Translated by Helen Zimmern. New York: Robert Carter & Brothers.

———. [1892] 1968. *Bernardino Ochino von Siena: Ein Beitrag zur Geschichte der Reformation.* 2. verb. Aufl. Braunschweig: Schwetschke. Reprint, Neiuwkoop: B. de Graaf.

———. 1903. "Morata, Olimpia." In *Realencyklopädie für protestantische Theologie und Kirche.* 3d ed. 13:461–64.

Bertoni, Giulio. 1933. "Documenti sulla dimora di Clément Marot a Ferarra." In *Mélanges de philologie offerts à Jean-Jacques Salverda de Grave* (Groningue: J.-B. Wolters), 9–11.

———. 1936. "Clément Marot à Ferarre: Documents nouveaux." *Revue des études italiennes* 1:188–93.

Bietenholz, Peter G., and Thomas B. Deutscher, eds. 1985–87. *Contemporaries of Erasmus.* Toronto: University of Toronto Press.

Biondi, Albano. 1970. "Il 'Pasquillus extaticus' di C. S. Curione nella vita religiosa italiana della prima metà del '500.'" *Bollettino della società di studi Valdesi* 128:29–38.

———. 1974. "La giustificazione della simulazione nel cinquecento." In *Eresia e riforma nell'Italia del Cinquecento: Miscellanea I,* edited by Albano Biondi. DeKalb: Northern Illinois University Press; Chicago: Newberry Library.

Blaisdell, Charmarie Jenkins [Webb]. 1969. "Royalty and Reform: The Predicament of Renée de France." Ph.D. diss., Tufts University.

———. 1972. "Renée de France between Reform and Counter-Reform." *Archiv für Reformationsgeschichte* 63:196–226.

———. 1975. "Politics and Heresy in Ferrara, 1534–1559." *Sixteenth Century Journal* 6:67–93.

———. 1982. "Calvin's Letters to Women: The Courting of Ladies in High Places." *Sixteenth Century Journal* 13:67–84.

Blume, Friedrich. 1974. *Protestant Church Music: A History.* New York: Norton.

Bonafede, Carolina. 1845. *Cenni biografici e ritratti d'insigni donne bolognesi.* Bologna: Sassi. Reproduced on microfilm, "History of Women," reel 191, no. 1268 (New Haven, Conn.: Research Publications, 1975).

Bonnet, Jules. 1856. *Vie d'Olympia Morata, épisode de la renaissance et de la réforme en Italie.* 3d ed. rev. and aug. Paris. Reproduced on microfilm, "History of Women," reel 245, no. 1634 (New Haven, Conn.: Research Publications, 1975).

———. 1878. "Lettera inedita di Olimpia morata." *Rivista Christiana* 6:3–7.

———, ed. 1872. "Mémoires de la vie de Jéhan de l'Archevesque, sieur de Soubise." *Bulletin de la société de l'histoire du protestantisme français* 23:15–22, 305–12, 452–62, 495–503, 549–54. Separately published as *Mémoires de la vie de Jean Parthenay-Larchevêque, sieur de Soubise, accompagnés le lettres relatives aux guerres d'Italie sous Henri II et au siége de Lyon (1562–1653)*. Paris: L. Willem, 1879.

Bourdieu, Pierre. 1977. *Outline of a Theory of Practice*. Cambridge: Cambridge University Press.

———. 1986. "The Forms of Capital." In *Handbook of Theory and Research for the Sociology of Education*, edited by John Richardson, 241–58. New York: Greenwood Press.

Borsetti Ferranti Bolani, Ferrante. 1735. *Historia almi Ferrariae gymnasu in duas partes divisa*. 2 vols. Ferrariae: Typis Bernadini Pomatelli. Reproduced on microfilm, Manuscripta, list 30, no. 3 (St. Louis: Pius XII Memorial Library, 1961).

Bozza, Tommaso. 1985. "Italia calvinista: Traduzioni italiane di Cavino nel secolo XVI." In *Miscellanea in onore di Ruggero Moscati*, 237–51. Naples: Edizioni scientifiche italiane.

Braun, Gabriel. 1988. "Le marriage de Renée de France avec Hercule d'Este: Une inutile mésalliance, 28 juin 1528." *Histoire, Economie et Société* 7:147–68.

Brown, George Kenneth. 1933. *Italy and the Reformation to 1550*. Oxford: B. Blackwell.

Bryant, Gwendolyn. 1987. "The Nuremburg Abbess: Caritas Pirckheimer." In Wilson 1987, 287–303.

Büsser, Fritz. 1994. "Humanismus im Zürich des 16. Jahrhunderts. In *Die Prophezei: Humanismus und Reformation in Zürich. Ausgewählte Aufsätze und Vorträge*, 56–73. Zürcher Beiträge zur Reformationsgeschichte 17. Bern: P. Lang.

Bussi, Rolando, ed. 1987. *Libri, idee e sentimenti religiosi nel Cinquecento italiano*. Modena: Panini.

Cameron, Euan. 1991. *The European Reformation*. Oxford: Oxford University Press.

———. 1992. "Italy." In Pettegree, ed. 1992, 188–214.

Cammelli, Giuseppe. 1941. Olimpia Morato." *Rinascita* 4:543–58.

Cantimori, Delio. 1990. "Italy and the Papacy." In *The New Cambridge Modern History*, edited by G. R. Elton, 2:288–312. 2d ed. (1990–). Cambridge: Cambridge University Press.

———. 1992. *Eretici italiani del Cinquecento e altri scritti*. Edited by Adriano Prosperi. Torino: Einaudi. [Ed. of 1939 reissued with other works]

Caponetto, Salvatore. 1999. *The Protestant Reformation in Sixteenth-Century Italy*. Translated by Anne C. Tedeschi and John Tedeschi. Kirksville, Mo.: Thomas Jefferson University Press.

Capori, marchese Giuseppe. 1875. "Fulvio Pellegrino Morato." *Atti e Memorie delle r. r. deputazioni di storica patria per le provincie modenesi e parmenesi*, ser. 1, vol. 8:361–71. [Available in the Vatican Library as an extract: Stampati: Ferraioli.IV.8941 (int.20)]

Casadei, Alfredo. 1934. "Fanino Fanini da Faenza. Episodio della Riforma protestante in Italia con documenti inediti." *Nuova Risvista Storica* 18:168–99.

———. 1937. "Donne della Riforma italiana: Isabella Bresegna." *Religo* 13:6–63.

Castelli, Patrizia, ed. 1991. *La Rinascita del sapere: libri e maestri dello studio ferrarese*. Venezia: Marsilio.

Catalano, Michele. 1930. *Vita di Ludovico Ariosto, ricostruita su nuovi documenti.* 2 vols. Geneve: L. S. Olschki.

Chiellini, Sabrina. 1991. "Contributo per la storia degli insegnamenti umanistici dello Studio ferrarese." In Castelli 1991, 210–45.

Church, Frederic Cross. 1932. *The Italian Reformers, 1534–1564.* New York: Columbia University Press.

Ciammitti, Luisa, Steven F. Ostrow, and Salvatore Settis, eds. 1998. *Dosso's Fate: Painting and Court Culture in Renaissance Italy.* Los Angeles: Getty Research Institute for the History of Art and the Humanities.

Cignoni, Mario. 1982–84. "Il pensiero di Olimpia Morata nell'ambito della Riforma protestante." *Atti dell'Accademia delle scienze di Ferrara* 60–61:191–204.

———. 1990–92. "Madame de Soubise alla corte di Ferrara (1528–36)." *Atti dell'Accademia delle scienze di Ferrara* 68–69:91–99.

Cole, Alison. 1995. *Art of the Italian Renaissance Courts: Virtue and Magnificence.* London: Weidenfeld and Nicolson.

Comba, Emilio. 1895–97. *I nostri Protestanti.* 2 vols. Firenze: Claudiana.

Crouzet, Denis. 1996. *La genèse de la Réforme française: 1520–1560.* Paris: SEDES.

Cruciani, Fabrizio. 1983. *Teatro nel Rinascimento, Roma 1450–1550.* Roma: Bulzoni.

D'Ascia, Luca. "Humanistic Culture and Literary Invention in Ferrara at the Time of the Dossi." In Ciammitti et al. 1998, 309–32.

Davis, Natalie Zemon. 1975. *Society and Culture in Early Modern France: Eight Essays.* Stanford, Calif.: Stanford University Press.

Del Col, Andrea. 1980. "Per una sistemazione critica dell'evangelismo italiano e di un'opera recente." *Critica storia* 17:266–76.

Donvito, Luigi. 1983. "La 'relgione cittadina' e le nuove prospettive sul Cinquecento religioso italiano." *Rivista di storia e letteratura religiosa* 19:431–74.

Düchting, Reinhard et al. 1998. *Olympia Fulvia Morata: Stationen ihres Lebens: Ferrara, Schweinfurt, Heidelberg.* Katalog zur Ausstellung im Universitätsmuseum Heidelberg, 26 März—8 Mai 1998. Ubstadt-Weiher: Verlag Regionalkultur.

Dykema, Peter A., and Heiko A. Oberman, eds. 1993. *Anticlericalism in Late Medieval and Early Modern Europe.* Leiden and New York: Brill. [The 2d ed. (1994) contains an expanded bibliography.]

Eire, Carlos M. 1979. "Calvin and Nicodemism: A Reappraisal." *Sixteenth Century Journal* 10:45–69.

Fahy, Conor, 1961. "Un tratato di Vincenzo Maggi sulle donne e un'opera sconosciuta di Ortensio Landi." *Giornale storico della letteratura italiana* 138:254–72.

Fantuzzi, Giovanni. 1781–94. *Notizie degli scrittori bolognesi.* 9 vols. Bologna: Stamperia di S. Tommaso d'Aquino.

Fenlon, Dermot. 1972. *Heresy and Obedience in Tridentine Italy. Cardinal Pole and the Counter Reformation.* Cambridge: Cambridge University Press.

Firpo, Massimo. 1988. "Vittoria Colonna, Giovanni Morone e gli 'spirituali.'" *Rivista di storia e letteratura religiosa* 24:211–61. Reprinted in Firpo 1992, 119–75.

———. 1992. *Inquisizione romana e controriforma.* Bologna: Il Mulino.

———. 1993. *Riforma protestante ed eresie nell'Italia del Cinquecento: un profilo storico.* Roma: Laterza.

———. 1996. "The Italian Reformation and Juan de Valdés." *Sixteenth Century Journal* 27:353–64.

Flood, John L. 1997. "Olympia Fulvia Morata." In *German Writers of the Renaissance 1280–1580*, edited by James Hardin and Max Reinhart, 178–83. Dictionary of Literary Biography 179. Detroit: Gale Research.

Flood, John L., and David J. Shaw. 1997. *Johannes Sinapius (1505–1560): Hellenist and Physician in Germany and Italy*. Geneva: Droz.

Fontana, Bartolommeo. 1889–99. *Renata di Francia, Duchessa di Ferrara*. 3 vols. Rome: Forzani.

Fragnito, G. 1997. "Die religiöse Heterodoxie in Italien und Vittoria Colonna." In *Vittoria Colonna: Dichterin und Muse Michelangelos*, edited by Sylvia Ferino-Pagden, 225–310. Vienna: Kunsthistorisches Museum/Skira.

Frizzi, Antonio. [1847–48] 1982. *Memorie per la storia di Ferrara*. 5 vols. Ferrara: Abram Servado. Reprint, Ferrara: Libro Editore.

Gauna, Max. 1992. *Upwellings: First Expressions of Unbelief in the Printed Literature of the French Renaissance*. Rutherford, N.J.: Fairleigh Dickinson University Press

Gibaldi, Joseph. 1987. "Child, Woman, and Poet: Vittoria Colonna." In Wilson 1987, 22–46.

Gilmore, Myron Piper. 1963. *Humanists and Jurists: Six Studies in the Renaissance*. Cambridge, Mass.: Harvard University Press.

Gleason, Elisabeth G. 1978. "On the Nature of Sixteenth Century Italian Evangelism: Scholarship, 1963–78." *Sixteenth Century Journal* 9:3–25.

———. 1981. *Reform Thought in Sixteenth-Century Italy*. Chico, Calif.: Scholars Press.

———. 1992. "Italy and the Reformation." In Maltby 1992, 281–306.

———. 1993. *Gasparo Contarini: Venice, Rome, and Reform*. Berkeley and Los Angeles: University of California Press.

Goodman, Anthony, and Angus MacKay, eds. 1990. *The Impact of Humanism on Western Europe*. New York: Longman.

Gordon, Bruce. 2000. "Italy." In Pettegree 2000, 277–95.

Grafton, Anthony, and Lisa Jardine. 1986. *From Humanism to the Humanities: Education and the Liberal arts in Fifteenth- and Sixteenth-Century Europe*. Cambridge, Mass.: Harvard University Press. [Contains revised and expanded versions of Jardine 1983, 1985]

Greengrass, M. 1987. *The French Reformation*. Oxford: Blackwell.

Grell, Ole Peter, and A. I. C. Heron. 1996. "Calvinism." In Hillerbrand, ed. 1996, 1:240–47.

Grendler, Paul F. 1977. *The Roman Inquisition and the Venetian Press, 1540–1605*. Princeton, N.J.: Princeton University Press.

———. 1989. *Schooling in Renaissance Italy: Literacy and Learning 1300–1600*. Baltimore: Johns Hopkins University Press.

Guillory, John. 1993. *Cultural Capital: The Problem of Literary Canon Formation*. Chicago: University of Chicago Press.

Gundersheimer, Werner L. 1973. *Ferrara: The Style of a Renaissance Despotism*. Princeton, N.J.: Princeton University Press.

Harrington, Joel F. 1995. *Reordering Marriage and Society in Reformation Germany*. Cambridge: Cambridge University Press.

Hautz, Johann Friedrich. [1862–64] 1980. *Geschichte der Universität Heidelberg*. 2 vols. Mannheim: J. Schneider. Reprint, Hildesheim: Georg Olms.

Head, Thomas. "A Propagandist for the Reform: Marie Dentière." In Wilson 1987, 260–83.

Heinsius, Maria. 1951. *Das unüberwindliche Wort. Frauen der Reformationszeit,* 96–133. Munich: C. Kaiser.

Hendrix, Scott H. 1993. "Deparentifying the Fathers: The Reformers and Patristic Authority." In *Auctoritas Patrum: Zur Rezeption der Kirchenväter im 15. und 16. Jahrhundert = Contributions on the Reception of the Church Fathers in the 15th and 16th Century* [sic], edited by Leif Grane, Alfred Schindler, and Markus Wriedt, 55–68. Mainz: Philipp von Zabern.

Hess, Ursula. 1983. "Oratrix Humilis: Die Frau als Briefpartnerin von Humanisten, am Beispiel der Caritas Pirckehimer." In *Der Brief im Zeitalter der Renaissance,* edited by Franz Josef Worstbrock, 173–203. Weinheim: Acta humaniora.

Hillerbrand, Hans J., ed. 1996. *The Oxford Encyclopedia of the Reformation.* New York: Oxford University Press.

Hofstadter, Douglas R. 1997. *Le Ton Beau de Marot: In Praise of the Music of Language.* New York: Basic Books.

Holzberg, Niklas. 1982. "Olympia Morata." In *Veröffentlichungen der Gesellschaft für Fränkische Geschichte. Reihe 7A, Frankische Lebensbilder.* Neustadt/Aisch. 141–56.

———. 1987. "Olympia Morata und die Anfänge des Griechishen an der Universität Heidelberg." *Heidelberger Jahrbücher* 31:77–93.

Horne, Philip Russell. 1962. *The Tragedies of Giambattista Cinthio Giraldi.* Oxford: Oxford University Press.

Hughes, Philip Edgcumbe. 1984. *Lefèvre: Pioneer of Ecclesiastical Renewal in France.* Grand Rapids, Mich.: W. E. Eerdmans.

Huizinga, Johan. 1952. *Erasmus of Rotterdam.* London: Phaidon.

Humfrey, Peter, and Mauro Lucco. 1998. *Dosso Dossi: Court Painter in Renaissance Ferrara.* New York: The Metropolitan Museum of Art.

Imbart de La Tour, Pierre. 1914. *Les origines de la reforme.* Vol. 3., *L'évangélisme,* 1521–1538. Paris: Hachette.

Irwin, Joyce L. 1979. *Womanhood in Radical Protestantism, 1525–1675.* New York: E. Mellen Press.

Jardine, Lisa. 1983. "Isotta Nogarola: Women Humanists—Education for What?" *History of Education* 12:231–44.

———. 1985. "'O decus Italiae virgo' or The Myth of the Learned Lady in the Renaissance." *Historical Journal* 28:799–820.

———. 1996. *Worldly Goods: A New History of the Renaissance.* New York: Doubleday.

Jedin, Hubert. 1937. *Girolamo Seripando.* Würzburg: Rita-Verlag.

———. 1949. *Geschichte des Konzils von Trient.* Bd. 1. *Der Kampf um das Konzil.* Freiburg: Herder.

Jensen, Kristian. 1996. "The Humanist Reform of Latin and Latin Teaching." In Kraye, ed. 1996, 63–81.

Jung, Eva-Maria. 1951. "Vittoria Colonna: Between Reformation and Counter-Reformation." *Review of Religion* 15:144–59.

———. 1953. "On the Nature of Evangelism in Sixteenth-Century Italy." *Journal of the History of Ideas* 14:511–27.

Kelley, Donald R. 1981. *The Beginning of Ideology: Consciousness and Society in the French Reformation.* Cambridge: Cambridge University Press.

King, Margaret L. 1976. "Thwarted Ambitions: Six Learned Women of the Italian Renaissance." *Soundings* 59:280–304.

———. 1978. "The Religious Retreat of Isotta Nogarola (1418–1466): Sexism and Its Consequences in the Fifteenth Century." *Signs* 3:807–22.
———. 1980. "Book-Lined Cells: Women and Humanism in the Early Italian Renaissance." In Labalme 1980, 66–90. Reprinted in Rabil, ed. 1988, 2:434–53.
———. 1991. *Women of the Renaissance*. Chicago: University of Chicago Press.
Knecht, R. J. (Robert Jean). 1994. *Renaissance Warrior and Patron: The Reign of Francis I.* Cambridge: Cambridge University Press.
Kößling, Rainer, and Gertrud Weiss-Stählin, eds. and trans. 1990. *Olympia Fulvia Morata. Briefe*. Leipzig: Reclan.
Krause, Karl. [1879] 1963. *Helius Eobanus Hessus, sein Leben und seine Werke: ein Beitrag zur Cultur- und Gelehrtengeschichte des 16. Jahrhunderts*. 2 vols. Gotha. Reprint, Nieuwkoop: B. De Graaf.
Kraye, Jill. 1988. "Moral Philosophy." In *The Cambridge History of Renaissance Philosophy*, edited by Charles B. Schmitt, Quentin Skinner, Eckhard Kessler, and Jill Kraye, 303–86. Cambridge: Cambridge University Press.
———, ed. 1996. *The Cambridge Companion to Renaissance Humanism*. Cambridge: Cambridge University Press.
Kristeller, Paul Oskar. 1963–. *Iter Italicum. A Finding List of Uncatalogued or Incompletely Catalogued Humanistic Manuscripts of the Renaissance in Italian and Other Libraries*. 7 vols. London: Warburg Institute.
———. 1964. *Eight Philosophers of the Italian Renaissance*. Stanford, Calif.: Stanford University Press.
———. 1965. "The European Diffusion of Italian Humanism." In *Renaissance Thought II. Papers on Humanism and the Arts*. New York; Harper & Row.
Kühlmann, Wilhelm, and Hermann Wiegand, eds. 1989. *Parnassus Palatinus: Humanistische Dichtung in Heidelberg und der alten Kurpfalz: Lateinisch-Deutsch*. Heidelberg: Manutius.
Kutter, Markus. 1955. *Celio Secondo Curione: sein Leben und sein Werk (1503–1569)*. Basel: Helbing & Lichtenhahn.
Labalme, Patricia H., ed. 1980. *Beyond Their Sex: Learned Women of the European Past*. New York: New York University Press.
Larsen, Anne R. 1987. "The French Humanist Scholars: Les Dames Des Roches." In Wilson 1987, 232–59.
Lindberg, Carter. 1996. *The European Reformations*. Oxford: Blackwell.
Logan, Gabriella Berti. 1994. "The Desire to Contribute: An Eighteenth-Century Italian Woman of Science." *The American Historical Review* 99:785–812.
Logan, O. M. T. 1969. "Grace and Justification: Some Italian Views of the Sixteenth and Early Seventeenth Centuries." *Journal of Ecclesiastical History* 20:67–78.
Macchiavelli [sic], Carolus Antonius. 1722. *Bitisia Gozzadina, seu, De mulierum doctoratu*. Bononiae: Jo. Baptista Blanchus. Reprinted on microfiche, "History of Education," fiche 21, 548 ff. (Woodbridge, Conn.: Research Publications, 1990).
McNair, Philip Murray Jourdan. 1967. *Peter Martyr in Italy: An Anatomy of Apostasy*. Oxford: Oxford University Press.
———. 1981. "The Reformation of the Sixteenth Century in Renaissance Italy." In *Religion and Humanism*, edited by Keith Robbins. Oxford: Blackwell.
M'Crie, Thomas. [1856] 1974. *History of the Progress and Suppression of the Reformation in Italy in the Sixteenth Century: Including a Sketch of the History of the Reformation in the*

Grisons. 2d ed. Edinburgh: Blackwood. Reprint, New York: AMS Press. [Numerous editions and reprints]

Maddison, Carol. 1965. *Marcantonio Flaminio: Poet, Humanist and Reformer*. London: Routledge and Kegan Paul.

Maltby, William S., ed. 1992. *Reformation Europe: A Guide to Research II*. St. Louis: Center for Reformation Research.

Marchetti, Valerio. 1975. *Gruppi ereticali senesi del Cinquecento*. Firenze: La nuova Italia.

Martin, John. 1987. "Popular Culture and the Shaping of Popular Heresy in Renaissance Venice." In *Inquisition and Society in Early Modern Europe*, edited and translated by Stephen Haliczer, 115–28. Totowa, N.J.: Barnes & Noble.

———. 1988. "Salvation and Society in Sixteenth-Century Venice: Popular Evangelism in a Renaissance City." *Journal of Modern History* 60:205–33.

———. 1993. *Venice's Hidden Enemies: Italian Heretics in a Renaissance City*. Berkeley and Los Angeles: University of California Press.

Martineau, Christine, and Michel Veissière. 1975. *Guillaume Briconnet, Marguerite d'Angoulême: Correspondance, 1521–1524*. Genève: Droz.

Mayer, Claude Albert. 1956. "Le départ de Marot de Ferrare." *Bibliothéque d'Humanisme et de la Renaissance* 18:197–221.

———. 1972. *Clément Marot*. Paris: A.-G. Nizet.

Mayer, Evan. 1952–53. "Daniel Stibar von Buttenheim und Joachim Camerarius." In *Würzburger Diözesangeschichtesblätter* 14–15:485–99, cited from Flood and Shaw 1997, 125 n. 49.

Mentz, Georg. 1903–8. *Johann Friedrich der Grossmütige 1503–1554. Festschrift zum 400 jährigen Geburtstage des Kurfürsten*. 3 vols. Jena: G. Fischer.

Miccoli, Giovanni. 1974. "La storia religiosa. X. Crisi e restaurazione cattolica nel Cinquecento." In *Storia d'Italia*, edited by Ruggiero Romano and Corrado Vivanti. Torino: G. Einaudi. Vol. 2, *Dalla caduta dell'Impero romano al secolo XVIII.*, 975–1079.

Mitchell, Bonner. 1979. *Italian Civic Pageantry in the High Renaissance: A Descriptive Bibliography of Triumphal Entries and Selected Other Festivals for State Occasions*. Biblioteca di bibliografia italiana. Supplementi periodici a La Bibliofilia 89. Firenze: Olschki.

Moreschini, Claudio. 1991. "Per una storia dell'umanismo latino a Ferrara." In Castelli 1991, 168–88.

Morsolin, Bernardo. 1878. *Giangiorgio Trissino; o, monografia di un letterato nel secolo XVI*. Vicenza: G. Burato.

Mulazzi, Virginia. 1875. *Olimpia Morato, scene della Riforma: Racconto storica del secolo XVI*. 2 vols. Milano: L. Bortolotti. [non vidi.]

Music, David W. 1996. *Hymnology: A Collection of Source Readings*. Lanham, Md.: Scarecrow Press.

Neumüllers-Klauser, Renate. 1970. *Die Inschriften der Stadt und des Landkreises Heidelberg*. Die Deutschen Inschriften 12. Heidelberger Reihe 4. Stuttgart: A. Druckenmüller.

Nichols, John Gough, ed. [1857] 1964. *Literary Remains of King Edward the Sixth. Edited from his autograph manuscripts*. London: Roxburghe Club. Reprint, New York: B. Franklin.

Nicholls, David. 1992. "France." In Pettegree, ed. 1992, 120–41.

Nischan, Bodo. 1999. *Lutherans and Calvinists in the Age of Confessionalism*. Aldershot, England: Ashgate Publishing.

Nolten, Georg Ludwig (Geo. Lud. Noltenii). 1775. *Commentaria historia critica de Olympiae Moratae vita, scriptis, fatis et laudibus*. Frankfort: Impensis Carol. Theophil. Strausii.

Nugent, George. 1990. "Anti-Protestant Music for Sixteenth-Century Ferrara." *Journal of the American Musciological Society* 43:228–91.

Olivieri, Achille. 1967. "Alessandro Trissino e il movimento calvanista vicentino del cinquecento." *Rivista di storia della chiesa in Italia* 21:54–117.

———. 1992. *Riforma ed eresia a Vicenza nel Cinquecento*. Roma: Herder.

Olson, O. K. 1981. "Matthias Flacius Illyricus." In *Shapers of Religious Traditions in Germany, Switzerland, and Poland, 1560–1600*, edited by Jill Raitt, 1–17. New Haven, Conn.: Yale University Press.

Pade, Marianne, Lene Waage Petersen, and Daniela Quarta, eds. 1990. *La Corte di Ferrara e il suo mecenatismo, 1441–1598. The Court of Ferrara and its patronage*: Atti del convegno internazionale, Copenhagen, maggio 1987. Modena: Panini.

Pardi, Giuseppe. 1900. *Titoli dottorali conferiti dallo studio di Ferrara nei sec. XV e XVI*. Lucca: A. Marchi.

Parker, Holt N. 1997. "Latin and Greek Poetry by Five Renaissance Italian Women Humanists." In *Sex and Gender in Medieval and Renaissance Texts*, edited by Paul Allen Miller, Barbara K. Gold, and Charles Platter, 247–85. Albany: State University of New York Press.

———. Forthcoming. "Angela Nogarola," "Isotta Nogarola," "Costanza Varano," "Olympia Fulvia Morata." In *Women Writing in Latin*, edited by Anne Clark Barlett, Laurie J. Churchill, and Jane Jeffery. New York: Garland Publishing.

Perosa, Alessandro, and John Sparrow, ed. 1979. *Renaissance Latin Verse: An Anthology*. London: Duckworth.

Perrone, Lorenzo, ed. 1983. *Lutero in Italia*. Casale Monferato: Marietti.

Pettegree, Andrew. 1992. "The Early Reformation in Europe: A German Affair or an International Movement?" In Pettegree, ed. 1992, 1–22.

———. 2000. *The Reformation World*. London and New York: Routledge.

———, ed. 1992. *The Early Reformation in Europe*. Cambridge: Cambridge University Press.

Peyronel Rambaldi, Susanna. 1979. *Speranze e crisi nel Cinquecento modenese: Tensioni religiose e vita cittadina ai tempi di Giovanni Morone*. Milano: F. Angeli.

———. 1982. "Ancora sull'evanglismo italiano. Categoria o invenzione storiografica?" *Società e storia* 18:935–67.

Pfeiffer, Rudolf. 1976. *History of Classical Scholarship from 1300 to 1850*. Oxford: Oxford University Press.

Pidoux, Pierre. 1962. *Le psautier huguenot du XVIe siecle. Melodies et documents*. Bâle: Baerenreiter.

Pirovano, Donato. 1998. "Olimpia Morata e la traduzione latina delle prime due novelle del Decameron." *Acme* 51:73–109.

Press, Volker. 1979. "Die Grafen von Erbach und die Anfänge des reformierte Bekenntnisses in Deutschland." In *Aus Geschichte und ihren Hilfswissenschaften. Festschrift für Walter Heinemeyer zum 65. Geburtstag*, edited by Hermann Bannasch and Hans-Peter Lachmann, 667–78. Marburg: Elwert.

Prine, Jeanne. 1987. "Poet of Lyon: Louise Labé." In Wilson 1987, 132–57.

Prosperi, Adriano. 1968. "Di alcuni testi per il clero nell'Italia del primo Cinquecento." *Critica Storia* 7:137–68.

———. 1990. "L'eresia in città e a corte." In Pade et al. 1990, 267–81.

———. 1996. "Italy." In Hillerbrand, ed. 1996, 2:324–29.

Puttin, Lucio. 1974. "L'umanista mantovan Fulvio Pellegrino Morato fra letterature e riforma." *Civiltà manovana* 45:113–25, 46:196–213.

Rabil, Albert. 1994. "Olympia Morata (1526–1555)." In Russell 1994:269–78.

———, ed. 1988. *Renaissance Humanism: Foundations, Forms, and Legacy.* Vol. 1: *Humanism in Italy;* vol. 2: *Humanism beyond Italy;* vol. 3: *Humanism and the Disciplines.* Philadelphia: University of Pennsylvania Press.

Raff, Diether. 1983. *Die Ruprecht-Karls-Universität in Vergangenheit und Gegenwart.* Heidelberg: Heidelberger Verlagsanstalt und Druckerei.

Rahner, Hugo. 1956. "Ignatius und die Bekehrung der Doña isabel Briceño: Ein Beitrag zur Geschichte des italienischen Protesantismus." *Archivum Historicum Societatis Iesu* 25: 99–118.

Rice, Eugene F. 1974. "The Meanings of 'Evangelical.'" In *The Pursuit of Holiness in Late Medieval and Renaissance Religion*, edited by Charles Trinkaus, with Heiko A. Oberman, 472–75. Leiden: Brill.

Rodocanachi, E. (Emmanuel). [1896] 1970. *Une protectrice de la Réforme en Italie et en France: Renée de France, duchesse de Ferrare.* Paris: Ollendorff. Reprint, Geneve: Slatkine Reprints; reproduced on microfilm: "History of Women," reel 596, no. 4712. New Haven, Conn.: Research Publications, 1976.

Roelker, Nancy Lyman. 1972. "The Role of Noblewomen in the French Reformation." *Archiv für Refomationsgeschichte* 63:168–95.

Roffi, Mario. 1984. "Un concorso di poesia francese a Ferrara alla corte estense di Renata di Francia." In *The Renaissance in Ferrara and Its European Horizons*, edited by J. Salmons, 263–69. Cardiff: University of Wales Press.

Roth, Cecil. 1959. *The Jews in the Renaissance.* New York: Harper & Row.

Rotondò, Antonio. 1967. "Atteggiamenti della vita morale italiana de Cinquecento: La practica nicodemetica." *Rivista Storica Italiana* 79:991–1030.

Rozzo, Ugo, and Silvana Seidel Menchi. 1998. "The Book and the Reformation in Italy." In *The Reformation and the Book*, edited by Jean-François Gilmont and translated by Karin Maag, 319–67. Aldershot, England: Ashgate Publishing.

Rummel, Erika. 1994. "Voices of Reform from Hus to Erasmus." In *Handbook of European History, 1400–1600: Late Middle Ages, Renaissance, and Reformation*, edited by Thomas A. Brady Jr., Heiko A. Oberman, and James D. Tracy, 2:61–91. New York: Brill.

———. 1995. *The Humanist-Scholastic Debate in the Renaissance and Reformation.* Cambridge, Mass.: Harvard University Press.

———. 2000. *The Confessionalization of Humanism in Reformation Germany.* Oxford: Oxford University Press.

Russell, Rinaldina, ed. 1994. *Italian Women Writers: A Bio-Bibliographical Sourcebook.* Westport, Conn.: Greenwood.

Saffert, Erich. 1993. *Studien zur Geschichte der Stadt Schweinfurt.* Schweinfurt: Historischer Verein.

Sandys, John Edwin. 1903–8. *A History of Classical Scholarship.* 3 vols. Cambridge: Cambridge University Press.

Savi, Ignazio. 1815. *Memorie antiche e moderne intorno alle pubbliche scuole in Vicenza.* Vinenza. Cited from Puttin 1974.
Schilling, Heinz. 1986. "Die 'Zweite Reformation' als Kategorie der Geschichtswissenschaft." In *Die reformierte Konfessionalisierung in Deutschland: Das Problem der "Zweiten Reformation": Wissenschaftliches Symposion des Vereins fur Reformationsgeschichte 1985*, edited by Heinz Schilling, 379–437. Gütersloh: Gütersloher Verlagshaus G. Mohn.
———. 1992. *Religion, Political Culture, and the Emergence of Early Modern Society: Essays in German and Dutch History.* Leiden: Brill.
———. 1998. *Aufbruch und Krise: Deutschland, 1517–1648.* Berlin: Siedler.
Schutte, Anne Jacobson. 1975. "The Lettere Volgari and the Crisis of Evangelism in Italy." *Renaissance Quarterly* 28:639–88.
———. 1977. *Pier Paolo Vergerio: The Making of an Italian Reformer.* Travaux d'humanisme et Renaissance, no 160. Genève: Droz.
———. 1989. "Periodization of Sixteenth-Century Italian Religious History: The Post-Cantimori Paradigm Shift." *Journal of Modern History* 61:269–84.
Screech, M. A. (Michael Andrew). 1964. *Jacques Lefèvre d'Etaples. Épistres & Évangiles pour les cinquante & deux sepmaines de l'an.* Facsimile of 1st ed., with introduction. Travaux d'humanisme et Renaissance, no. 63. Genève: Droz.
———. 1978. "Rabelais, Erasmus, Gilbertus Cognatus and Boniface Amerbach: A link through the *Lucii Cuspidii Testamentum*." *Études Rabelaisiennes* 14:43–46.
———. 1984. "Celio Calcagnini and Rabelaisian Sympathy." In *Neo-Latin and the Vernacular in Renaissance France*, edited by Grahame Castor and Terence Cave, 26–48. Oxford: Oxford University Press. Reprinted in Screech 1992, 278–300.
———. 1992. *Some Renaissance Studies: Selected Articles 1951–1991*, edited by Michael J. Heath. Genève: Droz.
———. 1994. *Clément Marot. A Renaissance Poet Discovers the Gospel: Lutheranism, Fabrism, and Calvinism in the Royal Courts of France and of Navarre and in the Ducal Court of Ferrara.* Leiden: Brill.
Seidel Menchi, Silvana. 1977. "Le traduzioni italiani di Lutero nella prima metà del cinquecento." *Rinascimento* 17:31–108.
———. 1987. *Erasmo in Italia, 1520–1580.* Torino: Bollati Boringhieri.
———. 1993. *Erasmus als Ketzer: Reformation und Inquisition im Italien des 16. Jahrhunderts.* Studies in Medieval and Reformation Thought 49. Leiden: Brill.
———. 1994. "Italy." In *The Reformation in National Context*, edited by Bob Scribner, Roy Porter, and MikulásÙ Teich. Cambridge: Cambridge University Press.
Shaw, David J. 1998. "Clément Marot's Humanist Contacts in Ferrara." *French Studies* 51:279–90.
Simon, Mattias, ed. 1962. *Pfarrerbuch der Reichsstädte Dinkelsbühl, Schweinfurt, Weissenburg i. Bay. und Windsheim.* Nürnberg: Verein für Bayerische Kirchengeschichte.
Smyth, Amelia Gillespie. 1834. *Olympia Morata: Her Times, Life and Writings.* London: Smith, Elder. [Published anonymously; often ascribed to Caroline Anne (Bowles) Southey; but the list of other titles by the same author makes her identity clear.]
Spitz, Lewis W. 1988. "Humanism and the Protestant Reformation." In Rabil, ed. 1988, 3:380–411.
Stevenson, Jane. 1998. "Women and Classical Education in the Early Modern Period." In *Pedagogy and Power: Rhetorics of Classical Learning*, edited by Yun Lee Too and Niall Livingstone, 83–109. Cambridge: Cambridge University Press.

Sutherland, N. M. (Nicola Mary). 1979. *The Huguenot Struggle for Recognition*. New Haven, Conn.: Yale University Press.
Tagmann, P. M. 1978. "Ferarras Festivitäten von 1529." *Schweitzer Beiträge zur Musikwissenschaft* 3:85–105.
Tedeschi, John A. 1974. "Italian Reformers and the Diffusion of Renaissance Culture." *Sixteenth Century Journal* 5:79–94.
———. 1987. "The Cultural Contributions of Italian Protestant Reformers in the Late Renaissance." In Bussi, ed. 1987, 81–107.
———, ed. 2000. *The Italian Reformation of the Sixteenth Century and the Diffusion of Renaissance Culture: A Bibliography of the Secondary Literature, ca. 1750–1997*. Ferrara : ISR (Istituto di studi rinascimentali).
———. 2001. *The Prosecution of Heresy: Collected Studies on the Inquisition in Early Modern Italy*. Binghamton, N.Y.: Medieval and Renaissance Texts and Studies.
Teissier, Antoine. 1696. *Les éloges des hommes scavans tirez de l'histoire de M. de Thou*. Rev. ed. Utrecht: Francois Halma.
Tiraboschi, Girolamo. 1822. *Storia della letteratura italiana*. 9 vols. in 16. Milano: Società tipografica de' classici italiani.
Trinkaus, Charles, ed., with Heiko A. Oberman. 1974. *The Pursuit of Holiness in Late Medieval and Renaissance Religion*. Leiden: Brill.
Tucker, George Hugo. 1992. "Didacus Pyrrhus Lusitanus (1517–1599), Poet of Exile." *Humanistica Lovaniensia* 41:175–98.
Turchetti, Mario. 1987. "Nota sulla religiosità di Celio Secondo Curione (1503–1569) in relazaione al 'nicodemismo.'" In *Libri, idee e sentimenti religiosi nel Cinquecento italiano*, edited by Rolando Bussi. Modena: Panini.
Uglow, Jennifer, ed. 1998. *The Macmillan Dictionary of Women's Biography*. London: Macmillan.
Veblen, Thorstein. 1899. *The Theory of the Leisure Class: An Economic Study of Institutions*. New York: Macmillan.
Veissière, Michel. 1986. *L'évêque Guillaume Briçonnet (1470–1534): contribution à la connaissance de la Réforme catholique à la veille du Concile de Trente*. Provins: Société d'histoire et d'archéologie.
Vorländer, Dorothea. 1970. "Olympia Fulvia Morata—eine evangelische Humanistin in Schweinfurt." *Zeitschrift für bayerische Kirchengeschichte* 39:95–113.
Weiss-Stählin, Gertrud. 1961. "Olympia Fulvia Morata und Schweinfurt." *Zeitschrift für bayerische Kirchengeschichte* 30:175–83.
———. 1976. "Per una biografia di Olimpia Morata." In *Miscellanea di studi in memoria di Cesare Bolognesi*, edited by Lucio Puttin, 79–99. Schio: Ascledum.
———. 1982. "Dr. Andreas Grundler (ca. 1506–1555)." *Mainfränkisches Jahrbuch für Geschichte und Kunst* 34:1–32.
Wiesner, Merry E. 1992. "Studies of Women, Family, and Gender." In Maltby 1992, 159–87.
———. 1998. *Gender, Church, and State in Early Modern Germany*. New York: Longman.
———. 2000. *Women and Gender in Early Modern Europe*. New York: Cambridge University Press.
Williams, George H. 1965. "Camillo Renato (c. 1500–?1575)." In *Italian Reformation Studies in Honor of Laelius Socinus*. Università di Siena. Facolta di Giurisprudenza, Collana di studi "Pietro Rossi," n.s., 4 (Firenze, F. Le Monnier), 103–83.

———. 1992. *The Radical Reformation.* 3d ed. Kirksville, Mo.: Sixteenth Century Journal Publishers.

Wilson, Katharina M., ed. 1987. *Women Writers of the Renaissance and Reformation.* Athens: University of Georgia Press.

Woodward, William Harrison. [1897] 1963. *Vittorino da Feltre and Other Humanist Educators.* Cambridge: Cambridge University Press. Reprint, New York: Teachers College Press.

SERIES EDITORS' BIBLIOGRAPHY

PRIMARY SOURCES

Alberti, Leon Battista (1404–72). *The Family in Renaissance Florence*. Translated by Renée Neu Watkins. Columbia: University of South Carolina Press, 1969.

Arenal, Electa, and Stacey Schlau, eds. *Untold Sisters: Hispanic Nuns in Their Own Works*. Translated by Amanda Powell. Albuquerque: University of New Mexico Press, 1989.

Astell, Mary (1666–1731). *The First English Feminist: Reflections on Marriage and Other Writings*. Edited and with an introduction by Bridget Hill. New York: St. Martin's Press, 1986.

Atherton, Margaret, ed. *Women Philosophers of the Early Modern Period*. Indianapolis: Hackett Publishing Co., 1994.

Aughterson, Kate, ed. *Renaissance Woman: Constructions of Femininity in England: A Source Book*. London: Routledge, 1995.

Barbaro, Francesco (1390–1454). *On Wifely Duties*. Translated by Benjamin Kohl. In *The Earthly Republic*, edited by Benjamin Kohl and R. G. Witt. Philadelphia: University of Pennsylvania Press, 1978, 179–228. Translation of the preface and book 2.

Behn, Aphra. *The Works of Aphra Behn*. Edited by Janet Todd. 7 vols. Columbus: Ohio State University Press, 1992–96.

Boccaccio, Giovanni (1313–75). *Corbaccio or the Labyrinth of Love*. Translated by Anthony K. Cassell. Rev. ed. Binghamton, N.Y.: Medieval and Renaissance Texts and Studies, 1993.

———. *Famous Women*. Edited and translated by Virginia Brown. The I Tatti Renaissance Library. Cambridge, Mass.: Harvard University Press, 2001.

Bruni, Leonardo (1370–1444). "On the Study of Literature (1405) to Lady Battista Malatesta of Moltefeltro." In *The Humanism of Leonardo Bruni: Selected Texts*, translated and with an introduction by Gordon Griffiths, James Hankins, and David Thompson, 240–51. Binghamton, N.Y.: Medieval and Renaissance Studies and Texts, 1987.

Castiglione, Baldassare (1478–1529). *The Book of the Courtier*. Translated by George Bull. New York: Penguin, 1967.

Cerasano, S. P., and Marion Wynne-Davies, eds. *Readings in Renaissance Women's Drama: Criticism, History, and Performance 1594–1998*. London: Routledge, 1998.

Christine de Pizan (1365–1431). *The Book of the City of Ladies.* Translated by Earl Jeffrey Richards, with a foreword by Marina Warner. New York: Persea Books, 1982.

———. *The Treasure of the City of Ladies.* Translated by Sarah Lawson. New York: Viking Penguin, 1985. Also translated and with an introduction by Charity Cannon Willard, and edited with an introduction by Madeleine P. Cosman. New York: Persea Books, 1989.

Clarke, Danielle, ed. *Isabella Whitney, Mary Sidney and Aemilia Lanyer: Renaissance Women Poets.* New York: Penguin Books, 2000.

Crawford, Patricia, and Laura Gowing, eds. *Women's Worlds in Seventeenth-Century England: A Source Book.* London: Routledge, 2000.

Daybell, James, ed. *Early Modern Women's Letter Writing, 1450–1700.* Houndmills, England: Palgrave, 2001.

Elizabeth I. *Elizabeth I: Collected Works.* Edited by Leah S. Marcus, Janel Mueller, and Mary Beth Rose. Chicago: University of Chicago Press, 2000.

Elyot, Thomas (1490–1546). *Defence of Good Women: The Feminist Controversy of the Renaissance.* Facsimile reproductions, edited by Diane Bornstein. New York: Delmar, 1980.

Erasmus, Desiderius (1467–1536). *Erasmus on Women.* Edited by Erika Rummel. Toronto: University of Toronto Press, 1996.

Ferguson, Moira, ed. *First Feminists: British Women Writers 1578–1799.* Bloomington: Indiana University Press, 1985.

Galilei, Maria Celeste. *Sister Maria Celeste's Letters to Her Father, Galileo.* Edited and translated by Rinaldina Russell. Lincoln, Nebr., and New York: Writers Club Press of Universe.com, 2000.

Gethner, Perry, ed. *The Lunatic Lover and Other Plays by French Women of the 17th and 18th Centuries.* Portsmouth, N.H.: Heinemann, 1994.

Glückel of Hameln (1646–1724). *The Memoirs of Glückel of Hameln.* Translated by Marvin Lowenthal, with a new introduction by Robert Rosen. New York: Schocken Books, 1977.

Henderson, Katherine Usher, and Barbara F. McManus, eds. *Half Humankind: Contexts and Texts of the Controversy about Women in England, 1540–1640.* Urbana: University of Illinois Press, 1985.

Joscelin, Elizabeth. *The Mothers Legacy to her Unborn Childe.* Edited by Jean leDrew Metcalfe. Toronto: University of Toronto Press, 2000.

Kallendorf, Craig W., ed. and trans. *Humanist Educational Treatises.* The I Tatti Renaissance Library. Cambridge, MA: Harvard University Press, 2002.

Kaminsky, Amy Katz, ed. *Water Lilies, Flores del agua: An Anthology of Spanish Women Writers from the Fifteenth through the Nineteenth Century.* Minneapolis: University of Minnesota Press, 1996.

Kempe, Margery (1373–1439). *The Book of Margery Kempe.* Translated and edited by Lynn Staley. Norton Critical Edition. New York: W. W. Norton, 2001.

King, Margaret L., and Albert Rabil Jr., eds. *Her Immaculate Hand: Selected Works by and about the Women Humanists of Quattrocento Italy.* Binghamton, N.Y.: Medieval and Renaissance Texts and Studies, 1983; rev. pbk. ed., 1991.

Klein, Joan Larsen, ed. *Daughters, Wives, and Widows: Writings by Men about Women and Marriage in England, 1500–1640.* Urbana: University of Illinois Press, 1992.

Knox, John (1505–72). *The Political Writings of John Knox: The First Blast of the Trumpet against the Monstrous Regiment of Women and Other Selected Works.* Edited by Marvin A. Breslow. Washington, D.C.: Folger Shakespeare Library, 1985.

Kors, Alan C., and Edward Peters, eds. *Witchcraft in Europe, 400–1700: A Documentary History.* Philadelphia: University of Pennsylvania Press, 2000.

Krämer, Heinrich, and Jacob Sprenger. *Malleus Maleficarum* (ca. 1487). Translated by Montague Summers. London: Pushkin Press, 1928. Reprint, New York: Dover, 1971.

Larsen, Anne R., and Colette H. Winn, eds. *Writings by Pre-Revolutionary French Women: From Marie de France to Elizabeth Vigée-Le Brun.* New York: Garland Publishing Co., 2000.

Lorris, William de, and Jean de Meun. *The Romance of the Rose.* Translated by Charles Dahlbert. Princeton, N.J.: Princeton University Press, 1971. Reprint, University Press of New England, 1983.

Marguerite d'Angoulême, Queen of Navarre (1492–1549). *The Heptameron.* Translated by P. A. Chilton. New York: Viking Penguin, 1984.

Mary of Agreda. *The Divine Life of the Most Holy Virgin,* abridgment of *The Mystical City of God.* Abridged by Fr. Bonaventure Amedeo de Caesarea, M.C. Translated from French by Abbé Joseph A. Boullan. Rockford, Ill.: Tan Books, 1997.

Myers, Kathleen A., and Amanda Powell, eds. *A Wild Country Out in the Garden: The Spiritual Journals of a Colonial Mexican Nun.* Bloomington: Indiana University Press, 1999.

Russell, Rinaldina, ed. *Sister Maria Celeste's Letters to Her Father, Galileo.* San Jose: Writers Club Press, 2000.

Teresa of Avila, Saint (1515–82). *The Life of Saint Teresa of Avila by Herself.* Translated by J. M. Cohen. New York: Viking Penguin, 1957.

Travitsky, Betty S., and Anne Lake Prescott, eds. *Female and Male Voices in Early Modern England: An Anthology of Renaissance Writing.* New York: Columbia University Press, 2000.

Weyer, Johann (1515–88). *Witches, Devils, and Doctors in the Renaissance: Johann Weyer, De praestigiis daemonum.* Edited by George Mora with Benjamin G. Kohl, Erik Midelfort, and Helen Bacon. Translated by John Shea. Binghamton, N.Y.: Medieval and Renaissance Texts and Studies, 1991.

Wilson, Katharina M., ed. *Medieval Women Writers.* Athens: University of Georgia Press, 1984.

———. *Women Writers of the Renaissance and Reformation.* Athens: University of Georgia Press, 1987.

Wilson, Katharina M., and Frank J. Warnke, eds. *Women Writers of the Seventeenth Century.* Athens: University of Georgia Press, 1989.

Wollstonecraft, Mary. *A Vindication of the Rights of Men and a Vindication of the Rights of Women.* Edited by Sylvana Tomaselli. Cambridge: Cambridge University Press, 1995. Also *The Vindications of the Rights of Men, The Rights of Women,* edited by D. L. Macdonald and Kathleen Scherf. Peterborough, Ontario: Broadview Press, 1997.

Women Critics 1660–1820: An Anthology. Edited by the Folger Collective on Early Women Critics. Bloomington: Indiana University Press, 1995.

Women Writers in English 1350–1850: 15 vols. published through 1999 (projected 30-vol. series suspended). Oxford University Press.

Wroth, Lady Mary. *The Poems of Lady Mary Wroth*. Edited by Josephine A. Roberts. Baton Rouge: Louisiana State University Press, 1983.

———. *Lady Mary Wroth's "Love's Victory": The Penshurst Manuscript*. Edited by Michael G. Brennan. London: The Roxburghe Club, 1988.

———. *The Countess of Montgomery's Urania*. 2 parts. Edited by Josephine A. Roberts. Tempe, Ariz.: MRTS, 1995, 1999.

Zayas, Maria de. *The Enchantments of Love: Amorous and Exemplary Novels*. Translated by H. Patsy Boyer. Berkeley and Los Angeles: University of California Press, 1990.

———. *The Disenchantments of Love*. Translated by H. Patsy Boyer. Albany: State University of New York Press, 1997.

SECONDARY SOURCES

Akkerman, Tjitske, and Siep Sturman, eds. *Feminist Thought in European History, 1400–2000*. London: Routledge, 1997.

Backer, Anne Liot. *Precious Women*. New York: Basic Books, 1974.

Barash, Carol. *English Women's Poetry, 1649–1714: Politics, Community, and Linguistic Authority*. New York: Oxford University Press, 1996.

Battigelli, Anna. *Margaret Cavendish and the Exiles of the Mind*. Lexington: University of Kentucky Press, 1998.

Beasley, Faith. *Revising Memory: Women's Fiction and Memoirs in Seventeenth-Century France*. New Brunswick N.J.: Rutgers University Press, 1990.

Beilin, Elaine V. *Redeeming Eve: Women Writers of the English Renaissance*. Princeton, N.J.: Princeton University Press, 1987.

Benson, Pamela Joseph. *The Invention of Renaissance Woman: The Challenge of Female Independence in the Literature and Thought of Italy and England*. University Park: Pennsylvania State University Press, 1992.

Bissell, R. Ward. *Artemisia Gentileschi and the Authority of Art*. University Park: Pennsylvania State University Press, 2000.

Blain, Virginia, Isobel Grundy, and Patricia Clements, eds. *The Feminist Companion to Literature in English: Women Writers from the Middle Ages to the Present*. New Haven, Conn.: Yale University Press, 1990.

Bloch, R. Howard. *Medieval Misogyny and the Invention of Western Romantic Love*. Chicago: University of Chicago Press, 1991.

Bornstein, Daniel, and Roberto Rusconi, eds. *Women and Religion in Medieval and Renaissance Italy*. Translated by Margery J. Schneider. Chicago: University of Chicago Press, 1996.

Brant, Clare, and Diane Purkiss, eds. *Women, Texts and Histories, 1575–1760*. London: Routledge, 1992.

Briggs, Robin. *Witches and Neighbours: The Social and Cultural Context of European Witchcraft*. New York: HarperCollins, 1995; Viking Penguin, 1996.

Brink, Jean R., ed. *Female Scholars: A Tradition of Learned Women before 1800*. Montréal: Eden Press Women's Publications, 1980.

Brown, Judith C. *Immodest Acts: The Life of a Lesbian Nun in Renaissance Italy*. New York: Oxford University Press, 1986.

Cervigni, Dino S., ed. *Women Mystic Writers. Annali d'Italianistica* 13 (1995) (entire issue).

Cervigni, Dino S., and Rebecca West, eds. *Women's Voices in Italian Literature. Annali d'Italianistica* 7 (1989) (entire issue).

Charlton, Kenneth. *Women, Religion and Education in Early Modern England.* London: Routledge, 1999.

Chojnacka, Monica. *Working Women in Early Modern Venice.* Baltimore: Johns Hopkins University Press, 2001.

Chojnacki, Stanley. *Women and Men in Renaissance Venice: Twelve Essays on Patrician Society.* Baltimore: Johns Hopkins University Press, 2000.

Cholakian, Patricia Francis. *Rape and Writing in the "Heptameron" of Marguerite de Navarre.* Carbondale and Edwardsville: Southern Illinois University Press, 1991.

―――. *Women and the Politics of Self-Representation in Seventeenth-Century France.* Newark: University of Delaware Press, 2000.

Clogan, Paul Maruice, ed. *Medievali et Humanistica: Literacy and the Lay Reader.* Lanham, Md.: Rowman and Littlefield, 2000.

Crabb, Ann. *The Strozzi of Florence: Widowhood and Family Solidarity in the Renaissance.* Ann Arbor: University of Michigan Press, 2000.

Davis, Natalie Zemon. *Society and Culture in Early Modern France.* Stanford, Calif.: Stanford University Press, 1975. Especially chapters 3 and 5.

―――. *Women on the Margins: Three Seventeenth-Century Lives.* Cambridge, Mass.: Harvard University Press, 1995.

De Erauso, Catalina. *Lieutenant Nun: Memoir of a Basque Transvestite in the New World.* Translated by Michele Ttepto and Gabriel Stepto, with a foreword by Marjorie Garber. Boston: Beacon Press, 1995.

DeJean, Joan. *Tender Geographies: Women and the Origins of the Novel in France.* New York: Columbia University Press, 1991.

―――. *Ancients against Moderns: Culture Wars and the Making of a Fin de Siècle.* Chicago: University of Chicago Press, 1997.

Dixon, Laurinda S. *Perilous Chastity: Women and Illness in Pre-Enlightenment Art and Medicine.* Ithaca, N.Y.: Cornell University Press, 1995.

Dolan, Frances, E. *Whores of Babylon: Catholicism, Gender and Seventeenth-Century Print Culture.* Ithaca, N.Y.: Cornell University Press, 1999.

Donovan, Josephine. *Women and the Rise of the Novel, 1405–1726.* New York: St. Martin's Press, 1999.

Erickson, Amy Louise. *Women and Property in Early Modern England.* London: Routledge, 1993.

Ezell, Margaret J. M. *The Patriarch's Wife: Literary Evidence and the History of the Family.* Chapel Hill: University of North Carolina Press, 1987.

―――. *Writing Women's Literary History.* Baltimore: Johns Hopkins University Press, 1993.

―――. *Social Authorship and the Advent of Print.* Baltimore: Johns Hopkins University Press, 1999.

Ferguson, Margaret W., Maureen Quilligan, and Nancy J. Vickers, eds. *Rewriting the Renaissance: The Discourses of Sexual Difference in Early Modern Europe.* Chicago: University of Chicago Press, 1987.

Fletcher, Anthony. *Gender, Sex and Subordination in England 1500–1800*. New Haven, Conn.: Yale University Press, 1995.

Frye, Susan, and Karen Robertson, eds. *Maids and Mistresses, Cousins and Queens: Women's Alliances in Early Modern England*. Oxford: Oxford University Press, 1999.

Gallagher, Catherine. *Nobody's Story: The Vanishing Acts of Women Writers in the Marketplace, 1670–1820*. Berkeley and Los Angeles: University of California Press, 1994.

Garrard, Mary D. *Artemisia Gentileschi: The Image of the Female Hero in Italian Baroque Art*. Princeton, N.J.: Princeton University Press, 1989.

Gelbart, Nina Rattner. *The King's Midwife: A History and Mystery of Madame du Coudray*. Berkeley and Los Angeles: University of California Press, 1998.

Goldberg, Jonathan. *Desiring Women Writing: English Renaissance Examples*. Stanford, Calif.: Stanford University Press, 1997.

Goldsmith, Elizabeth C. *Exclusive Conversations: The Art of Interaction in Seventeenth-Century France*. Philadelphia: University of Pennsylvania Press, 1988.

———, ed. *Writing the Female Voice*. Boston: Northeastern University Press, 1989.

Goldsmith, Elizabeth C., and Dena Goodman, eds. *Going Public: Women and Publishing in Early Modern France*. Ithaca, N.Y.: Cornell University Press, 1995.

Greer, Margaret Rich. *Maria de Zayas Tells Baroque Tales of Love and the Cruelty of Men*. University Park: Pennsylvania State University Press, 2000.

Hackett, Helen. *Women and Romance Fiction in the English Renaissance*. Cambridge: Cambridge University Press, 2000.

Hall, Kim F. *Things of Darkness: Economies of Race and Gender in Early Modern England*. Ithaca, N.Y.: Cornell University Press, 1995.

Hampton, Timothy. *Literature and the Nation in the Sixteenth Century: Inventing Renaissance France*. Ithaca, N.Y.: Cornell University Press, 2001.

Hardwick, Julie. *The Practice of Patriarchy: Gender and the Politics of Household Authority in Early Modern France*. University Park: Pennsylvania State University Press, 1998.

Harth, Erica. *Ideology and Culture in Seventeenth-Century France*. Ithaca, N.Y.: Cornell University Press, 1983.

———. *Cartesian Women. Versions and Subversions of Rational Discourse in the Old Regime*. Ithaca, N.Y.: Cornell University Press, 1992.

Haselkorn, Anne M., and Betty Travitsky, eds. *The Renaissance Englishwoman in Print: Counterbalancing the Canon*. Amherst: University of Massachusetts Press, 1990.

Herlihy, David. "Did Women Have a Renaissance? A Reconsideration." *Medievalia et Humanistica*, n.s., 13 (1985): 1–22.

Hill, Bridget. *The Republican Virago: The Life and Times of Catharine Macaulay, Historian*. New York: Oxford University Press, 1992.

A History of Women in the West:

Volume 1: *From Ancient Goddesses to Christian Saints*. Edited by Pauline Schmitt Pantel. Cambridge, Mass.: Harvard University Press, 1992.

Volume 2: *Silences of the Middle Ages*. Edited by Christiane Klapisch-Zuber. Cambridge, Mass.: Harvard University Press, 1992.

Volume 3: *Renaissance and Enlightenment Paradoxes*. Edited by Natalie Zemon Davis and Arlette Farge. Cambridge, Mass.: Harvard University Press, 1993.

Hobby, Elaine. *Virtue of Necessity: English Women's Writing 1646–1688*. London: Virago Press, 1988.

Horowitz, Maryanne Cline. "Aristotle and Women." *Journal of the History of Biology* 9 (1976): 183–213.

Hufton, Olwen H. *The Prospect before Her: A History of Women in Western Europe, 1: 1500–1800.* New York: HarperCollins, 1996.

Hull, Suzanne W. *Chaste, Silent, and Obedient: English Books for Women, 1475–1640.* San Marino, Calif.: The Huntington Library, 1982.

Hunt, Lynn, ed. *The Invention of Pornography: Obscenity and the Origins of Modernity, 1500–1800.* New York: Zone Books, 1996.

Hutner, Heidi, ed. *Rereading Aphra Behn: History, Theory, and Criticism.* Charlottesville: University Press of Virginia, 1993.

Hutson, Lorna, ed. *Feminism and Renaissance Studies.* New York: Oxford University Press, 1999.

James, Susan E. *Kateryn Parr: The Making of a Queen.* Aldershot and Brookfield, England: Ashgate Publishing Co., 1999.

Jankowski, Theodora A. *Women in Power in the Early Modern Drama.* Urbana: University of Illinois Press, 1992.

Jansen, Katherine Ludwig. *The Making of the Magdalen: Preaching and Popular Devotion in the Later Middle Ages.* Princeton, N.J.: Princeton University Press, 2000.

Jed, Stephanie H. *Chaste Thinking: The Rape of Lucretia and the Birth of Humanism.* Bloomington: Indiana University Press, 1989.

Jordan, Constance. *Renaissance Feminism: Literary Texts and Political Models.* Ithaca, N.Y.: Cornell University Press, 1990.

Kelly, Joan. "Did Women Have a Renaissance?" In *Women, History, and Theory.* Chicago: University of Chicago Press, 1984. Also in Renate Bridenthal, Claudia Koonz, and Susan M. Stuard, eds., *Becoming Visible: Women in European History,* 3d ed. Boston: Houghton Mifflin, 1998.

———. "Early Feminist Theory and the *Querelle des Femmes.*" In *Women, History, and Theory.*

Kelso, Ruth. *Doctrine for the Lady of the Renaissance.* Foreword by Katharine M. Rogers. Urbana: University of Illinois Press, 1956, 1978.

King, Carole. *Renaissance Women Patrons: Wives and Widows in Italy, c. 1300–1550.* New York: Manchester University Press, 1998; distributed in U.S. by St. Martin's Press.

King, Margaret L. *Women of the Renaissance.* Foreword by Catharine R. Stimpson. Chicago: University of Chicago Press, 1991.

Krontiris, Tina. *Oppositional Voices: Women as Writers and Translators of Literature in the English Renaissance.* London: Routledge, 1992.

Kuehn, Thomas. *Law, Family, and Women: Toward a Legal Anthropology of Renaissance Italy.* Chicago: University of Chicago Press, 1991.

Kunze, Bonnelyn Young. *Margaret Fell and the Rise of Quakerism.* Stanford, Calif.: Stanford University Press, 1994.

Labalme, Patricia A., ed. *Beyond Their Sex: Learned Women of the European Past.* New York: New York University Press, 1980.

Laqueur, Thomas. *Making Sex: Body and Gender from the Greeks to Freud.* Cambridge, Mass.: Harvard University Press, 1990.

Larsen, Anne R., and Colette H. Winn, eds. *Renaissance Women Writers: French Texts/American Contexts.* Detroit: Wayne State University Press, 1994.

Lerner, Gerda. *The Creation of Patriarchy* and *Creation of Feminist Consciousness, 1000–1870.* 2-vol. history of women. New York: Oxford University Press, 1986, 1994.

Levin, Carole, et al. *Extraordinary Women of the Medieval and Renaissance World: A Biographical Dictionary.* Westport, Conn.: Greenwood Press, 2000.

Levin, Carole, and Jeanie Watson, eds. *Ambiguous Realities: Women in the Middle Ages and Renaissance.* Detroit: Wayne State University Press, 1987.

Lindsey, Karen. *Divorced Beheaded Survived: A Feminist Reinterpretation of the Wives of Henry VIII.* Reading, Mass.: Addison-Wesley Publishing Co., 1995.

Lochrie, Karma. *Margery Kempe and Translations of the Flesh.* Philadelphia: University of Pennsylvania Press, 1992.

Lougee, Carolyn C. *Le Paradis des Femmes: Women, Salons, and Social Stratification in Seventeenth-Century France.* Princeton, N.J.: Princeton University Press, 1976.

Love, Harold. *The Culture and Commerce of Texts: Scribal Publication in Seventeenth-Century England.* Amherst, Mass.: University of Massachusetts Press, 1993.

MacCarthy, Bridget G. *The Female Pen: Women Writers and Novelists 1621–1818.* Preface by Janet Todd. New York: New York University Press, 1994. (Originally published by Cork University Press, 1946–47.)

Maclean, Ian. *Woman Triumphant: Feminism in French Literature, 1610–1652.* Oxford: Clarendon Press, 1977.

———. *The Renaissance Notion of Woman: A Study of the Fortunes of Scholasticism and Medical Science in European Intellectual Life.* Cambridge: Cambridge University Press, 1980.

Matter, E. Ann, and John Coakley, eds. *Creative Women in Medieval and Early Modern Italy.* Philadelphia: University of Pennsylvania Press, 1994. (Sequel to the Monson collection, below)

McLeod, Glenda. *Virtue and Venom: Catalogs of Women from Antiquity to the Renaissance.* Ann Arbor: University of Michigan Press, 1991.

Meek, Christine, ed. *Women in Renaissance and Early Modern Europe.* Dublin: Four Courts Press, 2000.

Mendelson, Sara, and Patricia Crawford. *Women in Early Modern England, 1550–1720.* Oxford: Clarendon Press, 1998.

Merrim, Stephanie. *Early Modern Women's Writing and Sor Juana Inés de la Cruz.* Nashville: Vanderbilt University Press, 1999.

Miller, Nancy K. *The Heroine's Text: Readings in the French and English Novel, 1722–1782.* New York: Columbia University Press, 1980.

Miller, Naomi J. *Changing the Subject: Mary Wroth and Figurations of Gender in Early Modern England.* Lexington: University Press of Kentucky, 1996.

Miller, Naomi, and Gary Waller, eds. *Reading Mary Wroth: Representing Alternatives in Early Modern England.* Knoxville: University of Tennessee Press, 1991.

Monson, Craig A., ed. *The Crannied Wall: Women, Religion, and the Arts in Early Modern Europe.* Ann Arbor: University of Michigan Press, 1992.

Newman, Karen. *Fashioning Femininity and English Renaissance Drama.* Chicago: University of Chicago Press, 1991.

Okin, Susan Moller. *Women in Western Political Thought.* Princeton, N.J.: Princeton University Press, 1979.

Ozment, Steven. *The Bürgermeister's Daughter: Scandal in a Sixteenth-Century German Town.* New York: St. Martin's Press, 1995.

Pacheco, Anita, ed. *Early [English] Women Writers: 1600–1720.* New York: Longman, 1998.
Pagels, Elaine. *Adam, Eve, and the Serpent.* New York: HarperCollins, 1988.
Panizza, Letizia, ed. *Women in Italian Renaissance Culture and Society.* Oxford: European Humanities Research Centre, 2000.
Panizza, Letizia, and Sharon Wood, eds. *A History of Women's Writing in Italy.* Cambridge: Cambridge University Press, 2000.
Perry, Ruth. *The Celebrated Mary Astell: An Early English Feminist.* Chicago: University of Chicago Press, 1986.
Rabil, Albert. *Laura Cereta: Quattrocento Humanist.* Binghamton, N.Y.: MRTS, 1981.
Rapley, Elizabeth. *A Social History of the Cloister: Daily Life in the Teaching Monasteries of the Old Regime.* Montreal: McGill-Queen's University Press, 2001.
Raven, James, Helen Small, and Naomi Tadmor, eds. *The Practice and Representation of Reading in England.* Cambridge: Cambridge University Press, 1996.
Reardon, Colleen. *Holy Concord within Sacred Walls: Nuns and Music in Siena, 1575–1700.* Oxford: Oxford University Press, 2001.
Reiss, Sheryl E., and David G. Wilkins, eds. *Beyond Isabella: Secular Women Patrons of Art in Renaissance Italy.* Kirksville, Mo.: Truman State University Press, 2001.
Rheubottom, David. *Age, Marriage, and Politics in Fifteenth-Century Ragusa.* Oxford: Oxford University Press, 2000.
Richardson, Brian. *Printing, Writers and Readers in Renaissance Italy.* Cambridge: Cambridge University Press, 1999.
Riddle, John M. *Contraception and Abortion from the Ancient World to the Renaissance.* Cambridge, Mass.: Harvard University Press, 1992.
———. *Eve's Herbs: A History of Contraception and Abortion in the West.* Cambridge, Mass.: Harvard University Press, 1997.
Rose, Mary Beth. *The Expense of Spirit: Love and Sexuality in English Renaissance Drama.* Ithaca, N.Y.: Cornell University Press, 1988.
———. *Gender and Heroism in Early Modern English Literature.* Chicago: University of Chicago Press, 2002.
———, ed. *Women in the Middle Ages and the Renaissance: Literary and Historical Perspectives.* Syracuse, N.Y.: Syracuse University Press, 1986.
Rosenthal, Margaret F. *The Honest Courtesan: Veronica Franco, Citizen and Writer in Sixteenth-Century Venice.* Foreword by Catharine R. Stimpson. Chicago: University of Chicago Press, 1992.
Sackville-West, Vita. *Daughter of France: The Life of La Grande Mademoiselle.* Garden City, N.Y.: Doubleday, 1959.
Schiebinger, Londa. *The Mind Has No Sex?: Women in the Origins of Modern Science.* Cambridge, Mass.: Harvard University Press, 1991.
———. *Nature's Body: Gender in the Making of Modern Science.* Boston: Beacon Press, 1993.
Schutte, Anne Jacobson, Thomas Kuehn, and Silvana Seidel Menchi, eds. *Time, Space, and Women's Lives in Early Modern Europe.* Kirksville, Mo.: Truman State University Press, 2001.
Shannon, Laurie. *Sovereign Amity: Figures of Friendship in Shakespearean Contexts.* Chicago: University of Chicago Press, 2002.
Shemek, Deanna. *Ladies Errant: Wayward Women and Social Order in Early Modern Italy.* Durham, N.C.: Duke University Press, 1998.

Sobel, Dava. *Galileo's Daughter: A Historical Memoir of Science, Faith, and Love.* New York: Penguin Books, 2000.

Sommerville, Margaret R. *Sex and Subjection: Attitudes to Women in Early-Modern Society.* London: Arnold, 1995.

Spencer, Jane. *The Rise of the Woman Novelist: From Aphra Behn to Jane Austen.* Oxford: Basil Blackwell, 1986.

Spender, Dale. *Mothers of the Novel: 100 Good Women Writers before Jane Austen.* London: Routledge, 1986.

Sperling, Jutta Gisela. *Convents and the Body Politic in Late Renaissance Venice.* Foreword by Catharine R. Stimpson. Chicago: University of Chicago Press, 1999.

Steinbrügge, Lieselotte. *The Moral Sex: Woman's Nature in the French Enlightenment.* Translated by Pamela E. Selwyn. New York: Oxford University Press, 1995.

Stephens, Sonya, ed. *A History of Women's Writing in France.* Cambridge: Cambridge University Press, 2000.

Stuard, Susan M. "The Dominion of Gender: Women's Fortunes in the High Middle Ages." In *Becoming Visible: Women in European History,* edited by Renate Bridenthal, Claudia Koonz, and Susan M. Stuard. 3d ed. Boston: Houghton Mifflin, 1998.

Summit, Jennifer. *Lost Property: The Woman Writer and English Literary History, 1380–1589.* Chicago: University of Chicago Press, 2000.

Teague, Frances. *Bathsua Makin, Woman of Learning.* Lewisburg, Pa.: Bucknell University Press, 1999.

Todd, Janet. *The Secret Life of Aphra Behn.* London: Pandora, 2000.

———. *The Sign of Angelica: Women, Writing and Fiction, 1660–1800.* New York: Columbia University Press, 1989.

Van Dijk, Susan, Lia van Gemert, and Sheila Ottway, eds. *Writing the History of Women's Writing: Toward an International Approach.* Proceedings of the Colloquium, Amsterdam, 9–11 September. Amsterdam: Royal Netherlands Academy of Arts and Sciences, 2001.

Wall, Wendy. *The Imprint of Gender: Authorship and Publication in the English Renaissance.* Ithaca, N.Y.: Cornell University Press, 1993.

Walsh, William T. *St. Teresa of Avila: A Biography.* Rockford, Ill.: TAN Books and Publications, 1987.

Warner, Marina. *Alone of All Her Sex: The Myth and Cult of the Virgin Mary.* New York: Knopf, 1976.

Warnicke, Retha M. *The Marrying of Anne of Cleves: Royal Protocol in Tudor England.* Cambridge: Cambridge University Press, 2000.

Watt, Diane. *Secretaries of God: Women Prophets in Late Medieval and Early Modern England.* Cambridge, England: D. S. Brewer, 1997.

Welles, Marcia L. *Persephone's Girdle: Narratives of Rape in Seventeenth-Century Spanish Literature.* Nashville: Vanderbilt University Press, 2000.

Whitehead, Barbara J., ed. *Women's Education in Early Modern Europe: A History, 1500–1800.* New York: Garland Publishing Co., 1999.

Wiesner, Merry E. *Women and Gender in Early Modern Europe.* Cambridge: Cambridge University Press, 1993.

Willard, Charity Cannon. *Christine de Pizan: Her Life and Works.* New York: Persea Books, 1984.

Wilson, Katharina, ed. *An Encyclopedia of Continental Women Writers*. New York: Garland, 1991.

Woodbridge, Linda. *Women and the English Renaissance: Literature and the Nature of Womankind, 1540–1620*. Urbana: University of Illinois Press, 1984.

Woods, Susanne. *Lanyer: A Renaissance Woman Poet*. New York: Oxford University Press, 1999.

Woods, Susanne, and Margaret P. Hannay, eds. *Teaching Tudor and Stuart Women Writers*. New York: MLA, 2000.

BIBLICAL REFERENCES INDEX

Genesis, xvi
Gen. 1:27, xv
Gen. 2:21–23, xv
Gen. 22: 1–18, 79

Exod. 16:3, 68, 114, 132, 137
Exod. 20:7, 135

Lev. 11:16, 85

Num. 21:4–9, 183

Deut. 8:3, 149
Deut. 32:5, 149
Deut. 32:15, 123

1 Sam. 2:6, 166
1 Sam. 15:22, 79
1 Sam. 25, 121

1 Kings 10, 71
1 Kings 18:6, 179

1 Chron. 29:15, 142

Esther, 121

Job 5:18, 166
Job 8:9, 142
Job 14:2, 142
Job 14:12, 142

Psalms, 9, 16, 27, 145, 147, 181, 182, 184, 185, 186
Ps. 13:3, 151
Ps. 17:5, 151
Ps. 18:1, 145
Ps. 19:14, 145
Ps. 22:19, 145
Ps. 25:4, 151
Ps. 26:5, 150
Ps. 27:1, 145
Ps. 37:1, 142
Ps. 37:20, 142
Ps. 42:1, 32
Ps. 45, 114
Ps. 46, 62, 108
Ps. 51:10, 151
Ps. 68:2, 142
Ps. 89, 146
Ps. 90:12, 146
Ps. 91:11–12, 108
Ps. 92:7, 142
Ps. 102:3, 142
Ps. 103:15 (102:15), 142, 145
Ps. 110:2 (109:2), 129
Ps. 115:11–13, 147
Ps. 119:23, 142
Ps. 119:98, 152
Ps. 119:105, 142, 152
Ps. 125:1, 68
Ps. 140, 145
Ps. 141:4, 145

Biblical References Index

Ps. 144:4, 142
Ps. 147, 121
Ps. 147:11, 147
Ps. 151, 185

Prov. 3:12, 124, 166
Prov. 16:9, 119
Prov. 17:3, 132

Eccles. 3:4, 172
Eccles. 6:12, 142
Eccles. 8:13, 142

Isaiah, 147, 148, 149, 172
Isa. 9:6, 149
Isa. 22:13, 170
Isa. 40:6–7, 142
Isa. 40:7–8, 142
Isa. 42:3, 148, 149
Isa. 43:2, 147
Isa. 51:6, 142
Isa. 51:12, 142
Isa. 55:6, 146

Jeremiah, 147, 178

Lamentations, 160

Ezek. 18:23, 136
Ezek. 18:32, 136
Ezek. 33:11, 136

Dan. 5:27, 132

Hos. 6:6, 79
Hos. 13:3, 142

Zech. 13:9, 132

Tob. 13:2, 166

Wisd. of Sol. 16:5–8, 183

Ecclus. 37:11, 138

2 Macc. 9:5–28, 135

Matt. 4:1–13, 151
Matt. 4:4, 149
Matt. 4:6, 108
Matt. 5:13, 135
Matt. 5:35, 135
Matt. 6:19–20, 154
Matt. 6:24, 67
Matt. 6:30, 142
Matt. 6:33, 145
Matt. 7:7, 144, 152
Matt. 7:23, 136
Matt. 10:22, 67, 153
Matt. 10:28, 142, 170
Matt. 10:30, 152
Matt. 10:38, 125
Matt. 11:28, 117, 124, 148
Matt. 16:24, 125
Matt. 17:17, 149
Matt. 17:21, 151
Matt. 18:19, 149
Matt. 19:26, 147, 167
Matt. 21:22, 144
Matt. 24:13, 153
Matt. 25:34–40, 111
Matt. 25:40, 105
Matt. 26:41, 135

Mark 8:34, 125
Mark 8:38, 169
Mark 9:29, 151
Mark 10:21, 125
Mark 10:27, 147, 167
Mark 11:24, 144
Mark 13:13, 153

Luke 1:1, 118
Luke 1:37, 147
Luke 4:1–13, 151
Luke 4:4, 149
Luke 4:10–11, 108
Luke 9:23, 125
Luke 9:41, 149
Luke 11:9, 152
Luke 12:5, 142
Luke 12:7, 152
Luke 12:28, 142

Biblical References Index

Luke 12:33, 154
Luke 14:27, 125
Luke 16:13, 67
Luke 18:27, 147
Luke 21:18, 152

John 2:8, 133
John 3:2, 15
John 3:14, 182, 183
John 3:16, 43, 183
John 4:10, 4
John 4:13–14, 124
John 6:44, 50
John 10:26, 50
John 14:3, 149
John 14:13, 170
John 14:13–14, 152
John 15:7, 152
John 15:16, 152
John 16:23–26, 152

Acts 2:21, 42, 126
Acts 8:5–25, 149
Acts 9:10–19, 13
Acts 10:44, 43, 145
Acts 20:9–12, 109
Acts 27:34, 152

Rom. 1:16, 68
Rom. 3:23, 135
Rom. 6:6, 142
Rom. 8:13, 170
Rom. 8:26, 140, 148
Rom. 8:28, 175
Rom. 8:29–30, 148
Rom. 8:37, 152
Rom. 10:13, 42, 126
Rom. 10:17, 42, 145, 153
Rom. 14:13, 135
Rom. 14:22, 15
Rom. 16:1–3, xvi

1 Cor. 3:13, 132
1 Cor. 3:16–17, 135
1 Cor. 4:16, 135
1 Cor. 6:10, 136

1 Cor. 7:31, 143
1 Cor. 8:9, 145
1 Cor. 8:11–13, 136
1 Cor. 9:24–25, 148
1 Cor. 9:25, 152
1 Cor. 9:27, 135
1 Cor. 10:12, 153
1 Cor. 10:29, 145
1 Cor. 11:1, 135
1 Cor. 11:3, xvi
1 Cor. 11:32, 175
1 Cor. 15:32, 170
1 Cor. 15:58, 126
1 Cor. 16:19, xvi

2 Cor. 1:7, 166
2 Cor. 2:4, 148
2 Cor. 2:11–16, 126

Galatians, 43, 145
Gal. 2:20, 13
Gal. 3:2–5, 43, 145
Gal. 3:28, xvi
Gal. 5:6, 169
Gal. 5:24, 135

Eph. 4:30, 135
Eph. 5, 151
Eph. 5:2, 126
Eph. 5:18, 134
Eph. 5:22–23, xvi, 180
Eph. 6:11–17, 151
Eph. 6:16–17, 68

Philippians, 151
Phil. 1:23, 174
Phil. 2:15, 149
Phil. 2:23, 183
Phil. 3:12, 150
Phil. 3:12–13, 151
Phil. 3:19, 120
Phil. 4:2–3, xvi

Col. 3:18, xvi

1 Tim. 2:4, 136

Biblical References Index

1 Tim. 2:9–15, xvi
1 Tim. 2:12, 52
1 Tim. 3:8, 134
1 Tim. 4:3, 134
1 Tim. 5:3–16, 111

2 Tim. 2:12, 166
2 Tim. 4:8, 152

Titus 1:2, 117, 124, 145
Titus 2:3, 134

Hebrews, 51, 145
Heb. 6:1, 150
Heb. 6:4, 14
Heb. 6:18, 117, 124, 145
Heb. 11:1, 147
Heb. 11:6, 145
Heb. 11:10, 13–14, 139
Heb. 11:13–14, 139
Heb. 11:15–16, 139
Heb. 11:19, 109
Heb. 11:26, 68
Heb. 12:6, 124, 166
Heb. 13:20, 109

James, 110
James 1:10–11, 142
James 1:12, 152
James 1:27, 111
James 4:14, 125
James 5:12, 135
James 5:16, 110
James 5:17, 110

1 Pet. 1:23, 132
1 Pet. 1:24, 142
1 Pet. 2:8, 152
1 Pet. 3:7, xvi
1 Pet. 3:13, 132
1 Pet. 5:4, 152

1 John 3:22, 144
1 John 5:14, 152

Rev. 2:10, 152

CLASSICAL REFERENCES INDEX

Agathon, frag 11 (Athen. 5.185a), 133
Anthologia Palatina 11.321, 92
Apostolius: Cent. IV.52, 91; Cent. VI.13, 95
Aristophanes, 85
Aristotle, xii, xiii, xiv, 70, 85, 86, 91, 211; *E.N.* 1139b18 ff., 69; *Gen. an.* 2.3.737a 27–28, xiii; *N.E.* 1098b6, 91; *N.E.* 1099a3–7, 92; *Phy.*, 161; *Phy.* 1.9.192a 20–24, xii; *Pol.* 1252a–1260b, 69; *Rh.*, 10
Athenaeus 5.185a, 133

[Ps. Cato], *Dicticha Catonis (Brev. Sent.)* 42, 77
Catullus 84, 85
Cicero: *Acad.* 2.200, 80; *Amic.* 91, 119; *Amic.* 104, 125; *Arch.* 13, 102; *Att.*, 165, 166; *Att.* 1.14.3, 177; *Att.* 4.15.6, 80; *Att.* 10.18.1, 115; *Brut.* 172, 86; *Cael.* 28, 133; *De Or.* 1.493, 128; *De Or.* 2.86, 90; *De Or.* 2.186, 129; *De Or.* 2.233, 90; *De Or.* 3.40–41, 89; *De Or.* 3.138, 87; *De Or.* 3.171, 89; *De Or.* 3.185, 89; *De Or.* 3.213, 85; *De Or.* 3.213–27, 89; *Div.*, 37; *Div.* 1.78, 86; *Div.* 2.66, 86; *Fam.* 2.3.1, 162; *Fam.* 4.5.5, 96; *Fam.* 5.16, 118; *Fam.* 15.12.2, 129; *Fam.* 15.16.2, 117; *Fin.* 2.110, 90; *Inv.* 1.9, 85; *N.D.* 1.23, 124; *Off.*, 15; *Off.* 1.30, 125; *Off.* 1.158, 93; *orat.* 10, 125; *Orat.* 56, 85; *Para.*, 2, 4, 17, 57, 62, 75, 76; *Para.* 1.1.8–9; 154; *Part.* 21, 89; *Rep.* 6.15, 90; *Senec.* 73, 198; *Somn.*, 76; *Tusc.* 1.34, 198; *Tusc.* 1.76, 169; *Tusc.* 1.117, 198; *Tusc.* 5.62, 121

Dio 47.49.3, 209
Diogenes Laertius 5.38, 86; 8.17, 128
Dionysius of Halicarnassus 5.27–31, 80; 5.35, 80

Ennius, 89, 198; *Andromache*, 80

Galen, xii, 211; 9.292, 133; 15.422, 133
Gellius 4.2.1, 205; 11.8, 75; 13.5.3–12, 85

Hesiod, 220; *Op.* 361, 131
Homer, 1, 16, 70, 75, 92, 160, 177, 181, 185, 216, 220; *Il.* 1.18, 217; *Il.* 3.237, 179; *Il.* 3.65, 129; *Il.* 17.514, 102; *Il.* 20.347, 217; *Od.* 1.82, 217; *Od.* 1.189, 101; *Od.* 4.833, 133; *Od.* 5.269, 78; *Od.* 10.495, 92; *Od.* 15.343, 139; *Od.* 16.137–41, 101; *Od.* 19.455–58, 87; *Od.* 24.209 ff., 101
Horace, 75; *Ars Poetica*, 4; *Ars Poetica* 38–40, 76; *Ars Poetica* 234, 276; *Ep.* 1.2.3, 129; *Ep.* 1.5.15, 135; *Ep.* 2.1.79, 80; *Ep.* 2.1.82, 80; *Ep.* 2.2.125, 80; *Epod.* 1.11–14,

Classical References Index

Horace (continued)
128; Odes 1.24.19–20, 124; Odes 1.28.16, 169; Odes 1.123–24, 69; Odes 2.1.6, 77; Odes 3.1.38–39, 142; Odes 3.3.7–8, 154; Odes 3.4.65, 78; Sat. 1.5.63, 80; Sat. 1.10.76, 80

Isocrates, 75; 1.1, 107; 1.43, 81

Jerome: *Against Jovinian*, xvi; Ep. 20, 72; Ep. 30, 72; Ep. 31, 72; Ep. 33, 72; Ep. 39, 72; Ep. 46, 72; Ep. 108, 72; Ep. 69.2, 87; Ep. 130.17, 87
Justinian: *Corpus of Civil Law*, xiv
Juvenal, 75; 1.44, 79

Lactantius: *Phoenix*, 88
Livy 1.12, 80; 4.28.5, 161
Lucian, 75, 210; 5 (Herc.) 3, 86; 11 (Patr. Enc.) 7, 80; 25 (Tim.) 12, 85; 31 (Ind.), 95
Lucretius, 21, 26, 27, 37, 38, 39, 75, 100, 101, 118; 2.69, 125; 2.416, 80; 2.417, 80; 2.559, 78; 5.1104, 78
Lysias, 77

Macrobius 2.7.2–9, 127
Martial 11.37.1, 66

Ovid, 10, 211; AA 2.4, 212; AA 2.11, 129; Ep. (Heroides) 1.12, 98; Fasti 1.493, 128; Met. 1.12–13, 87; Met. 10.4.2, 88; Met. 11.530, 196; Pont. 3.3.31, 212; Rem. 366, 66; Tr. 5.7.61, 220

Pacuvius: *Antiope*, 80
Persius 1.14, 85; 1.109, 89; 3.30, 168
Pindar, 113, 222
Plato, xiii, 16, 37, 66, 70, 85, 86; Leg., 72; Leg. 6.753e, 91; Rep., xiii, 72, 180; Rep. 5.451–56, 65; Symp., 93
Plautus: Amph. 505, 126; Trim. 32, 128
Pliny the Elder: N.H. 11.55, 86; N.H. 33.11, 78
Pliny the Younger, 129; 1.20.18, 87; 3.5.16, 101; 9.29.1, 129

Plutarch, 75, 157; Lives, 29, 154; Alex. 8.4, 91; Anthony 28, 101; Lyc. 20, 87; Popl. 17, 80; De garrul. 5 (Mor. 504c), 77; Reg. Et Imp. Apoth. (Mor. 181b), 77
Propertius, 75; 2.10.6, 79
Publius Syrus: Sententia 1.6, 113

Quintilian 1.5.32, 88; 1.8.2, 88; 1.11.5, 85; 11.3.6, 85; 12.5.5, 85

Seneca: Ag. 502, 196; Cont. 7.3.9, 127; Dial. 2.2.1, 124; Ep. 94.23, 177; Herc. Fur. 208, 140; Herc. Fur. 588, 99
Sophocles: Ant. 1126, 179; Electra, 18
Stobaeus 2.46, 92
Suetonius: Aug. 84.2, 88; Gaius 20, 79

Terence: Adelphi, 18; Adelphi 34, 119; Andria, 18; Andria 161, 198; Andria 310, 124; Eun., 85; Eun. 181–87, 99; Eun. 236, 78; Eun. 301, 115; Eun. 761, 111; Heaut. 225, 118; Heaut. 575, 119; Phorm. 493, 134; Phorm. 856, 129
Tertullian, xvi; Apol. 33.4, 78; On the apparel of women, xvi
Theocritus 12.2, 100

Ulpian, xv

Valerius Maximus 4.6.5, 209
Varro: RR 1.1.1, 125
Vergil, 36, 37, 70, 87, 212; Aen. 1.30, 66; Aen. 1.204, 218; Aen. 1.491–94, 71; Aen. 1.630, 105; Aen. 2.428, 159; Aen. 3.2, 159; Aen. 7.803–7, 71; Aen. 8.664, 206; Aen. 11.715, 89; Ecl. 2.65, 69; Ecl. 4.53–57, 95; Ecl. 8.35, 37, 101; G. 1.109, 89; G. 1.388, 88; G. 2.475–77, 70; G. 3.8–9, 70

Xenophon, 75; Agesil. 11.3, 92; Cyrop. 1.27, 92; Mem. 4.4.24, 92

Zen. 5.91, 78

GENERAL INDEX

Abigail, 121, 123
Abraham, 79
Acciaiuoli, Andrea, xxv
Achilles, 66, 76
Act of Uniformity, First (Church of England), 186
Adam, xv, xvi, xxiii, xxviii, 43, 142, 166
Adamus (Adam), Melchior, 34
Aemilia, 86
Aesclepius, 222
Agapitus, Saint, 11
Agesilaos, 91
Agnese (wife of Valentino Carchesio), 133
Agrippa, Cornelius, 39
Agrippa, Henricus Cornelius, xxiii, xxiv, xxv; *On the Nobility and Preeminence of the Female Sex*, xxiii
Ahasuerus, 122
Alberti, Leon Battista: *On the Family*, xxiii
Albrecht II Alcibiades, margrave of Brandenberg-Kulmbach, 28, 111, 137, 139, 140, 171, 217, 221
Alcman, 222
Alcaeus, 222
Aldhelm, Saint: *De laude virginum*, 218
Alexander the Great, 70, 76, 91
Alfonso della Viola, 7
Alps, 1, 26, 41, 128
Amazon(s), xxviii, 2, 34, 70, 76
ambassadors for Ferrara, 45

Amerbach, Basil, 204, 205, 207
Amerbach, Boniface, 96, 175, 197, 204
Amphictyonic League, 176
Amphion, 85
Anabaptists, 28
Ananias, 13
Andromache, 87
Angenoust, Jerôme (Hieronymus Angenosios), 171, 208, 213
Angla, 71
Anne of Brittany, xxv
Anne of Denmark, xxv
Antichrist, 12, 44, 45, 115, 127
Antonio del Cornetto, 7
Anyte, 71
Apennines, 219
Apollinaris (bishop of Laodicea), 185
Apollo, 87, 95, 210, 219
Aquinas, Saint Thomas, xiv, xvi
Arabia, 214
Arbuscula, 80
Arcadia, 209
Archilochus, 222
Ariosto, xxviii, 7, 14; *Orlando Furioso*, xxviii; *Orlando Furioso* 42.90, 14
Aristarchus, 177
ark of the Covenant, 11
Artemisia, xxvii
Ascra, 220
Aspasia, 71, 93, 211
Astell, Mary, xxv, xxvii, xxix; *Serious Proposal to the Ladies*, xxv

General Index

atheism, 38–39. *See also* Epicurus/Epicureanism; Lucretius
Athena, 209
Atlas, 76
Aubigné, Agrippa d', 25
Augsburg, 26, 62, 97, 104, 106, 112, 113, 114
Augsburg, Council of, 105
Augsburg Interim, 28, 29, 112, 133, 203
Augustus, 88
Augustine, Saint: *The Literal Meaning of Genesis*, xvi
Augustinians, 11
Aulus Albinus, 75
Autolycus, 87
Avicenna, 130
Avila y Zuñiga, Luis de, 123

Babylon, 168
Bacchelli, Franco, 38
Baldenburger, Jakob, 63
Bamburg, 29, 108, 137
Banz, 156
Barbara (maid to Olympia Morata), 158
Barbaro, Francesco, xxiii, xxviii; *On Marriage*, xxiii
Barotti, Giovanni Andrea, 34
Basel, 13, 54, 61, 63, 74, 107, 113, 155, 159, 161, 162, 174, 202, 205, 206, 211
Bassi, Laura Marina Caterina, 30
beast of the Apocalypse, 46
Bellermann, Johannes, 155
Bembo, Pietro, 3, 17, 52, 178, 180
Bentivoglio, Elena Rangoni, 115
Betuleius, Sixtus (Xystus, Sixt Birk), 14, 61, 108, 114
Bèze, Theodore de, 33, 40; *Icones*, 33
Bias of Priene, 154, 160
Bible: need for study, 26, 27, 32, 40, 43, 108, 118, 119, 121, 126, 138, 145, 151, 152, 166; Scripture, xxi, 1, 15, 18, 21, 26, 27, 32, 34, 36, 40, 41, 42, 43, 45, 63, 68, 75, 108, 118, 119, 121, 126, 133, 138, 142, 145, 146, 147, 150, 151, 152, 153, 166, 185, 204. *See also* Gospel; Word of God; *and* Biblical References Index
Biblical Humanism, 36, 40, 184–85
Boccaccio, Giovanni, xvii, xviii, xxi, xxii, xxv, 207; *Concerning Famous Women*, xxi; *Decameron*, 16; *Il Corbaccio*, xvii, xviii, xxi
Bodin, Jean, xxiv
Bologna/Bolognese, 89, 130
Bolsec, Jerôme, 19
Bonadus, Franciscus (Bonade, François), 185
Book of Common Prayer, 186
Borgia, Lucrezia, 7
Borsetti Ferranti Bolani, Ferrante, 34
Bouchefort, Jehannet de, 9, 46
Boussiron de Grande Rys, Françoise de, 19, 46, 111
Brantôme, Pierre de: *Lives of Illustrious Women*, xxii
Braunschweig, duke of (Heinrich, 1514–68), 29, 137
Bresegna [Briseña, de Briceño], Isabella Manriquez, 33, 65, 67, 68
Brigida (niece of Johannes Sinapius), 139, 155
Britain/Britons, 71, 73. *See also* England/English
Brixius, Magnolus, 154
Bruni, Leonardo, xxviii
Brutus, 87, 209
Bucer, Martin, 41, 50, 184
Buchanan, George, 185
Bullinger, Heinrich, 96; *Commentary on Matthew*, 12
Burton, Robert, 14

Cabianca, Domenico, da Bassano, 23
Caesar (Julius), 70, 87, 88
Calcagnini, Celio, 4, 5, 6, 14, 15, 16, 37, 38, 39, 66, 93, 94, 100, 103; "Coelii Secta," 37; "De imitatione," 16; "De libero animi motu," 14; "De lusu puellarum," 14; "De Trinitate et Sapentia Divina sermo," 103; "Descriptio culi," 14; "Descriptio

cunni," 14; "In impudicum," 14;
"Priapi fortitudo," 14; "Somatia,"
103
Caligula, 79
Calliope, 95, 212
Calvin, Jean, 9, 10, 15, 19, 27, 29,
32, 39, 40, 49, 51, 53, 55, 63–64,
131, 184; *Commentaries on Isaiah*, 29,
147; *Commentaries on the Lamentations
of Jeremiah*, 29, 141; *Commentary on
Jeremiah 38:15*, 39; correspondence
of, 12, 20, 32, 55, 131; *Excuse à
Messieurs les Nicodémites*, 15; *Institutio
Christianae religionis*, 15; *Institutio
Christianae religionis 1.2.2*, 39; *Institutio
Christianae religionis 1.3.2*, 39; *Institutio
Christianae religionis 1.16*, 39; *Institutio
Christianae religionis 3.14.17*, 43;
Institutio Christianae religionis 3.21.1,
50; *On Avoiding Superstitions* (De
vitandis superstitionibus), 47; *On
Scandals* (De Scandalis), 39
Calvinism/Calvinist, 2, 34, 40, 47, 48
Cambridge, 186
Camerarius, Joachim, 27, 55, 190
Cameron, Euan, 52
Camilla, 70
Campanus (Glock), Andreas, 27, 43,
57, 161, 163, 164, 165, 166, 195,
198, 202
Cantelma, Margherita, of Mantua, xxv
Cantimori, Delio, 51, 53
Capra, Galeazzo Flavio: *On the Excellence
and Dignity of Women*, xxiii
Capuchins, 42
Caracciolo (di Vico), Galeazzo,
marchese, 46
Carchesio, Valentino, 26, 131, 132
Carnesecchi, Pietro, 21, 53
Castiglione, Baldassare: *The Courtier*,
xxii, 1
Castile, xxv
Castor, 179
Catherine of Alexandria, Saint, 218
Catherine of Aragon, xxv
Catholic/Catholicism, xii, xix, xxii,
xxvi, 22, 40, 44, 45, 55, 178

Cato, Marcus Porcius, 75
Caucasus, 128, 222
Celtis, Konrad, 34
Cerberus, 87
Cereta, Laura, xxv, 34
Cesena, 4
Champagne, 171
Charles V (emperor), 28, 112, 123, 130
Charles V (king of France), xxv
Charles VIII, King of France, xxv
Chavanus, 133
Chiavenna, 33
Chiron, 96
Christ. *See* Jesus
Christian(s)/Christianity, xi, xii, xv,
xvi, xix, xxii, xxiii, xxix, 5, 6, 27, 34,
37, 38, 44, 45, 48, 49, 76, 102, 114,
115, 118, 119, 127, 128, 134, 136,
141, 149, 158, 165, 168, 170, 176,
180, 181, 200, 215
Christine de Pizan, xvii, xx, xxi, xxii,
xxv, xxvii, xxix, 71; *Book of the City of
Ladies*, xvii, xx, xxv; *Book of the City of
Ladies 1.1.1–2*, xxi; *Book of the City of
Ladies 2.61.3*, 71; *The Treasure of the
City of Ladies*, xxv
Chrysostomus, 86
Church of Christ/Church of God, 45,
69
church fathers, 21, 37, 41, 75
Cibo, Caterina, 52
Cicero, 1, 15, 16, 36, 37, 66, 70, 75,
78, 80, 85, 89, 94, 95, 180. *See also*
Classical References Index
Cicilia, 115
Clement VII, 8
Cleobulina, 71
Cleon, 85
Cognatus, Gilbertus (Gilbert Cousin),
Nozerenus, 211
Col, Gontier, xxii
Colomies, Paul, 34
Colonna, Vittoria, 9, 52
Communion, 18, 33. *See also* Eucharist;
Mass
Confessio Pentapolitana, 28
confessionalization, 47–48, 51

confraternities, lay, 53, 54
Consensus Tigurinus, 49
Constantia (Costantina), 218
Contarini, Gasparo, 52
Cook, Sir Anthony, 73
Copernicus/Copernican, 14, 34, 87
Corinna, 35, 71, 211, 212, 213
Cornaro Piscopia, Elena Lucrezia, 30
Cornelia, 89
Cornelius, 43, 145
Correr, Gregorio, 36, 37
Cortonaeus, Petrus, 211
Council of Ten (Venice), 5
Counter Reformation, 25
Cramer, Anna Maria, 35
Cremer, Johannes, 27, 92, 134, 155, 156, 157, 172
Cumaean, Sibyl, 217
Cupid, 178
Curio (Curione), Caelius Secundus, 2, 5, 11, 12, 13, 16, 17, 18, 19, 27, 31, 33, 40, 44, 46, 48, 54, 55, 57, 61, 63, 65, 69, 71, 73, 75, 84, 91, 93, 105, 106, 113, 114, 116, 134, 139, 142, 143, 145, 147, 155, 159, 162, 173, 174, 176, 177, 178, 180, 181, 183, 196, 197, 198, 199, 201, 202, 204, 205, 206, 207, 208, 214, 215, 218; *Commentary on Cicero's Philippics*, 73; *De Amplitudine Beati Regni Dei*, 198; *De liberis pie Christianeque educandis*, 27, 116, 178; "Dedication to Elizabeth I," 69–74, 93; "Dedication to Isabella of Bresengna," 2, 65–69, 94; *Enneades ab orbe condito*, 73; *Pasquillus Ecstaticus*, 12, 27, 116
Curio, Horatius (Orazio), 73, 161
Curio, Violantis, 175
Cyclops, 80

Danaans, 66
Dante, 12, 38
David, 70, 114, 121, 123, 145, 149, 150, 151, 152, 192
Deborah, 71
Delfini, G. Antonio, 22
della Rovere Orsini, Lavinia, 21, 22, 26, 27, 31, 39, 43, 50, 96, 97, 98, 99, 100, 101, 102, 105, 106, 109, 112, 115, 116, 117, 118, 137, 141, 143, 146, 150, 152
Demosthenes, 70, 84, 85
Dentière, Mariem, 52
Des Périers, Bonaventure: *Cymbalum Mundi*, 39
Des Roches, Catherine Fredonnoit: "Dialogue de Placide et Severe," 35
Des Roches, Madelaine: "Ode 1," 17, 71
Devil, 112, 118, 124, 142, 143, 149, 152, 153, 169, 197
Dianti, Laura, 6
Diotima, 93
Dolet, Étienne, 39
Dominicans, xxiv, 22
Donne, John: "On the Sacrament," 49
Doricism, 88
Dossi, Dosso, 7

Eberti, Johann Caspar, 34
Echo, 87
edict of Chateaubriant, 32, 170
edict of Nantes, 34
Edward VI, 73
Egypt/Egyptians, 26, 43, 68, 132, 137
Ehrenfriedersdorf, 171, 173
election. *See* predestination
Elenora of Aragon, xxv, 10
Elephant, Christopher, 207
Elijah, 110
Elizabeth I, xxvii, 33, 49, 69, 72
Elyot, Sir Thomas: *Defense of Good Women*, xxvii
England/English, xxii, xxv, xxvii, xxix, 9, 12, 33, 72, 143, 144. *See also* Britain/Britons
Enns, 28
Eobanus (Hessus, Helius Eobanus), 185, 186
Epicureanism/Epicurus, 16, 34, 36–39, 101, 134, 144, 145, 175. *See also* atheism; Lucretius
Episcopius (Bischoff, Nikolaus), 162
Epistles (Pauline), xv, xvi, 21
Equicola, Maria: *On Women*, xxiii, xxv

General Index

Erasmianism/Erasmus, xxiii, 4, 5, 10, 14, 15, 34, 38, 40, 41, 42, 46, 89, 90; *Adages* 1.1.61, 66; *Adages* 2.3.3, 78; *Letters*, 38; *On the Free Will*, 14
Erbach, Countess Elizabeth von, 144
Erbach, Count Georg II von and Count Eberhard XIV von, 29, 48, 51, 141, 150, 156, 157, 202, 203
Ercole I d'Este, duke of Ferrara, xxv, 7
Ercole II d'Este, duke of Ferrara, 6, 7, 8, 22, 62, 63, 95
Eretrians, 89
Eridanus, 219
Esslingen, 176
Este, Alfonsino d', 6
Este, Alfonso d', 6
Este, Anna d', 10, 11, 12, 18, 20, 32, 51, 62, 76, 93, 94, 95, 168
Este, Eleanora d', 10
Este, Francesco d', Prince of Massa, 3, 62
Este, Ippolito d', cardinal, 3, 20, 62
Este, Lucrezia d', 10
Este, Luigi d', cardinal, 10
Este, Sigismondo d', 3
Esther, 27, 118, 121, 122
Eton, 186
Etruscans, 81, 82
Eucharist, 1, 49, 103. *See also* Communion; Mass
Euclid, 10
Eumenides, 221
Euripides, 87
Eustochium, 72
Eutychus, 109
evangelism, 2, 36, 41–54; as aristocratic, 52
Eve, xv, xvi, xxi, xxiii, xxvii, xxviii

Faenza, 21, 22
faith/justification by faith, 8, 9, 15, 19, 27, 42, 43, 44, 47, 52, 121, 126, 135, 136, 144, 145, 147, 149, 150, 153, 166, 169, 197
Faius, 156, 157
Fanini, Fanino (Fanio Camillo), 21, 22, 23, 28, 45, 53, 105, 109, 112, 115

Fate(s), 216, 219
Faust, 34
Fedele, Cassandra, xxv, 17, 30, 34, 72
Ferdinand I, 19, 28, 97, 109, 126, 128
Ferrara/Ferrarese, xxv, 3, 4, 6, 7, 8, 9, 10, 12, 13, 15, 18, 19, 24, 27, 31, 33, 34, 50, 55, 57, 61, 64, 75, 84, 90, 91, 93, 94, 95, 96, 97, 98, 99, 100, 105, 107, 115, 116, 130, 131, 141, 165, 168, 178, 186, 204, 205, 208, 211, 213, 222, 224; University of, 6, 14
Ferrara, dukes of: Alfonso I d'Este, 3, 6, 7, 10, 62, 84; Alfonso II d'Este, 10
Ferreri, Bonifacio, cardinal, 11
Filippo da Bergamo: *On Illustrious Women*, xxii
Firpo, Massimo, 49
Flacius Illyricus, Matthias, 27, 49, 133
Flaminio, Marcantonio, 52, 185
Flanders, xix
Florence, xxv
Fonte, Moderata (Modesta Pozzo), xxvii, 34
Fortune, 77, 78, 79, 93, 160
France, xvii, xxii, xxiv, xxv, xxvii, xxix, 2, 7, 8, 9, 20, 21, 24, 32, 38, 41, 54, 55, 66, 117, 171
Franciotti, Niccolo, 21
Franciscans, 42
François I, King of France, 7, 9, 18, 96, 171
Franconia/Franks, 107, 215, 217, 221
Frankfurt, 160, 175, 197
Friedrich II, duke and elector Palatine (Pfalzgraf and Kurfürst), 30, 64, 138, 139, 144, 168, 221
Friedrich III, duke and elector Palatine (Pfalzgraf and Kurfürst), 48, 203
Froben, Hieronymus, 162
Froment, Antoine, 52
Fugger family, 19, 97, 98
Furstenau 155, 156

Gagny (Gaigny), Jean de, 185
Gallus, Eutychus Pontanus, 175, 179
Geneva, 48, 144

German(s)/Germany, xxii, xxiv, 1, 2, 11, 12, 19, 23, 24, 25, 26, 27, 28, 34, 40, 41, 42, 45, 49, 50, 51, 55, 61, 62, 64, 66, 68, 97, 98, 100, 104, 105, 106, 107, 109, 112, 117, 131, 132, 133, 144, 149, 169, 180, 199, 205, 210, 215, 222

Gerson, Jean, xxii

Giraldus (Giraldi, Lilio Gregorio), 3, 11, 24, 61, 104, 132, 133, 208; *On the Poets of Our Time*, 3, 11, 24, 61

Glock, Andreas. *See* Campanus

God, xv, 13, 14, 15, 19, 26, 27, 29, 36, 37, 39, 43, 44, 45, 50, 51, 62, 65, 67, 68, 69, 70, 72, 73, 77, 78, 79, 90, 93, 96, 101, 102, 103, 107, 108, 109, 110, 111, 112, 113, 114, 116, 117, 118, 120, 121, 122, 123, 124, 126, 127, 128, 129, 132, 134, 135, 136, 137, 138, 139, 140, 141, 142, 143, 144, 145, 146, 147, 149, 150, 151, 152, 153, 154, 158, 159, 160, 162, 166, 167, 169, 170, 171, 172, 175, 177, 181, 182, 183, 186, 187, 188, 189, 190, 191, 192, 196, 197, 200, 201, 206, 212, 213, 218, 225; promises and providence of, 26, 27, 42, 50–51, 110, 112–13, 116, 117, 118, 124, 126, 132, 137, 140, 144–45, 149, 151–52

Goggio, Bartolommeo: *In Praise of Women*, xxiii, xxv

Gonzaga, Cecilia, 36

Gonzaga, Guilia, 33, 52

Gonzaga, Margherita, 1

Gorgon, 209

Gospel, 36, 42, 43, 46, 67, 72, 145; cities of the Gospel (*città del evangelo*), 42, 144. *See also* Bible; Word of God

Gotwald, Andreas, 139, 156, 165

Gotwald, Matthäus, 139

Gournay, Marie de, xxix

Goveanus (de Gouveia), Antonius, 39

Gozi, Teofila, 3

Gozzadini, Bittizia, 30

Gracchi, 89

Graces, 40, 66, 94, 211, 214

Greek(s), xi, xii, xiii, xiv, xvi, xx, xxi, xxiii, 1, 10, 11, 12, 16, 17, 18, 20, 24, 27, 30, 61, 62, 65, 66, 71, 75, 79, 80, 84, 86, 95, 102, 107, 114, 130, 132, 159, 160, 171, 173, 177, 184, 185, 186, 197, 210, 211, 212, 216, 218

Grey, Lady Jane, 33, 35

Grifolus, Jacobus: *Defense of Cicero*, 15, 16

Grisons, 31, 167

Grumbach, Vitus, 154

Grunthler, Andreas, 19, 24, 25, 26, 28, 29, 30, 31, 45, 56, 57, 61, 62, 63, 64, 92, 98, 100, 104, 107, 109, 110, 120, 131, 153, 157, 159, 161, 163, 164, 168, 169, 175, 176, 180, 195, 196, 198, 199, 201, 203, 204, 210, 215, 216, 217, 221, 224

Guarini, Battista, 14

Guazzo, Stefano, xxiv

Guillaume de Lorris: *Romance of the Rose*, xvii, xxii, xxv

Guilio de Milano, 18, 46; *Exhortation to Martyrdom*, 46

Guise, François de Lorraine, duc de (earlier duc d'Aumale), 20, 32, 168

Habsburg, 28

Hail Mary, 3

Haman, 122

Hammelberg, 140, 141

Harpocration, 91

Hartmann (Harmanni), Hartmann, 138, 153, 156

Hebrew, xi, 184, 185, 186

Hebrew Bible, xii, xv

Heidelberg, 1, 10, 24, 28, 29, 30, 31, 32, 48, 57, 64, 131, 138, 139, 141, 143, 144, 146, 147, 148, 153, 155, 156, 162, 163, 164, 165, 166, 168, 170, 171, 173, 174, 176, 177, 186, 195, 196, 204, 207, 208, 215, 217, 224; University of, 30, 141, 144, 150, 160, 163

Helicon, 212, 219

Hell, 142, 149. *See also* Devil

General Index

Henri II (king of France), 20
Henry VIII (king of England), xxv
Hercules, 76, 85, 86, 160
Hermes, 211
Herold, Basilius Johannes, 57, 173, 175, 197
Herold, Johannes, 33, 66, 161, 162, 173
Herwagen, 162
Hessus, Helius Eobanus. *See* Eobanus
Hippocrene, 220
Hirschhorn am Neckar, 203, 204
Holech, 156
Holland, xxix
Holy Spirit, 21, 42, 68, 124, 126, 135, 145, 146, 172
Hörmann, Anton, 127, 130
Hörmann, Georg, 26, 28, 61, 62, 63, 104, 105, 106, 107, 108, 126, 128, 131
Hörmann Chronicle, 104
Huguenots, 8, 9, 20, 55, 171, 184
Hyperides, 91

idolatry, 9, 44, 45, 146, 149, 169
Infantius, Johannes, 174, 183
Inquisition, 8, 11, 12, 18, 22, 26, 33, 52, 53, 54. *See also* Protestants, persecution of
Isaac, 79
Isingrin, Michael, 113, 155, 162
Israel/Israelites, 71, 123, 147
Italian(s), xxii, xxiii, xxiv, xxv, xxviii, xxix, 2, 3, 5, 12, 25, 27, 31, 33, 34, 53, 73, 186, 201, 205, 206, 215, 220
Italy, xix, xx, 2, 3, 8, 31, 41, 45, 46, 49, 50, 53, 62, 68, 84, 89, 104, 115, 127, 130, 139, 161, 165, 209, 222
Ixion, 87

Jael, 71
Jay, Claudio, 32
Jean de Meun: *Romance of the Rose*, xvii, xxii, xxv
Jerusalem, 135, 138, 192. *See also* Zion
Jesuit(s), 32

Jesus, xvi, 6, 13, 23, 37, 42, 43, 44, 45, 46, 48, 49, 50, 65, 67, 68, 69, 72, 85, 86, 105, 106, 111, 120, 124, 125, 126, 127, 129, 133, 134, 135, 136, 137, 139, 141, 142, 143, 144, 146, 148, 151, 152, 157, 160, 166, 167, 168, 169, 170, 172, 173, 174, 176, 177, 180, 182, 183, 195, 197, 198, 200, 206, 215, 217, 218
Jew(s), xvi, xxii, 122
Johann Friedrich (der Grossmütige), duke and elector of Saxony, 123
John, Saint, 13, 70, 152
Joseph from Brixen, 133
Joshua, 70
Jove, 219
Juan II, King of Castile, xxv
Judith, 71
Julius III, 115
Jung, Eva-Maria, 48, 52, 53
Jupiter, 222

Kaufbeuren, 26, 104, 105, 106
Knox, John, xxvii, 48; *First Blast of the Trumpet against the Monstrous Regiment of Women*, xxvii
Kornmann, Heinrich, 33
Krämer, Heinrich: *The Hammer of Witches*, xxiv
Kunigunde (mother of Barbara, Olympia Morata's maid), 158

Labé, Louise, 17
Laertes, 101
Langeac, Jean de (bishop of Limoges), 10
Latin, xvi, xvii, xviii, xx, xxi, xxix, 1, 2, 4, 11, 15, 16, 17, 24, 37, 56, 61, 62, 63, 64, 65, 66, 75, 84, 88, 95, 99, 102, 107, 110, 116, 123, 143, 155, 185, 186, 201, 210, 211, 212, 216, 217, 218, 220
Lefèvre d'Étaples, Jacques, 8, 40
Lehms, Georg Christian, 34
Leipzig, 24
Le Moyne, Pierre: *Gallerie of Heroic Women*, xxii

Leonora (niece of Johann Sinapius), 139, 155
Ligurians, 89
Lindemann, Johann, 48, 132, 159, 181, 182
Linus, 95
Linz, 28, 44, 126, 127, 131
Logeria, Lady, 96
London, 46
Lord's Prayer, 4
Lorraine, 20, 168
Lossius, Lucas, 186
Lotichius, Johann Peter, 34
Louis XII, King of France, 7
Lucca, 12, 13
Lucius, Thomas, 111
Luna, Alvaro de, xxv
Lurtzing, Oswald, 97, 100, 139
Luther, Martin, 4, 5, 8, 11, 15, 27, 31, 34, 39, 46, 48, 49, 53, 54, 117, 133, 167, 181, 186; *Commentary on Galatians*, 11; *Greater Catechism*, 167; *On the Bondage of the Will*, 15, 38; *Table Talk*, 50
Lutheranism/Lutherans, 8, 14, 28, 29, 34, 41, 42, 43, 44, 45, 47, 48, 133, 161, 171
Lyons, 79
Lysippa, 99

Machaon, 221
Machiavelli: *Discourses* 1.1–15, 39
McNair, Philip, 42, 46
Macrin, Salmon, 185
Maggi, Vincenzo, 96
Main (river), 215
Mainz, 176
Maius, Vincentius, 96
Majoragio, Marc Antonio, 16
Makin, Bathsua, 35
Malatesta, Battista, 17
Manichaean, 15
Manriquez, Garcia, 33, 67
Mantua, 3, 61, 62, 65
Marburg, Colloquy of, 49
Margaret, duchess of Austria and Netherlands, xxv

Margraves' War, 29
Marguerite d'Angoulême, 7, 8
Marguerite de Navarre, 9, 52
Maria, Queen of Castile, xxv
Marnix, Philips van, heer van Sint Aldegonde, 212
Marot, Clément, 8, 9, 14, 184
Mars, 206, 221
Martin le France: *The Champion of Women*, xxii
Martinengo, Massimiliano Celso, conte, 46
Mass, 5, 8, 9, 18, 19, 21, 32, 44, 45, 46, 186. *See also* Communion; Eucharist
Matheolus: *Lamentations*, xvii, xx
Maurice (Moritz), duke and elector of Saxony, 23, 28, 130, 137
Mazzolino, Bernardino, 14
Medici, Catherine de', xxvii
Medici, Giuliano de', xxii, xxiii
Melanchthon, 5, 11, 27, 34, 40, 41, 49, 54, 127, 186
Melchior, 163
Menchi, Seidel, 53
Mercury, 87, 212
Michelangelo, 9
Micyllus, Jacob, 208, 210, 215
Milan, 33, 67, 115, 116
Milichius, 127
Minerva, 71, 166, 211, 219, 225
Modena, 115
Mohammed, 136
Molitur, Ulrich, xxiv
Moloch, 178
Momus, 93
Montargis, 20
Monte, Hypsicratea a, 34
Montreuil, Jean de, xxii
Morata, Olympia, 2, 3, 4, 5, 7, 10, 11, 12, 14, 17, 18, 19, 20, 21, 23, 24, 25, 26, 27, 28, 29, 30, 31, 33, 34, 35, 36, 37, 38, 40, 41, 42, 43, 44, 45, 46, 47, 48, 49, 50, 51, 52, 53, 54, 55, 56, 57, 61, 62, 63, 64, 65, 68, 72, 74, 75, 80, 84, 88, 89, 90, 91, 93, 94, 95, 96, 97, 98, 99, 100, 101, 102, 104, 105,

General Index 271

106, 108, 109, 110, 111, 112, 113, 114, 117, 118, 120, 123, 126, 127, 128, 130, 131, 132, 133, 134, 137, 138, 139, 141, 143, 146, 147, 150, 153, 154, 155, 156, 157, 158, 159, 161, 162, 164, 165, 166, 167, 168, 171, 173, 174, 175, 176, 178, 181, 183, 184, 186, 190, 195, 199, 200, 201, 202, 203, 204, 207, 208, 209, 210, 211, 212, 213, 214, 215, 216, 217, 218, 219, 221, 222, 223, 224; authority of, 1, 51–52; and Bible study, necessity of, 26, 27, 32, 36, 40, 42, 43, 45, 102, 108, 119, 121, 126, 138, 145, 151, 152, 166, 169, 170; biblical humanism and, 40–41, 184–85; as "Calvinist Amazon," 1, 34; and confessionalization, 45, 48–52; "Defense of Cicero," 16, 66; "Dialogue between Lavinia della Rovere and Olympia Morata," 26, 31, 36, 40, 42, 100–103, 116, 175; "Dialogue between Theophila and Philotima," 27, 31, 117, 118–26; dialogues of, generally, 66; and domestic duties, 25, 31; and Epicureanism (*see also* Lucretius), 16, 26, 27, 36–39; and the Eucharist, 49; and evangelism, 41–44, 47–52; in Heidelberg, 29–32; and Heidelberg University, 26, 30–31; intellectual development of, 26, 35–49; isolation of, from court, 19–21; juvenilia of, 16–17, 75–83; marriage of, to Grunthler, 1, 23–25; "On True Virginity," 12, 17, 75, 178; posthumous reputation and reception of, 32–35; "Praise of Scaevola," 12, 17, 80–83, 91, 92; and predestination, 50–51, 145, 152–53; "Prefaces to Cicero's Paradoxes," 66, 75–80, 87; on promises of God, 26, 27, 42, 50–51, 110, 112–13, 116, 117, 118, 124, 126, 132, 137, 140, 144–45, 149, 151–52; and Protestantism, 44–47, 47–49; in Schweinfurt, 26–29; style

of, 1, 11, 24–25, 56; "To Bembo," 75; "To Eutychus Pontanus Gallus," 75, 179; youth and adolescence of, 2, 10–11, 12; "Wedding Prayer," 24, 116, 180–81
Morato, Alfonsino (brother), 6
Morato, Delia (sister), 14
Morato, Emilio (brother), 6, 26, 32, 84, 104, 120, 146, 150, 156, 163, 167, 178, 199, 202, 224
Morato (Moretto), Fulvio Pellegrino (father), 2, 3, 4, 5, 6, 12, 13, 14, 15, 61, 62, 65, 84, 90, 161, 199, 210, 215, 220, 224; *Carmina Quaedam Latina*, 3; "Da mihi bibere dilla Samaritana," 3; *Del Significato de' Colori*, 4; *De Socrate*, 4; "Dichiaratione dil nome di Giesù," 3; *Rimario di tutte le candentie di Dante e Petrarca*, 3
Morato, Lucrezia Morata (mother), 3, 10, 199, 200, 201, 215
Morato, Vittoria (sister), 42, 50, 143, 149, 152
Mordecai, 122
Morel, François, 32
Morone, Giovanni, 52
Mosbach am Neckar, 161, 165, 198, 199, 202, 204
Moses, 146
Moulin, Charles du, 173
Mucius Scaevola, 75, 80–83
Mühlberg, battle of, 28, 123
Müntzer, Thomas, 184
Muses, 17, 69, 70, 87, 90, 92, 93, 94, 104, 179, 210, 211, 212, 214, 216, 220, 221, 222
Mytilene, 222

Naples, 67
Navarre, 7
Neander, Michael, 34
Neckar River, 216
Nerác, 7, 9
Nestor, 85, 212
Neustadt, 161
New Testament, xii, xv, xvi. *See also* Bible; Gospel; Word of God

Niceron, Jean-Pierre, 34
Nicodemism, 15, 44, 47
Nicolaus N. of Michelstadt, 203
Nogarola, Angela, 25
Nogarola, Isotta, xxv, xxviii, 34
Nolten, Georg Ludwig, 35
Numa, 206
Nuremberg, 29, 137, 140

Ochino, Bernardino, 9, 12, 21, 31, 33, 44, 46, 53, 144, 173, 175
Ofemianus, 216
Olympic Games, 92
Olympus, 35, 188, 214
Oporin, Johannes, 162
Opsopaeus (Opsopäus, Obsopaeus), Vincentius, 167, 185
Orpheus, 85, 88, 95, 220
Orsini, Camillo, 21, 22, 99, 109, 116
Orsini, Cherubina, 50, 106, 146, 147, 148, 149
Orsini, Guilia, 115
Orsini, Laura, 21
Orsini, Lavinia. *See* della Rovere Orsini, Lavinia
Orsini, Magdalena, 106
Orsini, Paolo, 21, 109
Ory, Matthieu, 32
Oxford, 186

Padua, 11, 107, 130, 131
Palatine, count and elector of, 30, 64, 138, 139, 144, 168, 221. *See also* Friedrich II
Paleario, Aonio, 11, 38; *On the Immortality of the Soul*, 38
Pallas, 87, 212, 214
Pallavicino, Gasparo, xxii
Panchaia, 80
Papal States, 8
Paris, 8, 9, 24
Parma, 109
Parnassus, 17, 179, 220
Paros, 222
Parthenay-Soubise, Anne de, 8
Pasithea, 209
Pasquino, Roman statue of, 12

Passau, treaty of, 28, 130
Paul, Saint, xvi, 13, 15, 21, 43, 51, 70, 109, 135, 136, 145, 148, 150, 151, 153, 170, 175
Paul III, 18, 22, 97, 109, 115
Paul IV, 18
Paula, 71
Pegasus, 220
Peitho, 85
Pelletier, Jean, 32
Pelorus, 222
Penthesilea, 70, 76
Pericles, 85, 86, 93
Perna, 54
Peter, Saint, 125, 151
Phaeton, 79
Phemius, 87
"philo-Protestants," 52
Philotheus, 174
Phoebus, 212, 219, 223
"Phonascus," 88
Piacenza, 23, 33, 67
Pico della Mirandola, Giovanni, 4
Pierides, 219, 221, 222. *See also* Muses
Pirkheimer, Caritas, 25
Po (river), 115, 220, 221
Pole, Reginald, cardinal, 52
Polydeuces, 179
Pomponazzi, Pietro, 38, 40
Pomponius, Mela, 10
Pontano, Giovanni, 17; *De magnificentia*, 17; *De splendore*, 17
pope, 12, 44, 45, 128
Porcia, 209
Porsena, 81
Portuguese, 209
prayer, 14, 110, 117–18, 126, 142, 145–46, 149, 150, 151, 153, 166, 170
Praxilla, 35, 71, 211, 212, 213
predestination, 19, 49, 50, 51, 117–18, 145, 152–53
Protestant(s)/Protestantism, xix, xxii, 1, 2, 5, 11, 12, 19, 20, 21, 22, 25, 26, 27, 28, 29, 31, 32, 33, 35, 36, 41, 42, 43, 44, 47, 49, 51, 53, 73, 105, 123, 130, 173, 178, 184;

persecution of, 6, 11, 21–23, 26, 28, 31, 32, 44, 46, 53–54, 127
Ptolemy, 10
Pyrrhus, Didacus (Diogo Pires), 208, 209
Pythagoras, 98, 128

Rabelais, François, 14, 39
Rangoni, Baldassarre, 115
Rangoni, Elena, 115
Rascalon, Guillaume, 66, 168, 224, 225
Reformation/Reform, 1, 3, 4, 25, 41, 45, 47, 48, 49, 54, 167, 185
Reineck, count of, 138, 155, 158
Remy, Nicolas, xxiv
Renaissance, xi, xvii, 17, 24, 38
Renato, Camillo, 18, 19, 46
Renée de France, duchess of Ferrara, 7, 10, 12, 17, 18, 20, 22, 24, 31–32, 33, 45, 54, 94, 96, 97, 107, 111, 116, 208; Academy of, 2, 66
Rhine Palatinate, 29, 48
Rhodiginus, Lodovicus Caelius, 89
Rhône (river), 79
Ribera, Pietro Paolo de: *Immortal Triumphs and Heroic Enterprises of 845 Women*, xxii
Rice, Eugene, 42
Richardot, François, 19
Rieneck, Philipp III, Graf von, 29, 141, 156
Rive, George de, 41
Robinson, Mary, 35
Rodriguez de la Camara, Juan (Juan Rodriguez del Padron): *The Triumph of Women*, xxii
Romagna, 21, 22
Roman(s), xi, xii, xiv, xv, xxi, xxiii, 12, 66, 71, 75, 78, 81, 82, 83, 107, 196
Rome, xiv, xx, 9, 18, 19, 22, 44, 45, 105, 106, 112, 116, 142
Rosa, Andreas, 27, 157, 158, 165, 181
Roscius, 80, 87
Rupprecht, Wolfgang, 171

Saba, Queen of the Ethiopians (Queen of Sheba), 71

Sabellicus (Marcus Antonius Coccius): *History*, 73
Sadoleto, Jacopo, 52
Salii, 206
Samaria, 149
San Begnino, 11
Sansovino, Francesco, 21
sapphic meter, 27, 62, 190
Sappho, 30, 35, 71, 114, 209, 211, 212, 213, 216, 222, 224
Sardi, Gasparo: *On the Three-Fold Philosophy*, 20, 38
Satan. *See* Devil
Saubonne, Michelle de. *See* Soubise, Michelle de Saubonne, baronne de
Sauerbrei, Johannes, 33
Savonarola, 4, 37
Saxony/Saxons, 28, 71, 123, 130, 184. *See also* Johann Friedrich (der Grossmütige); Moritz; Sibylle of Cleves
Scala, Alessandra, 18
Scheffer, Ludovic, 157
Schleenried, Laurenz, 130, 131
Schlosser, Anna, 139
Schlosser, Margareta, 139
Schmalkaldic League, 28
Schmalkaldic War, 130
Scholastic/Scholasticism, xx, xxiii, 41
Schurman, Anna Maria van (Anna), xxix, 10, 35
Schwaz, 26, 104
Schweinfurt, 1, 16, 26, 27, 28, 29, 35, 43, 48, 55, 64, 66, 92, 104, 110, 111, 112, 114, 116, 117, 126, 127, 128, 130, 131, 132, 133, 134, 137, 139, 140, 141, 144, 147, 154, 155, 156, 157, 158, 159, 163, 164, 165, 166, 177, 178, 180, 181, 186, 199, 204, 224
Scioppius (Schoppe), Kaspar, 34
Scripture. *See* Bible; Gospel; Word of God
Scythia, 222
Seidel Menchi, Silvana, 52, 53
Semiramis, 70
Septuagint (LXX), 114, 179, 185

Seripando, Girolamo, 52
Serres, Jean de, 185
Servetus, Michael, 39
Seso, Carlos de, count, 5
Sibyl, 218
Sibylle of Cleves, duchess of Saxony, 123
Sidney, Sir Philip: *Arcadia*, 39
Silva, Paulus, 154
Simler, Iosia, 33
Simon Magus, 149
Sinapius (Senf), Chilian, 11, 19, 64, 100, 205
Sinapius (Senf), Johannes, 10, 11, 18, 19, 24, 26, 28, 29, 30, 32, 49, 62, 63, 84, 90, 91, 96, 97, 98, 99, 100, 103, 105, 108, 110, 111, 112, 113, 116, 120, 127, 131, 138, 153, 155, 156, 157, 164, 176, 204, 205, 206, 207, 208, 217
Sinapius, Theodora, 24, 120, 138, 139, 155, 156, 157
Sirens, 87, 90
Socrates, 65
Solomon, 70, 71
Soubise, Michelle de Saubonne, baronne de, 8
Spangenberg, Johann, 186
Spaniard/Spanish, xxii, 28, 112, 123
Spenser, Edmund, *Faerie Queene*, xxviii
Speyer, 19, 64, 153, 155, 204, 206, 207
Spira, Francis, 167
spirituali, 33, 44, 47
Sprenger, Jacob: *The Hammer of Witches*, xxiv
Stiber, Daniel, 155
Stiblin, Caspar, 219
Strassburg, 161, 175
Stuttgart, 173
Swiss/Switzerland, 5, 9, 41, 46, 49, 167

Telesilla, 71
Ten Commandments, 120
Testa, Bartolomeo, 5
Thalia, 220
Themis, 222
Theophrastus, 85, 86

Thiene, Alessandro, 5
Thiene, Marco, 5
Thiene, Niccolo, 5
Thirty-Nine Articles (Church of England), 50
Thomas, Hubert, of Liege, 30, 139, 156
Thou, Jacques-Auguste de: *Universal History*, 34
Thrax, George, 107
Thucydides, 85
Tiber (river), 83
Tibertius, Saint, 11
Titian, 7
Titius, Casper: *Theologisches Exempel Buch*, 34
Tivoli, 10
Tobias, 13
Tolomeo, Claudio, 52
Tomasini, Giacomo Filippo, 34
Trent, Council of, 6, 12, 112, 168, 186
Treuthugerus, Georg, 203
Trissino, Alessandro, 5
Trissino, Guilio, 5
Tübingen, 33, 130
Turin, 11
Turk(s), 136
Tuscan/Tuscany, 12, 212

Ulysses, 87, 90, 210
Urbino, 10

Vadianus, Joachim, 63
Valdes, Juan de, 33, 52, 53
Valentini, Filippo, 46
Valla, Lorenzo, 11, 38; *On Pleasure*, 38
Vashti, 122
Venetian/Venice, 3, 4, 5, 6, 8, 9, 12, 18, 21, 45, 72, 178, 180
Venus(es): 94, 178, 180, 209, 210, 211, 219
Verano, Costanza, 17
Vergerio, Pietro Paolo, 18, 31, 32, 33, 44, 46, 49, 56, 167, 173; *Concilium non modo Tridentinum sed omne Papisticum perpetuo fugiendum esse*, 167
Vermigli, Pietro Martire, 33, 44, 46; *On Flight*, 46

Verona, 52
Vesta, 178
Vicenza, 4, 6
Vittorino da Feltre, 36
Vives, Juan Luis, xxiii, xxv, xxviii; *On the Education of a Christian Woman*, xxix
Vossius (Voss), Gerardus Joannes, 33
Vulgate Bible, 67, 85, 108, 114, 129, 133, 134, 138, 142, 143, 169, 186

Weber, Michael, 128
Wehner, Valentin, 166
Wertheim, Prefect of, 64
Weston, Elizabeth Jane, 34, 35; *Parthenica*, 35
Weyer, Johann, xxiv
Wiesbaden, 176
Winchester, 186
Wittenberg, 11, 127, 203
women, learned, xi–xxix, 17–18, 23, 25, 33, 65, 69–72, 90–91, 93, 100–102, 179

Word of God: 40, 42, 43, 49, 68, 118, 120, 121, 132, 137, 138, 142, 145, 146, 149, 151, 152, 153, 166, 197. *See also* Bible; Gospel
Worms, 173, 176
Wroth, Sir Thomas, 73
Würzburg, 19, 26, 28, 61, 63, 105, 108, 110, 112, 116, 137, 138, 139, 153, 156, 207

Zanchius, Hieronymus (Zanchi, Girolamo), 46, 161
Zenobia, 71
Zeul, Leonard, 157
Zeus, 179
Zion, 68, 187, 192
Zobel, Melchior, of Guttenberg, 105
Zoilus, 66
Zurich, 33
Zwinger, Theodor, 93, 211
Zwingli, Ulrich/Zwinglian, 5, 11, 40, 45, 48, 54